The Bulldozer in the Countryside

The concern today about suburban sprawl is not new. In the decades after World War II, the spread of tract-house construction changed the nature of millions of acres of land, and a variety of Americans began to protest against the environmental costs of suburban development. By the mid-1960s, indeed, many of the critics were attempting to institutionalize an urban land ethic. *The Bulldozer in the Countryside* is the first scholarly work to analyze the successes and failures of the varied efforts to address the environmental consequences of suburban growth from 1945 to 1970. For scholars and students of American history, the book offers a compelling new insight into two of the great stories of modern times – the mass migration to the suburbs and the rise of the environmental movement. The book also offers a valuable historical perspective for participants in contemporary debates about the alternatives to sprawl.

Adam Rome is assistant professor of history at Pennsylvania State University.

STUDIES IN ENVIRONMENT AND HISTORY

Editors

Donald Worster, University of Kansas
Alfred W. Crosby, University of Texas at Austin

Other books in the series

The Bulldozer
in the Countryside

Suburban Sprawl and the Rise
of American Environmentalism

ADAM ROME

Pennsylvania State University

CAMBRIDGE
UNIVERSITY PRESS

PUBLISHED BY THE PRESS SYNDICATE OF THE UNIVERSITY OF CAMBRIDGE
The Pitt Building, Trumpington Street, Cambridge, United Kingdom

CAMBRIDGE UNIVERSITY PRESS
The Edinburgh Building, Cambridge CB2 2RU, UK
40 West 20th Street, New York, NY 10011-4211, USA
10 Stamford Road, Oakleigh, VIC 3166, Australia
Ruiz de Alarcón 13, 28014 Madrid, Spain
Dock House, The Waterfront, Cape Town 8001, South Africa

http://www.cambridge.org

First published 2001

Printed in the United States of America

Typeface Sabon 11/13 pt.   *System* QuarkXPress 4.04   [AG]

A catalog record for this book is available from the British Library.

Library of Congress Cataloging in Publication Data
Rome, Adam Ward.
The bulldozer in the countryside : suburban sprawl and the rise of American
environmentalism / Adam Rome.
p. cm. – (Studies in environment and history)
Includes bibliographical references and index.
ISBN 0-521-80059-5 – ISBN 0-521-80490-6 (pb)
1. Environmentalism – United States – History.   2. Suburbs – Environmental
aspects – United States – History.   I. Title.   II. Series.
GE197 .R66 2001
333.73'15'0973 – dc21   00-058526

ISBN 0 521 80059 5 hardback
ISBN 0 521 80490 6 paperback

For Robin

Contents

Illustrations

Illustrations follow page 152.

Preface

As my subtitle suggests, *The Bulldozer in the Countryside* is about the relationship between two of the great stories of modern American history, the mass migration to the suburbs and the rise of the environmental movement. Each story has inspired a considerable scholarly literature. Yet scholars so far have not recognized the important connections between the two stories. The construction of tract-house subdivisions after World War II changed the nature of millions of acres of land, and a variety of people soon began to complain about the environmental costs of suburban development. *The Bulldozer in the Countryside* argues that the elaboration of an environmental critique of homebuilding in the period from 1945 to 1970 played an important role in the emergence of environmentalism.

When I started my research, however, I did not expect to write a book about the environmental movement: I simply saw a chance to help overcome a serious shortcoming in the literature of environmental history. The scholarship in the field has focused mainly on rural forms of production – farming, ranching, mining, lumbering, fishing, and hunting. Yet the enterprises of the metropolis also have had profound environmental consequences. Since I wanted to write about suburbia, I decided to focus on homebuilding. How had the environmental impact of residential development changed over time? In answering that question, I hoped to contribute to scholarly understanding of urban environmental history.

I found abundant evidence that the environmental cost of homebuilding rose sharply after 1945. But that fact by itself seemed lifeless to me. What problems did people notice first? Who took the initiative in trying to reduce the environmental costs of tract-house construction? How did the critics define the issues? What solutions did they propose? Which problems proved relatively easy to overcome, and which problems proved relatively intractable? I realized that my analysis of the environmental impact of homebuilding no longer was the heart of my work. I was most interested instead in how environmental problems became part of the public agenda. As a result, I began to plan a book that would join intellectual, political, and environmental history.

I thought at first that I would write about a particular place. Like social historians, environmental historians often have used case studies to examine big changes, and many of the issues I consider here were discussed in countless cities and counties across the country. I soon concluded, however, that a case study would not allow me to discuss all the intellectual and political changes that interested me. The postwar transformation of the homebuilding industry received national attention, and the most important debates about the environmental impacts of tract-house development took place in national forums: journals published by trade and professional organizations, congressional hearings, conferences sponsored by federal agencies. I therefore decided to focus on national trends.

With the exception of the introduction and conclusion, *The Bulldozer in the Countryside* proceeds roughly in chronological order. The first chapter considers the political, social, and economic forces behind the rise of tract housing. The next five chapters discuss different stages in the evolution of the environmental critique of homebuilding. Because I am most interested in the course of environmental activism, I make no attempt to consider all the environmental consequences of suburban development: I only discuss the problems that became important subjects of public debate. The seventh chapter analyzes a remarkably ambitious attempt in the early 1970s to institutionalize a new way of thinking about metropolitan land use. The introduction suggests how my work challenges influential interpretations of the history of the environmental movement; the conclusion reflects on the strengths and weaknesses of the early efforts to reduce the environmental costs of homebuilding.

Throughout the book, I use "tract-house construction" and "suburban development" interchangeably, but I recognize that the two phrases are not strictly synonymous. Many tract-house subdivisions lay within the borders of large cities. Because mass building required large and inexpensive tracts of land, however, the great majority of the homes built after World War II were in the suburbs – the communities surrounding long-established urban centers. The typical tract house was a suburban house.

Though I write mostly about the period from 1945 to 1970, the environmental impact of suburban development continues to be a source of controversy. I chose not to carry the story to the present because I saw my work principally as a contribution to the historical literature on environmentalism. Yet I hope *The Bulldozer in the Countryside* will help people think more clearly about the state of the environment today.

Acknowledgments

I began this project as a graduate student at the University of Kansas, where I worked under Donald Worster, and I cannot imagine a more wonderful mentor. Don is wise, inspiring, and supportive. He helped me to find my way in the field, and he continues to offer much wisdom, inspiration, and support. Now he is a wonderful friend.

Joel Tarr and Martin Melosi each read several versions of this book, and I appreciate their insightful suggestions. I also owe much to their work. Joel's ideas about retrospective technology assessment initially gave me the idea of doing a historical environmental-impact study of homebuilding. For years, both Joel and Marty have argued for the importance of urban environmental history, and their pioneering work in the field made my research possible.

I have presented material from this book at conferences of the American Society for Environmental History, the Society for the History of Technology, the Society for City and Regional Planning History, and the Urban History Association. I also gave talks about my research at the University of Kansas, Columbia University, the University of Virginia, Pennsylvania State University, and the University of Pennsylvania. I am grateful to all who shared thoughts on those occasions.

In addition, I received thoughtful criticism from the editors and reviewers of several journals. I particularly appreciate the suggestions I received from Joel Tarr and Christine Rosen, co-editors of a special *Journal of Urban History* issue on "the environment and the city"; Paul Starrs, editor of *Geographical Review;* and John Staudenmaier, editor of *Technology and Culture.* I also thank the

American Geographical Society for giving me permission to use material from my article "William Whyte, Open Space, and Environmental Activism," which appeared in *Geographical Review* 88 (April 1998): 259–274.

As a graduate student, I was helped greatly by a three-year University Fellowship and a one-year University Dissertation Fellowship. John Clark, William Tuttle, and Pete Shortridge offered thoughtful suggestions as members of my doctoral committee. From the start, Peter Mancall, Lisa Bitel, and Victor Bailey gave me all kinds of encouragement. Because Don Worster attracted a talented group of students to Kansas, I also had the advantage while in graduate school of belonging to a lively community of environmental historians. I am especially grateful for the good company of Brian Black – a friendly basketball foe and a relaxing conference roommate.

I owe much to Penn State too. To ensure that I had sufficient time for research and writing, I was given a term off from teaching. The staff in the Interlibrary Loan office enabled me to use a wealth of hard-to-find books, articles, and government documents. The University Photo / Graphics shop produced the prints of most of my illustrations. My department heads and deans – A. Gregg Roeber, Roger Downs, John Dutton, and Susan Welch – have given me helpful counsel and strong support. I have also enjoyed the chance to work with so many fine colleagues.

At Cambridge University Press, Frank Smith was a model editor. He was enthusiastic about the project from the time of our first conversation, and he was a fine guide on the trail to publication. I also appreciate the work of all the people involved in the production of the book.

I have always felt blessed in my family, and I owe more than I can say to my parents and my siblings – Donald and Sheila, Ethan and Lisa. I also have been fortunate in my friends. I especially thank Ben Fine, Alina Macneal, and Randy Scholfield. All became friends long ago, during formative periods of my life, and all continue to enrich my years.

Robin Schulze has lived with this book as long as I have. She is a true scholar, and her example and sage advice have helped me immeasurably. But I am grateful for much more. For me, Robin is home: comfort, joy, love. I dedicate this book to her with thanks for everything.

Introduction

In 1950, photographer William Garnett made a series of aerial photographs of the construction of Lakewood Park, a California suburb. Four of Garnett's images soon became iconic. The first was a bulldozed landscape – a large tract of earth with no topographical features, no trees or grass, indeed no visible life of any kind. In the second photograph, the tract had dozens of foundations in lines stretching indefinitely beyond the frame. Except for the utility poles and the piles of lumber by each foundation, nothing rose more than a few feet above the ground. The third photograph showed the wood skeletons of the houses-to-be. In the fourth photograph, the roofs and walls were done. The ground was still bare and the streets unpaved. But the tract was about to become a neighborhood.[1]

The photographs were commissioned by the developers. Like Levittown, Lakewood Park exemplified a revolutionary new way of building, and the developers took great pride in the project. "This is planning as businessmen can do it," one told *Time* magazine. The development was a gigantic undertaking, covering 3,500 acres and costing $135 million. The plans called for the assembly line construction of 17,000 homes. The community would also have 17 churches, 20 schools, 37 playgrounds – and a shopping center with department stores, supermarkets, banks, service stations, offices, movie theaters, and recreation facilities. In two years, the developers predicted, more than 70,000 people would live in Lakewood Park. To promote the project, the developers

---

1. I first saw the four photographs in Dolores Hayden, *Redesigning the American Dream: The Future of Housing, Work, and Family Life* (New York: W. W. Norton & Company, 1984), 36–37. But the series has appeared in many places, as I explain later in the text.

bound enlargements of Garnett's photographs in a beautiful presentation book.[2]

The national media also published Garnett's photographs in stories about "the world's largest planned housing development." In a two-page piece entitled "New Homes: 1,000 a Month," *Business Week* reproduced all four images, from the barren tract to the framed homes on the grid of unpaved streets. The photographs dwarfed the text. In a matter-of-fact tone, the captions highlighted the audacity of the developers. "Earthmoving job involved more than 3-million cu. yd. for drainage, streets, sewers, and water supply. . . ." "Construction timetable is the key to success. . . ." "Framing is done by new methods aimed at speeding work. . . ." "It'll look like this on completion. . . ." Together, the photographs suggested the remarkable energy of American business in meeting a vital need.[3]

By 1970, however, the Garnett photographs had become symbols of environmental devastation. The first sign of revisionism came in a 1964 book, Peter Blake's *God's Own Junkyard*. The book was a biting pictorial attack on "the planned deterioration of America's landscape" – a kind of anticoffee-table book – and Blake included the four Garnett views of Lakewood Park. Each photograph was half a page, with no caption. The introduction to the book made clear how Blake interpreted the images: The suburbs were "wastelands." Blake was not alone. In 1969, architect Nathaniel Owings used Garnett's photographs to illustrate a call for a new conservation aesthetic. For Owings, the bulldozed landscape was an object lesson in "what we want to avoid." Now we needed to "salvage what we have damaged" and "save what is still unspoiled." We needed to build communities that would "thrive in harmony with the surrounding land."[4]

---

2. The quotation comes from "Birth of a City," *Time* 55 (April 17, 1950): 100. D. J. Waldie describes the presentation book in *Holy Land: A Suburban Memoir* (1996; reprint, New York: St. Martin's Press, 1997, 4. For the project statistics, see also "New Homes: 1,000 a Month," *Business Week* (September 9, 1950): 52–53; Ray Day, "Lakewood Park: The City They Built in 6 Months," *American City* 66 (May 1951): 100–102.
3. "New Homes: 1,000 a Month," 52–53. In addition, see Day, "Lakewood Park," 101; William Garnett, "Over California," *Fortune* 49 (March 1954): 112.
4. Peter Blake, *God's Own Junkyard: The Planned Deterioration of America's Landscape* (New York: Holt, Rinehart and Winston, 1964), 8, 106–107; Nathaniel Alexander Owings, *The American Aesthetic* (New York: Harper & Row, 1969), 14, 24, 27, 29, 105, 107.

The radical rereading of Garnett's work reflected a dramatic change in the way many Americans reckoned the costs and benefits of suburban development. In the years after World War II, the nation's biggest homebuilders were hailed as heroes: By making the United States a nation of homeowners, the boosters argued, tract housing would help lay the foundation for a booming mass-consumption economy. Yet, just a generation later, a host of critics were calling the sprawl of suburbia an environmental disaster – and arguing that the problem of environmentally destructive development demanded far-reaching government action. The causes and consequences of that momentous shift in thinking are the subject of *The Bulldozer in the Countryside.*

The story begins with the postwar revolution in construction. The adoption of mass production techniques greatly intensified the environmental impact of homebuilding. For the first time, builders put hundreds of thousands of homes in environmentally sensitive areas, including wetlands, steep hillsides, and floodplains. Builders also began to use new earth-moving equipment to level hills, fill creeks, and clear vegetation from vast tracts. The result was more frequent flooding, costly soil erosion, and drastic changes in wildlife populations. The postwar subdivisions typically had little open space. Because the cheapest and largest tracts were beyond the reach of municipal sewer systems, the use of septic tanks increased sharply, yet septic tanks were a problematic method of disposing of household wastes in densely settled areas: Septic-tank failures caused outbreaks of disease, groundwater contamination, and eutrophication of lakes. In designing homes, builders abandoned regional traditions that kept homes warmer in winter and cooler in summer. Instead, the ranch house became the norm in places as diverse as Minnesota, Arizona, Florida, and Kansas – and residential use of energy skyrocketed.[5]

The problems did not become apparent all at once. Though the postwar building boom was an environmental catastrophe on the scale of the Dust Bowl, the signs of trouble were not nearly so striking as in the 1930s. No black clouds darkened suburban streets at

5. I first made this argument in "Building on the Land: Toward an Environmental History of Residential Development in American Cities and Suburbs, 1870–1990," *Journal of Urban History* 20 (1994): 407–434.

midday, no dust swept from the plains of Lakewood Park to the committee rooms of the nation's capitol. Yet, one by one, the environmental costs of tract-house development became subjects of debate. Even before the end of World War II, a variety of people were talking about the need for energy-conserving "solar houses." The septic-tank problem began to concern federal housing administrators in the late 1940s. The first questions about the wisdom of building on sensitive lands came a few years later, in the mid-1950s. *Fortune* and *Life* published influential essays about the loss of open space in the late 1950s. In the early 1960s – before the publication of *Silent Spring,* and long before the first Earth Day – the U. S. Geological Survey began to investigate the effects of suburban growth on water and soil.

The arrival of bulldozers in the countryside also inspired protests. By the mid-1960s, indeed, the sprawl of the tracts had provoked hundreds of grass roots campaigns to stop "the rape of the land." The protests struck classic chords. For more than a century, the nation's most gifted writers had expressed anxiety about the sudden appearance of "the machine in the garden." Would Nature survive the advance of Civilization? The antisprawl activists asked a similar question. Yet the outcry against the bulldozer was something new, because the concern no longer was limited to a tiny minority. From New York to California, countless suburbanites began to have doubts about the virtue of "progress."[6]

The activism of the 1950s and 1960s had profound consequences. The critics of tract-house development sought to encourage "a land ethic." To reduce the environmental costs of homebuilding, public officials challenged the near-sacred rights of property owners. Cities and counties passed ordinances to limit the spread of septic tanks, to restrict building on sensitive lands, and to check erosion during construction. Several states established programs to regulate how and where developers could build large subdivisions. The nation's courts also reinterpreted property law to allow greater public control over the use of privately owned land. Together, the initiatives made "a quiet revolution."

6. Both the title of my book and the argument of this paragraph play off Leo Marx, *The Machine in the Garden: Technology and the Pastoral Ideal in America* (New York: Oxford University Press, 1964).

To readers acquainted with the historical literature on environmentalism, the story of *The Bulldozer in the Countryside* should seem both familiar and unfamiliar. The basic plot is one of the archetypal narratives of the rise of environmental awareness: the introduction of a new product or process, welcomed as a miracle, that people eventually come to see as the source of disturbing environmental problems. That is the story of DDT and nuclear power and detergents – and that is the story of tract housing. In several ways, however, a study of the changing response to tract-house development provides important new insights into the history of the environmental movement.[7]

First, the homebuilding story illuminates the relationship between the two great explanations of the origins of environmentalism. On the one hand, scholars see the movement as a response to postwar changes in the world of production. The chemical revolution in agriculture, the proliferation of synthetic materials, the development of atomic energy, the increased scale of power-generation and resource-extraction technology – all created new environmental hazards. On the other hand, scholars argue that environmentalism followed a dramatic shift in the world of consumption. The unprecedented affluence of the postwar years encouraged millions of Americans to put a premium on the environmental elements of "quality of life." How did people come to see the new machinery of production as a threat to the new dream of consumption? The question deserves more scholarly attention. Certainly the popularization of ecological ideas helped people to understand how new technologies might undermine the promise of affluence: In *Silent Spring*, Rachel Carson took pains to bring the hazards of pesticides home to suburban readers. The televised horror of the Santa Barbara oil spill also was important as a symbol of the ability of modern industry to turn the grace and beauty of nature into something grotesque. But the history of suburban development suggests that

7. For the controversies over DDT, nuclear power, and detergents, see Thomas R. Dunlap, *DDT: Scientists, Citizens, and Public Policy* (Princeton: Princeton University Press, 1981); Thomas Raymond Wellock, *Critical Masses: Opposition to Nuclear Power in California, 1958–1978* (Madison: University of Wisconsin Press, 1998); William McGucken, *Biodegradable: Detergents and the Environment.* (College Station: Texas A & M University Press, 1991).

science and disaster were not the only ways by which Americans could come to see production as a threat to consumption. In new subdivisions, the bulldozer seldom was far from the living room, so the environmental destructiveness of postwar industry often intruded on the comfort of postwar prosperity.[8]

Second, the homebuilding story sheds light on the evolution of the environmental agenda. In *Beauty, Health, and Permanence,* Samuel Hays argues for a three-stage chronology of environmental activism. During the first stage, from the mid-1950s to the early 1960s, the major environmental issues were outdoor recreation, open space, and wilderness preservation. The issue of pollution dominated the environmental agenda from the mid-1960s to the early 1970s. Then environmentalists took up a new set of issues, ranging from energy conservation to preservation of endangered species. But Hays does not explain the progression from stage to stage. How did concern about the loss of open space lead to concern about pollution? *The Bulldozer in the Countryside* helps to fill the gaps in Hays's analysis. Because the critique of tract housing evolved over several decades – and because tract housing caused a remarkably broad range of environmental problems, including almost all the problems Hays emphasizes – the homebuilding story explains much about how the concerns of environmentalists changed over time.[9]

Third, the homebuilding story contributes to a more complex understanding of "the environmental opposition." Many historians see economic interests as the heart of resistance to the movement, and their arguments often are compelling. In the late 1960s and early

8. The first interpretation derives from a classic work of environmental criticism, Barry Commoner's *The Closing Circle: Nature, Man and Technology* (New York: Alfred A. Knopf, 1971). For a recent summary of the argument, see Hal K. Rothman, *The Greening of a Nation?: Environmentalism in the United States Since 1945* (Fort Worth: Harcourt Brace College Publishers, 1998), 11–15. The second interpretation comes from Samuel P. Hays, *Beauty, Health, and Permanence: Environmental Politics in the United States, 1955–1985* (New York: Cambridge University Press, 1987). Andrew Hurley's *Environmental Inequalities: Class, Race, and Industrial Pollution in Gary, Indiana, 1945–1980* (Chapel Hill: University of North Carolina Press, 1995) is the best study so far of the effects of postwar changes in production and consumption. For Rachel Carson's appeals to suburban readers, see *Silent Spring* (Boston: Houghton Mifflin, 1962), 155–161, 173–184. Robert Easton describes the oil disaster in *Black Tide: The Santa Barbara Oil Spill and Its Consequences* (New York: Delacorte Press, 1972).
9. Hays, *Beauty, Health, and Permanence,* 54–57.

1970s, for example, coal producers joined with a number of coal-dependent interests to form a coal coalition that fought against tough air pollution laws. Though builders never formally established a housing coalition, the building industry also had a diverse and powerful group of allies. Homebuilding was a driving force in the economy – the core of a "suburban-industrial complex." But the power of the industry went beyond jobs and profits, because the single-family home was one of the defining symbols of "the American way of life." The issue of homeownership was also tied to ideas about democracy, freedom, and civic order. In the effort to reduce the environmental costs of homebuilding, therefore, activists and officials often faced a combination of economic, social, and political arguments.[10]

But *The Bulldozer in the Countryside* does not merely fill gaps in the historical literature on environmentalism. The argument here recasts or revises a number of well-accepted conclusions about the movement's roots, evolution, and limits. Six points stand out.

1. **Though a growing concern about the loss of wilderness obviously contributed to the rise of environmentalism, the movement also was a response to environmental change at the edges of the nation's cities.** In *The Greening of a Nation?*, Hal Rothman argues that the battle in the mid-1950s to preserve Echo Park was the great catalyst of the environmental movement. His argument follows a number of works – from Roderick Nash's *Wilderness and the American Mind* to Stephen Fox's *John Muir and His Legacy* – that root environmentalism in the preservationist tradition exemplified by the Sierra Club. Yet scholars have not explained fully why Americans were more concerned about the fate of wilderness after World War II than before. In a fine study of the Echo Park controversy, Mark Harvey argues that the rapidly growing population of suburbia gave new strength to the wilderness cause. That argument accords with the common view that the environmental movement has always relied on the support of affluent suburbanites. Yet *The Bulldozer in the Countryside* shows that suburban environmentalism

---

10. Hays devotes a chapter of *Beauty, Health, and Permanence* to the antienvironmental lobbying of agriculture, labor, and industry. See 287–328. The coal story is the subject of Richard H. K. Vietor's *Environmental Politics and the Coal Coalition* (College Station: Texas A & M University Press, 1980).

was much more than a function of affluence. The residents of post-war suburbs lived in the midst of one of the most profound environmental transformations in the nation's history. Every year, a territory roughly the size of Rhode Island was bulldozed for urban development. Forests, marshes, creeks, hills, cornfields, and orchards all were destroyed in order to create subdivisions. Though some of the environmental consequences of suburban development were invisible to untrained observers, others were obvious. Again and again, the destruction of nearby open spaces robbed children of beloved places to play – and the losses hit home more vitally than the threats to far-off sites like Echo Park ever could. The desire to preserve wilderness was the tip of an iceberg, the most visible part of a much larger concern about the destructive sprawl of urban civilization.[11]

   2. **Though the environmental movement differed in some key respects from the conservation movement, the ideas of the conservationists nevertheless shaped environmentalist thought well into the 1960s.** The conservation movement was devoted to efficient use of productive resources, Samuel Hays argues in *Beauty, Health, and Permanence,* whereas environmentalism was a consumer movement keen to secure and protect a more satisfying environment. That contrast is overdrawn. The conservationist "gospel of efficiency" called for both restraint of private resource exploitation and promotion of wise public development. The environmental movement

11. For the preservationist roots of environmentalism, see Rothman, *The Greening of a Nation?,* 33–55; Roderick Nash, *Wilderness and the American Mind* [3d edition] (New Haven: Yale University Press, 1982); Stephen Fox, *The American Conservation Movement: John Muir and His Legacy* (1981; reprint, Madison: University of Wisconsin Press, 1985). The argument about suburban support for the wilderness cause is from Mark W. T. Harvey, *A Symbol of Wilderness: Echo Park and the American Conservation Movement* (Albuquerque: University of New Mexico Press, 1994), 242–243. In *Beauty, Health, and Permanence,* Hays notes the importance of postwar suburbanization for the environmental movement in a discussion of the "paradox" of suburbia: "Amenities purchased there often soon became threatened by the increase in people, traffic, and pollution. The world seemed to close in and destroy what one had sought to secure. This experience shaped much environmental concern. One spoke of the problems of growth. How to approach the problem was another matter. The confrontation with environmental degradation in the city now was augmented by a confrontation with threatened degradation in the suburbs." See 91. In *Forcing the Spring: The Transformation of the American Environmental Movement* (Washington: Island Press, 1993), Robert Gottlieb makes a powerful argument for an urban industrial tradition of environmentalism. But Gottlieb does not discuss the postwar rise of suburbia.

certainly challenged the second element of the conservation creed. To environmentalists, the conservationists took a terribly narrow view of the nonhuman world, seeing only raw materials and power sources to be used in the long-term interest of the nation. Yet environmentalists continued to draw on many of the conservationists' insights into the costs of unregulated private exploitation of the land. Indeed, *The Bulldozer in the Countryside* describes the urbanization of conservation – the recognition, over the course of two decades, that a range of problems once identified only with forests and farms also plagued the nation's metropolitan areas. As a presidential task force on suburban problems argued in 1968, "it is time to affirm an urban conservation ethic to match the concern for wise use of the nation's land and water resources expressed by Pinchot, Roosevelt, and others a half century ago."[12]

3. **Though ecologists played a prominent role as advocates for environmental activism, other scientific and technical professionals were also important in drawing attention to environmental problems.** Almost three decades ago, in a pioneering study of the intellectual roots of environmentalism, Donald Fleming gave special attention to scientists who popularized ecological ideas, from Rachel Carson to Barry Commoner. Since the publication of Fleming's work, scholars have shown in many ways how the insights of ecology shaped popular perceptions of the environment. *The Bulldozer in the Countryside* adds to that story, since ecological ideas played a part in the environmental critique of homebuilding. The language of ecology offered a way for activists to generalize a number of specific criticisms of tract-house development: Builders needed to have more respect for natural patterns and processes. But the arguments of ecologists directly shaped only a few of the campaigns to reform the development process. The critique also required the insights of architects, urban planners, landscape architects, hydrologists, geologists, soil scientists, public health officials, and

12. Hays begins *Beauty, Health, and Permanence* with a chapter titled "From Conservation to Environment." See 13–39. Hays is also the author of a classic work on the conservation movement: *Conservation and the Gospel of Efficiency: The Progressive Conservation Movement, 1890–1920* (Cambridge: Harvard University Press, 1959). For the quotation, see Charles M. Haar, editor, *The President's Task Force on Suburban Problems: Final Report* (Cambridge: Ballinger, 1974), 13; the task force findings originally appeared in several volumes in 1968.

geographers. *The Bulldozer in the Countryside* suggests that a neglected factor in the rise of environmentalism was the increase after
World War II in the number of people who looked at the environment not as commodity producers or consumers but as professionals committed to an ideal of service.[13]

4. **Though some federal agencies repeatedly battled with environmentalists, other federal agencies were instrumental in putting
environmental problems on the public agenda.** The overdrawn
contrast between the conservation and environmental movements
has also caused historians to miss the important role of the federal
government in the rise of environmentalism. As several scholars
have argued, the government's conservation and land-management
agencies often pursued policies that were anathema to environmentalists. But officials in the government's scientific agencies were
often the first to sound alarms about the environmental problems
caused by suburban development. At the request of the Federal
Housing Administration, the U.S. Public Health Service conducted
a pioneering set of studies of the hazards of septic-tank use in
densely settled areas. The U.S. Geological Survey, the Soil Conservation Service, and the Bureau of Sport Fisheries and Wildlife
drew public attention to the ways suburbanization affected water,
soil, and wildlife. At a time when the nation had few institutional
sources of environmental information, the government's research
centers and outreach networks often were catalysts to action. The
leadership provided by federal agencies was not due solely to ex-
ceptional resources. Though Americans now distrust "big government," federal officials in the 1950s and early 1960s enjoyed great
respect, and their recommendations had considerable influence.[14]

13. Donald Fleming, "Roots of the New Conservation Movement," *Perspectives in Amer-
    ican History* 6 (1972): 7–91. In *Nature's Economy: A History of Ecological Ideas* [2d
    edition] (New York: Cambridge University Press, 1994), Donald Worster calls the pe-
    riod since World War II "the age of ecology." See 340–433. Historians have done a num-
    ber of excellent case studies of the role of ecological ideas in environmental politics. The
    most influential are by Thomas Dunlap: In addition to *DDT*, see *Saving America's Wildlife*
    (Princeton: Princeton University Press, 1988).
14. Hays, *Beauty, Health, and Permanence*, 13–21; Rothman, *The Greening of a Nation?*,
    57–81; Paul W. Hirt, *A Conspiracy of Optimism: Management of the National Forests
    Since World War Two* (Lincoln: University of Nebraska Press, 1994). In a fine essay on
    "Lyndon Johnson and Environmental Policy," Martin V. Melosi argues that scholars
    have neglected the federal environmental initiatives of the mid-1960s. See Robert A. Di-
    vine, editor, *The Johnson Years: Vietnam, the Environment, and Science* (Lawrence:

5. Though a well-organized antienvironmental movement came out of a struggle over public lands in the West, the effort to control urban and suburban development also led to a powerful antienvironmental movement – the movement to defend "property rights." The few scholarly works on the organized opposition to environmentalism suggest that the countermovement has come largely from the West – the home of the Sagebrush Rebellion and the Wise Use movement. Though a number of journalists have noted that property-rights activism transcends regional boundaries, almost all the recent commentary on the environmental opposition treats the property-rights issue as a plank in the Wise Use platform. The rest of the literature sees the property-rights movement as an offshoot of the conservative crusade against government regulation in the 1980s. But the relationship between regulation and property rights had become a subject of public debate well before Ronald Reagan became president. With the help of Richard Epstein's 1985 book on takings, the Reagan administration certainly gave the property-rights cause a boost. Yet, as *The Bulldozer in the Countryside* demonstrates, the issue was rooted in the debates of the late 1960s and early 1970s over land use in fast-growing cities and suburbs.[15]

University Press of Kansas, 1987), 113–149. Melosi focuses almost entirely on the passage of legislation, however, not the daily work of federal bureaucrats.
15. C. Brant Short, *Ronald Reagan and the Public Lands: America's Conservation Debate, 1979–1984* (College Station: Texas A&M University Press, 1989) exemplifies the scholarly emphasis on the western roots of the environmental opposition. For a sampling of recent analysis of the backlash against environmentalism, see David Helvarg, *The War Against the Greens: The 'Wise-Use' Movement, the New Right, and Anti-Environmental Violence* (San Francisco: Sierra Club Books, 1994); John Echeverria and Raymond Booth Eby, editors, *Let the People Judge: Wise Use and the Private Property Rights Movement* (Washington: Island Press, 1995); Philip D. Brick and R. McGreggor Cawley, editors, *A Wolf in the Garden: The Land Rights Movement and the New Environmental Debate* (Lanham, MD: Rowman & Littlefield, 1996); Jacqueline Vaughn Switzer, *Green Backlash: The History and Politics of Environmental Opposition in the U.S.* (Boulder, CO: Lynne Rienner Publishers, 1997); Harvey M. Jacobs, editor, *Who Owns America?: Social Conflict Over Property Rights* (Madison: University of Wisconsin Press, 1998). The commentators often describe Richard A. Epstein's *Takings: Private Property and the Power of Eminent Domain* (Cambridge: Harvard University Press, 1985) as the intellectual foundation of the property rights movement. As one concluded, "Epstein has played a critical intellectual role in raising the takings issue to its current prominence. Many of his colleagues and students form the cadre of policy entrepreneurs and public interest litigators who have pushed for revisions in the judicial takings doctrine and new statutory limits on regulatory impacts on property values." See Brick and Cawley, *A Wolf in the Garden*, 125–126. In a frequently quoted passage, the solicitor general in the second Reagan administration also pointed to Epstein's influence: "Attorney General [Edwin] Meese and his young advisers – many drawn from the ranks of the then

6. **Though environmentalism was partly a form of consumer politics, the consumer mindset has limited the movement in critical ways.** The relationship between consumerism and environmentalism is not at all clear. According to Samuel Hays, the environmental movement was a consumer effort to counter the irresponsibility of producers. For the first time, millions of Americans demanded that industry stop scarring the land, polluting the air, and fouling the water. Yet a handful of scholars have begun to complicate Hays's argument. The demands of the newly affluent were not all laudable: Knowingly and unknowingly, consumers routinely made choices that intensified rather than diminished the human impact on the environment.

In *The Greening of a Nation?*, Hal Rothman concludes that the desire for environmental quality is often outweighed by conflicting desires. Americans "embrace environmentalism when it is convenient and inexpensive," Rothman writes, "but when it challenges the comforts to which they are accustomed, they ignore or avoid it." Though not a book about the environmental movement, William Cronon's *Nature's Metropolis* also suggests that consumers can be environmentally irresponsible. In nineteenth-century Chicago, few people could see the changes in the land required to produce a balloon-frame house or a side of beef or a loaf of bread. "The ecological place of production grew ever more remote from the economic point of consumption," Cronon writes, "making it harder and harder to keep track of the true costs and consequences of any particular product." In Cronon's view, that problem is even more profound today.[16]

The Bulldozer in the Countryside offers a further qualification of Hays's argument about the relationship between consumerism and

fledgling Federalist Societies and often devotees of the extreme libertarian views of Chicago law professor Richard Epstein – had a specific, aggressive, and, it seemed to me, quite radical project in mind: to use the Takings Clause of the Fifth Amendment as a severe brake upon federal and state regulation of business and property. The grand plan was to make government pay compensation as for a taking of property every time its regulations impinged too severely on a property right – limiting the possible uses for a parcel of land or restricting or tying up a business in red tape. If the government labored under so severe an obligation, there would be, to say the least, much less regulation." See Charles Fried, *Order and Law: Arguing the Reagan Revolution – A Firsthand Account* (New York: Simon and Schuster, 1991), 183.

16. For the quotations, see Rothman, *The Greening of a Nation?*, xii; William Cronon, *Nature's Metropolis: Chicago and the Great West* (New York: W. W. Norton & Company, 1991), 340.

environmentalism. Even when homeowners protested against threats to environmental quality, the protests had limited aims. In the late 1950s, for example, suds began to pour out of the faucets of thousands of suburban homes – the residue of nonbiodegradable detergents in septic tanks had contaminated drinking wells – and the resulting outcry helped to make water pollution a national concern. Yet the desire for a better quality of life only partially restrained the disruptive impact of septic tanks on the nonhuman world. The nation's lawmakers ultimately protected consumers from the principal domestic problems caused by the sprawl of septic-tank suburbs, but backyard waste-disposal systems continue to harm life in lakes and streams across the country. The consumer perspective was myopic: Homeowners only cared about certain elements of the environment.

The popularity of suburbia makes that clear. In the nineteenth century, the well-to-do had begun to build homes in parklike grounds at the edge of the city, and the suburban dream became more common after World War II. Though millions of postwar migrants to the suburbs simply sought affordable shelter – buying a tract house frequently cost less per month than renting a city apartment – suburban homebuyers often wanted a chance to be closer to nature. The developers of subdivisions acknowledged that hope by naming developments for natural features, but the names evidenced a brutal contradiction. To create tracts of houses, builders in the 1950s and 1960s routinely destroyed the meadows, woods, and hills they honored in their place names.[17]

The Bulldozer in the Countryside is the story of how Americans tried to resolve that contradiction.

17. The historical literature on the appeal of suburbia is vast. The best known works include Kenneth T. Jackson, *Crabgrass Frontier: The Suburbanization of the United States* (New York: Oxford University Press, 1985); Robert Fishman, *Bourgeois Utopias: The Rise and Fall of Suburbia* (New York: Basic Books, 1987); John Stilgoe, *Borderland: Origins of the American Suburb, 1820–1939* (New Haven: Yale University Press, 1988); Rosalyn Baxandall and Elizabeth Ewen, *Picture Windows: How the Suburbs Happened* (New York: Basic Books, 2000). For the post-1945 suburbs, see also Barbara M. Kelly, *Expanding the American Dream: Building and Rebuilding Levittown* (Albany: State University of New York Press, 1993); Clifford Edward Clark, Jr., *The American Family Home, 1800–1960* (Chapel Hill: University of North Carolina Press, 1986), 193–236; Gwendolyn Wright, *Building the Dream: A Social History of Housing in America* (Cambridge: MIT Press, 1981), 240–261; Karal Ann Marling, *As Seen on TV: The Visual Culture of Everyday Life in the 1950s* (Cambridge: Harvard University Press, 1994), 242–283; Thomas Hine, *Populuxe* (New York: Alfred A. Knopf, 1986), 15–58; Elaine Tyler May, *Homeward Bound: American Families in the Cold War Era* (New York: Basic Books, 1988), 162–182.

1

Levitt's Progress:
The Rise of the
Suburban-Industrial Complex

On 1,200 flat acres of potato farmland near Hicksville, Long Island, an army of trucks sped over new-laid roads. Every 100 feet, the trucks stopped and dumped identical bundles of lumber, pipes, bricks, shingles and copper tubing – all as neatly packaged as loaves from a bakery. Near the bundles, giant machines with an endless chain of buckets ate into the earth, taking just 13 minutes to dig a narrow, four-foot trench around a 25-by-32 ft. rectangle. Then came more trucks, loaded with cement, and laid a four-inch foundation for a house in the rectangle.

After the machines came the men. On nearby slabs already dry, they worked in crews of two and three, laying bricks, raising studs, nailing lath, painting, sheathing, shingling. Each crew did its special job, then hurried on to the next site. Under the skilled combination of men & machines, new homes rose faster than Jack ever built them; a new one was finished every 15 minutes.

Three years ago, little potatoes had sprouted from these fields. Now there were 10,600 houses inhabited by more than 40,000 people, a community almost as big as 96-year-old Poughkeepsie, N.Y., Plainfield, N.J., or Chelsea, Mass. Its name: Levittown.

In those excited words – the introduction to a cover story in 1950 – *Time* heralded a revolution in American life. Instead of building houses one at a time, the new leaders of the housing industry had begun to use factorylike methods of mass production. The results were astonishing. In 1949, the number of housing starts topped a million for the first time, and 1950 promised even more: In May alone, the nation's homebuilders had started over 140,000 units. Soon the industry would overcome the desperate postwar shortage of housing.[1]

1. "Up from the Potato Fields," *Time* 56 (July 3, 1950): 67, 68, 72.

In fact, the statistics cited by *Time* understated the record-breaking output of the late 1940s. According to a revised Bureau of the Census tabulation, the number of housing starts in 1949 topped 1.4 million. The final tally for 1950 was even higher – over 1.9 million, more than twice the pre-1945 record.[2]

As *Time* acknowledged, the federal government had played a key role in the housing revolution. To provide housing for workers in defense plants during World War II, the government encouraged builders – including the builders of Levittown – to experiment with mass-production techniques. By providing loan guarantees, the government also helped builders obtain the capital needed to operate on a large scale. Perhaps most important, the government's mortgage-insurance programs expanded the market for housing. The 30-year mortgage became standard, with a 5 percent down payment – veterans could buy a home with no money down. As a result, owning was often cheaper than renting: An ex-G.I. could realize the American dream in Levittown for $56 a month. "No longer must young married couples plan to start living in an apartment, saving for the distant day when they can buy a home," *Time* explained. "Now they can do it more easily than they can buy a $2,000 car on the installment plan."[3]

For *Time,* however, the heart of the postwar housing story was the innovative approach of a new breed of builder-entrepreneurs. The exemplar was William Levitt, the visionary behind Levittown. Levitt was "the most potent single modernizing influence in a largely antiquated industry," the magazine proclaimed, and Levitt and Sons was fast becoming "the General Motors" of housing. Across the country, a host of builders were using Levitt's methods to produce houses quickly and cheaply.[4]

The most conspicuous Levitt innovation involved the division of the construction process into 26 tasks, each performed by a different crew of workers. Since each crew did the same job over and over again, the work went amazingly fast. In many cases, the crews simply installed fixtures or pieces prefabricated in a central shop,

2. U. S. Department of Commerce, *Housing Construction Statistics* (Washington: USGPO, 1966), 18.
3. "Up from the Potato Fields," 68.
4. Ibid., 67, 68.

so only a few of the crews required highly skilled laborers. Because Levitt and Sons did not use union workers, the firm also avoided costly and time-consuming work rules. Instead of painting by hand, for example, Levitt's workers used spray guns. To cut costs further, Levitt forced suppliers to sell building materials to the firm directly. For a few key items, Levitt and Sons even eliminated that step: The Levitts bought a lumber mill and set up a nail-making plant. According to Levitt, the combination of "size plus organization" allowed the firm to save $1,000 a house on homes selling for $7,990. The savings opened the door to more young dreamers.[5]

The *Time* story was tardy yet typical. By 1950, William Levitt had become a national hero. Though a few critics warned that Levittown would become a new kind of slum, the warnings were lost among the dozens of admiring profiles of Levitt published in the late 1940s. In a 1947 essay entitled "The Industry Capitalism Forgot," *Fortune* promoted Levitt's methods as the solution to the costly conservatism of the building trades, and the magazine returned to the subject a few years later with a lengthy piece on "Levitt's Progress." *Reader's Digest* republished both the 1947 *Fortune* piece and the 1950 *Time* profile. *Life* also published several photo essays on Levittown. In one, the magazine called Levitt's houses "probably the best value currently on the market." In another, the magazine posed a family of five in Sunday best on the grass in front of a Levitt house, and the photograph soon became one of the iconic images of the postwar period: The wife smiles radiantly, the oldest child – a boy – has a slight but unmistakable grin, the two young girls stand transfixed before the camera, while the husband looks resolutely ahead, arms bent at his side – a little nervous, perhaps, but proud. For millions of young families, the photograph argued, the great American dream of homeownership was becoming real.[6]

5. Ibid., 71. Though Levitt was hailed as a pioneer, a few California builders anticipated many of the "Levitt" innovations in the late 1930s and early 1940s. See Greg Hise, *Magnetic Los Angeles: Planning the Twentieth-Century Metropolis* (Baltimore: Johns Hopkins University Press, 1997), 137–151, 165–175.
6. For a sample of the dozens of Levitt-as-hero stories in the late 1940s and early 1950s, see "The Industry Capitalism Forgot," *Fortune* 36 (August 1947): 61–67, 167–170; "Levitt's Progress," *Fortune* 46 (October 1952): 155–168; "The Way to More – and Cheaper – Houses," *Reader's Digest* 51 (October 1947): 45–50; "The Levitts of Levittown," *Reader's Digest* 57 (October 1950): 105–108; "Nation's Biggest Housebuilder," *Life* 25 (August 8, 1948): 75–78; "Levitt Adds 1950 Model to His Line," *Life* 28 (May 22, 1950):

In part, the enthusiastic response to Levitt's work was due to the peculiar circumstances of the postwar period. The demobilization of 14 million men and women in the armed forces led to a record demand for housing. Everywhere, newly married and recently reunited couples keenly desired the space to start families. Yet, because of the turmoil of the Depression and the war, almost a generation had passed with little homebuilding. According to government estimates, the nation needed 5 million new homes and apartments to satisfy the demand.[7]

For two years, newspapers, magazines, radio shows, and movie newsreels told horror stories about the housing shortage. The city of Chicago sold 250 streetcars as homes. In California, people were living in the unfinished fuselages of bombers. The photographs in a 1945 *Life* report showed a veteran sitting by a tent with a sign appealing for a home; a truck transformed into a shelter; a crowd lined up at a funeral parlor to find the addresses of newly vacated apartments; and a pair of men heading down the stairs of a Turkish bath with suitcases. The text cited a classified ad published in the Omaha newspaper: "Big Ice Box, 7 by 17 feet. Could be fixed up to live in." Official reports added the weight of statistics to the anecdotal evidence in the mass media. A congressional investigation found that hundreds of thousands of veterans could find shelter only in garages, trailers, barns, or chicken coops. The government also estimated that as many as two and a half million families were living "doubled up" with relatives.[8]

When Levitt set production records at Levittown, therefore, the news had obvious appeal. Almost all the pieces about Levittown mentioned residents grateful just to have a place to call home. But

141–147. The most notable contemporary critique of Levittown is Eric Larrabee, "The Six Thousand Houses That Levitt Built," *Harper's* 197 (September 1948): 79–88. For a thoughtful scholarly discussion of the Levitt "myth," see Barbara M. Kelly, *Expanding the American Dream: Building and Rebuilding Levittown* (Albany: State University of New York Press, 1993), 147–161.

7. For descriptions of the postwar housing crisis, see Gwendolyn Wright, *Building the Dream: A Social History of Housing in America* (Cambridge: MIT Press, 1981), 242–243; Joseph C. Goulden, *The Best Years: 1945–1950* (New York: Atheneum, 1976), 132–133; Richard O. Davies, *Housing Reform During the Truman Administration* (Columbia: University of Missouri Press, 1966), 40–41; Davis R. B. Ross, *Preparing for Ulysses: Politics and Veterans During World War II* (New York: Columbia University Press, 1969), 238–274.

8. In addition to the sources cited above, see "The Great Housing Shortage," *Life* 19 (December 17, 1945): 27–35; "Mr. Wyatt's Shortage," *Fortune* 33 (April 1946): 105.

the postwar housing crisis explains only a small part of Levitt's aura in the late 1940s and early 1950s. Like Henry Ford, Levitt had found a way to offer "the great multitude" a piece of the good life once reserved for the well-to-do, and the achievement promised to transform the country. Indeed, the mass-produced house fulfilled a set of needs first articulated almost 30 years before, when a handful of political and business leaders began to ponder the importance of affordable housing to the nation's economic, social, and political order.[9]

The Macroeconomic Importance of Homebuilding

Throughout the Progressive era, a variety of urban reformers campaigned vigorously to improve the quality of working-class housing. But the state of the nation's housing did not become a national issue until 1921, when Herbert Hoover became Secretary of Commerce. Hoover's interest in housing went beyond the condition of tenements and slums. He believed that widespread homeownership was "the foundation of a sound economy and social system," and he argued that the structure of the housing industry made home-ownership impossible for millions of Americans.[10]

At the time, the building of homes was still largely a craft. Most builders built only one or two houses a year. In the period from 1890 to 1920, the total number of housing starts in the nation's cities, suburbs, and small towns generally ranged between 250,000 and 400,000 a year. Though a handful of people had begun to integrate building and land development, the vast majority of builders

9. In a famous mission statement, Ford promised to "build a motor car for the great multitude." See Warren I. Susman, *Culture as History: The Transformation of American Society in the Twentieth Century* (New York: Pantheon, 1984), 136. Joseph Goulden notes that Levitt enjoyed a reputation as the Henry Ford of builders; see *The Best Years*, 139.
10. The quotation is from Hoover's introduction to John M. Gries and James S. Taylor, *How to Own Your Own Home: A Handbook for Prospective Home Owners* (Washington: USGPO, 1925), v. Though I focus here on the work of the Department of Commerce in the 1920s, the federal government briefly had attempted to promote more efficient methods of homebuilding during World War I. To address the problem of housing shortages in war centers, the federal government had also created two agencies to build houses. But the agencies were abolished at the end of the war. For a good account of the wartime programs, see Gail Radford, *Modern Housing for America: Policy Struggles in the New Deal Era* (Chicago: University of Chicago Press, 1996), 16–17, 37–43.

did not sell lots or install utilities. The purchase of a home was also quite complicated, since there were two markets for new housing, one for business and professional people and one for workers and shopkeepers. In the first market, a buyer often had to put 50 percent down, with the remainder due the bank in five years – ten at the most. In the second market, which operated mainly in ethnic neighborhoods, the building and financing processes were not so neatly separated: To become homeowners, working-class families had to rely on sweat equity and community self-help networks. For the nonfarm population as a whole, the homeownership rate in 1920 was 41 percent, a figure that had changed little since the government began to keep housing statistics in 1890.[11]

To Hoover, the large number of renters was intolerable. "Maintaining a high percentage of individual home owners is one of the searching tests that now challenge the people of the United States," he wrote in 1923. The discipline of ownership was critical to social order. "The home owner has a constructive aim in life," Hoover explained. "He works harder outside his home; he spends his leisure more profitably, and he and his family live a finer life and enjoy more of the comforts and cultivating influences of our modern civilization. A husband and wife who own their own home are more apt to save. They have an interest in the advancement of a social system that permits the individual to store up the fruits of his labor. As direct taxpayers they take a more active part in local government. Above all, the love of home is one of the finest instincts and the greatest of inspirations of our people."[12]

11. The literature on housing in the period from 1880 to 1920 is vast. For a succinct discussion of the small scale of building at the time, see Marc A. Weiss, *The Rise of the Community Builders: The American Real Estate Industry and Urban Land Planning* (New York: Columbia University Press, 1987), 38–40. The best discussion of the dual character of the housing market is Olivier Zunz, *The Changing Face of Inequality: Urbanization, Industrial Development, and Immigrants in Detroit, 1880–1920* (Chicago: University of Chicago Press, 1982), 129–176. For the construction and ownership statistics, see U.S. Department of Commerce, *Housing Construction Statistics*, 18; Paul F. Wendt, *Housing Policy – The Search for Solutions: A Comparison of the United Kingdom, Sweden, West Germany, and the United States since World War II* (Berkeley: University of California Press, 1963), 160. The homeownership figures for the nation as a whole were always several points higher than the nonfarm statistics I cite in the text, because a higher percentage of rural Americans owned their homes. For the national totals, see F. John Devaney, *Tracking the American Dream: 50 Years of Housing History from the Census Bureau* (Washington: U.S. Department of Commerce, 1994), 21.
12. Gries and Taylor, *How to Own Your Own Home*, v–vi.

Despite the social importance of homeownership, Hoover concluded, the United States never would become "a nation of home owners" unless the nation's builders began to produce houses more efficiently. For Hoover, indeed, the idea of efficiency was a kind of obsession. He had become a public hero by applying engineering principles to postwar problems, and he saw productive efficiency as the key to national prosperity. "The only road to further advance in the standard of living," he wrote in his best-selling credo *American Individualism,* "is by greater invention, greater elimination of waste, greater production and better distribution of commodities and services." As the first president of the Federation of American Engineering Societies in 1920, Hoover had organized a major investigation of waste in industry, and the study confirmed Hoover's judgment that the backwardness and disorganization of the building industry forced millions of hard-working Americans to live in rented quarters: Waste accounted for 53 percent of the cost of construction. To reduce waste – and to bring the price of new housing within reach of the average worker – the nation's builders had to learn new techniques of mass production.[13]

Hoover also was convinced that a more efficient building industry was essential to the achievement of "permanent prosperity." The exaggerated booms and busts in construction frequently threw the manufacturing sector out of step. In Hoover's view, therefore, homebuilding was one of a number of problem industries – along with agriculture, mining, and transportation – that weakened the entire economy. Hoover believed that a reformed construction industry could help create a new abundance. When he arrived in Washington in 1921, the country was struggling to overcome a severe slump that followed World War I, and he immediately convened a pioneering conference on unemployment. The conferees argued that builders might play a significant role in reviving the economy. "It

13. The quotation comes from Herbert Hoover, *American Individualism* (Garden City, NY: Doubleday, Page & Company, 1922), 32–33. For the waste study, see Committee on Elimination of Waste in Industry of the Federated American Engineering Societies, *Waste in Industry* (Washington: Federated American Engineering Societies, 1921), 52–93. The chart on 91 provides the statistical summary. For Hoover's views on the impact of wasteful practices in the housing industry, see Ellis W. Hawley, "Herbert Hoover and Economic Stabilization, 1921–1922," in Ellis W. Hawley, editor, *Herbert Hoover as Secretary of Commerce: Studies in New Era Thought and Practice* (Iowa City: University of Iowa Press, 1981), 54; Radford, *Modern Housing for America,* 51.

is recognized that the construction industry is a key industry," the conference report concluded, "that there is a vast amount of construction needed, and that this construction work would afford employment to a large number of men directly and indirectly and would result in the creation of permanent and useful wealth, translating wasting labor into earning capital." Of course, the power of builders to generate wealth was not limited to periods of economic adjustment.[14]

Accordingly, Hoover hoped to modernize and rationalize the housing industry. Though he was dead set against direct government intervention in the market, he thought that public officials could and should serve as facilitators of industrial progress. The federal government especially could help industry become more efficient by gathering economic statistics, conducting research, and promoting national trade associations. Because homebuilding was so critical to the social and economic future of the nation, Hoover quickly set out to demonstrate the benefits of a public-private partnership in the construction industry: In 1922, he established a division of building and housing in the Commerce Department.[15]

The new division focused on the problem of waste. The staff worked with industry officials to create national standards for building materials. At the same time, the housing division urged municipalities to adopt a uniform building code. In both cases, the goal was to lower construction costs by eliminating a serious obstacle to streamlined, large-scale operations.[16]

To encourage investment in the industry, the housing division pro-

14. The quotation comes from President's Conference on Unemployment, *Report of the President's Conference on Unemployment* (Washington: USGPO, 1921), 117. For Hoover's views on the economic ill effects of the housing industry, see Hawley, "Herbert Hoover and Economic Stabilization, 1921–1922," 54; Radford, *Modern Housing for America,* 51. For a discussion of Hoover's ideas about "permanent prosperity," see William Leach, *Land of Desire: Merchants, Power, and the Rise of a New American Culture* (1993; reprint, New York: Vintage Books, 1994), 355.
15. For Hoover's concern about the "modernization" and "rationalization" of the industry, see Ellis W. Hawley, "Herbert Hoover, the Commerce Secretariat, and the Vision of an 'Associative State,' 1921–1928," *Journal of American History* 61 (1974): 125. The notes below provide additional sources for the history of the building and housing division.
16. Wright, *Building the Dream,* 196–197; Radford, *Modern Housing for America,* 52; Hawley, "Herbert Hoover and Economic Stabilization, 1921–1922," 55.

duced a model zoning law designed to protect the value of residential property. Throughout the 1920s, the Commerce Department also worked with a private philanthropic organization – Better Homes for America – to promote the ideal of homeownership. The organization produced a film entitled "Home, Sweet Home" and distributed thousands of copies of the Commerce Department's *How to Own Your Own Home* booklet. By the end of the decade, Better Homes for America had over 7,000 local chapters, and each sponsored a variety of lectures and demonstrations, including construction of model homes.[17]

For a few years, the Hoover promise of "permanent prosperity" seemed real. The years from 1922 to 1928 set construction records. In 1925, the peak year, the number of housing starts reached 937,000. That was nearly twice the pre-1922 record. The nonfarm homeownership figure also increased during the 1920s, from 41 to 46 percent. But even before the stock market crashed in 1929, the pace of new construction had begun to slow. Then the Depression all but eliminated the demand. In 1933, the worst year for homebuilders since the government began to keep statistics, the industry put up only 93,000 homes. In the nation's cities, the number of home foreclosures reached a thousand a week. By 1940, the home ownership rate would fall back to 41 percent, the 1920 figure.[18]

The Depression did not change Hoover's approach to the housing problem. With one exception – a program to bolster the home mortgage market – he still refused to involve the government directly in the building sector. Instead, he intensified his call for voluntary action by builders, lenders, materials suppliers, and local officials to make homebuilding more efficient: In 1931, he organized a President's Conference on Home Building and Home Ownership, attended by more than 3,500 people. In part, Hoover hoped "to revitalize the building of homes as a factor of economic recovery." But he remained focused on his long-term goal. As he explained to his

17. Leach, *Land of Desire*, 369–370; Wright, *Building the Dream*, 197–198; Radford, *Modern Housing for America*, 52–53; Hawley, "Herbert Hoover, the Commerce Secretariat, and the Vision of an 'Associative State,' 1921–1928," 133–134; Hise, *Magnetic Los Angeles*, 38–40.
18. U.S. Department of Commerce, *Housing Construction Statistics*, 18; Wright, *Building the Dream*, 240; Wendt, *Housing Policy*, 160.

staff when he planned the conference, he wanted to inspire action to overcome the serious obstacles to the spread of homeownership.[19]

In his opening address at the conference, Hoover gave a similar charge to the participants. What could be done to facilitate the ownership of homes? That was the great question of the conference. "To own one's home is a physical expression of individualism, of enterprise, of independence, and of freedom of the spirit," Hoover explained. "This aspiration penetrates the heart of our national well-being. It makes for happier married life, it makes for better children, it makes for confidence and security, it makes for courage to meet the battle of life, it makes for better citizenship. There can be no fear for democracy or self-government or for liberty or freedom from home owners no matter how humble they may be."[20]

In response to Hoover's charge, the conference participants produced an 11-volume report. The published proceedings gave special emphasis to the problem of "mass production" – the phrase appeared dozens of times in the summary volume alone. By 1931, everyone knew about Ford's success with the automobile, and the conference committees on "technological developments" and "large-scale operations" both gave considerable thought to the best ways to incorporate Ford's insights into homebuilding. The committee on research also called for extensive study of the potential for mass production. As the committee concluded, the need was "self-evident," since new methods of organizing production held out the best hope of bringing costs within the budgets of the majority of workers. The committee on business and housing even included a lengthy proposal from the department store magnate Edward Filene calling for industrialists to create a "General Housing Corporation."[21]

19. The quotation is from John M. Gries and James T. Ford, editors, *Housing Objectives and Programs* [Publications of the President's Conference on Home Building and Home Ownership, Volume XI] (Washington: National Capital Press, 1932), 5. For Hoover's instructions to the staff, see xv.
20. Ibid., 1–2.
21. Gries and Ford, *Housing Objectives*, xiv, 8, 11, 35–40, 95, 283–285; John M. Gries and James T. Ford, editors, *Slums, Large-Scale Housing and Decentralization* [Publications of the President's Conference on Home Building and Home Ownership, Volume III] (Washington: National Capital Press, 1932), 66–88, 170–173; John M. Gries and James T. Ford, editors, *Home Ownership, Income and Types of Dwellings* [Publications of the President's Conference on Home Building and Home Ownership, Volume IV] (Washington: National Capital Press, 1932), viii. For Filene's interest in mass-produced hous-

The logic was straightforward. The automobile once was a symbol of wealth, but the use of modern mass-production methods had allowed a sharp decline in price. The trend was also evident in the price of almost every consumer good, from radios to refrigerators. Housing was the great exception. Despite the Depression, the cost of shelter continued to rise. As a result, new construction still was a luxury, affordable only by "the salaried class." That would not change – and the homebuilding industry would not meet the social and economic needs of the nation – until builders learned to follow the example of the automakers.

The call for mass-produced housing had a special urgency for boosters of private enterprise, since the argument for publicly supported shelter had grown stronger in the 1920s. Despite the boom in housing construction during the decade, at least a third of the nation still lived in terribly substandard dwellings. In the view of a prominent group of housing reformers, the failure of builders to satisfy the demand for decent and affordable shelter pointed to a fundamental flaw in the market – a flaw that more efficient methods of production would not overcome. In a book published just before the Hoover conference began, reformer Edith Wood argued bluntly that low- and middle-income Americans would never attain adequate housing without direct government action. "Except under pioneer conditions, where land and building materials are practically free, supply and demand, unaided, have never, at any time or at any place, furnished all classes of self-supporting families with a minimum health-and-decency grade of housing," Wood wrote. "Nor is there any reason to suppose they ever will." The alternative was clear. In Europe, a number of municipal and national governments had acted decisively after the war to provide subsidized housing for the masses, and Wood urged American officials to catch up to "the rest of the civilized world." Her voice was not alone, especially in the nation's largest cities.[22]

ing, see also Rosalyn Baxandall and Elizabeth Ewen, *Picture Windows: How the Suburbs Happened* (New York: Basic Books, 2000), 37–39.

22. Edith Elmer Wood, *Recent Trends in American Housing* (New York: Macmillan, 1931), 45. The possibility of using public funds to construct housing came up several times at the 1931 conference; see Gries and Ford, *Slums, Large-Scale Housing and Decentralization*, 49–50, 117–126. Radford provides a good summary of the public-housing argument in *Modern Housing for America*, 43–47, 53–56, 59–83.

The Hoover administration was quick to point out the potential threat to conservative economic values. In the foreword to the conference report on slums and blighted areas, for example, Secretary of the Interior Ray Wilbur issued a stern warning to "those who look upon government operations in housing construction with abhorrence." If the building industry failed to produce affordable housing for the working class, "it seems likely that American cities will be forced to turn to European methods of solution of this problem, through subsidization by State and municipal treasuries and probably through actual ownership and operation of housing projects by municipal authority." The issue surely would be decided in the next ten years, Wilbur concluded, and the business community needed to meet the challenge aggressively: "There is no compromise – no timid or partial solution."[23]

In 1932, a few months after the Hoover conference, the editors of *Fortune* made the point even more bluntly in the introduction to a six-part series on housing. "Housing is the one field where private enterprise and individual initiative have notoriously failed," the magazine proclaimed. As a result, the argument for socialism no longer seemed so foreign. The crescendos of rhetoric were not hard to imagine. The public-housing enthusiast easily "might declare that when an industry dealing in a fundamental commodity for which there is a constant real demand, and for which there is now and long has been a critical and crying need, confesses that it is unable to supply any part of the market but the richest third, and that the other two-thirds must satisfy themselves with a second-hand, resold product even though that product is in such condition as to endanger the health of the buyer and his wife and his children – when such an industry makes such a confession it admits industrial bankruptcy. And when it adds that it is suffering from overproduction within the limits of the market it *has* been able to reach, it confesses intellectual bankruptcy as well."[24]

The nation's best-known business magazine was not willing to concede the argument. The housing problem revealed only the stub-

23. Gries and Ford, *Slums,* xii. In addition, see 85.
24. "Housing I – The Need," *Fortune* 5 (February 1932): 88. The series ran through July, and then appeared as a book: Editors of "Fortune," *Housing America* (New York: Harcourt, Brace and Company, 1932).

born refusal of a single industry to accept the need for industrial production, the editors argued, not a fundamental flaw in the capitalist system. As the *Waste in Industry* study made clear, the costs of new housing could be cut substantially if builders operated at a larger scale: The small tradesman could not purchase materials in bulk or make efficient use of labor. Yet the problem surely was soluble. In the conclusion to the series, the editors described a number of promising ventures in mass production, including the first designs of General Houses, Inc., a newly formed consortium of manufacturing giants. The new corporation suggested that the nation's leading industrialists had recognized the social and economic importance of a modern housing industry. Within a few years, the editors predicted, a new breed of builders would enjoy the profits of supplying the vast demand for a well-built yet inexpensive house.[25]

The battle between the boosters of mass production and the supporters of public housing continued throughout the 1930s, but the election of Franklin Roosevelt changed the focus of the housing debate. Roosevelt did not care deeply about the rate of homeownership or the quality of the housing available to the working class, although his administration acted to improve both. He was not much interested in the structure of the homebuilding industry. His great goal was to lift the nation out of the misery of the Depression, and he viewed the housing problem as a small part of the all-important challenge of economic recovery. Yet the New Deal ultimately did much to encourage tract-house methods of construction.[26]

25. Editors of "Fortune," *Housing America*, 21–24, 45–70, 109–131.
26. For examples of the mass-production argument, see A. C. Shire, "The Industrial Organization of Housing: Its Methods and Costs," *Annals of the American Academy of Political and Social Science* 190 (March 1937): 37–49; Douglas Haskell, "Houses Like Fords," *Harper's* 168 (February 1934): 286–298; Clarence Arthur Perry, *Housing for the Machine Age* (New York: Russell Sage Foundation, 1939), 25–40, 181–204. For a good discussion of the campaign for "the minimum house," see Hise, *Magnetic Los Angeles,* 56–85. The call for mass-produced housing was also part of a broader cultural movement in the 1930s. See Brian Horrigan, "The Home of Tomorrow, 1927–1945," in Joseph Corn, editor, *Imagining Tomorrow* (Cambridge: MIT Press, 1986), 137–163. The public-housing argument is exemplified by Catherine Bauer, *Modern Housing* (Boston: Houghton Mifflin, 1934); Langdon W. Post, *The Challenge of Housing* (Farrar & Rinehart, 1938), 268–294; Coleman Woodbury, "Integrating Private and Public Enterprise in Housing," *Annals of the American Academy of Political and Social Science* 190 (March 1937): 162. For the public-housing campaigns of the 1930s, see also Baxandall and Ewen, *Picture Windows,* 57–66.

From the first, Roosevelt understood the macroeconomic importance of the housing industry. In late 1933, as New Dealer Marriner Eccles later recalled, Roosevelt asked five staff members to devise a program to stimulate construction:

He knew that almost a third of the unemployed were to be found in the building trades, and housing was by far the most important part of that trade. A program of new home construction, launched on an adequate scale, not only would gradually put these men back to work but would act as the wheel within the wheel to move the whole economic engine. It would affect everyone, from the manufacturer of lace curtains to the manufacturers of lumber, bricks, furniture, cement, and electrical appliances. The mere shipment of these supplies would affect the railroads, which in turn would need the produce of steel mills for rails, freight cars, and so on.

Because Roosevelt did not want to bust the budget, the staff members focused on ways to produce a maximum amount of private investment with a minimum outlay of public funds. The result was the National Housing Act of 1934.[27]

Roosevelt had already supported the creation of a Home Owners Loan Corporation to stem the flood of foreclosures, and he later approved a pioneering program to construct houses and apartments, but the National Housing Act had by far the greatest impact. The most important provision of the act created a mortgage-insurance program that revolutionized the nation's home finance system. If lenders and builders met a number of conditions, the newly created Federal Housing Administration would guarantee 20-year loans for up to 80 percent of the value of a home. In later years, a series

27. Marriner S. Eccles, *Beckoning Frontiers: Public and Personal Recollections* (New York: Alfred A. Knopf, 1951), 145–161. For the quotation, see 145–146. Several members of the Roosevelt administration spoke about the importance of the National Housing Act as a stimulus measure during congressional hearings on the legislation. Harry Hopkins, the Federal Emergency Relief Administrator, pointed out that "more than one-third of all the unemployed are identified, directly or indirectly, with the building trades. Now, a purpose of this bill, a fundamental purpose of this bill, is an effort to get these people back to work." Secretary of Labor Frances Perkins echoed Hopkins in stressing the need to provide employment for building tradesmen "who have long been out of work and who are themselves a basic part of our internal market, our purchasing power in this country, and also the importance arising from the stimulation of capital-goods industries, that will flow out of this bill, and the importance that that will be to the program of recovery in this country." Their testimony is reprinted in J. Paul Mitchell, editor, *Federal Housing Policy and Programs: Past and Present* (New Brunswick, NJ: Center for Urban Policy Research, 1985), 47–48, 60–61.

of amendments to the act allowed even more liberal loans, and the short-term mortgage with a large down payment became rare.[28]

Though the legislation won support principally as a prime-the-pump measure, the loan-guarantee provisions indirectly gave the government considerable power to shape the homebuilding process. To reduce the risk of loss, the FHA only insured mortgages on homes that met certain standards, and FHA officials used the power to establish minimum standards as a prod to innovation. The FHA quickly decided to promote large-scale construction for people of modest incomes. As a December 1934 circular explained, "the Administration seeks to encourage that type of operative builder who looks upon the production of homes as a manufacturing and merchandising process of high social significance and, who, preferably, assumes responsibility for the product from the plotting and development of the land to the disposal of the completed dwelling units." That was exactly the way Levitt and Sons operated in the late 1940s.[29]

The FHA inducements took several forms. If a builder submitted acceptable plans for a large-scale development, for example, the FHA might provide a "conditional commitment" that helped the builder to obtain working capital. In essence, the commitment was a promise to insure mortgages for the entire project as long as the buyers qualified for the program, so a lender could front the builder money at reduced risk. The commitment thus decreased the amount of capital a builder needed to undertake a big project. Though the program had little impact during the Depression years, a handful of postwar builders used conditional commitments to arrange financing for developments with thousands of homes.[30]

Because the administration and the public remained focused on

28. For summaries of New Deal housing legislation, see Ronald C. Tobey, *Technology as Freedom: The New Deal and the Electrical Modernization of the American Home* (Berkeley: University of California Press, 1996), 104–111; Gertrude S. Fish, "Housing Policy During the Great Depression," in Gertrude Sipperly Fish, editor, *The Story of Housing* (New York: Macmillan, 1979), 195–220, 232–239; Nathaniel S. Keith, *Politics and the Housing Crisis Since 1930* (New York: Universe Books, 1973), 22–39.
29. The FHA circular is quoted by Weiss, *The Rise of the Community Builders*, 147.
30. Ibid. In addition, see Kenneth T. Jackson, *Crabgrass Frontier: The Suburbanization of the United States* (New York: Oxford University Press, 1985), 238; Barry Checkoway, "Large Builders, Federal Housing Programmes, and Postwar Suburbanization," *International Journal of Urban and Regional Research* 4 (1980): 21–45.

the economic emergency, the FHA effort to encourage large-scale building went forward without fanfare. But the issue of mass production returned to prominence in the early 1940s, when "Dr. New Deal" became "Dr. Win the War." The mobilization for wartime production caused the population to explode in dozens of cities. To provide shelter for workers in defense plants, the federal government organized the construction of roughly a million and a half housing units, and the war administrators gave priority to builders willing and able to operate on a large scale. The contracts for defense housing also encouraged experiments with new techniques for speeding the construction process, including greater use of components "prefabricated" in factories or centralized workshops.[31]

In addition to creating a crying need for mass-produced housing, the war led New Deal planners to think anew about the economic importance of a vigorous homebuilding industry. Within months of the bombing of Pearl Harbor, the National Resources Planning Board began to ponder the likely needs of a postwar economy. The NRPB soon concluded that a sound transition to peacetime would require a dramatic change in the way Americans built homes.[32] "When the war is over," the planners reported in July 1942, "the need for housing in this country will challenge our industrial, financial, and political ingenuity." The dearth of construction during the Depression and the extraordinary increase in family formation during the war pointed toward a tremendous postwar demand for new homes. The ability of the industry to satisfy that demand would have a profound impact on the prospects for full employment. If builders could produce a million homes a year, the report argued, "the whole economy can be given a powerful support amid the shocks of the change-over from war production." On the other hand, a backward homebuilding industry would be "a major drag." The historical record proved that. In the mid-1920s, a building boom had helped the good times roll, but the inability of builders to produce

---

31. For a summary of the wartime housing effort, see Mary K. Nenno, "Housing in the Decade of the 1940s – The War and Postwar Periods Leave Their Marks," in Fish, *The Story of Housing*, 247–252. In addition, see Donald Albrecht, editor, *World War II and the American Dream: How Wartime Building Changed a Nation* (Cambridge: MIT Press, 1995).
32. National Resources Planning Board, *The Role of the Housebuilding Industry* (Washington: USGPO, 1942).

for a broad market eventually brought the economy down. Unfortunately, a number of forces were still retarding the growth of "a technically efficient industry geared to mass needs." Before the end of the war, therefore, the nation's leaders needed to make a choice about the future of homebuilding – to allow a return to traditions of inefficiency or to encourage "a large volume of low-priced production with its attendant social and economic benefits."[33]

In part, the NRPB report recast old arguments. The contribution of construction to employment was well known. Including the manufacture of building materials, the construction industry provided 10 percent of the nation's jobs, and homebuilding accounted for well over half of that total. But the emphasis on "broad markets" and "mass needs" was new. Like a growing number of Americans, the New Deal planners had found insight in the revolutionary economics of John Maynard Keynes.[34]

Even before Keynes published *The General Theory of Employment, Interest, and Money* in 1936, a few American economists had argued that the driving force in the economy was consumer spending, not capital investment. That meant that the great problem of the day was underconsumption, not overproduction. To bring the economy out of the doldrums, consumers needed to spend more, especially on durable goods. Keynes added the insight that government expenditures could counter economic downturns by ensuring that consumer spending did not fall. The new way of thinking began to win converts after the recession of 1937–38: The nation had seemed about to climb out of the Depression, but the economy fell back again after a sharp cutback in public spending. The war clinched the case for Keynes. As government spending on defense soared, the economy soared too. Unemployment all but disappeared. To the astonishment of countless officials, the gross national product grew at a record rate.[35]

For liberal Democrats, the Keynesian revolution resolved a particularly difficult dilemma. The early New Deal had drawn inspiration from a multifaceted critique of capitalism, but the political

33. Ibid., 1–3, 5–6, 10–11, 13–16, 26–29.
34. For the employment statistics, see Charles Abrams, *The Future of Housing* (New York: Harper & Brothers, 1946), 56–57.
35. Alan Brinkley, *The End of Reform: New Deal Liberalism in Recession and War* (New York: Alfred A. Knopf, 1995), 65–85, 227–264.

stalemate in Congress and the experience of mobilizing the nation for war had encouraged many New Dealers to search for a less confrontational program of reform. Keynes pointed the way. The state did not need to restructure the basic institutions of society in order to promote social welfare. Instead, the government could use a variety of Keynesian tools to achieve sustained economic growth, and the tool kit included policies to expand the housing market.[36]

The most vivid illustration of the importance of housing in the new liberal agenda came in 1946 in a best-selling call to action, *Tomorrow without Fear,* by the New Dealer Chester Bowles. In the first part of the book, Bowles offered a primer on Keynesianism. "It is in the increase of consumer spending on the things that consumers want and need that we must look for the basic and lasting solution to our economic future," he explained. "We must all learn to live constantly better, a lot better. Our standards of living must rise steadily year by year to match the increase in our productive capacity. Indeed, they must rise even more rapidly as the years go by, since, as we have seen, both the spending of business on private plant and the spending of government will, during the next twenty years, provide a steadily decreasing portion of the total spending we must have to keep our industrial machine running in high gear." The rest of the book outlined the full-employment program. To ensure adequate spending power, the government needed to pursue eight courses of action – sustain the consumer market by public spending; promote free competition; raise minimum wages; extend social security; revise the tax system to reduce the burden on most taxpayers; act boldly to promote homebuilding; foster foreign trade; and provide farmers with more purchasing power. The list was telling, since Bowles singled out just two sectors of the economy, and housing came first.[37]

"In the construction industry lies perhaps our greatest single opportunity, not only to correct our shocking lack of decent homes, but to increase the purchasing power of our people," Bowles explained. "Steady wages to 4 1/2 million workers will mean vastly increased sales in our grocery stores, our clothing and appliance

36. Ibid., 3–8.
37. Chester Bowles, *Tomorrow Without Fear* (New York: Simon and Schuster, 1946), 49, 57–65.

stores, in all the markets of our nation. There isn't a group in the land which is not certain to benefit from a vigorous program of homebuilding – benefit in increased farm income, higher pay checks, or better profits." Because the homebuilding industry was "shockingly backward," however, the postwar need for housing would go unmet without a vigorous effort by both public and private leaders. The government needed immediately to undertake a multiyear program of public construction. The government also needed to support research to develop more efficient building materials and building methods. Yet "the responsibility must rest largely with free enterprise." Accordingly, the housing industry needed "men of boldness and imagination" to come to the fore. "There are plenty of such men in the building field," Bowles concluded, "men who have already demonstrated the vision and daring to develop new engineering techniques and new building materials. It is time that they went to work."[38]

The liberal argument had considerable support in postwar debates about the future of housing. In scholarly studies, magazine articles, policy conferences, business meetings, agency memos, and congressional hearings, a variety of people argued that a full employment economy required a homebuilding industry capable of serving a mass market. The housing expert Charles Abrams made the point in especially dramatic terms in 1946. The notorious backwardness of the housing industry was "a major factor responsible for precipitating economic depressions as well as retarding recovery," Abrams wrote. "The challenge to the postwar democracy – whether it can employ its people and distribute its goods and services more equitably – cannot be met without a solution of the housing problem."[39]

---

38. Ibid., 61–62.
39. Abrams, *The Future of Housing*, 15, 17–18. In addition, see Charles Abrams, "Housing – The Ever-Recurring Crisis," in Seymour E. Harris, editor, *Saving American Capitalism: A Liberal Economic Program* (New York: Alfred A. Knopf, 1948), 192; Leon H. Keyserling, "Can We Do It? Yes, In an Integrated Economy," *The Nation* 166 (May 15, 1948): 542–544; Miles L. Colean, *American Housing: Problems and Prospects* (New York: Twentieth Century Fund, 1944), 10; Robert Lasch, *Breaking the Building Blockade* (Chicago: University of Chicago Press, 1946), ix–x, 267, 280–285; National Committee on Housing, *Proceedings of the National Conference on Postwar Housing* (New York: National Committee on Housing, 1944), 7, 58, 95; Keith, *Politics and the Housing Crisis Since 1930*, 52, 56–57; Hise, *Magnetic Los Angeles*, 162–163.

sten the industrialization of homebuilding, Abrams called
ssive program of public construction. The wartime mo-
a of industry provided the model. Instead of contracting
for ships and airplanes, the government could order as many as
500,000 homes a year, and the sheer size of the contracts would
stimulate construction companies to achieve unprecedented cost
efficiencies. "When mass orders are given," Abrams wrote, "mass
production will follow." The contractors would be able to borrow
money on favorable terms, purchase building materials at wholesale
prices, use standardized parts, and manage labor and equipment
efficiently. Eventually, the government contracts would force the
entire industry to learn the lessons of large-scale operations.[40]

Though few commentators shared Abrams's enthusiasm for public construction, almost everyone who wrote about homebuilding
in the mid-1940s agreed that the industry needed help. Housing
was "the stepchild of industrial civilization," "the industry capitalism forgot," "a forgotten stepchild of the industrial era – a shabby
Cinderella creeping pitifully through the fairy tale of technology."
The nation could not tolerate the backwardness of builders much
longer. The unprecedented demand of new families for space, the
concern to smooth the return of veterans to civilian life, the fear of
a postwar depression – all made the old arguments for reform of
homebuilding seem more urgent. To preserve social order, to give
the average worker a chance to own property, to provide a healthy
environment for children, and to stimulate the economy, the housing industry needed to produce more homes at less cost than ever
before.[41]

The pages of *Fortune* suggest the extent of the postwar consensus. To make clear the need for action, the magazine published
dozens of articles in 1946 and 1947 on the housing shortage. In a
rare editorial – "Let's Have Ourselves a Housing Industry" – the

---

40. Abrams, *The Future of Housing,* 362–369. For the quotation, see 365–366. Seven years
    earlier, a New Deal economist had offered a similar vision of public housing as a spur
    to mass production. See Mordecai Ezekiel, *Jobs for All Through Industrial Expansion*
    (New York: Alfred A. Knopf, 1939), 138–150.
41. For the quotations, see Lasch, *Breaking the Building Blockade,* v; "The Industry Capi-
    talism Forgot," 61; Dorothy Rosenman, *A Million Homes a Year* (New York: Harcourt,
    Brace and Company, 1945), 48.

editors supported a handful of government initiatives to encourage builders to operate on a larger scale. The editors even risked the wrath of the building and real estate lobbies by endorsing a limited program of public construction. If the government acted prudently to strengthen the housing market, they argued, the result would be the best defense against socialism, not a defeat for free enterprise. That conclusion followed "from candid reflection on what an incompetent housing industry can do for the reputation of U.S. business," the editors declared. "A house is the most urgent, most valued, and most studied demand of an American family; failure by capitalism to satisfy this essential want will do more to undermine free institutions than ten thousand Union Square orators."[42]

The nation's leaders followed *Fortune*'s prescription. Between 1945 and 1955, Congress and the president approved a number of bills intended to expand the housing market and encourage large-scale operations. The G.I. Bill allowed veterans to become homeowners with no money down and monthly payments stretched over 30 years. The Housing Act of 1949 funded research on ways to reduce costs and increase production. In the early 1950s, a handful of unheralded amendments to the housing act offered special incentives to large builders. The amendments also liberalized the terms of the FHA loan program.[43]

The legislation worked. In the late 1940s and early 1950s, the homeownership rate skyrocketed, topping 60 percent in 1956. The number of housing starts reached record highs. Builders constructed over 15 million homes in the 1950s, more than twice the total for the 1940s and nearly six times the figure for the 1930s. In a remarkably short period of time, the tract-house developer became the dominant force in the industry. By 1959, large-scale builders were responsible for 64 percent of the housing market, compared to just 24 percent in 1949 and 5 percent in 1938.[44]

---

42. "Let's Have Ourselves a Housing Industry," *Fortune* 37 (September 1946): 2–4. The magazine devoted the April 1946 issue to housing. For the lead article, see "The Promise of the Shortage," *Fortune* 33 (April 1946): 101–103.
43. Checkoway, "Large Builders, Federal Housing Programmes, and Postwar Suburbanization," 31–33.
44. Ibid., 23, 24; Wendt, *Housing Policy – The Search for Solutions*, 160.

Laying the Foundation for a Consumer Society

In 1944, the federal Office of Civilian Requirements took a survey to determine the things Americans were most keen to buy when the war ended, and household appliances topped the list. The most commonly cited item was a washing machine. Then, in order, the survey respondents looked forward to buying electric irons, refrigerators, stoves, toasters, radios, vacuum cleaners, electric fans, and hot water heaters.[45]

The survey no doubt pleased the management of General Electric. The year before, the corporation had begun a major advertising campaign to promote the home of tomorrow. The campaign featured a full-page advertisement published in a number of national magazines. "It's a promise!" the headline proclaimed. In the center of the page, a young couple sat together on a park bench. With a stick, the man – a private in uniform – drew the outline of a house in the ground, while the woman, in Sunday best, held his arm and shoulder. Both looked at the sketch with dreamy intensity.

> Jim's going away tomorrow . . . and there will be long, lonely days before he comes back.
>
> But that little home sketched there in the sand is a symbol of faith and hope and courage. It's a promise, too. A promise of gloriously happy days to come . . . when Victory is won.
>
> Victory Homes of tomorrow will make up in part at least for all the sacrifices of today . . . *and that's our promise!*
>
> They will have *better living built in* . . . electrical living with new comforts, new conveniences, new economies to make every day an adventure in happiness.
>
> Plan for *your* Victory Home now . . . the one sure way is to buy War Bonds. Every Bond you buy is an investment in your future happiness and security . . . every dollar you put into Bonds helps bring our boys back sooner – *and safer.* Buy another Bond today.

In slightly smaller type, the ad then described the General Electric Consumers Institute, a modern facility "devoted to research on wartime home problems." At the bottom of the ad, under the Gen-

---

45. John Morton Blum, *V Was For Victory: Politics and American Culture During World War II* (New York: Harcourt Brace Jovanovich, 1976), 100.

eral Electric name and logo, a line of small drawings ran across the page – a light switch, a fan, a clock, a radio, a hot water heater, a washer and drier, a range, a refrigerator, a blender, an iron, a sewing machine, a vacuum cleaner, and more.[46]

Together, the government survey and the General Electric advertisement point to a second set of desires that Levitt-style homebuilding fulfilled. The chance to live in a new home was the great dream of millions of families. Beginning in the early 1930s, manufacturers of appliances and furnishings encouraged the dream, and the promotional effort intensified during the war. By 1945, the single-family home with a full complement of consumer goods had become the most common image of "the American way of life." Yet the image of a mass consumer culture could only become reality with mass production of housing.

The idea that the home could provide the foundation for a new consumer culture took almost a generation to develop. In a 1929 book entitled *Selling Mrs. Consumer,* home economist and advertising consultant Christine Frederick argued that first-time homebuyers could become a prime market for manufacturers of consumer goods. In the late 1920s and early 1930s, Herbert Hoover and *Fortune* both recognized that the purchase of a house led to the purchase of furniture, appliances, and gadgets. Yet the conventional wisdom of the time held that a working-class family could afford a home only by economizing on a range of small purchases, from clothes to movie tickets. The 1931 presidential conference on homebuilding and homeownership even called for a "frank recognition" that the power of modern consumer advertising made homebuying more difficult, since advertising sought "the stimulation of wants." As studies of working-class budgets proved, however, the members of successful homeowning families generally subordinated individual satisfactions to the collective need to save.[47]

The first companies to think seriously about the homebuyer's

---

46. The advertisement is reproduced in Albrecht, *World War II and the American Dream,* xxi.
47. For the salutary effect of homebuying on purchases of consumer goods, see Christine Frederick, *Selling Mrs. Consumer* (New York: Business Bourse, 1929), 388–395; Leach, *Land of Desire,* 369; Editors of "Fortune," *Housing America,* 24. The studies of working-class budgets are cited in Gries and Ford, *Home Ownership, Income and Types of Dwellings,* 5–6, 50–51, 56, 99–100. For the quoted passages, see 56.

dilemma were the giants of the electrical industry. In the 1920s, after years of slighting the household market, the industry's leaders concluded that future growth depended on sharply increased sales to residential customers. To achieve that goal, the industry needed to expand the market for household appliances. The establishment of the Federal Housing Administration suggested a new way to meet potential demand. Because appliances were easiest to sell as built-in components of new homes, utility companies and electrical equipment manufacturers lobbied the FHA to allow federally insured mortgages to cover the cost of refrigerators, ranges, dishwashers, and washing machines. The agency soon agreed. Eventually, the electrical industry persuaded the FHA to insure purchases of smaller appliances, including vacuum cleaners.[48]

Throughout the 1930s, the industry's giants aggressively promoted the all-electric house as "the home of tomorrow." In 1934, Westinghouse built a $12,000 showplace with 21 kitchen appliances and 140 electrical outlets. The next year, General Electric joined the FHA in sponsoring a national "Home of the Future" competition for architects. *McCall's, Good Housekeeping, House and Garden,* and *Ladies' Home Journal* published the winning plans, and General Electric used the designs to construct a handful of model homes around the country. The company also built a series of all-electric "New American Homes" in 1936.[49]

The industry's promotional effort had limited success. Even before the Depression, a $12,000 house was well beyond the reach of the ordinary worker. With millions unemployed, the wonders of the all-electric home seemed more illusory than Oz. Yet the war soon made promises of plenty appear possible, even plausible. In cities across the country, the average family income rose dramatically. Instead of earning $2,200 or $2,300 a year, millions of Americans suddenly were earning more than $4,000. In some cities, the

48. For the history of the residential market for electricity, see David E. Nye, *Electrifying America: Social Meanings of a New Technology* (Cambridge: MIT Press, 1990), 238–286. The role of the FHA is summarized in Tobey, *Technology as Freedom,* 118. I follow only a part of Tobey's argument here, since Tobey argues that the Roosevelt administration took the lead in promoting increased use of electricity in the nation's homes, especially by providing loans to homeowners to "modernize" their electrical wiring.
49. Nye, *Electrifying America,* 358–359.

average family income topped $5,000. The total assets of American families nearly tripled, rising from $50 billion to $140 billion in just three years.[50]

Visions of "the world of tomorrow" quickly became the most common form of advertising. Thousands of factories converted to defense production, so the consumer goods market was severely restricted: Manufacturers could only sell promises. Often, the promise was generic, a corporate effort to revive faith in a capitalist system shaken by depression. The world-of-tomorrow advertising almost always cited the miracles of wartime production. Forced to do or die, the ads proclaimed, the nation's engineers and scientists had invented dozens of new products and production processes, and their inventions would transform everyday life after the war.[51]

"Methods developed by war will improve products and short-cut their manufacture," the Sparton Company advertised in 1942. "An abundance of materials, new and old, will make things plentiful." The result would be a chance to regain lost comforts – and more. "Home will be truly a House of Wonders in this after-Victory world. Science already knows how to make it comfortable beyond our dreams. Invention will fill it with conveniences we have never known." The Celotex Corporation agreed. "As America drives under war's incentive," the company promised, "the products of our future greatness are being shaped. Housing will undergo tremendous change. . . . Out of undreamed-of progress . . . will emerge your 'Miracle House' of tomorrow." Best of all, the miracles would be "within reach of the *average* family."[52]

To encourage dreaming, the Anderson Window Company distributed personally embossed scrapbooks to women eager to imagine postwar houses. The scrapbooks had sections for the women to store magazine clippings about house plans, kitchens, living rooms, bedrooms, extra rooms, bathrooms, built-ins, porches, fireplaces,

---

50. Blum, *V Was for Victory,* 92, 100.
51. Frank W. Fox, *Madison Avenue Goes to War: The Strange Career of American Advertising, 1941–1945* (Provo: Brigham Young University Press, 1975). In addition, see Mark H. Leff, "The Politics of Sacrifice on the American Home Front in World War II," *Journal of American History* 77 (March 1991): 1307–1313.
52. For the Sparton advertisement, see *Life* 13 (October 5, 1942): 22–23. The Celotex advertisement is cited by Blum, *V Was for Victory,* 104.

gardens, and "Window Beauty Ideas." Before the end of the war, the company gave away 350,000 books.[53]

Often, the wartime advertisements defined the conflict as a fight for the comfort, freedom, and happiness of home. "We have so many things, here in America, that belong only to a free people," one ad observed: "Warm, comfortable homes. Automobiles and radios by the million. Electrical machines to keep and cook our food; to wash and clean for us." In another ad, with a headline proclaiming "These are fundamental," a single-family home was literally the centerpiece of a vision of the nation. A third ad depicted a living room with a fireplace – the family hearth – and asked: "Is This Worth Fighting For?"[54]

Even the government made the home a key part of the call to arms. In a 1942 radio drama sponsored by the Office of Facts and Figures, the agency responsible for explaining the war effort to the public, a boy and a girl talked about their dream of bliss. "That's one of the things this war's about," the boy said. "About us?" the girl asked. "About *all* young people like us," the boy replied. "About love and gettin' hitched, and havin' a home and some kids, and breathin' fresh air out in the suburbs . . . about livin' and workin' *decent*, like free people."[55]

The promise to fulfill the dreams of countless couples added up to a promise to transform the country. Again and again, the wartime visionaries argued that the construction of millions of new homes would be only a part of the postwar effort to achieve permanent prosperity. The hard times of the 1930s would never return. Soon, the nation would be rebuilt, almost reborn.

That theme was expressed perfectly in a series of advertisements sponsored by the Nash-Kelvinator Corporation. The ads all featured a soldier speaking about the future after recalling the most nightmarish and miraculous moments of the war. In the October 1944 ad, the weary soldier, holding a rifle, resolutely looked at the

---

53. Clifford Edward Clark, Jr., *The American Family Home, 1800–1960* (Chapel Hill: University of North Carolina Press, 1986), 195.

54. For the first and third advertisements, see Fox, *Madison Avenue Goes to War*, 70; Blum, *V Was for Victory*, 104. The second advertisement, sponsored by the Lee Rubber and Tire Corporation, appeared on the back cover of *Fortune* 30 (August 1944). In addition, see Baxandall and Ewen, *Picture Windows*, 83.

55. Blum, *V Was for Victory*, 28.

winding road to the horizon. He spoke with confidence, because the nation had regained the strength that made America great:

I've hugged my belly to the ground while regiments of big guns stood up hub to hub and split the night with flame . . .

I've felt the earth quake under a tidal wave of tanks that rolled out of our lines and engulfed the enemy and smothered him and beat him down into the ground . . .

I've seen the sky blacked out by a thousand bombers' wings . . . and heard it cracked wide open by the thunder of their bombs . . .

And yet . . . through the ruins of war, I've seen the road ahead.

Out here, I've seen the power of America at war, the might of free-born men who work and fight to keep their freedom. And I believe this power to destroy can be the power to create.

And looking down the victory road I see a new America . . .

I see new cities rising up . . . new farms . . . new roads, new homes, new schools . . . new factories that will plan and build for peace the way they planned and built for war.

I see a place for me, and for the kids I'll have someday . . . a place for every man . . . a future to look forward to . . . a job to do . . .

I see a chance to live and grow in a stronger America . . .

After we've won the war . . .

While we're winning the peace!

In italics, the voice of the corporation then explained Nash-Kelvinator's program "to convert all the new strength, all the new power to produce, all the new ability and skill and knowledge that have come to us so quickly under the driving necessity of war to production for peace." The company would build better cars, better refrigerators, better freezers and water heaters and ranges "than have ever served any household." That would be the Nash-Kelvinator contribution to "the building of a greater, happier nation," a strong, growing nation "where all men and women will have the freedom and the opportunity to make their dreams come true."[56]

56. Nash-Kelvinator Corporation advertisement, *Fortune* 30 (October 1944): Back Cover. In addition, the company's ads appeared in the August and September issues.

The themes of the Nash-Kelvinator advertisements resounded in more analytical discussions of the postwar world. The war proved that the nation's economy was not "mature," as economists had feared in the 1930s. The gross national product had doubled in just four years. Now, to fulfill the hopes of a generation that had suffered through a depression and a war, the nation needed to employ the productive power of wartime to build a new mass-consumption economy.

In a 1944 book, *Mobilizing for Abundance,* the Keynesian economist Robert Nathan succinctly summarized the postwar challenge. "[I]f we can so speedily and effectively mobilize our resources for such an immense war production," he asked, "can we not with equal effectiveness . . . mobilize our economic resources for peacetime consumption? If we can build vast quantities of battleships, airplanes, guns, ammunition, tanks, and other weapons to kill our enemy, can we not devote the same resources after the war to building houses, automobiles, electrical devices, schools, hospitals, and other goods so much needed to raise the standard of living of all our people?"[57]

The building boom that began in the late 1940s answered the question. Though Nathan did not make the point, the production of houses, automobiles, electrical devices, schools, and hospitals went hand in hand. Because the cheapest and largest tracts of land lay at the urban fringe, the residents of postwar subdivisions and suburbs depended on the automobile for transportation. Nearly nine of ten suburban families owned cars, in contrast to just six of ten urban households, and a much higher percentage of suburban families had two cars. The rise of tract-house methods of development thus helped the automobile industry put the pedal to the metal: Automobile production jumped from 2 million in 1946 to 8 million in 1955. The housing boom also boosted sales of household goods. In the five years after World War II, consumer spending increased 60 percent, but the amount spent on furnishings and appliances rose 240 percent. Lawn mower sales jumped nearly tenfold, from 139,000 in 1946 to roughly 1.3 million in 1951. To provide essential services to residents of new neighborhoods, local gov-

57. Robert R. Nathan, *Mobilizing for Abundance* (New York: McGraw-Hill, 1944), 10–11.

ernments built thousands of roads, schools, and hospitals. Churches and shopping centers soon followed.[58]

Years later, the journalist Godfrey Hodgson explained what happened in a memorable phrase. The driving force of the postwar boom, he wrote, was "the fusion of demographic trends, government policy and business interests into something like a suburban-industrial complex." A number of observers made a similar argument at the time. In June 1950, a month before *Time* put William Levitt on its cover, *Fortune* published a cautious celebration of the housing industry. The new breed of large-scale builders had taken advantage of the baby boom and the federal home-loan program to make a marvel, the magazine reported. "Building, for the first time in a quarter century, is the most exciting thing in the U S. economy. It has become the gaudiest of all the business booms within the Great American Boom, that postwar wonder now nearing five years old. It can be viewed as . . . the crucial prop beneath that boom."[59]

Like so many vital elements of the postwar economy, however, the building boom came at considerable environmental cost. The reckoning of those costs began almost immediately. By 1950, for example, a number of people had already become concerned about the energy-wasting design of the typical postwar home. Yet the critics of tract housing faced formidable obstacles, because the new way of building met so many economic, social, and political demands. The first complaints about the environmental impact of postwar construction seldom made the news. Instead, the media focused on a far more compelling story: The nation's largest builders were answering the prayers of millions.

58. For the statistics, see Richard Polenberg, *One Nation Divisible: Class, Race, and Ethnicity in the United States Since 1938* (New York: Viking Press, 1980), 130; Elaine Tyler May, *Homeward Bound: American Families in the Cold War Era* (New York: Basic Books, 1988), 165; David Groelinger, "Domestic Capital Equipment," in John E. Ullman, editor, *The Suburban Economic Network: Economic Activity, Resource Use, and the Great Sprawl* (New York: Praeger, 1977), 158, 159.
59. Godfrey Hodgson, *America in Our Time* (Garden City, NY: Doubleday and Company, 1976), 51; "How Sound Is the Building Boom?," *Fortune* 41 (June 1950): 67.

2

From the Solar House to the All-Electric Home: The Postwar Debates over Heating and Cooling

In September 1943, *Newsweek* offered a tantalizing glimpse of a possible postwar "dream house." "One way for America to hedge against future fuel shortages would be to build more solar homes like that of Mr. and Mrs. Hugh Duncan in Homewood, a Chicago suburb," the piece began. Designed by architect George Keck to receive a maximum amount of the sun's heat in winter and a minimum amount in summer, the Duncans' solar home saved money and resources. Even on the coldest January days, the magazine announced, the couple seldom had to turn on the furnace. This was indeed a home to grip "the imagination of postwar thinkers and builders."[1]

The *Newsweek* story was just one of dozens of articles about solar homes to appear before the end of World War II. In a 1944 feature titled "The Proven Merit of a Solar Home," *Reader's Digest* called Keck's work "probably the most exciting architectural news in decades." In movie theaters across the country, millions of Americans saw a newsreel about the exciting promise of solar design. From *Architectural Forum* to *American Builder*, the trade press also explored the possibilities. In 1945, a builder of prefabricated homes received nationwide publicity after announcing plans to sell a modern, affordable solar house. According to a *Popular Mechanics* reviewer, the new house was a breakthrough, the first application of "the solar principle to large-scale production of better, brighter, easily heated homes."[2]

---

1. "Dream Houses – U.S. and British," *Newsweek* 22 (September 6, 1943): 102–104.
2. For the quotations, see Ralph Wallace, "The Proven Merits of a Solar Home," *Reader's Digest* 44 (January 1944), 104; William E. Taylor, "Your Solar Home Is All Wrapped

As the *Newsweek* piece suggested, the appeal of energy-conserving construction was heightened by wartime restrictions on the use of coal and fuel oil. But the interest in solar housing lasted well beyond the end of the war. For more than a decade, from the mid-1940s to the mid-1950s, the best way to heat and cool buildings was a subject of vigorous debate. Could the nation's homes use less energy? Engineers and scientists at prestigious universities began research on the potential of solar technology, while architects and federal housing officials touted the importance of energy-conserving design. Thousands of people bought solar houses. The cliché seemed literally true: The future looked bright.

The predictions of a bright new day in housing proved false, however. From 1945 to 1970, the energy consumption of the average American household increased precipitously. In the 1960s alone, the jump in household energy use was 30 percent. That was unprecedented. The high-energy house – heated and cooled by fossil fuels – had become the norm.[3]

Up," *Popular Mechanics* 84 (August 1945): 13. In addition, see "It's Here – Solar Heating for Post-War Homes," *American Builder* 65 (September 1943): 34–36, 94; "Solar House for a Sunny Hilltop," *Architectural Record* 95 (March 1944): 58–65; "Solar Heating," *Architectural Forum* 79 (August 1943): 6–8, 114; "End of Fuel Bills?," *Architectural Forum* 82 (March 1945): 12; "Prefabrication," *Architectural Forum* 83 (July 1945): 125–144; "Did You Know that the Heat of the Sun Can Help Heat Your House in Winter?," *House Beautiful* 85 (September 1943): 59–66; "Can an Old House Be Remodeled for Solar Heating?," *House Beautiful* 87 (June 1945): 75–79; James Marston Fitch, "A Solar House Designed to the Compass," *House Beautiful* 87 (November 1945): 128–135; Frank Lopez, "What Is a Solar House?," *Parents Magazine* 20 (April 1945): 40–41, 97–100. The newsreel is mentioned in Maron J. Simon, editor, *Your Solar House* (New York: Simon and Schuster, 1947), 10. Simon also describes coverage of the solar house in newspapers and on radio programs.

3. There is no universally accepted way to measure household energy use. For the postwar period, especially, the analysis turns on a decision about the proper way to count the consumption of electricity. Unlike wood, coal, fuel oil, or natural gas, electricity is a secondary source of energy, and so most analysts measure the primary energy needed to produce the electricity used in homes. The figure I cite for energy use in the 1960s comes from such an analysis. See U.S. General Accounting Office, *Analysis of Trends in Residential Energy Consumption* (Washington: USGPO, 1981), 5–6. But a few analysts argue that the proper measure of residential electricity consumption should not include the energy lost in the generation and transmission process: It should include only the energy equivalent of the electricity used directly in the nation's homes. The difference is considerable. Even by the second method of accounting, however, the increase in household energy use in the 1950s and 1960s was more than 23 percent. See Bonnie Maas Morrison, "Household Energy Consumption, 1900–1980: A Quantitative History," in George H. Daniels and Mark H. Rose, editors, *Energy and Transport: Historical Perspectives on Policy Issues* (Beverly Hills: Sage Publications, 1982), 225. To some extent, of course, the new demand for energy was a function of affluence. In the booming years after World War II, the use

The obstacles to energy efficiency in the 1950s and 1960s were tremendous. The postwar housing industry was driven by the demand to produce as cheaply as possible: For both builders and buyers of homes, the mortgage payment was the critical concern, not the cost of utilities. By the early 1950s, the price of energy had reached all-time lows, so the economic argument for conservation lost force. The postwar economic boom brought the first taste of affluence to millions of Americans, and the conservation ideal soon ran up against a powerful desire to enjoy pleasures that once seemed extravagant or simply inconceivable for working-class families. The advocates of energy-efficient housing faced competition too from corporate leaders with a very different vision of the future.

The fate of the solar house also suggests the limits of the conservation ideal in the postwar decades. Even the most committed advocates of solar technology and design did not offer a truly environmentalist critique of tract housing. In the 1940s and 1950s, for example, almost no one argued for the energy-efficient house as a way to reduce air pollution from fossil-fuel use. Though a few supporters of the cause had a conservation ethic, the popular interest in solar housing did not go deep.[4]

Solar Technology and Solar Design

The postwar enthusiasm for the solar house led in two directions. The first was an effort to develop new technology for collecting and

of refrigerators, freezers, washing machines, and clothes dryers increased. The number of appliances on the market grew by about one-and-a-half a year, and a few new products – the television and the dishwasher – became common. See Roy H. Krause, editor, *Moody's Public Utility Manual 1971* (New York: Moody's Investor Services, 1971), a20; Edwin Vennard, *The Electric Power Business* (New York: McGraw-Hill, 1962), 162. Yet appliances accounted for less than half of the increased residential use of electricity between 1950 and 1970. See John Tansil and John C. Moyers, "Residential Demand for Energy," in Michael S. Macrakis, editor, *Energy: Demand, Conservation, and Institutional Problems* (Cambridge: MIT Press, 1974), 378.

4. According to two prominent advocates of solar energy, engineers and architects often dreamed of "communities of people who live in comfort without combustion, without chimneys, free from atmospheric pollution." See Eugene Ayres and Charles A. Scarlott, *Energy Sources: The Wealth of the World* (New York: McGraw-Hill, 1952), 218. I found only one tiny bit of evidence to support that view: In an essay on "Future Uses of Solar Energy," Maria Telkes noted that solar energy would not produce soot. See *Bulletin of the Atomic Scientists* 7 (1951): 219.

storing the sun's heat. The second was a campaign to encourage the use of energy-conserving principles of building design. Though the war gave a push in both directions, the technological and architectural projects had different histories and different fates.

The technologists often saw their work as a contribution to a new global conservation movement. During the war, a number of conservationists had begun to worry about the relationship between population growth and resource consumption. Could the earth sustain billions more people? That question was at the heart of two best-selling books, Fairfield Osborn's *Our Plundered Planet* and William Vogt's *Road to Survival,* both published in 1948. The last paragraph of Osborn's work put the challenge in especially stark terms:

The tide of the earth's population is rising, the reservoir of the earth's living resources is falling. Technologists may outdo themselves in the creation of artificial substitutes for natural subsistence, and new areas, such as those in tropical or subtropical regions, may be adapted to human use, but even such recourses or developments cannot be expected to offset the present terrific attack upon the natural life-giving elements of the earth. There is only one solution: Man must recognize the necessity of cooperating with nature. He must temper his demands and use and conserve the natural living resources of this earth in a manner that alone can provide for the continuation of his civilization. The final answer is to be found only through comprehension of the enduring processes of nature. The time for defiance is at an end.

Many of the scientists and engineers who worked on solar technology agreed.[5]

Farrington Daniels was typical. A veteran of the Manhattan Project, he initially hoped to develop peaceful uses for atomic power, but he soon concluded that solar energy was more promising. He secured funding from the Rockefeller Foundation to make the University of Wisconsin a leading center for solar research. By 1948, he was arguing that the development of solar technology was indispensable in a time of "profligate spending of the world's natural resources and uncontrolled increase in population." He often cited

5. For the quotation, see Fairfield Osborn, *Our Plundered Planet* (Boston: Little, Brown and Company, 1948), 201. Vogt's book ends with a similar warning. See William Vogt, *Road to Survival* (New York: William Sloane Associates, 1948), 288.

Osborn and Vogt to support his argument. "The days of easy geographical quest for more food, fuel, and power are over, and our frontiers now lie in science and engineering," he wrote in *Science*. "In the future, it will be necessary to increase the efficiency of our utilization of sunlight, to conserve all our resources, and to control the birth rate of the world's population."[6]

The effort to develop solar heating systems built on almost a half century of work on solar water heaters. In the 1890s, a Maryland inventor patented the first solar water heater, and the invention soon found a market in sunnier climates. In California in the first decades of the century, and then in Florida in the 1920s and 1930s, a number of companies installed thousands of solar water heaters in homes and apartments. In 1936, a Boston philanthropist took the next step, endowing a major research program in solar energy at the Massachusetts Institute of Technology. By 1939, the MIT researchers had designed and built a solar-heated house with the water heater as a model. Though the war soon ended the experiment, the wartime shortage of heating oil inspired a second demonstration project in Boulder, Colorado. With funding from the War Production Board, a University of Colorado engineer – George Lof – developed a solar hot-air system in 1943. The first winter, the system provided about a quarter of the heat in Lof's house. The second winter, Lof added a storage unit, using rocks to radiate the sun's heat at night and on cloudy days, and the fuel saving increased to a third. When the MIT research effort resumed after the war, the interest in solar technology was greater than ever. In 1948, an MIT researcher, Maria Telkes, persuaded a benefactor to build a solar house with no auxiliary heating system. Instead, the house used a lightweight salt to store heat. The next year, the MIT program began a new demonstration project. In addition to using a solar collector, the MIT house incorporated a number of solar design principles,

---

6. For the quotations, see Farrington Daniels, "Solar Energy," *Science* 109 (January 21, 1949): 51, 55–56. In addition, see Farrington Daniels, M. King Hubbert, and Eugene P. Wigner, "Our Energy Resources," *Physics Today* 2 (April 1949): 19, 21; Farrington Daniels and John A. Duffie, editors, *Solar Energy Research* (Madison: University of Wisconsin Press, 1955), 4, 7–11. Daniel Behrman provides a brief biography of Daniels in *Solar Energy: The Awakening Science* (Boston: Little, Brown and Company, 1976), 187–190. For the concern among solar technologists about population and resource exploitation, see also Association for Applied Solar Energy, *Proceedings of the World Symposium on Applied Solar Energy* (Menlo Park, CA: Stanford Research Institute, 1956), 17.

and the results were astounding: The sun provided three-quarters of the heating needs of a family in the cold climate of the Boston suburbs.[7]

The postwar demonstrations received considerable publicity. In 1949, *Life* showcased the Telkes project, while the *Saturday Evening Post* ran a long piece featuring the MIT house. Each magazine made the same point: If the experiments worked, the houses might point the way toward billions of savings in fuel. The *Saturday Evening Post* story also raised the specter of diminishing stocks of coal, oil, and natural gas. "Yet if even a fraction of the solar energy that reaches the earth can be utilized directly," the author argued, "the danger recedes into infinity." With less fanfare, the trade publications of the heating industry and the architectural profession also published periodic reports on the solar experiments.[8]

By the early 1950s, the work on solar heating seemed to have considerable momentum. Though only a handful of researchers specialized in the area, a dozen universities had projects on solar energy. The American Association for the Advancement of Science and the American Academy of Arts and Sciences both sponsored meetings on solar technology, and the subject was discussed at two mid-century conferences on resources and the environment. MIT organized a symposium devoted entirely to solar heating. The field also attracted researchers at a number of foundations and consulting firms. In 1955, a group of scientists, engineers, and business leaders formed the Association for Applied Solar Energy, and the association soon teamed with the Stanford Research Institute and the University of Arizona to sponsor a conference that attracted

7. Ken Butti and John Perlin, *A Golden Thread: 2500 Years of Solar Architecture and Technology* (New York: Van Nostrand Reinhold, 1980), 117–154, 197–214; Behrman, *Solar Energy,* 89–112, 205–206.
8. "World's First Sun-Heated Home," *Life* 26 (May 2, 1949): 90–93; John Kobler, "Like Living in a Macy's Window," *Saturday Evening Post* 222 (September 24, 1949): 42–43, 156, 160–162. For the quotation, see 161. In addition, see "How to Heat a House," *Fortune* 38 (September 1948): 112; Eric Hodgins, "Power from the Sun," *Fortune* 48 (September 1953): 134–135. For reports in the trade press, see Maria Telkes, "Solar House Heating – A Problem of Heat Storage," *Heating and Ventilating* 44 (May 1947): 68–75; Maria Telkes, "A Review of Solar House Heating," *Heating and Ventilating* 46 (September 1949): 68–74; "Space Heating with Solar Energy," *Heating and Ventilating* 47 (September 1950): 88–90; "Test House Heated Only by Solar Heat," *Architectural Record* 105 (March 1949): 136–137.

900 registrants from 37 countries. The association then began to publish a solar energy journal.[9]

The solar effort had support in Washington, too. In 1949, the Department of the Interior made a short study of the prospects for solar energy and the subject continued to come up in departmental discussions of conservation. Early in 1952, the department organized a solar energy conference with MIT's Maria Telkes as the keynote speaker. The Atomic Energy Commission also commissioned a study of alternative energy sources in 1949. Though solar energy was not yet competitive economically, the author of the study wrote later, the technology had great promise: "Ultimately, perhaps as much as one-fifth the total comfort-heating load, or 6 per cent of the total United States energy system, will be carried by solar collectors at costs no greater than two times present costs." Accordingly, the government should encourage research in the field. That conclusion was seconded by a 1952 presidential commission on materials use. In a landmark report, *Resources for Freedom,* the commission predicted that solar technology could be widely used for domestic heating in the southern part of the country within 25 years. "It is time," the report concluded, "for aggressive research in the whole field of solar energy – an effort in which the United States could make an immense contribution to the welfare of the free world."[10]

9. For succinct summaries of work in the field, see Farrington Daniels, *Direct Use of the Sun's Energy* (New Haven: Yale University Press, 1964), 12–15; D. S. Halacy, Jr., *The Coming Age of Solar Energy* [revised edition] (New York: Harper and Row, 1973), 59–62. Daniels, Hubbert, and Wigner discuss the AAAS meeting in "Our Energy Resources," 19. Other solar conferences are described in Association for Applied Solar Energy, *Proceedings of the World Symposium on Applied Solar Energy;* Daniels and Duffie, *Solar Energy Research;* Richard W. Hamilton, editor, *Space Heating with Solar Energy* (Cambridge: Massachusetts Institute of Technology, 1954); "Sun in the Service of Man," *Proceedings of the American Academy of Arts and Sciences* 79 (1951): 181–326; "The Trapping of Solar Energy," *Ohio Journal of Science* 53 (1953): 257–319. In addition, see Resources for the Future, *The Nation Looks at Its Resources* (Washington: Resources for the Future, 1954), 221–227; William L. Thomas, Jr., editor, *Man's Role in Changing the Face of the Earth* (Chicago: University of Chicago Press, 1956), 1010–1022.
10. For the interest of the Department of the Interior, see Craufurd D. Goodwin, "Truman Administration Policies Toward Particular Energy Sources," in Goodwin, editor, *Energy Policy in Perspective: Today's Problems, Yesterday's Solutions* (Washington: Brookings Institution, 1981), 202–203, note 383. The first quotation comes from Palmer Cosslett Putnam, *Energy in the Future* (New York: Van Nostrand, 1953), 181. In addition, see 255. For the second quotation, see President's Materials Policy Commission, *Resources*

But the federal government never made the effort. In 1951, only 0.01 percent of federal outlays for scientific work went to solar researchers. By one reckoning, the total federal investment in solar technology in the early 1950s was only $150,000 to $200,000. A handful of corporations undertook solar research, but the corporate effort also was marginal.[11]

In the 1950s, especially, the principal heating fuels were incredibly cheap. As a result, there was little likelihood that solar energy would be economically viable in the foreseeable future: The savings would not justify the capital investment. Even a number of solar-heating proponents acknowledged that. Though not yet economical here, they argued, the technology would be a boon abroad. With solar heating and cooking technology, Farrington Daniels suggested, the people of the developing world would not need to strip their lands of brush and firewood, and so their soils would be less vulnerable to erosion. Cow and camel dung could be used for fertilizer, not fuel. "Our descendants 1,000 years hence may curse us for using coal, oil, and gas to heat our homes, when we might as well have used the sun," he concluded. "It seems to me that even though we do not need solar energy in the United States now, we should use it to conserve our fuel for future generations and to raise the standard of living in other parts of the world." The director of the Association for Applied Solar Energy made a similar argument. "The first major market for solar equipment is likely to be in foreign lands where living standards must be raised despite permanent fuel shortages," he wrote. "We in the United States will follow as our fuel prices rise." But the argument was a dead end. The nation's corporate giants were not tempted by the possibility of an export market for solar collectors, and the nation's political leaders had no interest in developing new technology as a form of foreign aid.[12]

for Freedom [Volume IV] (Washington: USGPO, 1952), 220. The fourth volume of the commission's report discussed solar energy in two sections – one on new technology and one on building materials. The sections were written by different authors, but both concluded – with some caveats – that solar energy had great potential for home heating, especially in the south. See 152 and 217.

11. For the 1951 figure, see Ayres and Scarlott, *Energy Sources,* 280. The total for solar research comes from Hodgins, "Power from the Sun," 134.
12. The quotations come from Resources for the Future, *The Nation Looks at Its Resources,* 225; John I. Yellott, "Solar Energy Today and Tomorrow," *Journal of the American Institute of Architects* 29 (April 1958): 202. For similar comments about the role of solar

Throughout the 1950s, the vision of a solar future also had to compete with a mesmerizing alternative – the promise of atomic power "too cheap to meter." In postwar analyses of potential replacements for finite supplies of fossil fuels, solar and atomic energy almost always were listed first. For a time, the two technologies seemed to be compatible. In a 1953 book titled *Energy in the Future*, for example, analyst Palmer Putnam urged stepped-up research on both solar and atomic technology: The first was the most promising source of renewable "income" energy, while the second was the most abundant form of depletable energy "capital." But, in fact, the choice turned out to be either/or, and solar research lost out. Though a few scientists argued in the 1950s that solar technology should have priority – atomic energy was more complex, involved health hazards, and posed potentially insoluble problems of hazardous waste disposal – the advocates of nuclear energy enjoyed important advantages. Unlike solar power, nuclear technology had military applications, so development could be justified in terms of national security. Atomic energy also seemed to provide more opportunities for profit. The only saleable product of solar heating technology was the equipment, whereas atomic energy yielded kilowatts, too. For the major nuclear contractors, all giants of the electrical industry, the development of power reactors also supported a number of well-established lines of business.[13]

technology abroad, see Daniels, *Direct Use of the Sun's Energy,* 4; Daniels and Duffie, *Solar Energy Research,* 4; Association for Applied Solar Energy, *Proceedings of the World Symposium on Applied Solar Energy,* 19, 20, 22, 299; Telkes, "Future Uses of Solar Energy," 219; Resources for the Future, *The Nation Looks at Its Resources,* 222; Hodgins, "Power from the Sun," 184, 188; Thomas Markus, "Solar Energy and Building Design – 1," *Architectural Review* 135 (1964): 456. On the economic obstacles to the development of solar heating technology in a time of cheap fossil fuels, see also Harrison Brown, *The Challenge of Man's Future* (1954; reprint, New York: Viking Press, 1956), 181. Several historical works cite the low energy prices of the 1950s and 1960s as a major reason for the slow development of solar technology. See Butti and Perlin, *A Golden Thread,* 216; Behrman, *Solar Energy,* 14.

13. The chairman of the Atomic Energy Commission predicted energy "too cheap to meter" in 1954. See Michael Smith, "Advertising the Atom," in Michael J. Lacey, editor, *Government and Environmental Politics: Essays on Historical Developments since World War Two* (Washington: Woodrow Wilson Center Press, 1989), 244. Putnam's analysis is in *Energy in the Future,* 255. For postwar discussions of solar and atomic energy, see also Ayres and Scarlott, *Energy Sources,* 168–176, 186–218, 279–283; Daniels, Hubbert, and Wigner, "Our Energy Resources," 18–22; Farrington Daniels, "Atomic and Solar Energy," *American Scientist* 38 (October 1950): 521–548; George W. Rusler, "Nuclear or Solar Energy: Which Is More Practical for Space Heating?," *Heating, Piping, and*

At the federal level, the effort to develop solar technology was handicapped further by a change in the political climate after the election of Dwight Eisenhower. The Republicans had much more faith than the Democrats in the cornucopian promise of the free market. At the opening session of a 1953 conference sponsored by Resources for the Future, for example, the new president warned the participants about the danger of heeding the calls of "extremists." The federal funding for solar research soon went from a drop to a speck.[14]

Without a strong commitment of government or corporate funds, the dream of a mass market for solar technology soon dimmed. The MIT researchers called it quits in 1962. Though the number of demonstration homes continued to grow, the projects were too far removed from commercial reality to influence the homebuilding industry. In the early 1970s, when the oil embargo revived interest in alternative energy sources, the United States still had only about 75 buildings with solar heating equipment.[15]

In contrast, the campaign to encourage energy-conserving design had some success. The effort did not require a tremendous investment in product development. Though the designers of solar homes took advantage of sophisticated research, the basic architectural principles were relatively easy to grasp. By the late 1940s, dozens of architects had designed solar homes. At least two manufacturers of prefabricated homes offered units with solar designs. Throughout

Air Conditioning 31 (February 1959): 106–109; Brown, *The Challenge of Man's Future*, 172–182. The director of the Association for Applied Solar Energy acknowledged the lack of a military payoff as a hindrance to the development of solar technology. See Yellott, "Solar Energy Today and Tomorrow," 206. For a good discussion of the unequal competition between solar and atomic energy, see Butti and Perlin, *A Golden Thread*, 223–226. Brian Balogh also offers a subtle analysis of "the iron triangle" of elected officials, bureaucrats, and industry lobbyists behind the federal push for nuclear power. See *Chain Reaction: Expert Debate and Public Participation in American Commercial Nuclear Power, 1945–1975* (New York: Cambridge University Press, 1991), 60–119.

14. For the skepticism about government conservation efforts in the Eisenhower administration, see Stephen Fox, *The American Conservation Movement: John Muir and His Legacy* (1981; reprint, Madison: University of Wisconsin Press, 1985), 309; Robert Gottlieb, *Forcing the Spring: The Transformation of the American Environmental Movement* (Washington: Island Press, 1993), 39. In addition, see William J. Barber, "The Eisenhower Energy Policy: Reluctant Intervention," in Goodwin, *Energy Policy in Perspective*, 205–286.

15. For the fate of solar heating technology in the 1960s and 1970s, see Butti and Perlin, *A Golden Thread*, 216; Behrman, *Solar Energy*, 377.

the country, a number of builders erected solar developments – the largest had more than 100 homes.[16]

In simplest form, the solar house relied on a handful of techniques to maximize the sun's heat in winter. Because the sun was most intense from the south, the house had to be oriented in that direction. Usually, the house was long and narrow, to permit a larger number of rooms to have southern exposures. The nonliving spaces – the utility closet, the bathroom, the garage – were massed to the north. The southern walls all had large expanses of glass, and the windows were double-glazed to protect against heat loss when the sun was not shining. Last, the house needed roof overhangs on the south side to protect against the sun in the hotter months: The summer sun was higher in the sky than the winter sun, so the overhangs could keep out unwanted summer heat without shading the interior of the house in winter.

The first major backer of the solar house was a manufacturer of insulated glass. In the 1920s and 1930s, the architectural modernists of the Bauhaus school had encouraged the use of glass walls, but the modernist buildings often were terribly uncomfortable in the winter: The uninsulated windows allowed too much heat to escape. To overcome the difficulty, a handful of companies sought to perfect windows with a sealed cushion of air between two planes of glass. The new windows also solved a major problem for would-be builders of solar homes. During World War II, the leading manufacturer of the new windows – the Libbey-Owens-Ford Glass Company – began to promote solar design. The company provided money for the Illinois Institute of Technology to research the heating performance of a George Keck house outside of Chicago. In 1943 and again in 1945, the company issued booklets about solar houses. Though a few more manufacturers entered the market, Libbey-Owens-Ford continued to lead the way. After the war, the company commissioned a demonstration solar home for every state, and Simon and Schuster published a book about the project in 1947: *Your Solar Home.*[17]

16. For the solar-home market, see Butti and Perlin, *A Golden Thread*, 190–191; Jeffrey Ellis Aronin, *Climate and Architecture* (New York: Reinhold, 1953), 74.
17. Simon discusses Libbey-Owens-Ford's interest in solar design in *Your Solar House*, 7–13. In addition, see Libbey-Owens-Ford Glass Company, *Solar Heating for Post-War*

Though the solar house promised economy – perhaps even the end of fuel bills, as one headline proclaimed – the monthly savings were only part of the appeal. For people with vivid memories of wartime rationing and postwar fuel crises, the dependability of the sun's heat was comforting: The new way of building offered "freedom from concern over oil shortages and coal strikes." But the principal argument for solar design was "aesthetic satisfaction." The solar house united the indoors and the outdoors, and so brought people closer to the pleasures of nature.[18]

A Libbey-Owens-Ford brochure beautifully illustrated the aesthetic argument. The cover showed a solar house in Illinois with a wall of glass framing a brilliant view of a forest. At the foot of the picture window, inside the house, the owners had planted lilies. The chair nearest the window was upholstered in a fabric of birds, flowers, and butterflies. The message was clear: The solar house allowed the owners to enjoy a new bond with nature. To emphasize the point, the company quoted a letter from a Wisconsin housewife. "We have always lived in a suburban area," she wrote, "but until we built our Solar house I really didn't appreciate the stimulation of being able to observe the day-by-day routine of 'life' that fairly teems all around us. We have really come to know birds and appreciate them. We purchased a book on birds, and now we recognize them quick! We are able to study the every-day habits, the playfulness, the industry in squirrels and we have found a vast new interest in growing things."[19]

Dwellings (Toledo: Libbey-Owens-Ford Glass Company, 1943) and *Solar Houses: An Architectural Lift in Living* (Toledo: Libbey-Owens-Ford Glass Company, 1945). For a book of plans by a second company, see Solar Air-Flo Incorporated, *Solar Designs for Comfortable Living* (Elkhart, IN: Solar Air-Flo Incorporated, 1950). According to the *Reader's Digest* piece about Keck's work, the Revere Copper and Brass Company also published booklets of solar home plans. See Ralph Wallace, "The Proven Merits of a Solar Home," 104.

18. The article about the end of fuel bills is cited in note 2. For the wartime fuel shortages, see John G. Clark, *Energy and the Federal Government: Fossil Fuel Policies, 1900–1946* (Urbana: University of Illinois Press, 1987), 316–380. The winter of 1947–48 also brought a fuel oil crisis. See Richard H. K. Vietor, *Energy Policy in America Since 1945: A Study of Business-Government Relations* (New York: Cambridge University Press, 1984), 50. For the argument about security from fuel shortages, see Hamilton, *Space Heating with Solar Energy*, 2; Kobler, "Like Living in a Macy's Window," 161. The designers of solar houses often made the closer-to-nature argument. See Simon, *Your Solar House*, 7, 19, 22, 25.

19. Libbey-Owens-Ford Glass Company, *Solar Houses*, 22–23.

For a number of homeowners, a solar house expressed a philosophy of life. One of Keck's clients, Hugh Duncan, argued that the closeness to the outdoors encouraged "simplicity in living." The day-to-day drama of nature made traditional interiors – "picturesque walls, floor coverings, drapes, furniture" – seem feeble and irrelevant. "The solar designer opens up ways of living for American families where they can search deeply within themselves for what a house should mean as a place to reach greater intellectual and spiritual fulfillment," Duncan concluded. "This is designing in one of the great American traditions, the tradition of Thoreau who told us: 'Before we can adorn our houses with beautiful objects the walls must be stripped, and our lives must be stripped, and beautiful housekeeping and beautiful living be laid for a foundation.'"[20]

The advocates of solar design also argued that beauty derived from the "fitness" of a structure. The most elegant house was the house best suited to the environment. Indeed, the solar house embodied a sense of the proper human place in the world. "As life has arisen through the hidden aspects of natural laws," one architect wrote, "so for better or worse the rules of nature command that life make a close adjustment to natural background."[21]

The solar house soon won the endorsement of a number of influential architectural critics. In the first postwar book about design, the two senior editors of *Architectural Forum* devoted a chapter to solar heating. "From here on in," they concluded, "anyone who plans a house without giving serious consideration to the operation of the solar house principle is missing a wonderful chance to get a better house, a more interesting house, and a house that is cheaper to run." The most popular postwar books of homes also included examples of solar design. *The American House Today* featured a Keck home, while *McCall's Book of Modern Houses* praised a home designed by another solar pioneer: "A 30-inch roof overhang plus shade from the trees keeps the hot summer sun from the windows, and in winter sun rays fill the living room with solar heat. This

---

20. Hamilton, *Space Heating with Solar Energy*, 89.
21. The quotation comes from Victor Olgyay, *Design with Climate: Bioclimatic Approach to Architectural Regionalism* (Princeton: Princeton University Press, 1963), 1. In addition, see Katherine Morrow Ford and Thomas H. Creighton, *The American House Today* (New York: Reinhold, 1951), 208.

house is now several winters old and the owners report that it has been easy and inexpensive to heat even in the coldest New England weather."[22]

In the late 1940s and early 1950s, a variety of architects, journalists, and public officials also supported the solar house as part of a campaign to encourage a more ambitious ideal of environmental design. The solar home took advantage of a gift of nature – sunlight – to provide economical heat. But why work with nature only to provide winter warmth? The design of a house could help moderate the extremes of the weather anywhere if architects and builders adapted to regional climate conditions.[23]

Though expressed in a modern language, the ideal of environmental design was quite ancient. The boosters of the cause pointed out that the Greek writer Xenophon and the Roman author Vitruvius had advised builders to consider the location of the sun and the nature of the winds. Through trial and error, the fundamental principles of climate adaptation had become part of vernacular traditions of design throughout the world. The American continent was no exception, as the desert pueblos of the southwest demonstrated. The early buildings of European emigrants also were well suited to regional conditions. The design of the archetypal 18th-century New England farmhouse maximized warmth in winter, with centrally located chimneys, low ceilings, thick masonry walls, small windows – and few openings of any kind on the north side. In contrast, the typical antebellum southern plantation house was designed to minimize heat and humidity. The chimneys were usually on outside walls, the ceilings were high, the walls had many large windows with louvered shutters, the attic was ventilated, and the house was surrounded by shade-producing porches and balconies.[24]

22. The quotations come from George Nelson and Henry Wright, *Tomorrow's House: A Complete Guide for the Home-Builder* (New York: Simon and Schuster, 1945), 179; Mary Davis Gillies, *McCall's Book of Modern Houses* (New York: Simon and Schuster, 1951), 16. In addition, see Ford and Creighton, *The American House Today*, 177.
23. For the theory of environmental design, see Aronin, *Climate and Architecture;* Olgyay, *Design with Climate;* Groff Conklin, *The Weather Conditioned House* (New York: Reinhold, 1958). The subject also gave rise to an extensive periodical literature, which I cite below.
24. For the ancients, see "Insolation and House Design," *Pencil Points* 25 (February 1944): 77; Aronin, *Climate and Architecture,* 11–16; Simon, *Your Solar House,* 15. For the American traditions, see James Marston Fitch, "Our Ancestors Had More Savvy about Climate," *House Beautiful* 91 (October 1949): 156–157. In addition, see Victor G. Olgyay,

By 1950, however, the regional traditions of design were in decline. The rise of the balloon-frame form of construction, the mail-order house, and the mass-produced subdivision all had led to a more uniform architecture. The supporters of regionalism certainly saw the trend. Again and again, they criticized tract-house builders for disregarding regional conditions. As one critic wrote in 1949, Americans had "gone backward and unlearned things we used to know. We have built, in the South, little, low-ceilinged hotboxes without properly shaded roofs. We have built, in the North, houses with thin brick walls that are cold in winter and hot in summer. We have put Cape Cod houses into climates that are as different from Cape Cod as Cape Cod is from England." The advocates of environmental design hoped to reverse the course of history.[25]

In October 1949, *House Beautiful* began a 15-month campaign to revitalize regional traditions of design. Too often, the magazine argued, the nation's builders ignored a basic principle of good

"The Temperate House," *Architectural Forum* 94 (March 1951): 180, 182, 192; "House for Texas: Cheap to Build, It Is Especially Adapted to the State's Climate," 19 *Life* (September 10, 1945): 58–59. In the 1970s and 1980s, the energy crisis renewed interest in the vernacular traditions of design. See, for example, Richard G. Stein, *Architecture and Energy* (Garden City, NY: Anchor Press, 1977), 23–47; John A. Burns, *Energy Conserving Features Inherent in Older Homes* (Washington: U.S. Department of Housing and Urban Development, 1982); Suzanne Stephens and Janet Bloom, "Before the Virgin Met the Dynamo," *Architectural Forum* 139 (July/August 1973), 76–87; Vivian Loftness, "Architecture and Climate," *Weatherwise* 31 (December 1978): 212–217; Wilson Clark, *Energy for Survival: The Alternative to Extinction* (Garden City, NY: Anchor Books, 1974), 569–577.

25. The quotation is from Wolfgang Langewiesche, "So You Think You're Comfortable!," *House Beautiful* 91 (October 1949): 134, 230. For the environmental critique of tract-house design, see Wolfgang Langewiesche, "How to Manipulate Sun and Shade," *House Beautiful* 92 (July 1950): 43; Conklin, *The Weather Conditioned House*, 137, 141; Aronin, *Climate and Architecture*, ix; Fitch, "Our Ancestors Had More Savvy about Climate," 156; W. R. Woolrich, "Tropical Housing Research Studies: An Appraisal of Factual Investigations Needed for Design of Tropical Homes for Maximum Summer Livability," *Heating, Piping, and Air Conditioning* 24 (September 1952): 119–120; A. Quincy Jones and Frederick E. Emmons, *Builders' Homes for Better Living* (New York: Reinhold, 1957), 181. A number of scholars have also noted the increasing standardization of architecture in the 20th century. See Reyner Banham, *The Architecture of the Well-Tempered Environment* [2nd edition] (Chicago: University of Chicago Press, 1984), 190; Larry R. Ford, *Cities and Buildings: Skyscrapers, Skid Rows, and Suburbs* (Baltimore: Johns Hopkins University Press, 1994), 151, 154–155; Kenneth T. Jackson, *Crabgrass Frontier: The Suburbanization of the United States* (New York: Oxford University Press, 1985), 240. Even in 1950, however, a few important regional differences persisted. The basement was more common in the North, whereas the porch was more common in the South. See "Regional Design Characteristics of New Houses," *Housing Research* 4 (October 1952): 29.

architecture: "Different places need different houses." With the help of the latest scientific research on "Climate Control," houses in every region of the country could be designed to provide much greater comfort. To point the way, the magazine published dozens of articles about techniques for moderating the extremes of the weather – how to use the sun for warmth, how to insulate against cold, how to provide more summer shade, how to use the wind to best advantage. Every month, the magazine introduced a "pace-setter" house designed to suit a specific region of the country. Because the Climate Control project was led by a distinguished team of experts, including a nationally known authority on microclimates, the director of research for the American Institute of Architects, the Army's top specialists in climatology and environmental health, two Yale professors, and the senior economist at the Federal Housing Administration, the magazine's editors were able to persuade the National Academy of Sciences to convene a symposium on architecture and climate in 1950. The proceedings of the 1950 symposium were published by the National Research Council. To ensure that practicing architects could use the climate data gathered for the project, *House Beautiful* arranged with the American Institute of Architects to publish monthly technical bulletins on regional design. The magazine even organized regional conferences for architects and manufacturers of building materials.[26]

The *House Beautiful* project went hand-in-hand with the efforts of the Housing and Home Finance Agency, which actively promoted environmental design. "In a defense emergency," a federal official wrote in 1951, "when many of the materials normally used in

26. For a good taste of the *House Beautiful* project, see Elizabeth Gordon, "What Climate Does to YOU and What You Can Do to CLIMATE," 91 (October 1949): 131; James Marston Fitch, "How You Can Use House Beautiful's Climate Control Project," 91 (October 1949): 143; James Marston Fitch, "The Scientists Behind Climate Control," 91 (October 1949): 144; Miles Colean, "Climate Control Can Save You Money," 91 (October 1949): 145, 249; "How to Look at a Pace-Setter House," 91 (November 1949): 200–201; "Climate Control Goes to the National Academy," 92 (January 1950): 82; Wolfgang Langewiesche, "How to Control the Sun," 92 (March 1950): 105–107, 130–138; Wolfgang Langewiesche, "Why Does Insulation Insulate?," 92 (September 1950): 126–129, 163–166; Elizabeth Gordon, "Report on the Climate Control Project," 92 (October 1950): 173; Wolfgang Langewiesche, "A Quickie Course in Climate Control," 92 (November 1950): 216–219, 317–318; Wolfgang Langewiesche, "Different Places Need Different Houses," 93 (January 1951): 58–61, 108–110. The volume of proceedings from the National Academy conference is Building Research Advisory Board, *Weather and the Building Industry* (Washington: National Research Council, 1950).

dwelling construction are scarce, the conservation of materials, fuel and energy is essential. Therefore, it is doubly important now that climate assume its proper position as one of our natural resources." Accordingly, the agency compiled a bibliography of books and articles about climate and architecture. To provide technical help to builders, HHFA issued two brief guides to solar orientation. A properly oriented house would provide "comfort and economy for the home owner," one guide explained, and "contribute greatly to the conservation needs of the nation." The agency also commissioned a detailed study of the use of weather data to improve regional design. One of the study's authors – Victor Olgyay – later developed the study's insights in a classic work: *Design with Climate.*[27]

But the *House Beautiful* and Housing and Home Finance Agency campaigns ultimately failed. The vast majority of tract-house builders showed little sensitivity to climate. In most postwar subdivisions, the arbitrary geometry of the grid, not the principles of solar orientation, still determined the layout of the houses. The new techniques of mass building also increased the amount of energy needed to heat and cool homes. To speed the work of site preparation, the typical subdivision builder cleared away every tree in the tract, so millions of postwar homes had no shelter against bitter winter winds and brutal summer sun. Though basements helped to moderate the extremes of temperature in the central and northern states, the number of new single-family homes with basements fell from more than 50 percent in 1940 to just 36 percent in 1950. To avoid the cost and trouble of digging holes in the ground, the building industry began to use the concrete slab foundation. The percentage of multistory homes also fell, as builders sought to save time and money by avoiding staircase construction – and to satisfy a new demand for the one-story ranch or rambler. Again, the result was to increase the use of energy for heating and cooling, since a

27. The quotations are from Housing and Home Finance Agency, *Climate and Architecture: Selected References* [Housing Research] (Washington: Housing and Home Finance Agency, 1951), 1; Housing and Home Finance Agency, *House and Site United* [Construction Aid 3] (Washington: USGPO, 1952), 14, 27. In addition, see Bernard Wagner, "Design for Livability: A Discussion of Livability Problems Arising From Proper Orientation in Regard to Sunlight," *HHFA Technical Bulletin 15* (Washington: USGPO, 1950), 1–10. For the results of the HHFA study, see Victor Olgyay and Aladar Olgyay, *Application of Climatic Data to House Design* [Housing Research] (Washington: Housing and Home Finance Agency, 1954); Olgyay, *Design with Climate*.

one-story house has more exposed surface area per square foot than a one-and-a-half or two-story house.[28]

The structure of the homebuilding industry worked against the widespread adoption of design-with-climate ideas. The advocates of energy-conserving housing took for granted the need to employ experts in the field. As *House Beautiful* argued, the design of a climate-controlled house took "all the brains, imagination, and experience of a good architect." But the typical tract-house developer had little to do with the profession. "Few merchant builders used architects or took them seriously," recalled California builder Ned Eichler. "Plans were drawn by a draftsman or a building designer who specialized in such work. Their role was largely technical and limited to putting the builder's ideas and decisions into a form suitable for bidding, construction, and government processing." Even among builders of higher-priced houses, Eichler wrote, "few turned to architects for help."[29]

But the structural problem went deeper than the reluctance of builders to seek architectural advice. The requirements of environ-

28. For the persistence of the grid orientation, see Michael Southworth and Peter M. Owens, "The Evolving Metropolis: Studies of Community, Neighborhood, and Street Form at the Urban Edge," *Journal of the American Planning Association* 59 (1993): 279–281. The trade press of the building industry occasionally acknowledged the added heat load on homes in treeless tracts. "Air cooling is more important for new houses," *House and Home* wrote, "because it may take years for trees to grow up around them to help keep them cool." See "Round Table Report on Electrical Living: The Conditioned House," 19 (April 1961): 107. The magazine made a similar point in a piece on ways to cut air-conditioning costs: "A house in a treeless tract must handle about twice as big a heat load as the same house in the woods." See "Five Top Priorities for Designing an Air-Conditioned House," 4 (August 1953): 100. In addition, see Jules R. von Sternberg, "The Economics of Trees," *House and Home* 3 (April 1953): 130–135. For the statistics on basements and one-story homes, see "Surveying Materials Used in House Construction," *Housing Research* 1 (Fall 1951): 37. In addition, see "The Fully Insulated House," *Housing Research* 5 (March 1953): 43–51, which argues that several postwar trends in home design and construction increased the heat losses of houses. In the mid-1950s, the rise of the split-level countered the trend toward one-story construction, but the one-story house remained predominant.

29. The first quotation is from Langewiesche, "A Quickie Course in Climate Control," 216. In addition, see Simon, *Your Solar House*, 23; Aronin, *Architecture and Climate*, 280. For the second quotation, see Ned Eichler, *The Merchant Builders* (Cambridge: MIT Press, 1982), 86. In *Builders' Homes for Better Living*, Jones and Emmons cited the lack of collaboration between builders and architects as a principal reason for the inadequacies of tract housing: See 187–189. On the reluctance of builders to use architects, see also Thomas Hine, *Populuxe* (New York: Alfred A. Knopf, 1986), 45; Nelson H. Foote, Janet Abu-Lughod, Mary Mix Foley, and Louis Winnick, *Housing Choices and Housing Constraints* (New York: McGraw-Hill, 1960), 269.

mental design increased the cost of construction. To produce an energy-efficient house for the low-cost market, a builder had to sacrifice space or equipment, and tract-house builders knew that a house without a minimum of space and equipment would not sell. "It is not contemplated that many of the features of . . . climate control can as yet be incorporated to any great degree into lower cost developments," the 1956 edition of the *Community Builders Handbook* acknowledged. "At present it would appear that they will be confined for some time to higher cost homes on relatively large lots." That meant that the homebuyers most likely to care about the potential savings on utility bills – the people on the tightest budgets – did not have the choice of buying a solar home.[30]

For middle-class homebuyers, the argument for functional economy in a house became less compelling as the memory of wartime fuel shortages faded. Throughout the 1950s and 1960s, the main sources of energy were a bargain, so the average family did not worry much about heating bills. Indeed, the new consumer culture of the 1950s stood in opposition to the conservation ideal. Though wary of appearing too acquisitive, most Americans wanted the chance to indulge themselves, to revel in their new prosperity. They bought appliances with chrome gorp, TV dinners, and – above all – tail-finned, super-stylized, gas-guzzling cars. Habits of thrift began to seem old-fashioned.[31]

The solar house also met resistance on aesthetic grounds. Many of the leading solar designers were advocates of modern architecture – George Keck helped to found a Bauhaus school in Chicago – and opponents of the new "international style" often attacked the solar house too. In a celebrated 1953 treatise on the architecture of the home, for example, Robert Woods Kennedy attacked the

30. Community Builders' Council of the Urban Land Institute, *The Community Builders Handbook* (Washington: Urban Land Institute, 1956), 102.
31. The lack of concern in the 1950s and 1960s about utility bills is mentioned by Eichler, *The Merchant Builders,* 14. For price trends of the principal sources of home heat, see Eric Hirst, "Building Energy Use: 1950–2000," in Melvin H. Chiogioji and Eleanor N. Oura, editors, *Energy Conservation in Commercial and Residential Buildings* (New York: Marcel Dekker, 1982), 7. The title of Hine's book on the style of the 1950s – "Populuxe" – brilliantly captures the popular desire for a bit of the luxury once reserved for the well-to-do. Karal Ann Marling extends Hine's argument in *As Seen on TV: The Visual Culture of Everyday Life in the 1950s* (Cambridge: Harvard University Press, 1994). For the postwar rejection of thrift, see Susan Strasser, *Waste and Want: A Social History of Trash* (New York: Metropolitan Books, 1999), 265–278.

"esthetic brutality" of the typical solar design: "Here all rooms of
any importance face due south; all have all glass walls; all face the
same view; typically all the bed rooms are exactly the same size and
shape; all have exactly the same light conditions; and all, more
likely than not, lack cross ventilation. The housewife is condemned
to tend such a jail of the spirit for the sake of a few lengths of pipe,
a few gallons of oil."[32]

Even if a homebuyer appreciated the aesthetic arguments for
modern design, the requirements for energy efficiency often seemed
needlessly restrictive. A home could offer the new closeness to nature – the picture windows, the open layout – without the constraints of a solar house. Why orient all the important rooms to the
south? Why not have great expanses of glass everywhere? Except
for the handful of true believers, the answer was simply a matter of
taste.

The rise of air conditioning in the 1950s further undercut the
effort to encourage environmental design. For the first time, people
could conquer heat and humidity with the flick of a switch, so the
air conditioner gave a new meaning to the phrase "climate control." As journalists and advertisers often observed, a homeowner
now might choose "push-button climate control." The ability to
make your own weather did not necessarily negate the virtues of
sound design. The design-with-climate proponents argued that me-
chanical cooling should be used mainly as a backup: With or without air conditioning, a home should be designed to allow comfort
in hot weather. But the nation's builders chose a different path.[33]

32. Robert Woods Kennedy, *The House and the Art of Its Design* (New York: Reinhold,
1953), 478. The proponents of solar design often anticipated aesthetic objections. See
Fitch, "A Solar House Designed to the Compass," 128; Lopez, "What Is a Solar House?,"
100; Simon, *Your Solar House,* 49; Putnam, *Energy in the Future,* 178. For Keck's tie
to the Bauhaus, see James Sloan Allen, *The Romance of Commerce and Culture: Capitalism, Modernism, and the Chicago-Aspen Crusade for Cultural Reform* (Chicago:
University of Chicago Press, 1983), 47.
33. The phrase "push-button climate control" comes from the title of a piece in *Popular
Mechanics* 105 (June 1956): 158–163. The idea that air-conditioning allowed made-to-
order climate was a staple of popular reporting on the new technology in the mid-1950s.
The air-conditioning industry routinely advertised the virtues of man-made weather. In
one of a series of advertisements praising the innovativeness of the capitalist system, the
Bankers Trust Company also touted the new technology: "At the Touch of a Finger –
Man-Made Climate that's Better than Nature's." See *U.S. News & World Report* 37 (August 20, 1954), 1. For the approach of environmental design advocates to air-conditioning, see Olgyay, *Design with Climate,* 31; Langewiesche, "A Quickie Course in Climate

The Rise of Air Conditioning

In 1945, only a tiny fraction of American homes had air conditioning. Though a number of air-conditioning manufacturers had tried to create a residential market before the war, their efforts were dismal failures. The prewar units were gargantuan. The first Frigidaire was four feet high, and the early Westinghouse room coolers were as big as pianos. Carrier, the industry pioneer, introduced a household air conditioner in 1932, but the unit – the Atmospheric Cabinet – was expensive, hard to install, and unreliable: In three years, the company sold only a thousand, at a loss of more than a million dollars. Even in the first years after the war, despite the entry into the market of a handful of corporate giants, the sale of household equipment accounted for only about 2 percent of the total air-conditioning market. Then the new day dawned, as manufacturers introduced relatively cheap and compact equipment. The sales of room air-conditioning units rose from 43,000 in 1947 to 1,045,000 in 1953. By 1952, *Business Week* was asking if air conditioning would be "the next big boom."[34]

The new technology soon had influential advocates in the homebuilding industry. In 1952, the trade journal *House and Home* predicted that air conditioning would help builders adapt to a disturbing change in the housing market. In the late 1940s and early 1950s, the industry hardly needed to give a thought to marketing. The shortage of new housing after 15 years of depression and war, the baby boom, and the massive federal subsidies for homebuyers ensured that builders could sell whatever they could build. To meet the demand, the industry turned out the equivalent of Model Ts – cheap, no-frills houses produced with factorylike methods. But by

Control," 317; Fitch, "Our Ancestors Had More Savvy About Climate," 156; Conklin, *The Weather Conditioned House,* 10–11; Jones and Emmons, *Builders' Homes for Better Living,* 177.

34. For the history of the air-conditioner, see Gail Cooper, *Air-conditioning America: Engineers and the Controlled Environment, 1900–1960* (Baltimore: Johns Hopkins University Press, 1998); Robert Friedman, "The Air-Conditioned Century," *American Heritage* 35 (August-September 1984): 29–32; Raymond Arsenault, "The End of the Long Hot Summer: The Air Conditioner and Southern Culture," *Journal of Southern History* 50 (1984): 609–610; Banham, *The Architecture of the Well-Tempered Environment,* 183–187. Friedman, 26, has a photograph of the 1939 Westinghouse unit. For the sales figures, see Krause, *Moody's Public Utility Manual 1971,* a20. In addition, see "Air Conditioning: The Next Big Boom?," *Business Week* (February 2, 1952): 21.

1952 builders no longer could take sales for granted. "Now that the warborn housing shortage is over and the formation of new families has fallen to around 700,000 a year," the magazine wrote, "how can homebuilding keep on at 1,000,000 houses a year plus?" The marketing success of the automobile industry suggested the answer. Every year, the automakers introduced attractive new models so that "very few people who can afford a new car stick to the old one." The result was a vast "replacement" market. With a little imagination, the building industry could follow a similar strategy. Every year, builders could offer new layouts or build in new appliances. But a few small changes would not be enough. Right now, the magazine argued, "homebuilding needs something really dramatic to make the home-buying public sit up and take notice that yesterday's house is just as obsolete as yesterday's car," and air conditioning was most likely to fit the bill: "We can imagine no new sales feature which could do as much to . . . create a whole new market for tomorrow's house."[35]

To be sure, as *House and Home* acknowledged, the potential of air conditioning would take a lot of hard work to realize. In conjunction with equipment manufacturers, architects, mortgage lenders, and federal housing officials, builders would need to reduce the cost and improve the performance of the product. "We all hope that air conditioning is going to be the next big thing in homebuilding," a leader of the National Association of Home Builders told an air-conditioning round table organized by the magazine, "but it won't be unless a great many changes are made."[36]

Two years later, the assessments of homebuilders were still mixed. In a major survey conducted in 1954, almost everyone considered air conditioning indispensable in higher-priced homes, since well-to-do buyers demanded "the latest ideas." But builders disagreed about the appeal of the new technology for the rest of the market.

---

35. "Air Conditioning, Because –," *House and Home* 1 (June 1952): 81. Nine years later, the magazine made the same argument: "Round Table Report on Electrical Living," 107. In 1952, *Business Week* also predicted that air-conditioning would appeal to builders because of "a growing need for a gimmick to sell a house." See "How Hot Is Air Conditioning?," (March 7, 1953): 46. For the housing industry's adoption in the early 1950s of the model-year strategy of marketing, see Hine, *Populuxe,* 20, 45.
36. "What Do Builders Want – A Round Table Discussion on Residential Air Conditioning," *House and Home* 1 (June 1952): 102.

In the middle price range, many builders found that air-conditioned houses sold with astonishing speed. Others reported that people often liked air conditioning but felt they couldn't afford it – or they preferred to spend their money on new appliances. The sell was even more uncertain at the low end of the market. In the construction of cheap housing, the great challenge was to provide more room for the money, and the cost of air conditioning seemed to force a problematic trade-off. Though a number of builders boasted of success with air conditioning in low-priced homes, a majority in the industry were skeptical. "People want space in a house," a Houston builder argued, "and at a price under $15,000 you cannot provide both space and air conditioning."[37]

Despite the initial doubts, however, the leaders of the home-building industry soon became air-conditioning boosters. Indeed, the major trade organizations and publications were determined to turn air conditioning into a powerful tool for marketing new houses. The industry sought ways to reduce both installation and operating costs. The National Association of Home Builders co-sponsored a study comparing the attitudes of residents in air-conditioned and nonair-conditioned subdivisions. To prove the sales appeal of air conditioning, *House and Home* helped to organize a model promotional campaign in Wilmington, Delaware.[38]

By the late 1950s, the pitch had become quite elaborate. In a piece entitled "Are You SELLING Air Conditioning?," for example, the *Journal of Homebuilding* offered builders 57 arguments to help clinch sales. But the heart of the campaign was always the promise of a new family life. In a cooler, more comfortable house, everyone

37. For the survey of builder attitudes, see "Can Air Conditioning Sell Houses?," *House and Home* 5 (March 1954): 128–129. The quotation is on 129. The continuing uncertainty in the industry was reflected in the title of a piece in another trade journal – "Air Conditioning: Luxury or Necessity?," *Journal of Homebuilding* 13 (May 1959): 14–24. For earlier expressions of ambivalence about air conditioning, see also "What Do Builders Want?," 102–103. In 1946, *Fortune* also reported "a certain defensiveness" among builders about the air-conditioning industry's effort to sell central cooling. See "Fortune Shorts: Complete Home Air Conditioning," 33 (April 1946): 260.
38. For the National Association of Home Builders study of air-conditioning, see "Construction Begins at NAHB's Air-Conditioned Village," *House and Home* 5 (March 1954): 119; "Air Conditioning: Effect on Family Life," *NAHB Correlator* 9 (August 1955): 26. The Wilmington promotional campaign is described in "You'll Sell More Houses If You Sell Them Air Conditioned," *House and Home* 20 (September 1961): 174–177. I discuss the issue of installation and operating costs in the text below.

slept better, and so everyone was more likely to have a good disposition and tempers flared less often. Husbands and wives enjoyed "better relations." Families spent more time at home together. Indeed, everyone in an air-conditioned home felt "a keener sense of relaxation." The children invited friends over more often and the adults could entertain more frequently and more successfully. "When we have a party now," one testimonial explained, "the men leave on their coats and the women can dress as they want to."[39]

For a number of reasons, the sales campaign for air conditioning was targeted at women. According to some guides, men often worked in air-conditioned buildings, so they did not need to be sold on the advantages of a cooler, less humid environment. In contrast, women tended to have doubts about the health effects of air conditioning – they feared excessive cold, and they believed in the importance of fresh air. But the marketing guides all agreed that women would become the greatest advocates of air conditioning if builders worked hard to sell them, since women spent more time at home.[40]

Again and again, therefore, the building industry argued that air conditioning improved family health. Babies suffered less often from heat rash and everyone had fewer problems with colds and allergies. Like the promoters of gas heat and electrical appliances, who had marketed to women for decades, builders also promised greater cleanliness, comfort, and convenience. With windows closed, the house had less dust and cleaning took less time. Insects were less of a nuisance. With drier air, there was less mildew. Wooden furniture did not warp, and wallpaper did not peel or buckle. Suits and dresses stayed pressed longer. "Putting on stockings, or makeup, or getting into a girdle – all are easier." Cereal and crackers never became soggy. In the summer, the kitchen was cooler, so baking was not a burden: The children could enjoy more cakes and cookies. Because eating at home was more pleasant, the air-conditioned

39. "Air Conditioning: Luxury or Necessity?," 24; "Air Conditioning: It's Not a Gimmick But Part of the House," *Journal of Homebuilding* 12 (June 1958): 28–29; "What Are the Sales Arguments for Air Conditioning . . . and How Can They Sell Your Houses?," *House and Home* 5 (March 1954): 120–124.
40. "Advice to Builders: Air Conditioning," *House and Home* 1 (June 1952): 115; "What Are the Sales Arguments for Air Conditioning . . . and How Can They Sell Your Houses?," 121.

family saved on restaurant bills. Everyone had a better appetite. The family ate more hot, healthy, home-cooked meals. Even in the dog days of summer, the family could have sit-down dinners, so "children's manners at table can be trained year round." Because the air was cooler and drier, the task of keeping house was less stressful and tiring. It was also easier to get domestic help, since maids and baby-sitters preferred to work in air-conditioned homes. Builders even promised improved security: With windows closed, a house was less inviting to prowlers.[41]

To complete the argument, homebuilders stressed the economic and social value of air conditioning. The new technology would prove a sound investment. Because push-button climate was the way of the future, a home without built-in cooling would soon be outdated. The air-conditioned house would be much easier to sell – and would have a higher resale value. With central cooling, a house also had "greater prestige value in the neighborhood." Indeed, air conditioning was a sure sign of a fine home. It was, as the slogan of *House and Home*'s model promotional campaign proclaimed, "the crowning touch."[42]

In ever-increasing numbers, the nation's homebuyers agreed. Room-unit sales of air conditioners skyrocketed in the 1950s and 1960s. In 1970, the annual total was almost 6 million. For the building industry, the growth of central air conditioning was even more gratifying. In 1960, when the U.S. census first tallied the numbers, a million residential units were centrally cooled. Ten years later, the figure was nearly 8 million. Not surprisingly, the south led the nation. By the mid-1960s, more than 40 percent of all new homes in the region had central air. But the jump in the use of air

---

41. "Air Conditioning: Luxury or Necessity?," 23–24; "Air Conditioning: It's Not a Gimmick But Part of the House," 28–29; "What Are the Sales Arguments for Air Conditioning . . . and How Can They Sell Your Houses?," 121–124; "Is Air Conditioning in for a Boom?," *House and Home* 1 (June 1952): 84; "Advice to Builders," 115; "You'll Sell More Houses If You Sell Them Air Conditioned," 176; George Dusenbury, "The 'Magic Climate' House," *American Builder* 87 (November 1965): 80–81. For the marketing efforts of the gas and electric utilities, see Mark H. Rose, *Cities of Light and Heat: Domesticating Gas and Electricity in Urban America* (University Park: Penn State Press, 1995).

42. "Air Conditioning: It's Not a Gimmick But Part of the House," 29; "Air Conditioning: Luxury or Necessity?," 15; "You'll Sell More Houses If You Sell Them Air Conditioned," 174. Gilbert Burck also pointed to the argument about obsolescence in "The Air-Conditioning Boom," *Fortune* 47 (May 1953): 203.

conditioning was astonishing everywhere. In the 1960s, the percentage of homes and apartments with some form of air conditioning tripled, from 12 to 36. The figure was even higher in the nation's cities and suburbs.[43]

From the first, architects, builders, and commentators assumed that the growing popularity of air conditioning would transform the design of buildings. But how? From a purely technical point of view, the new technology freed architecture from the constraints of climate. As architectural critic Reyner Banham wrote in 1969, "it is now possible to live in almost any type or form of house one likes to name in any region of the world that takes the fancy." In practice, however, the new freedom of design was rarely unlimited, because architects and builders had to consider the economics of air conditioning.[44]

For the builders of tract housing, the subject of air-conditioned design was especially complicated. In the 1950s, the overriding goal of the industry was to make air conditioning cheaper, because the greatest obstacle to sales was the widespread perception that only the well-to-do could afford air-conditioned living. Accordingly, the major trade organizations and publications stressed the importance of designing homes to reduce heat loads. With proper design, the builder could install a smaller unit and promise prospective buyers lower operating costs. As one official explained, "the house and the air conditioning system must work together, if the results are to be within the economic range of homeowner acceptance." The most common recommendations were to insulate the roof and walls, shade southern walls with roof overhangs, install double-glazed windows, and orient the house to minimize the force of the sun. But the how-to guides sometimes offered additional suggestions: Paint the roof white, ventilate the attic, preserve trees for

43. The annual sales of room units held relatively steady at around 1.5 million in the late 1950s and early 1960s, and then rose sharply. For the totals, see Krause, *Moody's Public Utility Manual 1971*, a20. The census figures are summarized in U.S. Department of Commerce, *Current Housing Reports: Residential Energy Uses* (Washington: USGPO, 1983), 4. For the southern and metropolitan figures, see Arsenault, "The End of the Long Hot Summer," 610–611. The overall percentages come from F. John Devaney, *Tracking the American Dream: 50 Years of Housing History from the Census Bureau* (Washington: U.S. Department of Commerce, 1994), 41–42.
44. Banham, *The Architecture of the Well-Tempered Environment*, 187. Banham also notes the economic limits on air-conditioned design.

shade, or locate nonliving spaces where the burden of the sun was greatest. Often, the trade writers borrowed the language as well as the principles of the design-with-climate advocates. *American Builder* quoted from the work of Victor Olgyay and *House and Home* told builders to "work with, instead of against, nature."[45]

At the same time, the air-conditioning manufacturers encouraged builders to cut costs by eliminating a number of traditional ways of minimizing summer heat and humidity. Why include breezeways? And why bother with basements, or attics, or porches? Why include expensive, oddly shaped corners just to improve ventilation? And why install screens for doors and windows? According to the Carrier Corporation, the equipment in a climate-controlled house almost paid for itself. Eliminate the screened-in sleeping porch, and save $350. Eliminate the attic fan, and save $250 more. Since air conditioning eliminated the need for cross-ventilation, builders did not have to put windows in every wall, and windows cost $25 apiece. The windows also could be fixed in place, with no sashes or screens, at a savings of $20 a window. Eliminate ventilation louvers, and save another $125. To demonstrate the practicality of the advice, the company even sponsored inexpensive model homes with central cooling.[46]

Many builders followed Carrier's suggestions. In 1959, for

---

45. The first quotation comes from Randall A. Nelson, "House and System Must Work as Team," *NAHB Correlator* 9 (August 1955): 28. For the *American Builder* citation of Olgyay's work, see Dusenbury, "The 'Magic Climate' House," 80–81. The second quotation comes from "Round Table Report on Electrical Living," 114. The quotation is an unacknowledged paraphrase of Olgyay, *Design with Climate*, 10: "The desirable procedure would be to work with, not against, the forces of nature." In addition, see "Air Conditioning: It's Not a Gimmick But Part of the House," 30–34; "Five Top Priorities for Designing an Air-Conditioned House," 100–109; "These Ten Design Measures Lighten the Cooling Load," *House and Home* 5 (March 1954): 114–115; "How Are Architects Designing for Air Conditioning?," *House and Home* 1 (June 1952): 89–95; "How to Make Buyers Demand Air Conditioning," *House and Home* 9 (May 1956): 186; Harold Legge, "The Influence of Air Conditioning on Value of Dwellings," *Appraisal Journal* 23 (1955): 563.

46. "Air Conditioning: It's Always Fair Weather," *Newsweek* 41 (June 15, 1953): 87, describes Carrier's tally of cost savings. In addition, see Robert Lasch, "Will Your Next House Have Central Cooling?," *Popular Science* 162 (March 1953): 155; "Air Conditioning: The Next Big Boom?," 21; "Weather-Controlled Home . . . Draws 2,500 House-Hunters," *Business Week* (August 23, 1952): 58–60; "Air Conditioning: Now for Small Homes," *Newsweek* 40 (September 8, 1952): 73; Burton T. Kehoe, "Comfort Costs Less than You Think," *NAHB Correlator* 9 (August 1955): 11–14. The last article also recommends the use of architectural devices to reduce air-conditioning expenses – roof overhangs, proper orientation, insulation.

example, the largest builder in Florida abandoned the sleeping porch. "I figured that for the cost of building a Florida room," he explained, "I could air condition the whole house." The story was similar throughout the south. Year by year, the old architectural adaptations to climate became increasingly rare in new construction. In the north, too, builders began to do away with attic fans, screens, storm windows, and cross-ventilation in order to provide central cooling.[47]

In a variety of ways, therefore, the homebuilding industry produced a vast new demand for energy. The nation's builders constructed millions of homes ill-equipped to provide relief from intemperate weather. The typical subdivision had no mature trees, and the typical tract house was a hotbox. Indirectly, then, the industry increased the market for the air conditioner: The new room units made tract housing more habitable. The boom in room-unit sales then encouraged the homebuilding industry to push central air conditioning. To make central cooling more affordable, builders also eliminated traditional devices for providing shade and ventilation. Of course, the use of air conditioning allowed homeowners to enjoy a new degree of comfort, but a goodly portion of the residential air-conditioning load simply replaced the comfort once provided – at little environmental cost – by good design.[48]

The Campaign for Electric Heat

For the nation's electric utilities, the rapidly increasing popularity of air conditioning created a dilemma. To ensure the most profitable return on its investment in generating equipment, a utility

47. For the quotation – and for the architectural changes in the air-conditioned south – see Arsenault, "The End of the Long Hot Summer," 624. In addition, see Cooper, *Air-conditioning America*, 154.
48. In *Air-conditioning America*, Cooper draws similar conclusions about the hotbox design of the typical tract house and the elimination of traditional climate-control features. But she offers a different explanation for the rise of air conditioning after World War II, perhaps because she relies on sources from the heating, cooling, and ventilating industry rather than the building industry. She argues that "air conditioning was most often installed as a means of achieving affordable home ownership." Since the cheap tract house was uninhabitable without air conditioning, she concludes, "consumers were faced with a fait accompli that they had merely to ratify." See 142, 156. I think the process was more complicated. Central air conditioning certainly was not essential to achieving affordable housing for the masses – the opposite was true, as the building industry understood from the first – and consumers were not as passive as Cooper suggests.

company needed to balance the demand for power throughout the year, yet the air-conditioning load came primarily in the summer. The result was increasingly unbalanced loads. First in the south and southwest, then throughout much of the nation, a large number of electric utilities began to experience great peaks of demand in the summer. The symbolic turning point came in 1956, when the Consolidated Edison Company of New York first saw the summer load move above the peak winter demand. What could be done to restore balance to the system? To many utility executives, the answer seemed obvious: Promote electric heat.[49]

In addition to improving the seasonal balance of demand, a new market for electric heat would offer utility companies a number of benefits. It would help to solve "the wiring problem." In most older houses, and even in many new homes, the electrical circuitry could not provide the power needed to run dozens of appliances, and so utility executives worried about a slowdown in the growth of residential demand for electricity. To provide electric heat, however, homebuilders would need to install the most up-to-date wiring. The lure of electric heat also might persuade many homeowners to rewire. Either way, the number of potential customers for new appliances would grow. Once people were sold on the attraction of electrical heat, moreover, the promotion of new electrical gadgets would become much easier. "Space heating customers," one utility manager explained, "are electrically minded." The overall increase in sales would be tremendous. In the mid-1950s, the average American home used about 3,000 kilowatt hours a year; the owners of all-electric homes used between 20,000 and 30,000. As the president of the Edison Electric Institute told a 1958 industry sales conference, "we should view electric house heating as a principal means by which our rate of growth can be dramatically increased."[50]

49. For discussion of the subject by leaders of the electrical industry, see Philip Sporn, "All-Electric Home Seen at Hand," *Electrical World* 143 (April 25, 1955): 16–18; "Turn on the Electric Heat," *Electrical World* 144 (November 14, 1955): 105; "Evans Spurs Industry to Back All-Electric Home," *Electrical World* 146 (December 24, 1956): 70–71. In addition, see "The Case for Electric Heat," *House and Home* 15 (March 1959): 173; Lawrence Lessing, "Electric Heating Puts on the Heat," *Architectural Forum* 111 (October 1959): 169–170; "Warmth by Watts," *Newsweek* 44 (September 27, 1954): 77; "Switch to Electric Heating?," *Changing Times* 14 (September 1960): 15–16; C. Lester Walker, "Will You Heat With Electricity?," *Reader's Digest* 71 (October 1957): 151.
50. The first quotation comes from "A Progress Report: Electric Heating and Heat Pumps," *Electrical World* 149 (June 30, 1958): 43. For the second quotation, see "Never Thought

To build the market, however, the industry would have to make a determined effort. In the years after World War II, natural gas had become widely available to residential customers, and gas heat offered many of the same advantages as electric heat: Unlike coal and fuel oil, natural gas and electricity both were clean and "modern," delivered automatically to the home. Would the electric utilities be able to win customers in a brutally competitive market?[51]

The early history of electric heat was not encouraging. Before the 1950s, the technology had won support only in the Tennessee Valley and the Pacific Northwest. Neither region offered a strong precedent for a national promotional campaign. Because the two regions were supplied with power from federally subsidized hydroelectric authorities, electric rates were far below the average. In both regions, the climate was fairly moderate, and so no one could say for sure how electric heat would perform in bitter cold. But the leaders of the electric industry were undaunted. From the early years of the century, the nation's utility companies had relied on aggressive salesmanship to build demand, and the industry's leaders spoke confidently in the postwar years about their power to "invent the future." In a famous speech to utility managers, for example, the president of a New York power company argued that "the most important elements that determine our loads are not those that happen, but those that we project – that we invent – in the broad sense of the term 'invention.' You have control over such loads: you invent them, and then you can make plans for the best manner of meeting them." By the late 1950s, accordingly, a substantial number of power companies had decided to sell electric heat – and sell hard.[52]

I Would Live to See the Day When the President of EEI Would Say . . .," *Electrical World* 149 (April 28, 1958): 73. In addition, see "The Case for Electric Heat," 173; E. Bryson Sessions, "A Special Report: Characteristics of the All-Electric Home," *Electrical World* 145 (March 19, 1956): 123; "Big Push to Sell Electric Living," *Business Week* (February 11, 1956): 64–66. For comparisons of electricity use in average and all-electric homes, see Sessions, "A Special Report," 146; "A Progress Report: Electric Heating and Heat Pumps," 77; Vennard, *The Electric Power Business*, 161.

51. For the spread of gas heating, see John H. Herbert, *Clean Cheap Heat: The Development of Residential Markets for Natural Gas in the United States* (New York: Praeger, 1992), 85–125.

52. The quotation comes from Richard F. Hirsh, *Technology and Transformation in the American Electric Utility Industry* (New York: Cambridge University Press, 1989), 52–53. For the early history of electric heating, see Lessing, "Electric Heating Puts on the Heat," 170. The initial doubts about the future of electric heat also were described in "Wired

The utility companies had powerful allies. The most important were the manufacturers of electrical equipment, especially General Electric and Westinghouse. For the two industry giants, the creation of a new market for electric heat promised to increase profits in three ways. The two corporations sold electric heating units; the use of electric heat led to increased demand for a variety of household appliances, including air conditioners; and the overall growth of the power industry meant a growing market for electrical generating equipment, which the companies also manufactured. Accordingly, the two corporations sponsored multimillion-dollar campaigns to promote the construction of all-electric homes. General Electric provided the principal support for a nationwide "Live Better Electrically" promotion, beginning in 1956. A year later, the company also helped to launch the Medallion Home campaign. New homes with all-electric appliances – refrigerators, clothes dryers, hot water heaters – received a bronze medallion. Homes that also had electric heating and cooling received a gold medallion: The symbol of the best in modern living. In 1959, Westinghouse followed suit with a $2.5 million campaign to promote "the total-electric house." Both corporations advertised heavily in national publications, and both created television programs to sell the idea. Across the country, the two companies also joined with builders to sponsor model medallion homes.[53]

for Heat," *Business Week* (July 22, 1944): 48–50. In the 1950s, a number of people in the industry continued to express doubts. See "Almost Everywhere Utilities Like Electric House Heating," *Electrical World* 144 (November 14, 1955): 132; "A Progress Report: Electric Heating and Heat Pumps," 41. For a straightforward description of the way utilities thought about "getting new business," see Vennard, *The Electric Power Business*, 147–190. For the early history of the industry, see especially Harold L. Platt, *The Electric City: Energy and the Growth of the Chicago Area, 1880–1930* (Chicago: University of Chicago Press, 1991); Rose, *Cities of Light and Heat*. The emphasis on aggressive promotion was a distinctly American way of dealing with the issue of load balance. See Thomas P. Hughes, *Networks of Power: Electrification in Western Society, 1880–1930* (Baltimore: Johns Hopkins University Press, 1983). For decades, the regulatory structure of the industry also encouraged public utilities to build demand: The utilities were allowed a maximum rate of return on investment, so a company could earn more money by creating the need for new investments in generating capacity.

53. For General Electric, see "'Medallion Home' Spurs LBE Plans," *Electrical World* 148 (October 28, 1957): 47–49; "Big Push to Sell Electric Living," 64. For Westinghouse, see "Total-Electric Home Promotion Launched by Westinghouse," *Electrical World* 151 (January 19, 1959): 32–33; "5 Architects Design 'Gold Medallion Homes' for Westinghouse," *Architectural Record* 130 (August 1961): 14–15. The National Electrical Manufacturers Association also sponsored an electric-heat campaign. See "Electric Heat Goes Big Time," *Electrical World* 145 (June 25, 1956): 162.

The campaign for electric heat also had the support of people involved in the production and distribution of coal. Once the dominant source of home heat, coal lost out to natural gas and fuel oil after World War II – but electric heat offered a roundabout way to offset that loss because coal turned more than half of the nation's electrical generators. Accordingly, the United Mine Workers worked hard to promote electric heat. In a number of areas, coal suppliers joined utility companies in selling electric living. As one newspaper advertisement proclaimed, "King Coal, the mighty monarch of heat and power, carries the burden of producing the electricity Reddy Kilowatt requires to turn the wheels of progress, brighten homes, lighten housework, [and] make life more enjoyable for you!" The railroads also joined the fight, since coal constituted much of their freight.[54]

The pitch to consumers emphasized the hallowed themes of comfort and convenience. Unlike natural gas or fuel oil, electric heat could be controlled room by room with the simple flick of a switch. Especially in the late 1950s and early 1960s, when the nation's consumers were infatuated with the idea of push-button control, the comfort-and-convenience argument for electric heat automatically gave the technology the appeal of modernity. Often, the advertisements made the tie explicit: "Enjoy tomorrow's heat today." The advertisements for electric heat also claimed that the new technology was both cleaner and quieter than the alternatives. To clinch the argument, the utility companies tried to chip away at consumer confidence in the safety of natural gas. Electric heat was "flameless," the advertisements proclaimed. In face-to-face pitches, the sales staffs of some utilities were more aggressive. "Sometimes we used slogans that weren't exactly kosher, but they

54. For the support of the United Mine Workers, see Lessing, "Electric Heating Puts on the Heat," 170; "A Progress Report: Electric Heating and Heat Pumps," 77; "Warmth by Watts," 77; Walker, "Will You Heat With Electricity?," 152. In the mid-1960s, coal producers and coal-carrying railroads joined with utility companies, electrical equipment manufacturers, and insulation makers to form the Electric Heat Association. See "The All-Electric House: A Stronger Sales-Builder Than Ever Before," *House and Home* 27 (February 1965): 65. The King Coal advertisement ran in the *Kansas City Star* on January 4, 1953 – I found the ad in a clipping file on all-electric homes in the Johnson County (Kansas) Historical Museum. Between 1954 and 1970, coal generated about half of the nation's electric power, and electric utilities consumed more than half of the nation's coal output. See Martin V. Melosi, *Coping with Abundance: Energy and Environment in Industrial America* (Philadelphia: Temple University Press, 1985), 201.

helped to sell," recalled one electric company representative. "'Gas goes Boom.'"[55]

To build the market for electric heat, power companies also used promotional rates, although the practice was not universal. For a time, indeed, the industry debated the best way to approach the question of cost. According to a number of utility executives, the advertisements for electric heat should downplay the issue of economy and instead follow a "Cadillac" approach to marketing: Electric heat simply was better and customers should be willing to pay a premium for higher quality. But a majority in the industry took a different view. Though electric heat was more expensive than gas or oil, the situation would soon be reversed, and electric utilities should sell the future: With the coming of atomic energy, electricity would be incredibly cheap. In the meantime, because the higher cost of electric heat was the principal obstacle to higher sales, the industry had to sell Cadillacs at Pontiac prices. By the early 1960s, accordingly, almost 100 of the nation's utilities offered special rates for electric heat. The most common approach was to charge residential customers differently for different levels of demand. Below one hundred and fifty kilowatt hours a month, more or less – enough electricity to power lights and small appliances – the highest rate applied. The rate went down for the next step of demand, to reward customers with a few big-ticket appliances. Finally, for monthly use above three or four hundred kilowatt hours – a level only homes with electric heat would reach – the rates were rock-bottom.[56]

55. For the first quotation, see "Have Tomorrow's Heat – Today," *House Beautiful* 93 (November 1953): 280. The second quotation comes from Susan M. Stacy, *Legacy of Light: A History of the Idaho Power Company* (Boise: Idaho Power, 1991), 163, 166. A Kansas City Power and Light advertisement for the first all-electric home in the area promised "a home for modern family living," "comfortable and up-to-the-minute in every respect," and full of "convenience and gracious living." See the all-electric home file of the Johnson County Historical Museum. In addition, see "The All-Electric House," 60–67; "What's New in Electric Heat?," *House and Home* 16 (December 1959): 157; "What Builders Should Know about Electric Heat," *Practical Builder* 25 (March 1960): 110. For the push-button mania of the period, see Hine, *Populuxe*, 123–138.

56. *Electrical World* periodically conducted surveys of the promotional strategies of utilities, including rates. For a good discussion of the "Cadillac" question and the use of promotional rates, see "Electric Comfort Heating and Heat Pumps: 1959 Electric Heating Survey," *Electrical World* 152 (November 16, 1959): 72, 81. The promotional rates were also reported widely in the trade publications of the building industry, the business press, and the mass circulation magazines for consumers. See "Round Table Report on

Though the most visible part of the campaign for electric heat targeted consumers, the utilities also worked aggressively to win over the building industry. The effort built on a strong foundation. To increase sales of major electrical appliances, both power companies and electrical manufacturers had already begun to cultivate the developers of large subdivisions. The utilities regularly reduced wiring charges for each appliance builders installed. As the trade publication *Electrical World* explained, the industry needed to acknowledge "the growing importance of home builders to utilities," because built-ins accounted for a significant share of the market for water heaters, ranges, air conditioners, refrigerators, and clothes dryers. The importance of builders in the market for home heating was even greater than in the market for major appliances, and the utility outreach to builders became more emphatic once the campaign for electric heat began.[57]

In part, the promoters of electric heat promised builders the opportunity to sell cheaper and better houses. Electric heating systems usually cost less than gas or oil burners. Installation was simpler: With experience, the power companies argued, a builder could cut installation time in half. In a house without air conditioning or with room cooling units, a builder also could eliminate the costly and time-consuming work of installing a duct system. Because the electrically heated house did not need a chimney or a furnace room, the builder could offer more usable space. To help builders incorporate the new technology, a majority of utilities even offered free design-and-layout services. In all, therefore, the builder of a home with electric heat could advertise more house for the money.[58]

The builders of electrically heated subdivisions could also count

Electrical Living," 108–109; Lessing, "Electric Heating Puts on the Heat," 171; "Switch to Electric Heating?," 15–17; "Heating the Home with Electricity," *Consumer Bulletin* 44 (January 1961): 27. On the promise of atomic energy, see Sporn, "All-Electric Home Seen at Hand," 18; "The Case for Electric Heat," 172; "What's New in Electric Heat?," 157.

57. "Mass Home Builder Growing in Importance," *Electrical World* 144 (December 12, 1955): 144–146. The trade press of the building industry also discussed the industry's targeting of builders. "Courtship of builders by the electric utilities is entering a new phase – the promotion of electric heat," one article began. See "What Builders Should Know about Electric Heat," 110.

58. "Warmth by Watts," 77–78; Lessing, "Electric Heating Puts on the Heat," 171; "Electric Heat Goes Big Time," 162; "What Builders Should Know about Electric Heat," 110; "The Case for Electric Heat," 173; "Electric Heat . . . Can the Builder House Use It?," *House and Home* 7 (January 1955): 154; "Electric Space Heating: What Utilities Are Doing About It," *Electrical World* 147 (January 21, 1957): 75, 86.

on help with marketing. Often, the local power company sent people to staff model homes. Some utilities ran sales seminars for builders, and almost all provided free promotional materials. In at least one case, a power company organized a homebuilders association to ensure organizational backing for a gala "parade" of all-electric homes. Across the country, utility companies reinforced the nationwide campaigns for all-electric living with local advertising, including traveling exhibits, print ads, and radio and television spots. When a builder advertised electrically heated homes, the local utility frequently shared the cost.[59]

Perhaps most important, the utilities offered builders substantial discounts, payments, and financial benefits for installing electric heat. Occasionally, the incentives were included in rate schedules approved by state regulatory bodies. To cite one example from the late 1950s, Commonwealth Edison of Chicago charged $50 a house for underground wiring, but reduced the charge to $25 if the builder installed one major electrical appliance; with two built-in appliances, the wiring was free; and if a house had electric heat, the utility company paid the builder $100. Often, however, the utilities negotiated special deals with developers, and the terms were not subject to public scrutiny. In addition to cash payments, the arrangements often included cut-rate pricing on appliances. In some cases, the power company also provided low-interest loans to help builders acquire land. According to *House and Home,* the total value of the electric-heat incentives for subdivision homes generally ranged from $100 to $200, but went as high as $400. The range actually was greater: In a 1959 study, the Public Utilities Commission in New Jersey found that some builders received more than $500 a house, and one garnered $911.[60]

59. U.S. House of Representatives, *Promotional Practices by Public Utilities and their Impact Upon Small Business: Hearings Before the Subcommittee on Activities of Regulatory Agencies, Select Committee on Small Business,* 90th Congress, 2nd session, 1968, 4, 7, 30, 49–50; Stacy, *Legacy of Light,* 159, 161–163; Eichler, *The Merchant Builders,* 14; "If You Build for Electrical Living, Utilities Will Go All Out to Help You," *House and Home* 17 (April 1960): 139–141; "Round Table Report on Electric Living," 116; "Home Buyers Demand Quality Heating," *Practical Builder* 27 (October 1962): 63; "Mass Home Builder Growing in Importance," 144; "Electric Heat: WWP Gets on the Bandwagon," *Electrical World* 147 (May 20, 1957): 120–122; "Utilities Go All Out for Medallion Home Program," *Electrical World* 150 (July 28, 1958): 52–53, 92, 99.

60. On loans, see Eichler, *The Merchant Builders,* 14. The Chicago schedule is described in "The Case for Electric Heat," 173. The figures for the overall value of incentives come from "Round Table Report on Electric Living," 116. The New Jersey study is cited in

As a last resort, a number of utility companies apparently used coercive tactics. In one case, a gas utility sued to stop a power company from buying land for resale to developers with covenants requiring the use of electric heat. In several states, the electrical industry's competitors complained that builders were quoted extortionate rates for wiring if they planned to install gas or oil heat – since every house had to have electricity for lighting, the builders had no choice but to pay the penalty or install electric heat.[61]

The campaign to sell electric heat soon became controversial. By 1968, when a congressional subcommittee held hearings on utility promotional practices, 28 state regulatory bodies had investigated the issue. To critics of the electric companies, the incentives offered to builders were a kind of "payola," a form of bribery to secure the trade of a supposedly independent body of professionals. The industry's defenders countered that the system of promotional rates and payments to builders ultimately contributed to the public good: By allowing utility companies to build a more balanced and efficient load, the incentives helped to lower electric rates for everyone. Some states accepted the industry's argument; others did not. Thus, in much of the country, utility companies continued the hard sell until 1978, when federal legislation outlawed the most controversial marketing practices.[62]

Whether fair or foul, the promotional tactics of the electrical industry proved quite successful. Though natural gas quickly became the dominant source of home heating after World War II, electric heat gained rapidly. In 1960, only 2 percent of the nation's households were heated with electricity; a decade later, the figure was 8 percent; and by 1980, the total had reached 18 percent. The growth of electric heat in new construction was even more striking. In the 1950s, when the industry's big push began, builders installed electric heating in 8 percent of their units – by the early 1980s, 50 per-

U.S. House of Representatives, *Promotional Practices by Public Utilities*, 49. The House subcommittee hearing also had detailed evidence about the use of discounts, payments, and benefits. See, especially, 5, 6, 10, 19, 28, 30–31, 50, 78, 81, 93, 96, 97.

61. U.S. House of Representatives, *Promotional Practices by Public Utilities*, 21, 74, 93–95.
62. The *Promotional Practices by Public Utilities* hearings are a good source for the controversy. For a summary of state action on the promotional issue, see 50–62. For the charges of "payola" and "bribery," see 2, 29, 40, 77, 82. For the industry defense, see 62–70, 82–91. In addition, see Hirsh, *Technology and Transformation in the American Electric Utility Industry*, 245, note 80.

cent of new homes had electric heat, a stunning increase. As the leaders of the electrical industry had hoped, the growing reliance on electric heating also contributed to a sharp rise in the total residential demand for electricity: From 1950 to 1970, the increase was almost 400 percent.[63]

The increase might have been even greater, but the electric industry also pushed hard to improve household insulation. The need was great. Before World War II, the average home had almost no insulation. In 1941, as a wartime conservation measure, the Federal Housing Administration set a minimum standard for protection against heat loss in federally insured homes, but the requirement was lax. Because the standards only applied to FHA houses, moreover, a large number of houses still did not meet the minimum standard. In the 1950s, the agency revised the standard twice, each time requiring slightly more insulation, but the building industry successfully opposed a tougher requirement. In much of the country, therefore, a house built in 1960 could satisfy the FHA with a small amount of ceiling insulation – and no insulation in the walls or floor.[64]

To the electrical industry, a lax insulation standard was unacceptable. If electric-heat customers were shocked by their first monthly bills, the negative word of mouth would destroy the potential of the mass market. Accordingly, a number of utility companies refused to install electric heat in inadequately insulated homes. To insure the quality of insulation work, a few even sent out inspectors. In the late 1950s, the industry also pressed the Federal Housing Administration to adopt serious insulation standards. Though a majority of homebuilders opposed the insulation campaign, a few lobbied hard for tougher standards: If the monthly cost of electric

63. For the heating statistics, see Devaney, *Tracking the American Dream,* 42; U.S. Department of Commerce, *Current Housing Reports,* 1–2; Herbert, *Clean Cheap Heat,* 169. For the rise in residential electricity demand, see Tansil and Moyers, "Residential Demand for Energy," 378. Electric heating directly accounted for 20 percent of the increase.
64. For insulation use in 1940 and 1950, see "Metals Saving Trends in Domestic Heating," *Housing Research* 2 (Winter 1951–1952): 2–4. In addition, see Housing and Home Finance Agency, *The Materials Use Survey* [Housing Research] (Washington: Housing and Home Finance Agency, 1953), 12. The history of the FHA standard also is described in "How to Sell Quality Insulation," *House and Home* 15 (May 1959): 176–177. For the resistance of builders to higher insulation standards in the late 1950s, see "What's New in Electric Heat?," 184. For a discussion of the standards in 1960, see Hirst, "Building Energy Use," 17.

heat could be reduced, the boosters believed, the new technology might join air conditioning as a powerful way to sell the idea of the up-to-date home. The insulation industry naturally joined the fray too. By the late 1950s, indeed, the largest insulation manufacturers had decided to bet heavily on the appeal of "electric living." In display ads in national-circulation magazines, for example, Owens-Corning urged homebuyers to look for "Comfort Conditioned Homes," which were identified by medallionlike placards in the front yard. With full Fiberglas insulation, the ads proclaimed, home owners could enjoy "the comfort and convenience of Full House-power" – with heating and cooling costs "kept at the lowest level."[65]

Despite the efforts of the electric-heat promoters, the federal insulation standard remained lax until the 1970s, when the energy crisis provoked a new interest in conservation. But the insulation campaign of the late 1950s made a difference: The homes built after 1960 were better insulated than the homes built before.[66]

---

65. For discussion of the subject by people in the electrical industry, see "Electric Heating: Good Insulation Is the Utility's Responsibility," *Electrical World* 150 (August 18, 1958): 59; "How to Cut High Heating Bill Complaints: I & M Stresses Better Insulation," *Electrical World* 146 (October 1, 1956): 112; "Electric Space Heating," 74; "Electric House Heating – 1955," *Electrical World* 144 (November 14, 1955): 132; "Electric Comfort Heating and Heat Pumps," 78. The subject was also a staple of discussions of electric heat in the trade press of the homebuilding industry. See "Experts Urge Simple New Yardstick to Show If House Is Built to Save Heat," *House and Home* 7 (January 1955): 138–143; "How to Sell Quality Insulation," 175–177; "The Case for Electric Heat," 174; "What's New in Electric Heat?," 156, 164, 168, 172, 176, 182, 184; "Round Table Report on Electrical Living," 114; "The All-Electric House," 64; "What Builders Should Know about Electric Heat," 111–114. The Owens-Corning advertisement was in *Life* 46 (May 18, 1959): 120–121; in addition, see *Life* 46 (June 1, 1959): 88–89. In 1956, the trade organization of the insulation industry – the National Mineral Wool Association – issued a booklet on electric heat. See "Electric Heat in 100,000 Homes a Year Is Forecast," *Electrical World* 145 (April 2, 1956): 129. The articles on home heating in consumer magazines also described the electric industry's promotion of insulation. See "Switch to Electric Heating?," 16; "Heating the Home with Electricity," 24–25.
66. According to a recent federal study of 5,000 homeowners, the number of homes with wall insulation increased 5 percent from the 1950s to the 1960s; the percentage of homes with roof or ceiling insulation did not change. See Energy Information Administration, *Housing Characteristics 1990: Residential Energy Consumption Survey* (Washington: U.S. Department of Energy, 1992), xii. The federal study may have underestimated the change, however. In a more detailed survey of homeowners and homebuilders in North Carolina, the post-1960 increase in the number of homes with wall, ceiling, and floor insulation ranged from 20 to 30 percent. See Mary Ellen Marsden, "Structural Characteristics and Energy Efficiency of Existing Housing," in Raymond J. Burby and Mary Ellen Marsden, editors, *Energy and Housing: Consumer and Builder Perspectives* (Cambridge: Oelgeschlager, Gunn & Hain, 1980), 34. In 1959, a Johns Manville executive concluded that "The coming of age of electric heat has done more to improve insulation than any other thing that has happened." See "What's New in Electric Heat?," 164.

Yet the energy savings from the increased use of insulation were more than offset by the wastefulness of electric heat. The total amount of energy needed to heat a home with electricity was much higher than the amount required to heat with gas or oil. Though electric heat was a marvel of efficiency in the home – no energy escaped up a furnace flue – the production and distribution of electricity were terribly inefficient. Even in the 1980s, only 29 percent of the energy used to generate electricity ultimately was usable at the end of the line. With gas or oil heating, in contrast, the overall energy efficiency ranged from 50 to 65 percent.[67]

The relative inefficiency of electric heat was even greater in the early 1950s, as a number of analysts noted at the time. The President's Materials Policy Commission even advised against the use of electricity for home heating. "Electricity is of course the ideal fuel, in that it is easier to control than any other, and is more convenient," the commission concluded in 1952. "It is inherently a very wasteful form of heat, however, and from the viewpoint of social benefit and economy, should be used only for power purposes." But the recommendation went unheeded: The wastefulness of electric heat did not become a subject of public controversy until a generation later. In the 1950s and 1960s, the nation still seemed to have energy to burn.[68]

---

67. For the wastefulness of electric heat, see U.S. General Accounting Office, *Analysis of Trends in Residential Energy Consumption*, 1–6; Stein, *Architecture and Energy*, 197; Eric Hirst and John C. Moyers, "Efficiency of Energy Use in the United States," *Science* 179 (March 30, 1973): 1301; Clark, *Energy for Survival*, 186–189.

68. In 1952, two energy analysts calculated that electric heat was only 16 percent efficient, compared to 61 percent for oil or natural gas. But the two predicted that the use of heat pumps and solar-produced electricity would eventually allow electric heat to be both technically and economically superior to the alternatives. See Ayres and Scarlott, *Energy Sources*, 149–150. The quotation is from President's Materials Policy Commission, *Resources for Freedom* [Volume IV], 152. By 1973, a number of members of Congress were asking with concern how "a relatively inefficient way of producing heat" had become so common. See Behrman, *Solar Energy*, 63. One scholar also noted that the issue had become important to environmentalists.

   Almost all environmentalists would like to see some shackles upon the largely unregulated promotional advertising common to the electric utilities; they argue that the utilities incessantly, persuasively promote their product, create high demand for their services, and then use the demand as a justification for their continuing expansion to meet "consumer needs." Why not, suggest these critics, end the advertising for "all-electric living," with all the glamorous embellishments, that the industry has so long relied upon to escalate its sales. Finally, proposals have been made that governmental bodies set limits on the permissible power consumption in American homes.

   From Walter A. Rosenbaum, *The Politics of Environmental Concern* (New York: Praeger, 1973), 278.

The Obstacles to Energy Conservation

Neither the solar house nor the all-electric home ever dominated the housing market in the years from 1945 to 1970, yet the fates of the two types of houses shed light on a profound turning point in American environmental history. For a few years, many people looked forward to the mass production of energy-conserving homes. By the 1960s, in contrast, the dream of millions of families was the all-electric rancher: With cheap energy and modern heating-and-cooling technology, the residents of every part of the country could imagine life in a home designed to suit the Mediterranean temperateness of California. The high-energy house had become common.

The new way of living came at a considerable environmental cost. The use of electricity to heat and cool homes was especially destructive. The strip mining of coal to provide fuel for generators scarred thousands of acres of land. The emissions from power plants polluted the air, caused acid rain to fall on lakes and forests, and contributed to the prospect of global warming. Though the United States so far has had only one disastrous reactor accident, the use of nuclear generating technology routinely produced a host of environmental hazards, from uranium tailings to radioactive waste. The nation's utilities also created a new threat to aquatic life – the thermal pollution that resulted when the hot water produced during electricity generation was dumped into rivers.[69]

In the postwar decades, however, the critics of tract housing did not question the environmental impact of energy consumption. The campaign to develop solar technology was inspired by concern about population growth and resource depletion, but that concern never became common. For a few architects, the solar house made a statement about the importance of respecting natural limits. The popular interest in solar housing was, however, largely a response to fuel rationing during World War II, and the wartime enthusiasm for energy-conserving homes did not lead to a new environmental ethic. By 1950, even the principal author of *House Beautiful*'s Climate Control series acknowledged the practical irrelevance of the

69. Pace University Center for Environmental Legal Studies, *Environmental Costs of Electricity* (New York: Oceana Publications, 1991) is a good summary of the huge literature on the subject. For a comparison of the environmental costs of the major fuels, see also Clark, *Energy for Survival*, 92–110.

conservation argument: "[F]uel saving is really important only in wartime, when fuel is hard to get. As my friend, Dr. L. P. Herrington says, 'Fuel waste is like sin; everybody is against it in theory, but nobody really cares in practice.'"[70]

The unprecedented affluence of the postwar decades also undercut the conservation effort. The pitch for air conditioning assumed that a majority now could enjoy the pleasures once restricted to a small minority. You can afford real comfort, the advertisements suggested, and you should have real comfort! Electric heat was also sold as a newly affordable luxury – the Cadillac of home heating, at a Pontiac price.

But the transition from wartime concern about scarcity to postwar confidence in abundance cannot explain some of the most important heating-and-cooling decisions of the 1950s and 1960s. The story of air conditioning makes that clear. The ever-increasing amount of energy used for cooling was partly a sign that Americans could afford a higher level of comfort, but the air-conditioning load was also a consequence of decisions builders made in order to hold down the cost of new construction: To install air conditioning on a budget, builders eliminated traditional ways of providing shade and ventilation.

The success of electric heat similarly was not a simple function of affluence. In most cases, the decision to install electric heat was made by builders, not homebuyers, and builders often chose electric heat because the alternatives were less profitable. Electric heat was cheaper and easier to install, and electric utilities offered builders substantial financial incentives. When people really had a choice – when they hired contractors to build a home according to their specifications – they were much less likely to install electric heat than speculative builders were. But the electric houses still sold. Because a house was a complex and expensive product, almost all homebuyers had to make trade-offs, and many were willing to accept a second-choice heating system in order to get a house with a better kitchen or a bigger bedroom.[71]

---

70. For the quotation, see Langewiesche, "A Quickie Course in Climate Control," 317. In *Coping with Abundance,* Melosi concludes that the war did not lead to a lasting concern for conservation. See 188.
71. For evidence that people building homes were less likely to choose electric heat than builders, see Dorothy K. Newman and Dawn Day, *The American Energy Consumer: A*

The constraints on consumer choice also help to explain the environmental flaws of tract housing. In a survey of homeowners conducted in the early 1950s, a significant number said that they would have preferred a more efficiently heated and ventilated house, but that preference was not a priority. By one estimate, as much as 40 percent of the housing market in the years just after the end of World War II consisted of "distress buyers," families so desperate to find a house that they were willing to accept anything they could afford. The market also included a high percentage of first-time buyers – young families with more needs than income. The number of bedrooms and bathrooms, the layout, and the neighborhood came first.[72]

The postwar decades thus suggest the weakness of a consumer-based environmentalism. In the 1950s and 1960s, the nation's consumers were either unwilling or unable to conserve energy. The well-to-do were often drawn to homes designed to provide a new closeness with nature – yet they also wanted a host of high-energy comforts and conveniences. Working-class homebuyers often wanted homes that cost less to heat and cool – yet, as the price of homeownership, they had to accept places with little protection against the extremes of climate. The result in each case was a dramatic increase in energy consumption.

Report to the Energy Policy Project of the Ford Foundation (Cambridge: Ballinger, 1975), 42–43.
72. The survey results come from Glenn H. Beyer, Thomas W. Mackesey, and James E. Montgomery, *Houses are for People: A Study of Home Buyer Motivations* (Ithaca: Cornell University Housing Research Center, 1955), 38. For a superb discussion of the complexities of consumer choice in the postwar housing market, see Foote, Abu-Lughod, Foley, and Winnick, *Housing Choices and Housing Constraints*, 71–271.

3

Septic-Tank Suburbia: The Problem of Waste Disposal at the Metropolitan Fringe

About 20 years ago, the best-selling chronicler of American middle-class culture, Erma Bombeck, offered a succinct interpretation of the rise of suburbia:

> The suburbs were discovered quite by accident one day in the early 1940s by a Welcome-Wagon lady who was lost. As she stood in a mushy marshland, her sturdy Red Cross shoes sinking into the mire, she looked down, and exclaimed, "It's a septic tank. I've discovered the suburbs!"
>
> News of the discovery of a septic tank spread and within weeks thirty million city dwellers readied their station wagons and began the long journey to the edge of town in search of a bath and a half and a tree.

In that passage from *The Grass Is Always Greener Over the Septic Tank,* Bombeck humorously noticed what more scholarly observers have overlooked: Like the automobile and the highway, the septic tank was a key element in the suburbanization of the United States. With backyard systems for waste disposal, houses did not need to be near municipal sewer lines, so the area available for suburban development expanded tremendously.[1]

Because the census bureau did not begin to count the nation's septic tanks until 1960, historians have no sure way to gauge the

---

1. For the quotation, see Erma Bombeck, *The Grass Is Always Greener over the Septic Tank* (1976; reprint, New York: Fawcett Crest, 1977), 11. There is no mention of septic tanks in the standard history of suburbia: Kenneth T. Jackson, *Crabgrass Frontier: The Suburbanization of the United States* (New York: Oxford University Press, 1985). But some analysts of urban growth have noted the role of septic tanks in the spread of suburbia. See, for example, Robert C. Wood, *Suburbia: Its People and Their Politics* (Boston: Houghton Mifflin, 1958), 3; Marion Clawson and Peter Hall, *Planning and Urban Growth: An Anglo-American Comparison* (Baltimore: Johns Hopkins University Press, 1973), 16; Samuel Kaplan, *The Dream Deferred: People, Politics, and Planning in Suburbia* (1976; reprint, New York: Vintage Books, 1977), 3.

increase in numbers after World War II. But the available evidence makes clear that the increase was phenomenal. In 1945, according to one government estimate, only about 4.5 million homes had septic tanks. In 1960, the first census counted nearly 14 million. If the 1945 estimate was close to the mark, then the increase in just 15 years was over 300 percent. The two figures also suggest that roughly 45 percent of the new homes built in those years had septic tanks. In fact, that number is probably a bit high, but only a bit. In the years just after the war, more than 40 percent of the homes insured by the Federal Housing Administration relied on backyard waste-disposal systems. In the mid-1950s, government officials and builders were estimating that the number of septic tanks was increasing by 400,000 to 500,000 a year, a number representing roughly a third of the new houses built at the time. In some metropolitan areas, the reliance on backyard waste-disposal systems was even more pronounced: In metropolitan Phoenix, for example, a 1958 study found that more than 70 percent of subdivision homes had septic tanks. Thus, septic tanks were not found only on the large, isolated lots of the affluent. Builders installed them by the hundreds and thousands in tract developments. In one extreme case, a developer used septic tanks for a subdivision with more than 8,000 houses.[2]

Yet the widespread use of septic tanks in suburbia proved problematic. Because a substantial number of the backyard waste-disposal

2. For the 1945 estimate, see V. G. MacKenzie, "Research Studies on Individual Sewage Disposal Systems," *American Journal of Public Health* 42 (1952): 411. MacKenzie also provides the figure for septic tank use in FHA-insured housing. The 1960 census figure is cited by Arthur C. Nelson and Kenneth J. Dueker, "Exurban Living Using Improved Water and Wastewater Technology," *Journal of Urban Planning and Development* 115 (1989): 110–111. For estimates of the annual increase in septic tank numbers in the 1950s, see United States Public Health Service, *Manual of Septic-Tank Practice* [PHS Publication 526] (Washington: USGPO, 1957), v; "Do You Know the Economics of Sewage?," *House and Home* 7 (June 1955): 154. Later studies cite similar figures. See, for example, J. W. Patterson, R. A. Minear, and T. K. Nedved, *Septic Tanks and the Environment* (Chicago: Illinois Institute of Technology, 1971), 5. The Phoenix statistic comes from A. Anne Dunbar and Joseph J. Weinstein, "City-County Control of Subdivision Sewage Disposal," *Public Works* 89 (1958): 102. For the use of septic tanks in huge subdivisions, see David B. Lee, "Sewage Disposal in Mass Building," *Public Health Reports* 71 (1956): 555. The thousands of homes in Levittown also relied on backyard waste-disposal systems, although the precise nature of the technology is a subject of dispute. In *The Builders: Houses, People, Neighborhoods, Governments, Money* (New York: W. W. Norton, 1978), Martin Mayer writes that the Levittown waste-disposal systems were "concrete mortuary vaults converted to septic tanks by the ingenuity of Levitt's engineers." See 258. According to historian Barbara M. Kelly, however, the homes in Levittown were connected to cesspools. See *Expanding the American Dream: Building and Rebuilding Levittown* (Albany: State University of New York Press, 1993), 218, note 91.

systems failed in the first two or three years, homebuyers were often faced with foul and unsanitary messes. Many were stuck with steep repair bills, and some lost everything they had invested in their homes. The high failure rate also cost the nation's taxpayers, since the FHA and the Veteran's Administration insured millions of homes with septic tanks. Eventually, the federal government provided billions in subsidies to enable local governments to replace septic systems with sewers. In many areas of the country, septic tank failures were responsible for outbreaks of infectious disease. The technology also had a considerable environmental cost, since poor design, siting, and maintenance of septic tanks often led to contamination of groundwater, pollution of streams, and eutrophication of lakes.

The critique of septic tank suburbs evolved in three stages. From the late 1940s through the 1950s, the problem of failing septic tanks seemed largely a matter of protecting investments and preventing public-health hazards. The backyard waste-disposal system also became a symbol of the folly of unplanned growth. Though the owners of malfunctioning septic tanks often complained about the problem, the issue at first remained largely a concern of housing and public-health officials. In the 1960s, however, it became a more public concern. The misuse of septic tanks threatened to pollute a resource of growing importance – groundwater. In dramatic fashion, the spread of the septic tank began to taint drinking water. By the early 1970s, the septic tank problem had become part of a vast environmental crisis that threatened the well-being of many creatures, not just humans. In each period, the pressure to restrict the use of septic tanks intensified.

Yet the number of homes with septic tanks continued to increase. Though the most flagrant problems caused by backyard waste disposal were overcome, septic tanks continue to pollute the nation's waters. At every stage, from the 1950s to the 1970s, the effort to regulate septic tank use demonstrated the difficulty of controlling the process of urban and suburban development.

The First Concerns about Septic Tanks

In 1945, the nation's builders saw only the benefits of using the septic tank. The long years of depression and war had led to a severe housing shortage. The title of a 1948 "March of Time" newsreel summed up the postwar demand – "Needed: More Houses." To build on a large scale and thus to build cheaply, builders flocked to the suburbs, where large tracts of inexpensive land were readily available. But much of the land at the periphery of cities was well beyond the limits of sewer service. How would builders provide for waste disposal? The septic tank seemed a reasonable solution to a fundamental problem. It was not a new, untested technology. The first patent on the system dated from the early 1880s, and many farmers had relied on septic tanks for decades. Septic tanks were cheap – much cheaper, at least initially, than building a neighborhood or community sewage-treatment plant. In the 1950s, the installation of a septic tank cost less than $300 in many areas, whereas the alternatives might easily be double or triple that amount per house, depending on the size and character of the development.[3]

In engineering terms, the system also was quite simple. Household waste traveled from the house to the underground tank by a short sewer line. In the oxygen-less environment of the tank, the waste broke down through bacterial action. Some of the waste became gas, which was vented to the surface. A residue of greasy "scum" – as the experts called it – floated on the top of the tank, and a residue of "sludge" – unbroken-down solids – settled to the bottom. But much of the waste became liquid, and moved out into a soil-absorption field through a network of underground drainage pipes. If properly designed, the tank and the field both varied in size according to a number of factors, including the size of the household and the character of the soil. Thus, the network of drainage pipes might have been 500 square feet, 1000 square feet, even 1500 square feet. The liquid waste seeped into the soil, where it was disinfected naturally. The sludge in the tank, however, remained noxious. Periodically, both sludge and scum had to be removed for disposal elsewhere.

3. By most accounts, the use of the septic tank in the United States dates from 1883. See, for example, "Individual Sewage Disposal Systems – Part I," in *HHFA Technical Bulletin Number 7* (Washington: Housing and Home Finance Agency, 1948), 23. For the relative cost of septic tanks and community sewage treatment plants, see "Do You Know the Economics of Sewage?," 154–159; "Why Not Use Sewage Treatment Plants?," *House and Home* 9 (March 1956): 176–177; "What You Need to Know About Sewage," *House and Home* 13 (February 1958): 116–123.

In ecological terms, however, septic systems were quite complex. The possible causes of failure were legion. If the soil of a yard was too dense, the effluent from the tank might back up into the house or float to the surface of the yard. If the soil was too porous, or if the water table was close to the surface, the system might contaminate underground aquifers. If the drainage field was close to a drinking well, the well might be contaminated. Similarly, septic tanks could pollute nearby lakes and streams. If the land flooded periodically, if intense rains made the soil soggy, or if homeowners were too zealous in watering their lawns, the system also might fail. Both the septic tank and the drainage field had to be the right size for the quantity of waste produced by residents. If the builder compacted the soil in and around the drainage-pipe trenches, even a properly sized system might fail. If the tank was not cleaned of sludge and scum periodically, the system might not last more than a few years. Even if individual tanks in a subdivision "worked," the sheer density of septic systems might contaminate groundwater or pollute nearby lakes or streams. The disposal of sludge and scum also was problematic, since several methods of septage disposal could damage the environment.

The discovery of the ecological complexity of septic systems came slowly. In the years before 1945, only a handful of researchers had explored the subject, and without exception the early studies – almost all undertaken by scientists at agricultural colleges – had focused on rural installations. But the performance of septic systems in densely settled areas raised unprecedented questions. In farm country, there was little danger to the public or the environment from failing systems. Indeed, even the individual owner rarely had to be seriously concerned, because most farmers had enough land to replace a failing system if necessary. That was rarely the case in cities and suburbs, however, as federal officials began to realize in the late 1940s.[4]

Because the FHA was involved all over the country in financing housing construction, the agency became the first organization with responsibility for keeping track of hundreds of thousands of

4. For a review of the pre-1945 literature, see "Individual Sewage Disposal Systems – Part I," 34–41; "Individual Sewage Disposal Systems – Part II," in *HHFA Technical Bulletin Number 10* (Washington: Housing and Home Finance Agency, 1949), 17–22.

backyard waste-disposal systems. The FHA soon found that as many as one-third of the systems in suburban subdivisions failed within the first three years. Agency officials quickly understood that the failure of so many waste-disposal systems threatened both public and private investment in housing. "[We] viewed tracts of homes with failing septic-tank systems," one FHA inspector later recalled. "Children were playing in the surfaced effluents. I was told that these homes constituted the one major life's expenditure of most of the owners. They could neither sell their homes nor afford to sewer them. They could only live with their sewages or walk away from their investments and lose them." In one case, the agency had to repossess a 1,000-house development because of wholesale septic-tank failures. The tanks could not be fixed or replaced, so the houses were worthless: No one wanted to buy a home without a working toilet.[5]

In 1946, the FHA's overseer – the Housing and Home Finance Agency – asked the U.S. Public Health Service to study septic-tank operations. The list of unanswered questions was dauntingly long. What were the most important causes of septic-tank failures? Unsuitable soils? Faulty installation? Poor maintenance? Could septic tanks break down the organic mush produced by kitchen garbage disposals, which were just coming on the market? To what extent were the bacterial agents in the system affected by the soapy effluent from dishwashers and washing machines? Could malfunctioning septic tanks be fixed with special additives, or were the growing number of over-the-counter remedies little more than patent medicines? To provide answers, the PHS ultimately conducted both laboratory and field investigations over the course of 20 years, but both the HHFA and the PHS began to publish findings from the studies in the 1940s. The housing agency published a technical bulletin on septic tanks in 1948, for example, and the health service published a *Manual of Septic-Tank Practice* in 1957. The FHA also adopted

---

5. For the connection between septic tank failures and FHA repossessions, see P. H. Mc-Gauhey and John H. Winneberger, *Causes and Prevention of Failure in Septic-Tank Percolation Systems* (Washington: Federal Housing Administration, 1964), 3. The quotation comes from John H. Timothy Winneberger, *Septic Tank Systems: A Consultant's Toolkit* [Volume Two] (Boston: Butterworth Publishers, 1984), xv–xvi.

a set of PHS recommendations as minimum standards for builders and homebuyers seeking government insurance.[6]

The HHFA and PHS publications were primarily for builders and public health officials, but journalists quickly began to cite the official reports in primers for suburban homebuyers. *The American Home* provided "Facts about Septic Tanks" in 1952 and *Good Housekeeping* explained "The How and Why of Septic Tanks" in 1958. *Better Homes and Gardens, House and Garden,* and *Consumers' Research Bulletin* all published similar articles in the 1950s. Even *Popular Mechanics* offered a step-by-step homeowner's guide to "Safe Sewage Disposal."[7]

"Up to a few weeks ago," one of the magazine primers began, "a friend of mine who recently moved to the country was enthusiastic about his new home beyond the city limits. Then the septic tank overflowed – and his dream of peaceful country living went, literally, down the drain. Belligerently, he denounced septic tanks. Actually, he knew little about them. A typical city resident moving to the country, he had overlooked his duty (as a property owner) of sewage disposal."[8]

Was that story really typical? The evidence suggests that people who bought homes with septic tanks in fact had a range of expectations. Some evidently did not ask about waste disposal. "Highly educated, sophisticated people have confessed that they did not know their home had a septic tank system until it overflowed," one

6. In addition to the references cited above, see Laurance Schuman, "Septic Tank Studies," in *HHFA Technical Bulletin Number 4* (Washington: Housing and Home Finance Agency, 1948), 1–10; Housing and Home Finance Agency, *Septic Tanks – Their Use in Sewage Disposal* [Housing Research Paper 18] (Washington: USGPO, 1951); Housing and Home Finance Agency, *Septic Tank Soil Absorption Systems for Dwellings* [Construction Aid 5] (Washington: USGPO, 1954); "Individual Sewage Disposal Systems – Part III," in *HHFA Technical Bulletin Number 11* (Washington: Housing and Home Finance Agency, 1949), 19–37.
7. Jim Elliott, "Facts about Septic Tanks," *American Home* 48 (October 1952): 151–152; "The How and Why of Septic Tanks," *Good Housekeeping* 147 (October 1958): 159; William Kaiser, "Septic Systems," *Better Homes and Gardens* 28 (March 1950): 120–125; "The Septic Tank and Household Sewage Disposal," *House & Garden* 105 (April 1954): 191–205; "Sewage Disposal for the Individual Dwelling," *Consumers' Research Bulletin* 39 (February 1957): 19–22; and "Safe Sewage Disposal," *Popular Mechanics* 102 (August 1954): 166–171. *Consumers' Research Bulletin* also had short notes on septic tank operation throughout the 1950s.
8. Elliott, "Facts about Septic Tanks," 151.

public health official wrote. "Is there any law that requires a bill of sale, or property title to state that the property has a well or septic tank disposal system?" Other homebuyers accepted bland assurances about their systems from real estate agents or homebuilders. Even for those with doubts about septic tanks, the alternatives often seemed less desirable – either paying more for a home somewhere else or remaining in a city apartment. Many also expected to be able within a few years to hook up to a public sewer system. Despite those differences, the vast majority of suburban homebuyers in the 1950s apparently were alike in knowing too little about the implications of relying on backyard waste-disposal systems.[9]

Again and again magazine primers advised readers to be sure to obtain maps of their drainage fields. But the very frequency of the advice suggests that few homeowners even had that basic information about their waste-disposal systems. Indeed, one article noted that homeowners often unwittingly buried their tanks under concrete – thus making maintenance prohibitively expensive and disruptive – when they installed backyard patios. As *Changing Times* concluded in 1957, "every year thousands of families . . . buy or build homes equipped with septic tanks, often with misgivings and usually without knowing enough about what they are getting."[10]

The how-to articles themselves might have confused readers, since they offered differing assessments of the reliability of septic systems. Some claimed that any home could have one. According to others, however, septic tanks were acceptable only as a temporary expedient – and only if the design and installation were expertly done. "A septic tank system is neither economical nor foolproof nor trouble-free," one article began. "No homeowner who had a choice

---

9. For the quotation, see Robert M. Brown, "Urban Planning for Environmental Health," *Public Health Reports* 79 (1964): 202. In addition to the articles cited above, see Stan Schuler, "What You Should Know about Septic Tanks," *American Home* 63 (May 1960): 76–96; "Septic Systems for the House," *Good Housekeeping* 131 (October 1950): 380–382; "A Primer on Septic Tanks," *House & Garden* 135 (May 1969): 50–54; "Septic Tank Drain Field," *Sunset* 118 (April 1957): 232–234; "If You Plan to Install a Septic Tank," *Sunset* 132 (June 1964): 110–119; "Septic Tank Problems – What You Need to Forestall Trouble and Expense," *Changing Times* 11 (July 1957): 29–31; Committee on Fringe Area Sanitation Problems of the American Public Health Association, "Fringe Area Sanitation," *Public Health Reports* 76 (1961): 314.
10. For the quotation, see "Septic Tank Problems – What You Need to Forestall Trouble and Expense," 29. The description of septic tanks buried under patio concrete comes from "If You Plan to Install a Septic Tank," 112.

would prefer one to a public sewer system." But many other advice givers gave a qualified endorsement, arguing that the success of backyard waste-disposal systems depended on the nature of the land. Though unsuitable for certain kinds of sites, septic tanks often were "as good as city sewerage systems and as little trouble to keep working." Thus readers needed to inspect the land and test the soil before they invested.[11]

Beyond offering technical advice, city, county, and state officials were not much help to homebuyers. In 1945, the use of septic tanks was unregulated in most areas – the buyer simply had to beware. To be sure, many state health departments had issued recommendations for septic-tank installation, but apparently few cities and suburbs had made those standards binding. According to a U.S. Public Health Service survey conducted in 1948, only about 40 percent of the septic tanks in metropolitan areas were installed with any kind of regulatory oversight. Since the survey covered only communities with full-time health officials – the communities generally with the most sophisticated, best informed health departments – the number of unregulated septic tanks nationwide surely was much greater than the 60 percent reported by the PHS. The survey also suggested that most local regulatory ordinances only covered what might be termed engineering matters – the size of the tank and the drainage field, for example, or the distance from houses and water wells. Few communities required tests to ensure that soils were suitable for waste disposal, and few inspected septic-tank installations. None oversaw the disposal of sludge or required periodic maintenance. Perhaps most important, local authorities seldom sought to control the density of septic-tank use, to prevent builders from putting hundreds or thousands of septic tanks side by side.[12]

In the 1950s, however, sanitary engineers and public health officers began to campaign for stricter regulation of septic tanks in

---

11. The first quotation is from "Septic Tank Problems – What You Need to Forestall Trouble and Expense," 29. Fifteen years later, the magazine repeated the point: "Remember, septic tank systems in suburban developments are intended only as stop-gap methods of waste disposal until public sewers can be provided. If the wait for adequate sewers is a long one, as it sometimes is, you owe it to yourself to do all that's possible to have as good a system as you can get." See "If You Must Have a Septic Tank," *Changing Times* 26 (April 1972): 43. The second quotation comes from Kaiser, "Septic Systems," 120.
12. "Individual Sewage Disposal Systems – Part III," 19–20.

metropolitan areas. "To put it simply," a Florida official wrote in 1956, "the septic tank is a country cousin that came to town and promptly got into trouble. In its place – a rural setting – the septic tank and subsurface drain field is a suitable method of domestic sewage disposal, given adequate drainage, soil conditions, and water table; but it was never intended for use in settlements with more than one family dwelling per acre. Even this may be too dense for septic tanks if soil conditions and water tables are not ideal." To protect the public, therefore, officials needed to do more "to assure wise and orderly development of new neighborhoods." The use of septic tanks had to be limited, and the construction of neighborhood sewerage systems had to be encouraged.[13]

For sanitarians, indeed, the spread of septic tanks brought a nightmarish sense of déjà vu. The profession had grown to maturity fighting against private disposal of household wastes. Until the second half of the nineteenth century, the nation's cities had no sewers: People threw slop into the streets or buried waste in backyard pits. For decades, city engineers and doctors had struggled to persuade citizens to build public sewer systems, to prevent both disruptive nuisances and deadly outbreaks of disease, and the campaign had succeeded. Now the reliance on septic tanks in fast-growing suburbs seemed to threaten a dangerous turning back of the clock – "the recrudescence," in the words of two authorities, "of an old and presumably solved problem."[14]

The profession responded to the challenge with vigor. In speeches and articles, officials tried to stir people to act with provocative imagery. According to one sanitarian, the use of septic tanks in nice new subdivisions was "about like a person walking down the street with a silk hat on his head and a hole in the seat of his britches."

13. For the quotation, see Lee, "Sewage Disposal in Mass Building," 553 and 556.
14. The quotation is from Abraham Gelperin and Willard O. Fuller, "A Method of Simplifying Soil Percolation Tests for Septic Tank Systems," *Public Health Reports* 68 (1953): 693. According to one commentator, the postwar proliferation of septic tanks led to a "new sanitary movement." See Cornelius W. Kruse, "Our Nation's Water: Its Pollution Control and Management," in James N. Pitts, Jr. and Robert L. Metcalf, editors, *Advances in Environmental Sciences* [Volume I] (New York: Wiley-Interscience, 1969), 50–55. For the earlier campaigns against private waste disposal, see Martin V. Melosi, editor, *Pollution and Reform in American Cities, 1870–1930* (Austin: University of Texas Press, 1980), 35–57; Joel A. Tarr, *The Search for the Ultimate Sink: Urban Pollution in Historical Perspective* (Akron: University of Akron Press, 1996), 103–217.

Officials also described in nauseating detail a host of septic-tank disasters – houses filled with unbreathably foul gas, basements dank with backed-up effluent, roadside streams of sewage, lawns transformed into disgusting and unsanitary bogs. Who wanted to see family members mired in pestilential muck? To safeguard the public health, the speeches and articles invariably concluded, the nation's cities and counties needed to control the use of septic tanks.[15]

The call to regulate suburban waste disposal was seconded by the planning profession. Again and again, the nation's planners cited the spread of septic tanks as evidence of costly "chaos in the suburbs." Instead of paying once for a good waste-disposal system, the residents of new subdivisions often paid twice: They bought homes with septic tanks, and then, when their septic tanks failed, they had to pay the cost and suffer the inconvenience of digging up their yards and streets to install public sewers. To avoid future problems, the planners concluded, cities and counties needed to create metropolitan authorities to plan for growth and to ensure adequate provision of public services.[16]

In a highly regarded critique of suburban sprawl, geographer Edward Higbee offered a more dramatic example of the cost of poor waste-disposal planning:

For those dependent on septic tanks it is an advantage to be on flat ground. At least the houses themselves are not likely to slip away. Around Los Angeles many homes are built upon hillsides and some of these locations are underlain with sheets of shale rock tilted seaward. When the underground shale is slicked with sewage effluent or too much lawn sprinkling, the loose

15. The quotation is from John E. Kiker, Jr., "Fringe Area Sewerage Problems," *Journal of the Sanitary Engineering Division: Proceedings on the American Society of Civil Engineers* 84 (Paper 1714, 1958): 9. In addition, see James B. Coulter, "The Septic Tank System in Suburbia," *Public Health Reports* 73 (1958): 488–492; Frank L. Woodward, Franklin J. Kilpatrick, and Paul B. Johnson, "Experiences with Ground Water Contamination in Unsewered Areas of Minnesota," *American Journal of Public Health* 51 (1961): 1130–1136; Joseph A. Salvato, "Problems of Wastewater Disposal in Suburbia," *Public Works* 95 (1964): 120–121, 172–178; Brown, "Urban Planning for Environmental Health," 201–204; Lee, "Sewage Disposal in Mass Building," 556.
16. The quotation is from Lawrence Lader, "Chaos in the Suburbs," *Better Homes & Gardens* 36 (October 1958): 10. The "serious menace" of failing septic tanks is one of the first problems that Lader describes. In addition, see Thomas W. Ennis, "Suburban Areas Seen as Mazes," *New York Times* (March 20, 1958): 50; Melvin E. Scheidt, "Metropolitan Sprawl," in James B. Trefethen, editor, *Transactions of the Twenty-Fourth North American Wildlife Conference* (Washington: Wildlife Management Institute, 1959), 82–93; "How Good Is Our Land Development?," *Urban Land* 15 (April 1956): 1–6.

earth above it may be inclined to slip downhill a bit. Since this is one of Nature's ancient ways of leveling mountains, the leveling of a house is easy. The residents of Portuguese Bend, south of Los Angeles, learned this geologic truth the hard way. When the septic tanks of their new homes had saturated the shale beneath their 225-acre hillside community, everything began to respond slowly to the tug of gravity – lots, lawns, shrubbery, and 156 houses, each costing $25,000 to $50,000, gently slumped downhill as though they were so much custard pudding.

Though the landslide was unusual, Higbee concluded, the annals of suburbia were full of tales of septic-tank woes. Like many planners and public health officials, Higbee saw the disasters that befell septic-tank owners as compelling evidence that Americans needed to exercise more control over metropolitan development.[17]

The cultural critics of suburbia also attacked the septic tank. In the antisuburban literature of the 1950s, the crud of septic-tank failure often symbolized the baseness of life in mass-produced tracts. The suburbs oozed waste. Everywhere, you had to be careful not to step in "it." In a classic polemic, *The Crack in the Picture Window,* John Keats even imagined the possibility of suburbanites swimming in their own effluent. At one point in the book, a take-charge housewife in Keats's mythical community of Rolling Knolls convinced everyone to buy a nearby swamp to turn into a swimming pool. The community could divert the underground streams running into the swamp, she argued, and then use the diverted water to supply the pool. But the R K Pool was not to be. "Soon after the land had been purchased," Keats wrote, "it was discovered no underground streams fed the developing swamp in the low ground. The swamp was entirely fed by runoff from Rolling Knolls septic tanks, trickling across the clay hardpan not

17. The quotation is from Edward Higbee, *The Squeeze, Cities Without Space,* (New York: William Morrow and Company), 122. The tie between slick slopes and landslides continued to receive attention in both professional and popular forums. See U.S. Department of Agriculture and U.S. Department of Housing and Urban Development, *Soil, Water, and Suburbia* (Washington: USGPO, 1968), 57; F. Beach Leighton, "Landslides and Hillside Development," in Richard Lung and Richard Proctor, editors, *Engineering Geology in Southern California* (Glendale: Association of Engineering Geologists, 1966), 167; Leonard Downie, Jr., *Mortgage on America* (New York: Praeger, 1974), 96; Duncan Erley and William J. Kockelman, *Reducing Landslide Hazards: A Guide for Planners* [Planning Advisory Service Report Number 359] (Chicago: American Planning Association, 1981), 5–6; Robert D. Brown and William J. Kockelman, *Geological Principles for Prudent Land Use: A Decisionmaker's Guide for the San Francisco Region* [U.S. Geological Survey Professional Paper 946] (Washington: USGPO, 1983), 71.

far below the surface." The foundations of septic-tank civilization were shaky.[18]

The most self-consciously progressive homebuilders quickly acknowledged the mounting concern about septic tanks. The 1956 handbook of the Community Builders' Council warned that septic tanks were "rarely completely satisfactory." In many areas of the country, septic-tank subdivisions had begun to encounter "sales resistance." To satisfy homebuyers, the handbook concluded, subdivision builders should resort to septic tanks "only when absolutely necessary."[19]

In a series of articles in the mid-1950s, the trade publication *House and Home* also addressed "one of the toughest problems builders and developers have to meet." The editors were eager to avoid regulation of septic-tank use, since regulation would limit the amount of land available for building. Regulation also meant "red-tape trouble." Accordingly, *House and Home* encouraged homebuilders to act decisively to solve the waste-disposal problem. The first step was a forthright reckoning with the past. The magazine attributed the septic-tank failures of the late 1940s and early 1950s to inexperience and scientific ignorance. Now the leaders of the homebuilding industry had learned how to avoid disasters. When properly sited, constructed, and maintained, septic tanks could be acceptable. To ensure quality in construction, *House and Home* urged builders to meet FHA standards even on non-FHA projects. But meeting the FHA guidelines was merely a temporary expedient.[20]

For a few years, *House and Home* touted a technological fix – a self-contained, sewerless toilet. The new toilet had already worked wonders in tests at Purdue University, the magazine reported, and a number of experts expected the new technology to revolutionize the industry. Soon, indeed, the invention might free builders from the constraints of soil and terrain: "In short, it could help make

18. The quotation is from John Keats, *The Crack in the Picture Window* (Boston: Houghton Mifflin, 1956), 90–91. Though Rolling Knolls was fictional, Keats also cited evidence about septic tank failures taken from congressional hearings on the quality of housing for veterans. For a critical evaluation of the antisuburban literature of the 1950s, see Scott Donaldson, *The Suburban Myth* (New York: Columbia University Press, 1969).
19. Community Builders' Council of the Urban Land Institute, *The Community Builders Handbook* (Washington: Urban Land Institute, 1956), 21, 96–99.
20. "What You Need to Know About Sewage," 116; "Do You Know the Economics of Sewage?," 154.

the house autonomous – independent of the land on which it stands."[21]

House and Home was even more emphatic about the need for builders to reconsider "the economics of sewage." Though septic tanks usually looked cheaper than the neighborhood-sized "package" sewage-treatment plants sold by about 20 different manufacturers, the truth was more complicated. With new technology and new methods of financing projects, builders often could make sewage-treatment plants profitable for developments with as few as 25 to 50 units. Because knowledgeable buyers invariably preferred sewers to septic tanks, homes in subdivisions with sewerage systems sold faster. The likelihood of increasingly strict regulation also affected the calculus of costs. If city and county officials permitted septic tanks only on large lots, *House and Home* argued, then construction of a community sewerage facility would allow builders to build more houses per acre – and thus reduce per-unit costs for land, streets, storm drainage, and utility connections.[22]

In fact, regulation of septic tanks continued to be spotty throughout the 1950s and early 1960s. Because the supervision of sanitation remained largely the province of local boards of health, the response varied greatly from community to community. In some areas, authorities took action after conspicuous failures. Fairfax County, Virginia, enacted a tough regulatory ordinance after spending $20 million to replace hundreds of malfunctioning systems with sewers. Occasionally, officials banned the use of septic tanks in areas which, experience proved, were clearly unsuitable for back-

---

21. "Sewerless Toilet Without Chemicals," *House and Home* 1 (March 1952): 110. See also "Now You Can Buy a Sewerless Toilet," *House and Home* 9 (June 1956): 162–165. In addition, see Albert G. H. Dietz, "Housing Industry Research," in Burnham Kelly, editor, *Design and Production of Houses* (New York: McGraw-Hill, 1959), 255.

22. On the question of cost, see "Do You Know the Economics of Sewage?," 154–159; "Why Not Use Sewage Treatment Plants?," 176–177; "What You Need to Know About Sewage," 116–123; "You Can Act Big About Land Planning If You Think Big About Sewage Facilities," *House and Home* 13 (March 1958): 120–123; "Lagoons Like This May Solve Your Sewerage Cost Problem," *House and Home* 10 (November 1956): 174–175; "For $365 More Per House, Builder Adds Sewer System," *Practical Builder* 23 (October 1958): 157–159. The issue is also discussed by Sigurd Grava, *Urban Planning Aspects of Water Pollution Control* (New York: Columbia University Press, 1969), 70–73, who cites articles published in *Progressive Architecture* and *Public Works* in 1960 and 1961. Though the trade press of the building industry generally boosted the package treatment plant, there were a few dissenters. See, for example, Rodney M. Lockwood, "Community Facilities," *Urban Land* 18 (January 1959): 6–8.

yard waste-disposal systems. In a number of Florida communities, for example, officials acted once they realized that the ground was too swampy to allow proper functioning of soil-absorption fields. As *House and Home* pointed out, some cities and counties set minimum lot sizes for houses in unsewered districts. In many places, however, builders did not even need septic-tank permits.[23]

The obstacles in the way of regulation were considerable. In local debates about the wisdom of controlling septic-tank use, officials well knew, homebuilders had influential allies. Indeed, the supporters of regulation in the late 1950s and early 1960s readily enumerated the catchphrases of the opposition. "The prosperity of the community is at stake!" "Don't deny young couples their chance at the American dream!" Proposals to restrict the density or location of septic tanks often were opposed by people financially dependent on sales of new homes, from real estate agents to well diggers. Rural landowners also objected, since regulation might limit their ability to sell their land to developers.[24]

"Quite frequently we are told . . . that the cost of each lot would become prohibitive and make development of the land impractical," a public health official complained in 1957. "We may be accused of holding up sound development and of 'keeping the poor veteran out of a home.' Many people believe this propaganda. It must, therefore, be shown that these are half-truths, and proven to the skeptic what is more nearly the actual situation and cost." A decade later, the degree of opposition still troubled advocates of regulation. "Although public health officials and sanitary engineers have been disturbed by and opposed to the widespread use of temporary septic systems in suburban areas," a local administrator wrote in 1967, "they have been faced with the practical (and in many areas, the political) impact of owners who wished to develop or sell their

---

23. John W. Clayton, "An Analysis of Septic Tank Survival Data from 1952 to 1972 in Fairfax County, Virginia," in William J. Jewell and Rita Swan, editors, *Water Pollution Control in Low Density Areas: Proceedings of a Rural Environmental Engineering Conference* (Hanover, NH: University Press of New England, 1975), 75–76; Lee, "Sewage Disposal in Mass Building," 555; "Why Not Use Sewage Treatment Plants?," 176–177; Darryl R. Goehring and F. Robert Carr, "Septic System Problems on an Urban Fringe," *Journal of Water Resources Planning and Management* 106 (1980): 90.
24. In addition to the sources cited below, see U.S. Public Health Service, *Ground Water Contamination: Proceedings of the 1961 Symposium* (Cincinnati: Robert A. Taft Sanitary Engineering Center, 1961), 66.

properties for housing, and the pent-up needs and desires of a great number of families for new and better homes."[25]

Occasionally, the proponents of regulation urged a head-on assault on the fundamental assumptions of the opposition. "The impression that progress is inevitable and that certain areas have to be developed is a figment of the imagination," a county official wrote in 1957. "Certain areas are not suitable for development, and cannot be used for housing and at the same time provide full protection to the health of the people. Such land should remain as farm land, swamp, or whatever the existing natural condition may indicate. There is a widespread misconception that the owner of a farm has a certain inalienable right granted to him by the Constitution of the United States to become a subdivider if he so desires. Such a belief needs careful scrutiny in the light of the need for protection of the general welfare, the public health and the community's best interest."[26]

But that was a radical argument in the 1950s. Though some critics of septic-tank suburbs surely agreed, most were reluctant to argue so boldly in public. In debates about waste-disposal problems, local officials often sought to show that they understood the blessings of development and the pressures to provide housing for a growing population. They tried, as one noted in 1960, to find "a middle ground." Instead of pushing hard for waste-disposal regulations, many officials ultimately decided to rely on their powers of persuasion, to try to convince homebuilders to install neighborhood sewage-treatment plants rather than septic tanks.[27]

The division of the nation's metropolitan areas into dozens or even hundreds of political jurisdictions made the balancing act even more difficult. If a community enacted strict regulations on septic-

25. The first quotation is from J. A. Salvato, Jr., "Coping With Suburban Sewage Disposal: 3 – Legislation and Financing," *Modern Sanitation* 9 (April 1957): 55. For similar comments, see Salvato, "Problems of Wastewater Disposal in Suburbia," 120; "How Good Is Our Land Development?," 3. The second quotation comes from W. C. Dalton, "An Interim Sewage Plan," *Public Works* 98 (1967): 118.

26. For the quotation, see Morton S. Hilbert, "Coping With Suburban Sewage Disposal: 2 – Prevention of Sanitation Hazards," *Modern Sanitation* 9 (March 1957): 26.

27. The quotation comes from U.S. Public Health Service, *Ground Water Contamination*, 162–163. For the pressure not to support regulation, see "How Good Is Our Land Development?," 3. Officials also wrote about the importance of understanding the homebuilders' point of view. See Lee, "Sewage Disposal in Mass Building," 554–555.

tank use, homebuilders might build elsewhere, because land was almost always available nearby where oversight was negligible. Public health officials and urban planners recognized the problem: The difficulty of acting effectively in a world of fragmented authority was one of the basic arguments for the creation of regional planning authorities. But regional planning only became a reality in a few remarkable places. In most regions, the dream remained just that.[28]

Septic Tanks and the Environment

The real rush of regulation came only in the late 1960s and early 1970s. In large part, the stricter oversight of suburban waste disposal came in response to new evidence about the costs of inaction. Except for the risk to taxpayers of default on government-insured mortgages, the septic-tank problem had seemed to be largely a local concern. But the issue began to attract national attention in the late 1950s and early 1960s, when officials at all levels of government concluded that the widespread use of septic tanks threatened the nation's groundwater.

The issue of groundwater pollution was not new. In the 1930s, a number of geology and hydrology textbooks had noted the possibility of contamination from below-ground disposal of industrial wastes, but officials did not yet hold manufacturers responsible for preventing problems: The burden lay with the owners of wells to avoid potential contaminants. The issue began to seem more pressing in the 1940s. In several states – including Michigan, New York, and Virginia – officials discovered water wells contaminated by industrial chemicals. In the 1950s, the U.S. Geological Survey, the American Society of Civil Engineers, the American Water Works Association, and the trade organizations of the oil and chemical industries addressed the issue, yet the problem continued to become more acute. By 1960, industrial chemicals had tainted groundwater in at least 25 states. The FHA commissioned a review of research on groundwater contamination in 1960. The next year, the U.S.

28. For a discussion of one of the few successes in regional planning for sanitation, see Scheidt, "Metropolitan Sprawl," 82–93.

Public Health Service organized a symposium on the issue. The experts all came to a disturbing conclusion: The threat of contamination was increasing, while the nation was becoming more dependent on groundwater to meet residential, municipal, and industrial needs. Without preventive action, therefore, the pollution problem would cause a crisis.[29]

The experts also agreed that industrial wastes were no longer the only important threat to groundwater. In many metropolitan areas, the effluent from backyard waste-disposal systems had contaminated wells and aquifers. The participants in the 1961 symposium organized by the Public Health Service made that point repeatedly. In the introduction to the conference, the rapid growth of septic-tank subdivisions was first in a list of postwar developments that had made the groundwater issue more urgent. Many of the papers offered evidence of the impact of suburban growth on groundwater quality, and two papers focused entirely on that subject.[30]

Because a growing percentage of the nation's drinking water came from the ground rather than from rivers and reservoirs, the experts argued that groundwater contamination was first and foremost a conservation issue. Potable groundwater was a limited and increasingly precious resource, especially in metropolitan areas, yet groundwater was especially vulnerable to abuse, because polluted wells and aquifers were difficult or impossible to cleanse. If we did nothing to stop contamination of our underground supplies, we would suffer eventually from desperate scarcity. As one official noted, the danger could be summed up in an oft-repeated complaint: "Water, water, everywhere, but not a drop to drink."[31]

29. For a good summary of the history of the issue, see Craig E. Colten, "A Historical Perspective on Industrial Wastes and Groundwater Contamination," *Geographical Review* 81 (April 1991): 218–223; Craig E. Colten and Peter N. Skinner, *The Road to Love Canal: Managing Industrial Waste before EPA* (Austin: University of Texas Press, 1996), 42–43. In addition, see William E. Stanley and Rolf Eliassen, *Status of Knowledge of Ground Water Contaminants* (Washington: Federal Housing Administration, 1960); U.S. Public Health Service, *Ground Water Contamination*.
30. For discussion of the relationship between suburban growth and groundwater pollution at the 1961 symposium, see U.S. Public Health Service, *Ground Water Contamination*, 1, 35, 66–82, 130, 154–157, 166.
31. The quotation is from U.S. Public Health Service, *Ground Water Contamination*, 149. In addition, see Wood, *Suburbia*, 244. The foreword to the FHA's report on groundwater contaminants began by quoting President John Kennedy's first message on natural resources, which argued that many areas of the country needed new sources of water to meet the needs of a growing population – "but in all areas we must protect the

Others made the argument in more technical language. "Ground-water contamination should be considered not only as a hazard to public health but also as a threat to the water resource potential of the region and an economic problem of considerable magnitude," a scientist warned in the new journal *Ground Water* in 1965. "Widespread deterioration of ground-water quality can result in substantial increases in the cost of treatment of water preparatory to use. When treatment costs become prohibitive or treatment cannot be accomplished satisfactorily . . . other, more expensive sources of supply would then have to be obtained."[32]

As public health officials had recognized for years, the effluent from septic tanks often contained a variety of organic contaminants of drinking water, including bacteria and viruses. By 1960, a number of studies had traced outbreaks of hepatitis to contamination of drinking wells by nearby septic tanks. But the danger of disease was not the primary concern of officials in the early 1960s. Instead, the attention-getting contaminant was a new chemical component of laundry detergents.[33]

In the late 1950s, public health boards in a number of communities began to receive complaints from homeowners about foul odors and tastes in their drinking water. In many cases, people also noted a strange sudsing when they turned on their taps. When the authorities investigated, they found that most of the complaints came from people who lived in neighborhoods built after World War II with no public water supplies or sewers. Instead, the homes relied on backyard wells and septic tanks, and the wells were contaminated with septic-tank effluents. Though the foul odors and tastes might be attributable to the presence of unbroken-down sewage, the suds were something new. As chemical tests revealed,

supplies we have." The foreword also noted that the issue was particularly pressing in the suburbs, since fringe developments typically depended on groundwater. See Stanley and Eliassen, *Status of Knowledge of Ground Water Contaminants,* ii.

32. The quotation is from J. E. Hackett, "Ground-water Contamination in an Urban Environment," *Ground Water* 3 (July 1965): 30. In addition, see Earl Finbar Murphy, *Water Purity: A Study in Legal Control of Natural Resources* (Madison: University of Wisconsin Press, 1961), 15, 132; Woodward, Kilpatrick, and Johnson, "Experiences with Ground Water Contamination in Unsewered Areas of Minnesota," 1130–1136; John M. Cain and M. T. Beatty, "Disposal of Septic Tank Effluent in Soils," *Journal of Soil and Water Conservation* 20 (1965): 104.

33. For a good summary of the issue of biological contamination and disease, see U.S. Public Health Service, *Ground Water Contamination,* 35–43.

they were caused by synthetic detergents which had followed a liquid path from washing machines through septic tanks to drinking wells.[34]

By 1960, a rapidly growing body of evidence indicated that the problem of detergent pollution was widespread. In a review of 30 studies from 13 states, the director of water conservation studies at the U.S. Public Health Service reported that detergents had shown up in 37 percent of the drinking wells tested for contaminants. In some subdivisions, the figure was almost 100 percent. According to official estimates, the number of homes with contaminated wells approached 17,000 in one Long Island county – and 27,000 in metropolitan Minneapolis-St. Paul.[35]

The potential consequences of detergent pollution became a lively subject of professional debate. At the least, the telltale suds were a sign of the likelihood of biological contamination: The effluent from a nearby septic tank was probably seeping into the water supply. A number of scientists also suspected that detergents intensified the danger of disease outbreaks, since detergents seemed to allow both bacteria and viruses to travel farther in groundwater. But the tougher questions still were unanswerable. Was the threat largely a matter of water quality – because contaminated water looked and tasted bad, people were reluctant to drink from the tap? Or was there a threat to long-term health from exposure to the chemical itself? The professionals could not say. In 1960, a review of the state of knowledge about groundwater contamination concluded that the problem of synthetic detergents should be the top research priority in the field.[36]

34. Graham Walton, "ABS Contamination," *Journal of the American Water Works Association* 52 (1960): 1354–1362; John M. Flynn, Aldo Andreoli, and August A. Guerrera, "Study of Synthetic Detergents in Ground Water," *Journal of the American Water Works Association* 50 (1958): 1551–1562; Jerome Deluty, "Synthetic Detergents in Well Water," *Public Health Reports* 75 (1960): 75–77; M. Starr Nichols and Elaine Knapp, "Synthetic Detergents as a Criterion of Wisconsin Ground Water Pollution," *Journal of the American Water Works Association* 53 (1961): 303–306; Louis G. Campenni, "Synthetic Detergents in Ground Waters – Part 1" and "Synthetic Detergents in Ground Waters – Part 2," *Water and Sewage Works* 108 (1961): 188–191 and 210–213; Harry E. LeGrand, "Management Aspects of Groundwater Contamination," *Journal of the Water Pollution Control Federation* 36 (1964): 1134; U.S. Geological Survey, *A Study of Detergent Pollution in Ground Water* (Washington: Federal Housing Administration, 1959).
35. Walton, "ABS Contamination," 1354–1362.
36. The early research on synthetic detergents is summarized in Stanley and Eliassen, *Status of Knowledge of Ground Water Contaminants,* 69–70, 300–314, 462. For the possibility

The detergent problem went beyond the contamination of drinking wells. The engineers in charge of water- and sewage-treatment plants reported the presence of a froth which proved to be extraordinarily difficult to remove. Across the country, suds also began to appear in rivers and lakes – in the worst cases, the detergent residue formed floating mountains of foam. Without the threat at home, however, the problem might have concerned only civil engineers and conservationists. Instead, the environmental effects of detergents became a source of anxiety for millions of Americans.[37]

In the early 1960s, the issue received considerable attention in the popular press. "Synthetic detergents, and worse, are getting into our drinking water," warned the headline of a 1960 *Consumer Bulletin* article. In magazines devoted to the concerns of middle-class women, from *Redbook* to *Good Housekeeping* to *American Home,* the subject was especially prominent. The weekly newsmagazines also published pieces about the problem of drinking-water quality. Invariably, the popular articles pointed out the way septic tanks turned the sudsing ingredient of detergents – alkyl benzene sulfonate – into a hazard. "In areas where homes discharge sewage into septic tanks, the chemical seeps down into the underground water and then is pumped up from wells," *U.S. News and World Report* explained in 1963. "Tests have shown that ABS persists in underground water for years, and the concentration is building up rapidly."[38]

Occasionally, the problem was the subject of black humor. "One of the more familiar beverages in suburban areas is the 'detergent cocktail' – a glass of tap water foaming with suds," wrote one critic of septic-tank subdivisions. The author of a pioneering book about water pollution titled a chapter on detergents "white beer." But the

that detergents increased the threat of epidemic disease, see U.S. Public Health Service, *Ground Water Contamination,* 40–41.

37. I am departing here from the argument of the sole history of the detergent controversy – William McGucken's *Biodegradable: Detergents and the Environment* (College Station: Texas A & M University Press, 1991) – which ignores the connection between septic tanks and detergent residues in drinking water.

38. For the quotations, see "Synthetic Detergents, and Worse, Are Getting into Our Drinking Water," *Consumer Bulletin* 43 (October 1960): 20–21; "Just How Safe Is Your Drinking Water?," *U.S. News and World Report* 55 (July 15, 1963): 74. In addition, see Ruth Carson, "How Safe Is Your Drinking Water?," *Redbook* 117 (August 1961): 86; Alvin B. Toffler, "Danger in Your Drinking Water," *Good Housekeeping* 150 (January 1960): 128; Milton J. E. Senn with Evan McLeod Wylie, "We Must Stop Contaminating Our Water," *American Home* 66 (Winter 1963): 45–46, 72–74.

jokes always led to sober tabulations of the number of homes with contaminated wells. Often, the exposés of detergent pollution painted a picture of well-to-do families forced to rely on elaborate expedients to ensure a supply of sound water: "In the spring of this year two-year-old Gerald Colpas toddled into the kitchen of his new Lindenhurst, Long Island, home and asked for a drink of water. His mother drew it from a two-gallon camping jug that had been filled in another community. Beside the jug a covered fish tank held the reserve supply. Gerald's thirst quenched, Mrs. Colpas started to fill a cooking pot from the tap in the sink. Thick suds foamed up over the edge before it was half full."[39]

In a few cases, the popular work on detergents raised the possibility that drinking contaminated water might lead to stomach cancer. How great was the risk? There was no way to know for sure. According to one writer, the small number of studies on mice and rats were not conclusive, but research with clams and oysters showed that both were harmed by exposure to detergents. According to a second writer, the issue was "hotly disputed." A National Cancer Institute researcher had reported cancer in mice exposed to water with a variety of pollutants, including detergents, but "industry-slanted" scientists had challenged the results. Evidently, the U.S. Public Health Service also discounted the risk to humans, since the agency's recommended drinking-water standards allowed some detergent residue. Nevertheless, the author concluded, skepticism seemed appropriate, because detergents were chemically similar to a number of substances of unquestioned danger: "Although industry hygienists and sanitary engineers will loftily dismiss the stomach cancer scare, it is not to be dispelled by sneering. Until we have a much greater body of information that will comfort us we can regard this as a health hazard entirely as realistic as lung cancer from polluted air."[40]

39. Lewis Herber, *Crisis in Our Cities* (Englewood Cliffs, NJ: Prentice Hall, 1965), 16; Donald E. Carr, *Death of the Sweet Waters* (New York: W. W. Norton, 1966), 157–164; Frank Graham, Jr., *Disaster by Default: Politics and Water Pollution* (New York: M. Evans and Company, 1966), 169–170. In addition to the articles cited in the previous note, see also Vance Packard, *The Waste Makers* (New York: David McKay, 1960), 193; Edward Higbee, *The Squeeze*, 122; Mitchell Gordon, *Sick Cities* (New York: Macmillan, 1963), 90–91.
40. The analyses cited in the text are Graham, *Disaster by Default*, 174–175; Carr, *Death of the Sweet Waters*, 163–164.

In testimony before Congress after the publication of *Silent Spring,* Rachel Carson also cited the detergent risk. "I have pointed out before, and I shall repeat now, that the problem of pesticides can be properly understood only in context, as part of the general introduction of harmful substances into the environment," she said. "In water and soil, and in our bodies, these chemicals are mingled with others, or with radioactive substances. There are little understood interactions and summations of effect. No one fully understands, for example, what happens when pesticide residues stored in our bodies interact with drugs repeatedly taken. And there are some indications that detergents, which are often present in our drinking water, may affect the lining of the digestive tract so that it more readily absorbs cancer-causing chemicals."[41]

Even for many who did not share the concern about the potential cancer risks, the presence of detergent foam in drinking water was still troubling. By the early 1960s, the contamination of milk by fallout from atmospheric testing of atomic weapons and the devastating effects of the pesticide DDT on wildlife had raised doubts in the minds of many Americans about the unintended and unforeseen consequences of new technologies, and the detergent problem intensified those doubts. As one authority on water pollution argued, "A cardinal mistake had been made, and this oversight holds some lessons for the future. The experience shows how easily and suddenly a new, different, and widely used product can upset the already overloaded purification mechanism of the physical environment. It also points out that the manufacturers and responsible government agencies had neglected or had not thought of testing other characteristics of the product beyond its immediate use. The side effects in this case interfered with our well-being and aesthetic sensibilities; next time they may threaten our very survival." The detergent issue thus added force to the evolving environmentalist argument about the need for new institutions to assess the likely costs of technological development.[42]

41. For the quotation, see William O. Douglas, *A Wilderness Bill of Rights* (Boston: Little, Brown and Company, 1965), 163. Carson also mentioned the detergent threat in her published work. See *Silent Spring* (Boston: Houghton Mifflin, 1962), 238–239.
42. Grava, *Urban Planning Aspects of Water Pollution Control,* 44. For a succinct discussion of the fallout and DDT issues, see Samuel P. Hays, *Beauty, Health, and Permanence: Environmental Politics in the United States, 1955–1985* (New York: Cambridge University

In a more straightforward fashion, the new evidence about the dangers of septic tanks increased popular support for federal water-pollution legislation. Though a variety of conservation and public health groups had lobbied on the issue since the 1930s, the campaigns led only to two weak bills, in 1948 and 1956, which enabled the federal government to provide technical assistance to local governments. In part, the limited federal role in the 1950s expressed President Dwight Eisenhower's view that water pollution was essentially a local problem. There was little popular protest against Eisenhower's position. In the early 1960s, however, the water-pollution issue began to hit home. The number of articles and books on the subject rose dramatically, and many gave prominent play to the threats posed by septic tanks – the spread of infectious disease and the contamination of drinking water with detergents.[43]

The extreme example was a 1963 *American Home* piece, "We Must Stop Contaminating Our Water," which gave more space to the hazards of septic tanks than to the pollution problems caused by industry, agriculture, or municipal sewage systems. "The disturbing discoveries about the outbreaks of infectious hepatitis and the distasteful detergent suds problems plaguing many communities should drive home to all of us – physicians, home owners, and municipal authorities – that perils to family health from polluted water are steadily increasing," the authors argued. "We can no longer afford to enjoy the popular illusion that because we live in America our drinking water is safe. In fact, clean water has become one of the nation's major health problems."[44]

Over the course of a decade, from 1965 to 1974, Congress passed a series of major water-pollution measures. The first – the Water Quality Act – sought to ensure the fitness of surface waters for municipal, industrial, and recreational uses. In 1972, the Federal Water Pollution Control Act promised "to restore and maintain the

Press, 1987), 171–177. The concern about the unforeseen consequences of technological change led eventually to the establishment of the congressional Office of Technology Assessment.

43. Almost all the articles and books cited in notes 38 and 39 offer evidence that the proliferation of septic tanks was important in making water pollution a popular issue. For the history of federal water-pollution legislation from the late 1940s through the 1950s, see Leonard B. Dworsky, editor, *Pollution* (New York: Chelsea House, 1971), 203–290.

44. Senn, "We Must Stop Contaminating Our Water," 45.

chemical, physical, and biological integrity of the nation's waters." For the first time, Americans accepted responsibility for reducing the impact of pollution on the nonhuman life of rivers, lakes, and coastal waters. Two years later, the government made a commitment to protect underground sources of drinking water.[45]

Because septic tanks polluted water both above and below the ground, the new laws led to greater public scrutiny. What could be done to reduce the environmental impact of septic tanks? The federal government took three significant actions:

First, in 1965, the Department of Housing and Urban Development changed the rules governing federal aid to homebuilders in order to prevent the use of septic tanks in large subdivisions. The new rules included a significant loophole: If the extension of municipal sewers or the construction of neighborhood sewers was not economically feasible, a developer still might be permitted to use septic tanks. But the leaders of the building industry recognized that the change indicated that septic-tank subdivisions would be tougher to build.[46]

Second, the government subsidized suburban sewer construction. In the 1970s – the years of the most lavish outlays – the federal subsidy totaled $30 billion. Though a portion of that money enabled communities with sewer systems to build sewage treatment plants, a goodly share paid for replacement of septic tanks.[47]

Third, the Federal Water Pollution Control Act required states to draw up plans for controlling pollutants from nonpoint sources,

45. For a summary of federal water-pollution legislation, see Walter E. Westman, *Ecology, Impact Assessment, and Environmental Planning* (New York: John Wiley & Sons, 1985), 53–56.
46. The 1965 HUD rules are described by John C. Hancock, "Onsite Treatment Manuals," in Nina I. McClelland, editor, *Individual Onsite Wastewater Systems: Proceedings of the Fifth National Conference 1978* (Ann Arbor: Ann Arbor Science, 1979), 235. For the industry response, see J. Ross McKeever, editor, *The Community Builders Handbook: Anniversary Edition* (Washington: Urban Land Institute, 1968), 46–47, 178.
47. The figure for federal subsidies is cited by Brian J. O'Connell, "The Federal Role in the Suburban Boom," in Barbara M. Kelly, editor, *Suburbia Re-examined* (Westport: Greenwood Press, 1989), 188–189. I have not found a detailed breakdown of the federal outlays, so I cannot be more precise about the percentage of the total devoted to construction of sewers as replacements for septic tanks. But there is evidence to suggest that the percentage was sizeable. In official projections of spending requirements in the late 1970s, construction of new collector sewers generally accounted for almost 20 percent of all spending for waste-disposal facilities. See, for example, "1978 Needs Survey: Closing in on Clean Water," *Journal of the Water Pollution Control Federation* 51 (1979): 875–876.

including backyard waste-disposal systems. Like the new HUD rules, the act had a soft spot, since the states were not required to implement the plans. "You can plan forever and never achieve the objective of all that planning," a staff member of the National Commission on Water Quality complained in 1975. But the weakness was not crippling. Even before the act passed, a handful of states regulated septic-tank use, and the federal mandate encouraged many more to follow suit. By 1977, a majority of states had enacted regulations. Though several left enforcement to local authorities, many assigned oversight of waste disposal to new state environmental-protection agencies.[48]

The Environmental Protection Agency also took an active interest in the waste-disposal issue. Established in 1970, the agency quickly commissioned a study of the environmental effects of septic tanks. Beginning in 1975, the EPA cosponsored an annual conference to consider ways to remedy the problems caused by backyard waste-disposal systems. The agency conducted a second study of the septic-tank issue in 1977.[49]

The EPA was not alone. The late 1960s and early 1970s saw a resurgence of government and university research on septic tanks. The results were disturbing. A 1969 U.S. Department of the Interior study reported that roughly one-third of all septic tanks eventually

48. For the quotation, see Joe G. Moore, Jr., "Environmental Control Versus Unlimited Growth," in Nina I. McClelland, editor, *Individual Onsite Wastewater Systems: Proceedings of the Second National Conference 1975* (Ann Arbor: Ann Arbor Science, 1977), 7. The statistics about state regulation are in Environmental Protection Agency, *Report to Congress: Waste Disposal Practices and their Effects on Ground Water* (Washington: Environmental Protection Agency, 1974), 186. For state-by-state details, see Marion R. Scalf, William J. Dunlap, and James F. Kreissl, *Environmental Effects of Septic Tank Systems* (Ada, OK: Environmental Protection Agency, 1977), 8–11; Patterson, Minear, and Nedved, *Septic Tanks and the Environment*, 26.
49. The first EPA study of septic tanks was conducted by a team of consultants: S. N. Goldstein, V. D. Wenk, M. C. Fowler, and S. S. Poh, *A Study of Selected Economic and Environmental Aspects of Individual Home Wastewater Treatment Systems* (Washington: Mitre Corporation, 1972). The second study is Scalf, Dunlap, and Kreissl, *Environmental Effects of Septic Tank Systems*. The EPA also discussed the septic tank problem in the *Report to Congress* on groundwater contamination. The proceedings of the annual conferences which EPA cosponsored were published under the general title *Individual Onsite Wastewater Systems*. Eight volumes appeared between 1977 and 1982. The first six were edited by Nina I. McClelland; McClelland coedited volume seven with Joe L. Evans, and Evans coedited volume eight with Lawrence Waldorf. Ann Arbor Science published the first six volumes between 1977 and 1980, and the remaining volumes were published by the National Sanitation Foundation (Ann Arbor) in 1981 and 1982.

failed, while a 1971 Illinois Institute of Technology study found failure rates as high as 50 percent. In addition to strengthening the conservation and public health arguments against widespread reliance on septic tanks, the post-1970 research raised a number of new concerns.[50]

Investigators reported that unregulated disposal of sludge and scum was a serious source of water pollution. A few officials had pointed to the problem in the early 1960s. On Long Island, one reported, septic-tank "scavengers" simply deposited their haul at landfills and waste dumps. Though no one had evaluated the consequences, the official concluded, the groundwater in the vicinity of the disposal sites undoubtedly was "grossly contaminated." But the studies of the 1970s went beyond anecdote to demonstrate the magnitude of the problem. The quantity of sludge and scum was enormous, and the collectors held to few standards. In New England alone, over 400 million gallons of waste were pumped out of septic tanks every year, and much of that waste was simply poured by unscrupulous haulers into abandoned sand and gravel pits, buried in landfills, or dumped along roadways and streams.[51]

Throughout the 1970s, researchers found additional evidence about the harmful impact of septic tanks on public health. By increasing the levels of nitrates in suburban drinking water, septic tanks increased the threat to infants from blue-baby syndrome. The syndrome itself was not new: In the late 1950s, a sizable body of research on the problem already existed, but researchers had focused on the threat in farm areas, where nitrate-rich manure could contaminate wells. The new research made clear that blue-baby syndrome had become a problem in suburbia too. The pollution of both ground and surface water by septic-tank effluent also caused

50. For the first study of failure rates, see James R. Bailey, Richard J. Benoit, John L. Dodson, James M. Robb, and Harold Wallman, *A Study of Flow Reduction and Treatment of Waste Water from Households* (Washington: U.S. Department of the Interior, 1969), 30–31. The 1971 estimate was based on a survey of five midwestern states. See Patterson, Minear, and Nedved, *Septic Tanks and the Environment*, 5.

51. The account of scavenger operations in Long Island comes from U.S. Public Health Service, *Ground Water Contamination*, 157. For the statistics, see Environmental Protection Agency, *Report to Congress*, 196. In the 1980s, the EPA belatedly sought to remedy the problem of improper disposal of sludge and scum from septic tanks. See Joseph W. Rezek and Ivan A. Cooper, *Septage Management* (Cincinnati: Environmental Protection Agency, 1980); U.S. Environmental Protection Agency, *Handbook – Septage Treatment and Disposal* (Cincinnati: Environmental Protection Agency, 1984).

countless cases of infectious hepatitis, typhoid fever, dysentery, and gastrointestinal illness. According to a number of estimates, septic-tank failure caused roughly 40 percent of all outbreaks of water-borne diseases from 1945 to 1980.[52]

In addition to threats to human well-being, investigators reported disruptive effects on the nonhuman world. Salamanders and frogs seemed to be especially vulnerable. By the mid-1970s, a handful of studies pointed to septic-tank effluent as a cause of declines in suburban reptile and amphibian populations. The effluent from backyard waste-disposal systems also affected fish. In some places, septic-tank failures caused eutrophication of nearby ponds and lakes. Fed by the nutrients in urine and excrement, blue-green algae soon covered the water, and the algal bloom choked off aquatic life below. The septic tank truly was an environmental problem.[53]

The Difficulty of Restricting Development

In the course of a generation, from the mid-1950s to the mid-1970s, the case for septic-tank regulation became more elaborate and more compelling, and the critique clearly made a difference. The percent-

52. The best summary of the early studies on blue-baby syndrome is Stanley and Eliassen, *Status of Knowledge of Ground Water Contaminants*, 24–25, 272–274, 280–286. For later studies of the health effects of septic tank effluent, see Richard J. Perkins, "Septic Tanks, Lot Size and Pollution of Water Table Aquifers," *Journal of Environmental Health* 46 (1984): 298–304; Scalf, Dunlap, and Kreissl, *Environmental Effects of Septic Tank Systems*, 20; C. Hagedorn, E. L. McCoy, and T. M. Rahe, "The Potential for Ground Water Contamination from Septic Effluents," *Journal of Environmental Quality* 10 (1981): 1–8; Marylynn V. Yates, "Septic Tank Density and Ground-Water Contamination," *Ground Water* 23 (1985): 587–588; Patterson, Minear, and Nedved, *Septic Tanks and the Environment*, 3, 28.

53. The effects of septic tanks on reptiles and amphibians are discussed in Sherman A. Minton, Jr., "The Fate of Amphibians and Reptiles in a Suburban Area," *Journal of Herpetology* 2 (December 1968): 113–116; Craig A. Campbell, "Survival of Reptiles and Amphibians in Urban Environments," in John H. Noyes and Donald R. Progulske, editors, *A Symposium on Wildlife in an Urbanizing Environment* (Amherst: Massachusetts Cooperative Extension Service, 1974), 61–66; Dale L. Keyes, *Land Development and the Natural Environment: Estimating Impacts* (Washington: Urban Land Institute, 1976), 100. For septic tanks as a cause of eutrophication, see John Savini and J. C. Kammerer, *Urban Growth and the Water Regimen* [Geological Survey Water Supply Paper 1591–A] (Washington: USGPO, 1961), A-27; W. T. Edmondson, "Eutrophication in North America," in National Academy of Sciences, *Eutrophication: Causes, Consequences, Correctives* (Washington: National Academy Press, 1969), 135; Patterson, Minear, and Nedved, *Septic Tanks and the Environment*, 28.

age of new homes with septic tanks fell sharply from the levels of the late 1940s and early 1950s: Instead of 40 or 45 percent, the figure in the 1980s was roughly 25 percent. But the problem did not go away. Because builders kept adding to the nation's housing stock, the absolute number of septic tanks increased decade by decade despite the decline in the percentage of new homes with septic tanks. In 1970, nearly 17 million homes had septic tanks; in 1980, the tally was just shy of 21 million; and in 1990, the number rose to almost 25 million. Nearly a quarter of all homes still relied on backyard waste disposal. Throughout the country, septic tanks continued to contaminate groundwater, pollute streams, and threaten the health of lakes.[54]

What forces still worked against a solution to the waste-disposal problem? Why did the septic tank remain a fixture in the suburban landscape?

For the building industry, the choice of a waste-disposal system was always a business decision, although the factors weighing in the calculation changed over time. In the late 1940s and early 1950s, when there was little opposition to septic tanks, the technology often offered builders a number of advantages. Unlike neighborhood sewage-treatment systems, septic tanks did not tie up much capital, because they did not have to be installed all at once at the start of construction – they could be added one by one as each house was finished. The costs were easier to pass on to homebuyers, and the builder had no responsibility for maintenance. Indeed, as a number of observers pointed out, builders rarely had to pay any financial penalties if septic tanks failed in a few months or years. For the most self-consciously progressive builders, however, the calculus began to change in the mid-1950s. If the use of septic tanks caused problems, then the reputation of the industry might suffer. Worse yet, the problems might invite unwanted restrictions on land use.

54. For the 1970 and 1980 census figures, see Nelson and Dueker, "Exurban Living Using Improved Water and Wastewater Technology," 110–111. The 1990 figures are in U.S. Bureau of the Census, *1990 Census of Housing: Detailed Housing Characteristics* (Washington: USGPO, 1993), 12. For the estimate of the percentage of new homes with septic tanks, see Sierra Club Legal Defense Fund, *The Poisoned Well: New Strategies for Groundwater Protection* (Washington: Island Press, 1989), 41; Larry W. Canter, Robert C. Knox, and Deborah M. Fairchild, *Ground Water Quality Protection* (Chelsea, MI: Lewis Publishers, 1987), 77.

Accordingly, the trade publications of the building industry began to discuss new waste-disposal technologies. The National Association of Home Builders also sought ways to make the existing alternatives to the septic tank more financially attractive.

The response was similar in the mid-1960s, when the passage of federal water-pollution legislation led to renewed scrutiny of septic-tank use. In 1966, *House and Home* began a major piece on alternative sewage-treatment technologies by warning that builders soon would feel "new pressure" to stop solving the waste problem "the easy way." The 1968 edition of the Community Builders Handbook also warned about increasingly stringent regulations. But the first consideration of the industry remained financial: What waste-disposal system would give the greatest flexibility in the choice of building sites with the least trouble and expense? Because builders did not have to pay for the damage done to ground and surface waters by septic-tank effluent, environmental costs still did not figure directly in the waste-disposal decision – the problem of pollution entered the calculation only indirectly, when builders decided whether to respond to the concerns of homebuyers and public officials.[55]

For the homeowner, the performance of a waste-disposal system was basically a consumer issue, yet the consumer's perspective only took in a handful of environmental problems. If everything worked well, the benefits of a septic tank were often considerable: With a septic tank, a house might cost less and be in a more desirable location. If a septic tank failed, the result might be a nasty inconvenience, a family health hazard, perhaps even a serious financial blow – but, even in the worst case, the typical homeowner did not worry about the long-term environmental costs of septic-tank use.

55. For the quotation, see "Sewage Treatment: Why Homebuilders Won't Be Able To Duck the Problem Any More," *House and Home* 29 (April 1966): 118. Throughout the 1960s, *House and Home* urged builders to investigate both new and old alternatives to the septic tank. See "Package Sewerage Plant Saves a Subdivision . . . and Permits 44% More Lots on the Same Tract," 23 (February 1963): 53; "Add-a-Section Sewerage Plant Grows with Tract," 26 (September 1964): 73; "Sewage-Treatment Plants and Other New Sewage-Handling Techniques Are Fast Making the Septic Tank a Thing of the Past," 27 (March 1965): 124; "Is There a Future for the Single-House Sewage Treatment Plant?," 33 (February 1968): 98–100; "The Single-House Sewage Treatment Plant Finally Starts Winning Local Approval," 37 (February 1970): 26–28. In addition, see McKeever, *The Community Builders Handbook*, 46–47, 178.

As a result, the nation's lawmakers could alleviate the most urgent concerns of homeowners without addressing all the environmental problems caused by septic tanks. Over the years, that is exactly what happened. The banning of nonbiodegradable detergents stopped the flow of suds at the tap. The restrictions on the use of septic tanks in large subdivisions eliminated the cause of the worst waste-disposal disasters. The lavish federal subsidies for suburban sewer construction reduced the burden of replacing inadequate backyard systems. But the ever-increasing numbers of septic tanks still caused environmental damage. The concern of homeowners did not extend to salamanders and frogs.

Though homeowners often complained about septic-tank problems, the first call for regulation in many communities came from public health officials and urban planners. The national organizations of both groups began to discuss the problem of suburban waste disposal in the mid-1950s. As a result, a sanitary engineer in Wichita or a health department inspector in Hartford did not need to witness a local septic-tank disaster to become concerned about the issue. Yet local officials knew that they could not get too far out in front of their neighbors.

Almost from the start, indeed, the supporters of regulation understood that the septic tank was not just a waste-disposal technology. It was also a mechanism for facilitating the construction of single-family homes in the suburbs, and so it furthered a number of widely shared goals. The septic tank supported a popular domestic ideal. It increased the opportunity for people to profit from one of the great American paths to wealth – real estate speculation. Above all, the septic tank helped to stimulate economic growth. With so much at stake, the regulation of septic tanks was a difficult proposition. In a few areas, where waste-disposal problems were especially visible or costly, local officials managed to marshal support for crackdowns on septic tanks. But that was the exception, at least in the 1950s and early 1960s.

Even after the federal government set out to control water pollution, the fundamental dilemma of septic-tank regulation persisted. Congress delegated enforcement to the states, and both state and local officials continued to struggle to balance conflicting demands. In a series of waste-disposal conferences in the late 1970s and early

1980s, for example, a number of participants spoke about the pressure not to uphold strict standards. According to the director of Pennsylvania's Bureau of Community Environmental Control, the issuance of permits for septic tanks frequently was just "a paper exercise or a revenue collection scheme. It is often difficult to bite the bullet and deny permits where soil, slope, or geological conditions preclude the installation of subsurface disposal systems." The argument for development remained powerful.[56]

56. William Middendorf, "Management Guidelines for Conventional and Alternative On-site Sewage Systems – Pennsylvania," in Nina I. McClelland, editor, *Individual Onsite Wastewater Systems: Proceedings of the Third National Conference 1976* (Ann Arbor: Ann Arbor Science, 1977), 197. Two years before, Middendorf had described the protests against the state's first septic-tank standards because the regulations restricted building on certain types of land. See "Current Status of Regulations (Pennsylvania)," in Nina I. McClelland, editor, *Individual Onsite Wastewater Systems: Proceedings of the First National Conference 1974* (Ann Arbor: Ann Arbor Science, 1977), 65.

4

Open Space:
The First Protests against the
Bulldozed Landscape

"Take a last look," William Whyte told the readers of *Life* in 1959. "Some summer's morning drive past the golf club on the edge of town, turn off onto a back road and go for a short trip through the open countryside. Look well at the meadows, the wooded draws, the stands of pine, the creeks and streams, and fix them in your memory. If the American standard of living goes up another notch, this is about the last chance you will have."[1]

Why? What was the problem? "Go back toward the city five or 10 miles," Whyte wrote. "Here, in what was pleasant countryside only a year ago, is a sight of what is to come. No more sweep of green – across the hills are splattered scores of random subdivisions, each laid out in the same dreary asphalt curves. Gone are the streams, brooks, woods and forests that the subdivisions' signs talked about. The streams are largely buried in concrete culverts. Where one flows briefly through a patch of weeds and tin cans it is fetid with the ooze of septic tanks. A row of stumps marks the place where syca-mores used to shade the road and if a stand of maple or walnut still exists the men with power saws will soon be at it. Here and there a farm remains, but the 'For Sale' signs are up and now even the golf course is to be chopped into lots."[2]

The lament was common. In the years after World War II, as the nation's builders turned acre after acre into suburban subdi-visions, a large number of Americans became concerned about the transformation of the landscape. What could be done to stop the

1. William H. Whyte, Jr., "A Plan to Save Vanishing U.S. Countryside," *Life* 47 (August 17, 1959): 88.
2. Ibid., 88–89.

destruction of the countryside? By the end of the 1950s, the question was at the heart of a new kind of conservation effort – a multifaceted campaign to save the nation's "open space." Though scholars so far have written little about the subject, the campaign to save open space had profound consequences. It was the first broad attempt to deal with some of the problems caused by the postwar pattern of development, and it shaped later efforts to force builders to meet new environmental obligations. In a number of ways, the effort to preserve open space was also a critical stage in the evolution of the modern environmental movement.[3]

The open-space issue was rooted in the profound transformation of the building industry during and after World War II. For the first time, the industry was dominated by large-scale builders using mass-production techniques to transform tracts of hundreds or thousands of acres into new neighborhoods. The industry's output reached unprecedented levels: In the 1950s, builders put up more than 15 million homes, mostly located at the edge of the nation's cities. For a number of reasons, the average size of residential lots also increased considerably. As a result, the metropolitan area of the nation grew by leaps and bounds. In 1950, the U.S. Census considered only 5.9 percent of the nation's land to be urban or suburban; in 1960, the figure was 8.7 percent; and in 1970, the metropolitan share reached 10.9 percent. Throughout the 1950s, the nation's cities and suburbs took a million more acres every year – a territory larger than Rhode Island.[4]

3. Samuel P. Hays is one of the few historians of environmentalism to note the importance of the open-space issue. In his major work on the environmental movement, he devotes four pages to strategies for open-space preservation and concludes: "The urban fringe continued to be a major battleground in the conflict between environmental and developmental objectives. Out of this experience came many ideas about environmental quality, support for environmental organizations, and political action." See *Beauty, Health, and Permanence: Environmental Politics in the United States, 1955–1985* (New York: Cambridge University Press, 1987), 92–95.

4. The construction statistics are in U.S. Department of Commerce, *Housing Construction Statistics* (Washington: USGPO, 1966), 18. For the percentage of postwar homes in suburban areas, see F. John Devaney, *Tracking the American Dream: 50 Years of Housing History from the Census Bureau* (Washington: U.S. Department of Commerce, 1994), 13. The average house lot was roughly 3,000 square feet in the streetcar suburbs of the 1880s and 1890s and 5,000 square feet in the automobile suburbs of the 1920s; but in the subdivisions of the 1940s and 1950s, the lots generally were at least 6,000, 8,000, or 12,000 square feet. See Kenneth T. Jackson, *Crabgrass Frontier: The Suburbanization of the United States* (New York: Oxford University Press, 1985), 185, 239; Michael Southworth

Just as significantly, the face of development changed. Before 1945, builders often had to bypass large wetlands and steep slopes. But with the earth-moving machinery developed during the war, and with the new economies of large-scale construction, postwar builders could consider almost any kind of land. Indeed, as land costs skyrocketed in the 1950s, the trade publications of the building industry were full of exhortations to investigate lands once considered impossible to build on. "Need Land?" the headline of one article asked. "Then Take a Look at Marshland." Another told "How to Hit Paydirt on a Hillside." Builders avidly took the advice. From the mid-1950s to the mid-1970s, almost a million acres of marshes, swamps, bogs, and coastal estuaries were destroyed by urban development. Builders even began to subdivide wetlands the size of the Florida Everglades. Though there are no nationwide statistics on hillside development, there is no doubt that construction tore into the hills in many parts of the nation after 1945. One of the most popular houses of the 1950s – the split-level – was designed in part to suit lots on steeply sloped ground. Thus the new metropolitan landscape had fewer spaces left open because of the terrain.[5]

Within tracts, the bulldozer also made possible a new kind of monotony. To prepare the land for construction, builders often bulldozed all vegetation, leveled all rises, and filled or channeled all streams. For a few weeks or months, the result was a wasteland, a

and Peter M. Owens, "The Evolving Metropolis: Studies of Community, Neighborhood, and Street Form at the Urban Edge," *Journal of the American Planning Association* 59 (1993): 282; Christopher Tunnard and Boris Pushkarev, *Man-Made America: Chaos or Control?* (New Haven: Yale University Press, 1963), 92–95. The metropolitan land area statistics are from U.S. Bureau of the Census, *Statistical Abstract of the United States: 1986* (Washington: USGPO, 1985), 19. For the annual rate of increase in urban and suburban acreage, see Ann Louise Strong, *Open Space for Urban America* (Washington: U.S. Department of Housing and Urban Development, 1965), 1. I offer a slightly more detailed discussion of these trends in "Building on the Land: Toward an Environmental History of Residential Development in American Cities and Suburbs, 1870–1990," *Journal of Urban History* 20 (1994): 415–416. I also draw on my article in the next three paragraphs.

5. For a good sampling of the exhortations in the trade press, see "Need Land? Then Take a Look at Marshland," *House and Home* 13 (April 1958): 146–152; "How to Hit Pay Dirt on a Hillside," *House and Home* 4 (December 1953): 90–115; "Land – A Special Issue," *House and Home* 18 (August 1960): 106, 151–164. For the wetlands statistics, see Ralph W. Tiner, Jr., *Wetlands of the United States: Current Status and Recent Trends* (Washington: USGPO, 1984), vii. The origin of the split-level house is described by Joseph B. Mason, *History of Housing in the U.S., 1930–1980* (Houston: Gulf Publishing Company, 1982), 71. I discuss the development of wetlands and hillsides at length in the next chapter.

barren plain of dirt. But even after the tracts became neighborhoods of homes, the new landscape had little variety. Builders usually planted a few trees per lot – and laid sod or planted grass seed – but that was it.[6]

In laying out neighborhoods, builders rarely provided green space. In some cases, they argued that families with yards would not need parks. As one advertisement for the second Levittown explained, "Every house will have its own 'park' when all the trees are grown." In other cases, builders offered no justification – they simply wanted to maximize the number of lots per tract. Either way, the layout of new subdivisions marked a significant departure from older neighborhoods with single-family homes. In the New York metropolitan area, for example, the postwar tracts had just a tenth of the park acreage of neighborhoods established in the first four decades of the twentieth century – 2.7 out of every 100 acres instead of 27. For a while, the undeveloped land at the edge of a tract might serve as a kind of park. But as development spread, as nearby woods and streams disappeared, the absence of permanent open space became more noticeable.[7]

By the time Whyte published his call for action in *Life,* a diverse group of people had voiced concerns about the loss of open space. In the professions directly concerned with the shape of the metropolis – architecture and urban planning – the costs of sprawl were a topic of intense interest by the mid-1950s. In addition to worrying about the difficulty of providing adequate streets, sanitary systems, and schools in new communities, the professional critics of sprawl often complained about the lack of open space. The subject soon attracted the attention of civic clubs and foundations. The effort to preserve open space also included government officials, conserva-

6. Even the major organizations of the building industry acknowledged this change. See, for example, Jule R. von Sternberg, "The Economics of Trees," *House and Home* 3 (April 1953): 130–131; Urban Land Institute, American Society of Civil Engineers, and National Association of Home Builders, *Residential Erosion and Sediment Control: Objectives, Principles, and Design Considerations* (Washington: Urban Land Institute, 1978), 8–9.
7. The Levitt advertisement is cited by Cynthia L. Girling and Kenneth I. Helphand, *Yard-Street-Park: The Design of Suburban Open Space* (New York: John Wiley & Sons, 1994), 95. For the park statistics, see Edward Higbee, *The Squeeze: Cities Without Space* (New York: William Morrow and Company, 1960), 228–229. In addition, see Mel Scott, *American City Planning Since 1890* (Berkeley: University of California Press, 1969), 457–458; Southworth and Owens, "The Evolving Metropolis," 278–279.

tionists, and advocates of parks and playgrounds. In many communities, the advance of development led to the formation of grass-roots groups, often led by women, to "save our trees" or "stop the rape of the valley." Farmers sometimes joined the protests.[8]

The open-space activists made three kinds of arguments. In the words of the time, one was a "conservation" argument. Another argument, essentially aesthetic, focused on "amenity." The third argument dealt with "outdoor recreation." Though many advocates of open space sought to be comprehensive, the three lines of argument had different roots and often appealed to different sorts of people.[9]

Because the archetypical postwar subdivision was built on farmland, open-space advocates often argued that the nation was risking the loss of a vital productive resource. In California, especially, the growth of suburbs destroyed thousands of acres of unmatched productivity. To be sure, as a number of analysts argued, the acreage lost was only a small fraction of the nation's total agricultural land base, but the doubts about the wisdom of building houses on prime farmland persisted. For the doubters, the issue usually was a matter of culture, not just agricultural production. In the 1950s, more than 10 million people left farms, and the outcry against the suburbanization of the countryside was partly a way to express anxiety about the social consequences of a profound demographic change – if the city continued to swallow up the country, would Americans forget the "agrarian" virtues which had made the nation great? Though seldom raising that question directly, the advocates of open space

8. For a good summary of the professional critique of sprawl in the late 1950s and early 1960s, see Mitchell Gordon, *Sick Cities* (New York: Macmillan, 1963). The grassroots slogans are cited in Whyte, "A Plan to Save Vanishing U.S. Countryside," 90.

9. In the 1960s, a number of open-space advocates offered similar typologies. See William L. Slayton's foreword in Strong, *Open Space for Urban America,* iii; Charles E. Little and John G. Mitchell, editors, *Space for Survival: Blocking the Bulldozer in Urban America* [A Sierra Club Handbook] (New York: Pocket Books, 1971), 7; Regional Plan Association, *The Race for Open Space: Final Report of the Park, Recreation and Open Space Project* (New York: Regional Plan Association, 1960), 9. Other writers provided more elaborate outlines of the major arguments for open space. See, for example, Stanley B. Tankel, "The Importance of Open Space in the Urban Pattern," in Lowdon Wingo, Jr., editor, *Cities and Space: The Future Use of Urban Land* (Baltimore: Johns Hopkins University Press, 1963), 57–71; S. B. Zisman, "Open Spaces in Urban Growth," *AIA Journal* 44 (December 1965): 50–51; Edward A. Williams, *Open Space: The Choices Before California* [The Urban-Metropolitan Open-Space Study, 1965] (San Francisco: Diablo Press, 1969), 18–19.

often argued that conservation of prime agricultural lands in fast-growing areas would ensure that urban and suburban people retained "a sense of rural life."[10]

By 1960, a number of civil engineers and conservation officials were arguing that open space had a "functional" value as a check against flooding. Floodplains and wetlands were natural sponges, soaking up runoff after storms, and communities could reduce the need for expensive public works by preserving both types of land as open space. Woodlands served a similar function – by slowing runoff, trees allowed more water to soak into the ground. In part, the conservation argument for open space was a refashioning of the New Deal concept of watershed planning. As the New Dealers recognized, the way people used the land had direct effects on the hydrological system of a region. But the conservation argument also built on new scientific ideas. Open space was necessary to maintain "ecological balance" – that is, to preserve the complex community of living things which sustain human society. At least until the late 1960s, the new ecological thinking was confined to a few professional circles. But the argument eventually became more popular and more influential.[11]

10. The short quotation is from T. J. Kent, Jr., "The Meaning of Open Space in the Metropolitan Environment," in Frances W. Herring, editor, *Regional Parks and Open Space: Selected Conference Papers* (Berkeley: University of California Bureau of Public Administration, 1961), 12. In addition, see Luther Gulick, "The City's Challenge in Resource Use," in Henry Jarrett, editor, *Perspectives on Conservation: Essays on America's Natural Resources* (Baltimore: Johns Hopkins University Press, 1958), 127–128; Alice Harvey Hubbard, *This Land of Ours: Community and Conservation Projects for Citizens* (New York: Macmillan, 1960), 111; Wilfred Owen, *Cities in the Motor Age* (New York: Viking, 1959), 144–145; Raymond F. Dasmann, *The Destruction of California* (New York: Macmillan, 1965), 124–137; James P. Degnan, "Santa Clara: The Bulldozer Crop," *The Nation* 200 (March 8, 1965): 242–245. For a history of the debate about the fate of agricultural land, see Tim Lehman, *Public Values, Private Lands: Farmland Preservation Policy, 1933–1985* (Chapel Hill: University of North Carolina Press, 1995). In addition, see Rebecca Conard, "Green Gold: 1950s Greenbelt Planning in Santa Clara County, California," *Environmental History Review* 9 (1985): 5–18. The postwar exodus from the nation's farms is summarized in John L. Shover, *First Majority – Last Minority: The Transforming of Rural Life in America* (DeKalb: Northern Illinois University Press, 1976), 4.
11. U.S. Senate, *Housing Legislation of 1961: Hearings on S. 858 before the Subcommittee on Housing of the Committee on Banking and Currency,* 87th Congress, 1st session, 1961, 996, 1017, 1023, 1043, 1047; Strong, *Open Space for Urban America,* 7–11; Lawrence Levine, "Land Conservation in Metropolitan Areas," *Journal of the American Institute of Planners* 30 (1964): 207–208. For the argument about "ecological balance," see William A. Niering, *Nature in the Metropolis: Conservation in the Tri-State New York*

The aesthetic argument was potent from the start. To many people, the tracts simply were ugly. They were places with no character. The 1950s saw a fierce intellectual attack on "mass culture," and the aesthetic critique of tract-house development was partly a high-brow response to a new form of mass production. In the view of some critics, indeed, the postwar suburbs did not deserve the name, since they so manifestly lacked the parklike spaciousness of the suburbs built earlier for the wealthy. But the advocates of open space were proposing a solution to a specific problem, not simply deriding a general cultural phenomenon. To give life to new subdivisions, the critics argued, there had to be some open space. Open space provided much-needed contrast – "visual relief," as one advocate put it, from the monotony of sprawl. Open space also helped to define communities, to mark one place off from another, and so gave residents a sense of belonging, a vital rootedness.[12]

The aesthetic argument was usually more basic, however. People wanted and needed the chance to enjoy the beauty of nature. As one scientist wrote, "the average person wants more and more to conserve nature simply because it is there; because it is good to look at and be in." That argument was not new in the 1950s. A century before, the leaders of urban America had begun to worry that the growth of cities threatened to alienate people from nature, and many sought to preserve a bit of green in the metropolis by building land-scaped cemeteries and parks. In the decades around the turn of the century, well-to-do Americans began to devise new ways to get back to nature – camping and hiking in the wilds, hunting, moving to parklike suburbs. But if the appreciation for nature in the 1950s was

Metropolitan Area (New York: Regional Plan Association, 1960), 7, 57; Ian L. McHarg, "The Place of Nature in the City of Man," *Annals of the American Academy of Political and Social Science* 352 (March 1964): 1–12; Wallace Stegner, "What Ever Happened to the Great Outdoors?," *Saturday Review* 48 (May 22, 1965): 37–38; Joseph James Shomon, *Open Land for Urban America: Acquisition, Safekeeping, and Use* (Baltimore: Johns Hopkins University Press, 1971), 21–40. The ideal of watershed planning is well illustrated by Bernard Frank and Anthony Netboy, *Water, Land, and People* (New York: Alfred A. Knopf, 1950).

12. For the quotation, see U.S. Senate, *Housing Legislation of 1961*, 997. In addition, see "The City's Threat to Open Land," 88; John Brewer Moore, "Wanted: More Open Space in Growing Areas," *American City* 71 (1956): 94; "The Importance of Land," *Recreation* 50 (1958): 226; Owen, *Cities in the Motor Age*, 22–23. For a critique of the highbrow response to the suburbs, see Scott Donaldson, *The Suburban Myth* (New York: Columbia University Press, 1969).

not new, it certainly was more widespread than ever before. The dozens of best-selling books of nature writing; the popularity of television series about wild animals and wild places, especially the Disney documentaries about the prairie and the desert; the successful campaign to protect the canyon lands in Dinosaur National Monument from destruction by the proposed Echo Park dam, and the increasing strength of the movement to create a national system of wilderness areas – all made clear the growing appeal of natural beauty. For many Americans, in other words, it was increasingly important to have everyday opportunities to appreciate nature: The occasional weekend or vacation trip was no longer enough.[13]

The recreation profession took the aesthetic argument a step further. People needed a range of recreational spaces, from structured playgrounds to natural areas, and the postwar suburbs were not meeting those needs. But the argument really went deeper, because recreation was tied in the minds of many Americans with a number of profound social issues. The 1950s were marked by a major campaign against juvenile delinquency, and advocates of recreational open space often claimed that access to nature would help to ensure the healthy social development of children. The unprece-

13. For the quotation, see Niering, *Nature in the Metropolis*, 53. In addition, see D. B. Luten, "The Citizen's Stake in Preserving Open Space," in Herring, *Regional Parks and Open Space*, 17–20; U.S. House of Representatives, *The Housing Act of 1961: Hearings on H. R. 6028, H. R. 5300, and H. R. 6423 before the Subcommittee on Housing of the Committee on Banking and Currency*, 87th Congress, 1st session, 1961, 863; Sigurd F. Olson, "Our Need of Breathing Space," in Jarrett, *Perspectives on Conservation*, 147–148; Strong, *Open Space for Urban America*, 1; Arthur A. Davis, "Planning Our Open Space Land Resources for the Future," *Trends in Parks and Recreation* 2 (January 1965), reprinted in Phillip O. Foss, *Recreation* (New York: Chelsea House, 1971), 352–355; Catherine Bauer Wurster, "The Urban Octopus," in David Brower, editor, *Wilderness: America's Living Heritage* (San Francisco: Sierra Club, 1961), 118–122; Lewis Mumford, *The Urban Prospect* (New York: Harcourt, Brace & World, 1968), 79–91. For the antecedents, see David Schuyler, *The New Urban Landscape: The Redefinition of City Form in Nineteenth-Century America* (Baltimore: Johns Hopkins University Press, 1986); Peter J. Schmitt, *Back to Nature: The Arcadian Myth in Urban America* (New York: Oxford University Press, 1969). For the 1950s, see Stephen Fox, *The American Conservation Movement: John Muir and His Legacy* (1981; reprint, Madison: University of Wisconsin Press, 1985), 218–290; Thomas R. Dunlap, *Saving America's Wildlife: Ecology and the American Mind, 1850–1990* (Princeton: Princeton University Press, 1988), 98–110; Russel B. Nye, *This Almost Chosen People: Essays in the History of American Ideas* (Lansing: Michigan State University Press, 1966), 298–302. In *Wilderness and the American Mind* [3d edition] (New Haven: Yale University Press, 1982), Roderick Nash discusses both the back-to-nature movement and the campaign to establish a national system of wilderness areas; see especially 141–160, 200–237.

dented affluence of the postwar years also led to new concerns about the social consequences of increased leisure time. In 1958, as a result, the U.S. Congress voted to fund a massive multiyear study of the nation's "outdoor recreation resources."[14]

Often, the recreation issue was discussed in abstract statistical terms. The boom in population, the reduction in the industrial workweek, the intensified demands on existing parks and recreational facilities – all argued that the nation had to make a concerted effort to provide new recreational space. Thus recreational space became a resource, like trees or energy or water, which could be overexploited. Indeed, one of the first major studies of the issue was done by Resources for the Future, which also offered long-term analyses of the more conventional resources. For many residents of suburbia, however, the recreation issue was much more tangible and personal.[15]

In new subdivisions, children were often able to play in undeveloped land nearby – then one day the bulldozers would come to

14. The best example of the recreation argument is Walter A. Tucker, editor, *The Crisis in Open Land* (Wheeling, WV: American Institute of Park Executives, 1959), which speaks to the threat of juvenile delinquency as well as the broader anxiety about the new abundance of leisure. See, especially, page 9:

Here is one of the knottiest social problems of our age. How shall we dispose of these mounting surpluses of idle time? It must be employed in ways that will help promote the general welfare. Otherwise the dead weight of it will begin to pull us down. If it can not be used constructively, it must inevitably be used destructively. The devil can find work for idle hands and idle minds in more ways than our ancestors imagined were possible.

On the relationship of open space and juvenile delinquency, see also U.S. Senate, *Housing Legislation of 1961*, 594, 1017; Margo Tupper, *No Place to Play* (Philadelphia: Chilton Books, 1966), 38–84; Gordon, *Sick Cities*, 113–114; Lawrence Lader, "Chaos in the Suburbs," *Better Homes & Gardens* 36 (October 1958): 129. For the historical context, see James Gilbert, *A Cycle of Outrage: America's Reaction to the Juvenile Delinquent in the 1950s* (New York: Oxford University Press, 1986). The federal recreation study led to a series of publications; the summary report is Outdoor Recreation Resources Review Commission, *Outdoor Recreation for America* (Washington: USGPO, 1962). Samuel Hays argues that concern about outdoor recreation was a key element in the first phase of the modern environmental movement. See *Beauty, Health, and Permanence*, 54. For a similar argument about the evolution of environmental politics at the state level, see Thomas R. Huffman, *Protectors of the Land and Water: Environmentalism in Wisconsin, 1961–1968* (Chapel Hill: University of North Carolina Press, 1994), 32–61.

15. See, especially, Marion Clawson, *Statistics on Outdoor Recreation* (Washington: Resources for the Future, 1958); Marion Clawson, R. Burnell Held, and Charles H. Stoddard, *Land for the Future* (Baltimore: Johns Hopkins University Press, 1960); Marion Clawson, *Land and Water for Recreation: Opportunities, Problems, and Policies* [Resources for the Future Policy Background Series] (Chicago: Rand McNally and Company, 1963).

turn those playgrounds into lots for new houses, and people of all ages reacted with shock and outrage. In 1962, for example, a seven-year-old boy from California made national news when he sought the help of President John Kennedy after discovering that development was destroying his favorite place to hunt for lizards: "Dear Mr President," he wrote, "we Have no Place to go when we want to go out in the canyon Because there are going to Build houses So could you setaside some land where we could Play? thank you four listening love scott." In other cases, parents took action, joining together to try to save the woods or streams or hills that their children cherished.[16]

William Whyte's Campaign to Save Open Space

What could people do to save open space? For more than a decade, the writer William Whyte provided the most influential answers to that question, and a consideration of Whyte's work offers a concise way to understand the impact of the open-space campaigns of the 1950s and 1960s.[17]

Whyte's passion for open-space preservation came from dismaying personal experience. He had grown up in Chester County, Pennsylvania, about 20 miles from Philadelphia, in the rolling countryside of the Brandywine Valley – a place he considered the most beautiful in America – and every time he visited his family in the early 1950s he saw more signs of sprawl: The lush pastoral scene of his youth was giving way to a depressing new landscape of cinderblock ranchers and frozen custard stands. Many open-space ac-

16. The letter to President Kennedy was reproduced in U.S. Department of the Interior, *The Race for Inner Space* (Washington: USGPO, 1964), 19. The boy's plea received "a blaze of attention – column upon column of newsprint." See 21. The letter was reprinted in Open Space Action Committee, *Stewardship: The Land, the Landowner, the Metropolis* (New York: Open Space Action Committee, 1965), 8; Foss, *Recreation*, 753. In addition, see Ben H. Bagdikian, "The Rape of the Land," *Saturday Evening Post* 239 (June 18, 1966): 25–29, 86–94; Tupper, *No Place to Play*, 18–19; Whyte, "A Plan to Save Vanishing U.S. Countryside," 94.

17. Several of Whyte's contemporaries acknowledged his role in making open space a public issue. See Scott, *American City Planning Since 1890*, 568; F. Stuart Chapin, Jr., *Urban Land Use Planning* [2d edition] (Urbana: University of Illinois Press, 1965), 418; Bernard F. Hillenbrand, "America the Ugly," in James B. Trefethen, editor, *Transactions of the Twenty-Fifth North American Wildlife and Natural Resources Conference* (Washington: Wildlife Management Institute, 1960), 40.

tivists had similar experiences. But Whyte was better situated than most activists to press the issue. He was already famous as the author of *The Organization Man,* a best-selling social analysis of suburbia. As an assistant managing editor at *Fortune,* he was also able to enlist the resources of the vast Time-Life publishing empire to make his case for the importance of open space.[18]

In 1957, Whyte was one of two organizers of a roundtable discussion – published in *Fortune*'s sister publication, *Architectural Forum* – on "The City's Threat to Open Land." He edited a multipart *Fortune* series on "The Exploding Metropolis," republished as a book in 1958, and he wrote a piece for the series entitled "Urban Sprawl": "In the next three or four years," he argued, "Americans will have a chance to decide how decent a place this country will be to live in, and for generations to come." In 1959, he offered "A Plan to Save Vanishing U.S. Countryside" in *Life.* Whyte also made his case before a number of professional organizations, including the American Society of Planning Officials, the Urban Land Institute, and the American Society of Landscape Architects. In 1961, when the U.S. Senate held a hearing on a bill to encourage open-space preservation, Whyte was the first witness to testify. A year later, he wrote a report on "open space action" for a federal commission on outdoor recreation. Throughout the 1960s, he continued to publish influential work, culminating in a 1968 classic: *The Last Landscape.*[19]

18. For the Brandywine roots of Whyte's activism, see William H. Whyte, *The Last Landscape* (Garden City, NY: Doubleday, 1968), 15–19. *The Organization Man* was published by Simon and Schuster in 1956. For a succinct analysis of the book's importance, see Richard H. Pells, *The Liberal Mind in a Conservative Age: American Intellectuals in the 1940s and 1950s* [2nd edition] (Middletown, CT: Wesleyan University Press, 1989), 232–238.

19. "The City's Threat to Open Land," *Architectural Forum* 108 (January 1958): 87–90, 164–166; *The Exploding Metropolis* (1958; reprint, Berkeley: University of California Press, 1993), 133–156; "A Plan to Save Vanishing U.S. Countryside," 88–102; "Open Space and Retroactive Planning," in *Planning 1958* (Chicago: American Society of Planning Officials, 1958), 68–78; *Conservation Easements* (Washington: Urban Land Institute, 1959); "Open Space, Now or Never," *Landscape Architecture* 50 (1959): 8–13; U.S. Senate, *Housing Legislation of 1961,* 1002–1010; *Open Space Action: Report to the Outdoor Recreation Resources Review Commission* [ORRRC Study Report 15] (Washington: USGPO, 1962). The citation for *The Last Landscape* is in the previous note. The quotation from *The Exploding Metropolis* is on 133. Whyte's work was also reprinted in a number of trade, professional, and general interest magazines. See "How to Save Open Spaces While There Are Still Some Left to Save," *House and Home* 13 (February 1958): 102–106, 202; "Get That Land!," *Recreation* 51 (1959): 85; "Let's Save Our Vanishing Countryside," *Reader's Digest* 75 (November 1959): 198–204.

Whyte was able to win audiences in large part because he was especially effective in focusing attention on the possibilities for action. He also held out the appealing hope that Americans could solve the open-space problem without fundamentally changing the structure of the real-estate market and without rethinking the rights and responsibilities of property ownership. As Whyte himself argued, his proposals were "conservative."[20]

Whyte rejected as impractical the dream of many urban planners – the creation of regional planning agencies with the power to reserve land as green space. The need for action was too urgent, Whyte argued, to wait for perfect planning solutions. Whyte also rejected the use of zoning. Though zoning had a role in preserving open space, zoning decisions were too easy to overturn. More important, the use of regulation to enforce open-space preservation was unfair and probably unconstitutional. What could justify restrictions on the right of landowners to develop their property? The regulatory powers of a community should be used only to prevent property owners from doing tangible harm, Whyte argued, not to compel them to provide a community benefit. If a community wanted to enjoy open space, the taxpayers should expect to pay for the privilege. In many cases, communities simply should acquire desirable lands as quickly as possible. But Whyte also argued for the use of conservation easements. If citizens wanted to preserve a meadow or a marsh, they could buy the right to develop the property – and never use that right. The land would still be private property; the landowner would be compensated for the loss of potential profit from development. In return, the community would have the benefit of open space without the financial burden of acquiring the land outright.[21]

In his *Life* article, Whyte also argued briefly for a second approach – what would soon be known as cluster or planned unit development – to preserve open space within subdivisions, not just between them. The nation's zoning laws should be revised to allow

---

20. Whyte twice characterized his proposals as "conservative" in his urban sprawl essay: *The Exploding Metropolis,* 154, 156.

21. For Whyte's first statements on planning, regulation, and acquisition, see *The Exploding Metropolis,* 135, 150–151, 153–154; "A Plan to Save Vanishing U.S. Countryside," 95–96, 99, 102. Whyte develops each of these points at greater length in *The Last Landscape.*

subdivision builders to create large communal tracts of open space by clustering homes on smaller-than-standard lots. The developers would gain with such a layout because they would spend less per home on streets, land clearing, and utility hookups. The residents would also benefit – by giving up a bit of their yards, they would be able to enjoy a meadow, a hilly woodland, or a creek. Indeed, the cluster layout would turn potential annoyances into amenities. If a stream gully runs through a subdivision, Whyte explained, "it will not be chopped up into a patch of back lots that will only be a headache for the owners to keep up. Instead it will be left as a whole so that all the residents can use it. The density of the development will be the same as under the conventional pattern, but a lot more *space* will be created – and at less cost to the community, to the developer, and to the residents themselves."[22]

In the early 1960s, Whyte became even more convinced that builders needed to abandon "the land-wasting pattern" of subdivision design. He included a section on clusters in his 1962 openspace report to the outdoor recreation commission. With help from the Rockefeller Brothers Fund, he made a study of cluster developments, and he published a brief on the subject in 1964. Four years later, he devoted a chapter of *The Last Landscape* to cluster design. In his view, the point was inescapable: "People have to live somewhere, as it is often said, and if there is to be any hope of having open space in the future, there is going to have to be a more efficient pattern of building."[23]

The public debate about the best solutions to the open-space problem was not limited to the approaches championed by Whyte. By 1960, for example, a number of liberal Democrats were pushing for a federal program to help local governments acquire large "banks" of land at the frontiers of metropolitan settlement. In addition to preserving open space, the land banks would allow citizens to exercise more control over the timing and location of development, since public officials could sell or hold the fringe properties in accordance with public plans. The Kennedy administration

22. "A Plan to Save Vanishing U.S. Countryside," 94.
23. *Open Space Action*, 11–15; *Cluster Development* (New York: American Conservation Association, 1964); *The Last Landscape*, 199–224. For the quotation, see *The Last Landscape*, 199.

initially endorsed the land-bank idea, but the real estate and home-building industries blasted the proposal as a dangerous, untested meddling with the market, and the idea went nowhere.[24]

In contrast, Whyte's proposals won significant support. In Whyte's home state of New York, the legislature in 1960 created a $75 million program to help local governments acquire open space. "The disappearance of open and natural lands, particularly in and near rapidly growing urban and suburban areas, is of grave concern to the legislature and to the people of the State," the legislature declared. "Once such lands are used for residential or commercial purposes, they are often permanently rendered unsuitable for parks, conservation, or other recreational purposes. The present and future needs of the growing population of the State require the immediate acquisition of such lands."[25]

By 1965, six more states – including California – offered grants to local governments for open-space acquisition. Several other states had begun ambitious programs to acquire undeveloped tracts of land for outdoor recreation. Across the nation, local spending for park acquisition rose sharply in the early 1960s. The number of cities and counties with nature trails almost tripled from 1960 to 1965. A few cities and counties even acquired land solely to create "greenbelts."[26]

24. Catherine Bauer Wurster, "Framework for an Urban Society," in President's Commission on National Goals, *Goals for Americans: Programs of Action in the Sixties* (New York: Prentice-Hall, 1960), 234, 240; Scott, *American City Planning Since 1890,* 567–568; Mark I. Gelfand, *A Nation of Cities: The Federal Government and Urban America, 1933–1965* (New York: Oxford University Press, 1975), 319. Though rejected by Congress in 1961, the land-bank idea continued to have support. See National Commission on Urban Problems, *Building the American City* (Washington: USGPO, 1968), 251–253; Albert Mayer, "It's Not Just the Cities: Land as a Public Resource vs. Speculative Commodity," *Architectural Record* 147 (June 1970): 140–142; Charles Haar, "Wanted: Two Federal Levers for Urban Land Use – Land Banks and Urbank," in David Listokin, editor, *Land Use Controls: Present Problems and Future Reform* (New Brunswick, NJ: Center for Urban Policy Research, 1974), 365–379; Richard P. Fishman, "Public Land Banking: Examination of a Management Technique," in Randall W. Scott, editor, *Management and Control of Growth: Issues, Techniques, Problems, Trends* [Volume One] (Washington: Urban Land Institute, 1975), 61–85; Ann L. Strong, *Land Banking: European Reality, American Prospect* (Baltimore: Johns Hopkins University Press, 1979).
25. Strong, *Open Space for Urban America,* 75.
26. For statistics on programs and spending, see William K. Reilly, editor, *The Use of Land: A Citizens' Policy Guide to Urban Growth* (New York: Thomas Y. Crowell Company, 1973), 109; Davis, "Planning Our Open Space Land Resources for the Future," in Foss, *Recreation,* 354; George D. Butler, editor, *Recreation and Park Yearbook 1961* (New York: National Recreation and Park Association, 1961), 13, 15, 33, 36; Donald E. Hawkins,

The federal government also began to support open-space preservation. Though the land-bank proposal was killed, a pioneering program to aid city and county governments in acquiring open space was included in the Housing Act of 1961 despite opposition from fiscal conservatives in both parties. Federal aid for open-space acquisition increased significantly in the mid-1960s, when President Lyndon Johnson made a campaign for "natural beauty" a key part of the Great Society environmental agenda. Throughout the Kennedy and Johnson administrations, Secretary of the Interior Stewart Udall argued that his greatest task was "to hold open spaces against the sprawl of suburbia."[27]

By the early 1960s, the cluster-development idea also seemed to have considerable momentum. In 1960 the American Society of Planning Officials issued a report promoting cluster subdivisions. The administrator of the federal Housing and Home Finance Agency endorsed the idea, and the agency revised its minimum standards to allow open-space developments. Perhaps most important, the spokespeople for the nation's self-consciously progressive builders began to voice support for new subdivision layouts. The Urban Land Institute and the National Association of Home Builders encouraged cluster design in a number of publications, including a market study, and the trade press of the industry was soon filled with articles on the need for smarter, more sensitive land-use planning. The cluster concept also won laurels from commentators in a range of mass-circulation journals, from the *New York Times Magazine* to *Sports Illustrated*.[28]

editor, *Recreation and Park Yearbook 1966* (Washington: National Recreation and Park Association, 1967), 25, 27–28, 41–42, 48, 52, 57. For greenbelts, see Little and Mitchell, *Space for Survival*, 104–110.

27. The open-space provision of the Housing Act of 1961 is reprinted in Foss, *Recreation,* 333–335. For the Johnson administration, see Martin V. Melosi, "Lyndon Johnson and Environmental Policy," in Robert A. Divine, editor, *The Johnson Years: Vietnam, the Environment, and Science* (Lawrence: University Press of Kansas, 1987), 113–149; Lewis L. Gould, *Lady Bird Johnson and the Environment* (Lawrence: University Press of Kansas, 1988), 51–75, 199–221. Udall was quoted in Christian Science Monitor, *The Call of the Vanishing Wild* (Boston: Christian Science Publishing Society, 1967), 2. In addition, see U.S. Department of the Interior, *The Race for Inner Space.*

28. Jon Rosenthal, *Cluster Subdivisions* [Planning Advisory Service Information Report Number 135] (Chicago: American Society of Planning Officials, 1960); Federal Housing Administration, *Planned Unit Development with a Housing Association* (Washington: USGPO, 1963); Urban Land Institute and National Association of Home Builders, *New Approaches to Residential Land Development: A Study of Concepts and Innovations*

Despite a number of significant successes, however, the twofold strategy advocated by Whyte proved inadequate.

The acquisition effort was outpaced by development. As a number of officials acknowledged by the late 1960s, the taxpayers in most areas were not able or willing to provide the funds to ensure adequate open space. The cost of land kept rising at the metropolitan fringe, and the competition for public funds was keen, since many fast-growing suburbs also faced difficulties paying for such essential community facilities as sewers and schools. But the problem was not merely the rapidly rising cost of land: In many communities, local governments also faced the loss of existing parks and green spaces to public construction projects, especially interstate highways. Even when officials worked imaginatively to provide and preserve open space, the obstacles were often insurmountable. In 1974, for example, a study of the open-space issue in California concluded simply: "The impossibility of acquiring in fee the land area necessary for open space purposes has now become obvious."[29]

[Technical Bulletin 40] (Washington: Urban Land Institute, 1961) and *Innovations vs. Traditions in Community Development: A Comparative Study in Residential Land Use* [Technical Bulletin 47] (Washington: Urban Land Institute, 1963); Carl Norcross, *Open Space Communities in the Marketplace* (Washington: Urban Land Institute, 1966); "Better Land Use: From Research to Reality," *NAHB Journal of Homebuilding* 17 (July 1963): 45–76; "Land Use: A Progress Report," *NAHB Journal of Homebuilding* 18 (July 1964): 49–62; "Cluster Planning Is Good Business," *American Builder* 87 (May 1965): 65–68; "Land . . . Is Always Where You Find It," *Practical Builder* 27 (June 1962): 77–92; "Smart Land Planning," *Practical Builder* 31 (February 1966): 76–85; "The Changing Suburbs," *Architectural Forum* 114 (January 1961): 97–99; Tunnard and Pushkarev, *Man-Made America*, 55–156; White House Conference on Natural Beauty, *Beauty for America* (Washington: USGPO, 1965), 135–137, 439–467; Regional Plan Association, *The Race for Open Space*, 12; Tupper, *No Place to Play*, 182–199; Ada Louise Huxtable, "'Cluster' Instead of 'Slurbs,'" *New York Times Magazine* (February 9, 1964): 36–44; Robert H. Boyle, "America Down the Drain," *Sports Illustrated* 21 (November 16, 1964): 90.

29. For the quotation, see Edward Ellis Smith and Durward S. Riggs, editors, *Land Use, Open Space, and the Government Process: The San Francisco Bay Area Experience* (New York: Praeger, 1974), 143. On the financial obstacles to open-space acquisition, see also Davis, "Planning Our Open Space Land Resources for the Future," in Foss, *Recreation*, 354–355; Reilly, *The Use of Land*, 19–22. The journal *Recreation* regularly included reports on highway "encroachment" in the late 1950s and early 1960s, and the National Recreation Association made a major study of the subject. In 1961, the association's director submitted a summary of that study as part of his testimony on the open-space bill; see U.S. Senate, *Housing Legislation of 1961*, 1034–1036. In addition, see Outdoor Recreation Resources Review Commission, *Outdoor Recreation for America*, 152; Robert Rienow and Leona Train Rienow, *Moment in the Sun: A Report on the Deteriorating Quality of the American Environment* (New York: The Dial Press, 1967), 46; Huey D. Johnson, editor, *No Deposit – No Return: Man and His Environment: A View Toward Survival* (Reading, MA: Addison-Wesley, 1970), 197.

Despite the chorus of praise for the cluster concept in the early 1960s, the effort to transform the design of subdivisions failed even more obviously to live up to the hopes of open-space advocates. Cities and towns were often reluctant to change their zoning rules because of the fear that clustering would lead to undesirable densities and bring in undesirable residents. But even where developers were free to employ new site-planning concepts, the results were disappointing. Often the only "open spaces" were community facilities – pools, tennis courts, and landscaped clubhouses. As Whyte acknowledged, the site plan in most cluster developments was a "hack" job, usually done not by a landscape architect but by a surveyor or an engineer: The real purpose was to squeeze the maximum number of units out of the land. As a result, few cluster developers used the resources of terrain – hills, streams, woods, wetlands – to provide satisfactory green space. "What appeals most to them is the cluster, not the open space; the doughnut and not the hole," Whyte wrote in *The Last Landscape*. "Where they have been allowed to get away with it, some developers have compressed people to the point of claustrophobia, with mean little spaces labeled as commons largely given over to parking."[30]

Whyte still believed that the potential of clustering could be realized if public officials showed more care and imagination in reviewing site plans. By 1970, however, the momentum had shifted toward a far greater reliance on regulatory powers than Whyte thought wise. As the ecological point of view became more widespread, cities and counties turned increasingly to regulation to protect wetlands, streams, hillsides, and floodplains. More and more, both grassroots activists and government officials also saw the difficulty of acquiring open space as part of a larger problem – uncontrolled growth. The high cost of land was due partly to the speculation inherent in sprawl, while the competition for public funds was made more acute by the high cost of infrastructure in "spread city." Accordingly, cities and counties began to do more to try to control development and to force developers to pay a larger share of the public costs of growth.[31]

---

30. Whyte, *Cluster Development*, 14; *The Last Landscape*, 212. See also Little and Mitchell, *Space for Survival*, 48.
31. The literature on the rise of land-use and growth-control regulations is enormous. For

In part, then, the failure of Whyte's proposals was tied to a kind of paradigm shift. Whyte always believed that the strongest argument for open space was aesthetic. Even in 1968, when the science of ecology had begun to shape the thinking of millions of Americans, Whyte downplayed the conservationist and environmentalist arguments for open-space preservation. But Whyte underestimated the power of the idea that – in Barry Commoner's words – everything is connected. If the destruction of open space threatened the health of vital natural systems, then the issue no longer could be described in Whyte's terms. It was no longer a matter of how best to secure a benefit. Rather, it was a question of preventing a long-term disaster. According to a number of advocates, indeed, the preservation of open space was essential for "survival."[32]

But there was a more fundamental problem with Whyte's "conservative" approach. Though the loss of open space was a direct consequence of the ways postwar builders did business, Whyte was unwilling to challenge the basic premises of the industry. His argument for open-space acquisition did not touch the building industry at all: He simply called on citizens to act with foresight to promote the public good. Even his argument for cluster development was directed as much at public officials and homebuyers as builders. He urged cities and counties to give subdivision developers freedom from restrictive standards about lot size, minimum setbacks, and density in return for the inclusion of open space. He described for homebuyers the satisfactions of a cluster home. In both cases, he was more successful than not. But Whyte's pitch to builders – a dollars-and-cents appeal to self-interest – fell flat. Though Whyte demon-

a good summary of the trend toward land-use regulation, see Jon A. Kusler, *Regulating Sensitive Lands: A Guidebook* (Cambridge: Ballinger Publishing Company, 1980). For discussion of the problems posed by speculation, see Reilly, *The Use of Land,* 21, 111; Smith and Riggs, *Land Use, Open Space, and the Government Process,* 121–122; Mayer, "It's Not Just the Cities," 137–142; Leonard Downie, Jr., *Mortgage on America* (New York: Praeger, 1974), 81–134. For a wide-ranging collection of early writings on the growth-control issue, see Scott, *Management and Control of Growth* [Three Volumes].

32. For Whyte's continued defense of the aesthetic point of view, see *The Last Landscape,* 352–353. For arguments that the preservation of open space was a question of "survival," see Shomon, *Open Land for Urban America,* x; Little and Mitchell, *Space for Survival,* ix, 1–6. For Barry Commoner's argument that "everything is connected to everything else" is "the first law of ecology," see *The Closing Circle: Nature, Man, and Technology* (1971; reprint, New York: Bantam Books, 1972), 29–35.

strated that cluster developments could be profitable, a majority of builders evidently concluded that conventional site planning offered more profit with less trouble. No doubt, they were right. As the ecologist Aldo Leopold argued in a different context, "a system of conservation based solely on economic self-interest is hopelessly lopsided."[33]

By the early 1970s, therefore, even a number of Republican leaders were arguing in very unWhytian terms for a rethinking of "the rights and responsibilities that accompany property ownership." The new tenor of the debate is well illustrated by a 1973 report entitled *The Use of Land: A Citizens' Policy Guide to Urban Growth*. The work of a task force funded by the Rockefeller Brothers Fund, with a membership including Pete Wilson, then mayor of San Diego, and William Reilly, a conservationist later appointed by George Bush to head the Environmental Protection Agency, the report called for a new understanding of the proper uses of land. "It is time to change the view that land is little more than a commodity to be exploited and traded," the report declared. "We need a land ethic that regards land as a resource which, improperly used, can have the same ill-effects as the pollution of air and water, and which therefore warrants similar protection."[34]

Accordingly, the report argued at length for a dramatic expansion of public efforts to regulate private property. The argument rested on a matter-of-fact acknowledgment of the limitations of the profit motive as a tool of conservation: "Of course, in a market-based economic system, profitability and the public interest can and do diverge," the report noted. "Thus, it makes sense for governments to prevent conditions in which owners (or builders or lenders) have the opportunity to obtain greater profit by acting contrary to the public interest."[35]

To make sure that readers caught the implications of that point, the report also rejected outright the major legal and philosophical obstacles to regulation, especially the understanding of property rights embodied in the "takings" concept. If property owners were

33. Aldo Leopold, *A Sand County Almanac, and Sketches Here and There* (New York: Oxford University Press, 1949), 214.
34. Reilly, *The Use of Land*, 7.
35. Ibid., 222.

entitled to develop their lands in any way they saw fit, then they had to be compensated if regulation took away their right to profit from development. But that conclusion was based on a faulty understanding of the nature of land values. Traditionally, the report argued, Americans had believed that the value of land came from the "bottom up" – from the enterprise of the landowner. In truth, however, the value of land came from the "top down": It was created by society, which provided the context for economic development. Without the opportunities offered landowners by membership in a community, that is, a piece of property never could be worth more than the subsistence value of the land's harvest – it could never have a greater value as a site for subdivisions, factories, offices, or shopping centers. The members of society, therefore, had the right to define the obligations which all property owners must respect.[36]

Because the nation's courts had severely restricted regulation of private land use, the report devoted a chapter to the necessity of establishing new legal precedents. The report also called for a campaign to overcome the common view among property owners that restrictions on their right to develop land amounted to robbery. "Land whose development would be hazardous may be the place to begin," the report argued. "Surely it should be possible to develop a national consensus that profits from the residential development of a floodway are the moral equivalent of profits from selling tainted meat. Beyond this, though more slowly, it should be possible to develop an equivalent consensus with respect to land where development would damage valuable and irreplaceable resources or significantly interfere with natural processes." Eventually, then, the consensus would encompass a variety of lands, including "important open spaces."[37]

To be sure, the consensus envisioned by the authors of *The Use of Land* proved difficult to achieve. But the report makes clear how much had changed in a little over a decade, from the late 1950s to the early 1970s. At first, a majority of open-space advocates shared

36. Ibid., 16, 22.
37. Ibid., 124–125. In addition, see 145–175, which discuss the law and the "takings" concept.

Whyte's hope that the postwar pattern of development could be improved without reforming the process of homebuilding. But the experience of the 1960s failed to sustain that hope. Though Whyte's proposals won considerable support, the destruction of open space continued. As a result, the argument for regulation became more compelling.

Open Space and the Environmental Movement

The most direct legacy of the campaign to save open space was increased support for land-use regulation, but the effort also had a significant impact on the emerging environmental movement. The open-space issue pointed conservationists toward a broader, more "environmental" agenda. It created a new group of activists and a new set of grassroots organizations. Perhaps most important, the open-space issue contributed to the development of a distinctly environmentalist rhetoric and imagery.

Throughout the 1960s, the authors of environmentalist manifestos pointed to suburban sprawl as a critical problem. "Our cities have grown too fast to grow well, and today they are a focal point of the quiet crisis in conservation," Stewart Udall wrote in a 1963 call to arms. "We must act decisively – and soon – if we are to assert the people's right to clean air and water, to open space, to well-designed urban areas, to mental and physical health." Two years later, Raymond Dasmann blamed the postwar pattern of development for much of "the destruction of California."

Already we have filled the San Francisco Bay basin with housing, industry, airfields, and highways, from the tops of the hills to the edge of the water. The same thing has happened to Los Angeles. In the Central Valley, from the head in the sloughs leading to San Francisco Bay as far east as the Sierra foothills, one housing tract replaces another in a formless mass of suburbs that have been aptly termed 'slurbs.' If it could end at this it would be bad enough, but reparable. Instead, the process goes on. Housing and industry spread ever farther, engulfing farm and forest, marsh and pasture with no end in sight except the dismal one of a gigantic, disorganized megalopolis, filling much of the state and depending for its food on distant lands.

Similarly, Robert Rienow and Leona Train Rienow devoted a chapter to the problem of "space and sprawl" in *Moment in the Sun,* a best-selling 1967 work on "the deteriorating quality of the American environment." As the two explained, the monster of suburbia was an "insatiable land-eater," one of the great devourers of our most precious resource.[38]

For Lyndon Johnson, the first postwar president to make environmental issues a top priority, the loss of open space to suburban development was one of the principal justifications for a new federal role in protecting the environment. The structure of Johnson's 1965 address on conservation and restoration of natural beauty made that clear. In a list of modern forces which threatened the nation's natural heritage, Johnson put urbanization first. "Cities themselves reach out into the countryside, destroying streams and trees and meadows as they go," he explained. Then Johnson cited the damage done by pollution, the "darker side" of modern technology. "To deal with these new problems will require a new conservation," Johnson argued. "We must not only protect the countryside and save it from destruction, we must restore what has been destroyed and salvage the beauty and charm of our cities."[39]

Almost from the first, then, the loss of open space was a hot issue. It bothered many people deeply, and it became one of the most important arguments for a new kind of activism. As one writer argued in 1964, "conservation is no longer a distant, rural concern that can be left to the conservationists. During the postwar years it has sneaked up and come viciously to roost as a pressing suburban problem." The issue also had a kind of generative power. The more people thought about the destruction of open space, the higher the stakes seemed. Again and again, in different ways, the issue drew public attention to other environmental problems.[40]

By the early 1960s, a number of experts had concluded that the effort to preserve open space for recreational use forced a reckon-

38. Stewart L. Udall, *The Quiet Crisis* (New York: Holt, Rinehart and Winston, 1963), 159–160, 172; Dasmann, *The Destruction of California,* 19; Rienow and Rienow, *Moment in the Sun,* 45.
39. The message is reprinted in Foss, *Recreation,* 661–673; the quotations are on 661.
40. The quotation is from James Nathan Miller, "To Save the Landscape," *National Civic Review* 53 (1964): 355. For a similar argument, see Christian Science Monitor, *The Call of the Vanishing Wild,* 13.

ing with the problem of water pollution. "Although few surveys have been made of waters available for recreation," a technical report to the Outdoor Recreation Resources Review Commission argued in 1962, "widespread evidence indicates that water pollution is diminishing the number of recreation waters." Untreated sewage and industrial wastes often made rivers and lakes unsuitable for boating and swimming. By killing fish and waterfowl, pollution also destroyed opportunities for sport fishing and hunting. Even the banks of rivers could be ruined for recreation by noxious odors and unsightly scums. Accordingly, the commission's final report argued, recreational needs should be "a motivating purpose" in the fight for "pollution control." By 1964, the commission's argument had persuaded a cabinet-level committee of federal officials.[41]

For Lyndon Johnson, too, the threat to open space was a major justification for antipollution legislation. Johnson pointed to the health hazards of pollution, but he often put beauty first when justifying programs to clean up the nation's waters – and for Johnson beauty was tied to the outdoor recreation issue. Johnson made the point succinctly in a 1966 message about pollution in which he called for recognition of a number of new rights and duties, including "the right of easy access to places of beauty and tranquillity where every family can find recreation and refreshment – and the duty to preserve such places clean and unspoiled."[42]

The open-space issue also intensified concern about population growth. The threat of global overpopulation had become a part of conservationist discourse in 1948, with the publication of Fairfield Osborn's *Our Plundered Planet* and William Vogt's *Road to Survival*, but the public did not pay much attention until the late 1960s and early 1970s. In 1948, Americans had no near-at-hand image of uncontrolled population growth. The problem was most obvious

---

41. U.S. Geological Survey, *Water for Recreation – Values and Opportunities: Report to the Outdoor Recreation Resources Review Commission* [ORRRC Study Report 10] (Washington: USGPO, 1962), 14–18; Outdoor Recreation Resources Review Commission, *Outdoor Recreation for America*, 176; Recreation Advisory Council, *Policy Governing the Water Pollution and Public Health Aspects of Outdoor Recreation* [Circular Number 3] (Washington: USGPO, 1964), reprinted in Foss, *Recreation*, 504–506. In addition, see Tupper, *No Place to Play*, 85–126; Regional Plan Association, *The Race for Open Space*, 15. Hays, *Beauty, Health, and Permanence*, 53, notes this connection in passing.
42. The message to Congress is reprinted in Foss, *Recreation*, 517–519; the quotation is on 519.

abroad – in Asia, Africa, and South America. But by 1968, when Paul Ehrlich's *The Population Bomb* became a sensational bestseller, the danger no longer seemed so distant. Though Ehrlich followed Osborn and Vogt in dramatizing the explosion of people in distant lands – he began with a nightmarish description of the crowds on a "stinking hot night" in Delhi, India – Americans had begun to feel the pressure of population growth directly: The sprawling metropolis seemed to threaten much that the nation held dear.[43]

Well before Ehrlich popularized the bomb metaphor, analysts of metropolitan growth were writing with concern about "the population explosion." The open-space literature was full of references to the psychological costs of population growth. In 1959, for example, the author of a booklet on *The Crisis in Open Land* began by quoting from a report by the Twentieth Century Fund: "Being crowded is, indeed, the almost universal experience of today's citizen. . . . The highways are packed, recreation places are saturated, the open landscape is increasingly devoured." Yet people needed open space, especially in a world rapidly becoming more populated. "That crowded feeling – that growing sensation of suffocation – could easily become more and more painful until we reach the point where we can no longer deal with its social consequences," the author concluded. "That would mean a breakdown of our social structure."[44]

The geographer Edward Higbee wrote even more pointedly about population growth in a 1960 book on cities and space, *The Squeeze*. "A better organization of space for residence, for pleasure, and for business is absolutely imperative if the rising tides of population are not to make a complete shambles of the metropolitan habitat,"

43. The population classics are Fairfield Osborn, *Our Plundered Planet* (Boston: Little, Brown and Company, 1948); William Vogt, *Road to Survival* (New York: William Sloane Associates, 1948); Paul R. Ehrlich, *The Population Bomb* (New York: Ballantine Books, 1968). The best short discussion of the population issue is Fox, *The American Conservation Movement*, 306–313. In addition, see Hays, *Beauty, Health, and Permanence*, 210–216; Victor B. Scheffer, *The Shaping of Environmentalism in America* (Seattle: University of Washington Press, 1991), 100–109; Otis L. Graham, Jr., *Toward a Planned Society: From Roosevelt to Nixon* (New York: Oxford University Press, 1976), 149–159. But none of these authors considers the role of suburban sprawl in dramatizing the issue.

44. For the problems caused by "the population explosion," see Charles M. Haar, "Foreword," *Iowa Law Review* 50 (1965): 243; John E. Cribbet, "Changing Concepts in the Law of Land Use," *Iowa Law Review* 50 (1965): 246; Mumford, *The Urban Prospect*, 4. The quotations come from Tucker, *The Crisis in Open Land*, 5.

Higbee wrote in the introduction. "Within the next hundred years the United States will breed a population that will surpass that in China today. How will our children fare during the years of transition as the horde increases?" If the nation did not act decisively to change the pattern of metropolitan development, "it will not be long before there is standing room only in the cluttered heart of Metropolis." The foreword to the book – by Fairfield Osborn – made the same point.[45]

In a 1972 report on population and the American future, a presidential commission also highlighted the issue of urban and suburban development. "Population growth *is* metropolitan growth in the contemporary United States," the commission wrote, and the problem was especially acute because the growth of the metropolis loomed larger than the demographic statistics indicated: "The territory of metropolitan America has expanded even faster than its population." "During the rapid expansion of suburban areas since World War II," the commission concluded, "we failed to plan for anticipated growth; instead, we allowed it to spread at will. Whether or not we are past a population explosion, it is clear that the land-use explosion of 'spread city' is currently in full bloom. In the 1970's and 1980's, the baby-boom generation will marry, have children, and set up house in the suburbs, creating a tremendous demand for the conversion of rural land to urban use. Without proper efforts to plan where and how future urban growth should occur, and without strong governmental leadership to implement the plans, the problems of sprawl, congestion, inadequate open space, and environmental deterioration will grow on an ever-increasing scale."[46]

In addition to heightening concern about water pollution and population growth, the open-space issue led a number of conservationists to reconsider their mission. The professionals in conservation agencies had always focused on the fate of forests and farms, and

45. Higbee, *The Squeeze*, xii–xiii. The chapter on "space and sprawl" in *Moment in the Sun* also made the connection to population growth. See Rienow and Rienow, 43–53. In addition, see U.S. Department of the Interior, *The Race for Inner Space*, 5, 18, 69.
46. Commission on Population Growth and the American Future, *Population and the American Future* (New York: Signet, 1972), 25, 33, 35. In addition, see Anthony Bailey, *Through the Great City: Impressions of Megalopolis* (New York: Macmillan, 1967), 101–114.

the amateur activists in the old-line conservation organizations traditionally were most concerned about the preservation of wilderness. By the late 1950s, however, the explosive spread of the suburbs had begun to draw attention to the conservation problems of the metropolis.

One of the first signs of change came in a 1958 volume entitled *Perspectives on Conservation,* which included a section on "urban growth and natural resources." The main contribution to that section argued that the postwar pattern of settlement greatly intensified the pressures on the nation's vital resources. It filled valuable open space, destroyed prime agricultural lands, added to flood hazards, spread the problems of air and water pollution, increased the use of energy for transportation, and threatened water shortages. Accordingly, conservationists needed to think in new ways.[47]

The new thinking did not come easily. In 1961, the Sierra Club invited the housing reformer and urban planner Catherine Bauer Wurster to speak at the club's biennial wilderness conference, and Wurster began by acknowledging the peculiarity of the invitation. She too loved the outdoors, she said, but she had spent her life working on the problems of the city. What could she say to a group of wilderness lovers? But she believed that she needed to offer advice "from the camp of the enemy aggressor." Though urban planners and wilderness conservationists rarely joined hands in common cause, she argued, the two groups in fact faced a common enemy, "the urban octopus, spreading its tentacles farther and farther out into natural areas for all kinds of purposes." Wurster urged the audience to support the open-space legislation in Congress. But the club did not heed her plea.[48]

47. Jarrett, *Perspectives on Conservation,* 115–154. The major contribution to the section on urban growth was Gulick, "The City's Challenge to Resource Use," 115–137; the section also included three short responses to Gulick's essay. In addition, see "Urban Growth and Natural Resources," *American Forests* 64 (June 1958): 24–25. By 1965, the conservationist Wallace Stegner was arguing that the effort to preserve open space ultimately had to lead to a profound concern for "the total environment" – and, indeed, to

an environmental ethic that will reach all the way from the preservation of untouched wilderness to the beautification of industrial cities, that will concern itself with saving the still-savable and healing the half-ruined and cleansing the polluted, that will touch not only land but air and water, that will have as its purpose the creation of a better environment for men, as well as the creation or preservation of viable habitats for the species that our expansion threatens.

See "What Ever Happened to the Great Outdoors?," 38.
48. Wurster, "The Urban Octopus," 117–122.

During the congressional deliberations about the open-space provisions of the Housing Act of 1961, only four conservation organizations submitted evidence. The sole conservation official to appear at the Senate hearing was Spencer Smith of the Citizens Committee on Natural Resources, a coalition of conservation groups which had formed during the fight to save Dinosaur National Monument. Smith's testimony was significant. He began by apologizing for the absence of testimony from other conservation groups – the hearing conflicted with a National Watershed Conference – and assuring the senators that almost all the national conservation organizations were "very much in favor" of the effort to preserve open space. Smith then attacked head-on the traditional view of the scope of conservation. Though people generally assumed that conservation concerned the wise use of agricultural and public lands, Smith testified, that was wrong: "Actually conservation is of supreme importance within the cities too." To support that point, Smith offered all three major arguments for open-space preservation. Open space was a key to providing adequate opportunities for recreation and to meeting the need for the sort of refreshment that natural beauty provided. Open space also was vital as a tool in dealing with the problems of water supply and water management, since open space was a check against soil erosion and flooding.[49]

The National Audubon Society provided the best evidence that Smith truly spoke for the major conservation organizations. The society's president in the late 1950s, John Baker, was a leader of a task force which campaigned successfully for a major open-space-acquisition program in the New York metropolitan area. Baker's successor, Carl Buchheister, endorsed that campaign in one of his monthly reports to the membership in *Audubon Magazine*. His assistant also submitted a brief in favor of the open-space provisions of the Housing Act of 1961. "As the Nation's oldest citizen's organization concerned with the conservation of nature and wildlife," the brief explained, "we have been increasingly concerned with the

---

49. U.S. Senate, *Housing Legislation of 1961*, 1013–1018. For the quotation, see 1015. Smith submitted a similar statement to the House subcommittee which considered the issue: See U.S. House of Representatives, *The Housing Act of 1961*, 869–870. The other conservation organizations which submitted written testimony were the National Wildlife Foundation, the Wildlife Management Institute, and the National Audubon Society. For the Citizens Committee on Natural Resources, see Nash, *Wilderness and the American Mind*, 212.

importance – indeed, the dire necessity – of adequate planning and timely action to preserve open spaces and natural beauty in urban and suburban areas."[50]

For the Audubon Society, the open-space issue was a bridge between old and new missions in the early 1960s. As president, Buchheister wanted to take a more activist role on a wider range of issues, and the campaign to preserve open space was a way to move in that direction without breaking fundamentally with the traditions of the organization. The society had long maintained wildlife sanctuaries around the country and was just beginning to establish nature centers to educate children and adults. Since both activities involved preservation of land, the jump to open-space activism was easy. The land for the society's most celebrated nature center, Aullwood, was a gift from a woman concerned about the loss of open space around Dayton, Ohio, in the decade after World War II. But the open-space issue pointed Audubon members in new directions, too, since the arguments for urban green space ultimately drew on new ecological principles. According to a 1971 Audubon guidebook, *Open Land for Urban America,* Americans needed to see the city as a complex organism. The guide therefore included a long chapter on the function of open space in maintaining the carbon and hydrological cycles, reducing the effects of water and air pollution, and moderating the extremes of urban climate.[51]

In addition to nudging a few old-line conservation organizations in new directions, the open-space issue inspired the kind of grassroots activism that became the heart of the environmental movement after 1970. In the 1950s and 1960s, Americans formed countless organizations to preserve patches of green in fast-growing cities and suburbs. Californians created People for Open Space. New Yorkers

50. The brief is in U.S. House of Representatives, *The Housing Act of 1961,* 863. See also Carl W. Buchheister, "The President Reports to You," *Audubon Magazine* 62 (1960): 278–279; John H. Baker, "How Can Natural Areas Be Saved?," *Audubon Magazine* 61 (1959): 105. Baker was one of six members of the steering committee of the Parks, Recreation, and Open Space project sponsored jointly by the Regional Plan Association and the Metropolitan Regional Council. The project culminated in the publication of four influential reports in 1960 – *The Law of Open Space, Nature in the Metropolis, The Dynamics of Park Demand,* and *The Race for Open Space.*
51. For the refashioning of Audubon's mission, see Fox, *The American Conservation Movement,* 266. For a brief description of Aullwood, see Frank Graham, Jr., *The Audubon Ark: A History of the National Audubon Society* (New York: Alfred A. Knopf, 1990), 205–209. The guidebook chapter is Shomon, *Open Land for Urban America,* 21–40.

established the Open Space Action Institute, and citizens in St. Louis organized the Open Space Council. The threat of development also prompted ad hoc activism. "In every city and in thousands of towns and obscure neighborhoods," the *Saturday Evening Post* reported in 1966, "there are housewives and homeowners banding together to fight, block by block, sometimes tree by tree, to save a small hill, a tiny brook, a stand of maples."[52]

To encourage open-space preservation, activists wrote dozens of guides to community organizing. A short guide published in 1964 began with the story of one woman's successful campaign to preserve a marsh from development. "The war Ruth Rusch has been waging in her little corner of suburbia contains immense significance for all of us," the author wrote. "For it shows not only that we can win the fight to save our landscape from the despoilers, but also specifically how to go about it."[53]

In some cases, neighbors formed nonprofit organizations to acquire parcels of undeveloped land. Though the groups typically had staid names, the members often approached their task with a kind of militancy. "A suburban open space does not have to be glamorous or unique to be worth saving," argued a member of the Sudbury Valley Trustees, a Massachusetts open-space organization established in the 1950s. "Any unspoiled natural area in any suburb is threatened today and will be spoiled tomorrow unless someone starts fighting for it right now."[54]

52. For the three organizations, see Smith and Riggs, *Land Use, Open Space, and the Government Process*, 137; Degnan, "Santa Clara," 244–245; Shomon, *Open Land for Urban America*, 59; Open Space Action Committee, *Stewardship*. The quotation is from Bagdikian, "The Rape of the Land," 26.
53. For a sample of the organizing guides, see Hubbard, *This Land of Ours;* William Hard, "Save a Spot of Beauty for America," *Reader's Digest* 76 (January 1960): 148–153; Charles E. Little, *Challenge of the Land* (1968; reprint, New York: Pergamon Press, 1969); Rutherford H. Platt, *Open Land in Urban Illinois: Roles of the Citizen Advocate* (DeKalb: Northern Illinois University Press, 1971); Little and Mitchell, *Space for Survival;* Reilly, *The Use of Land;* Ruth Adams, *Say No!: The New Pioneers' Guide to Action to Save Our Environment* (Emmaus, PA: Rodale Press, 1971), vii–xi, 142–163. The quotation is from Miller, "To Save the Landscape," 355; Miller's article was reprinted in *Reader's Digest* 85 (August 1964): 161–169. In one of the first scholarly studies of environmental activism, three political scientists also gave considerable attention to open-space preservation: See Lynton K. Caldwell, Lynton R. Hayes, and Isabel M. MacWhirter, *Citizens and the Environment: Case Studies in Popular Action* (Bloomington: Indiana University Press, 1976).
54. Barbara B. Paine, "Challenge to Suburbia," *Nature Magazine* 51 (October 1958): 431.

In other cases, people organized to persuade local officials to act. The campaign to save the Holmes Run woods in Fairfax, Virginia, was typical. To protest against a proposal to turn the tract into housing, a group of 12-year-olds brought a petition to school: "Us boys would like to save our woods." When the principal refused to let the boys pass the petition around, the boys went door-to-door in their neighborhood. The neighborhood recreation association then began to lobby for public acquisition of part of the woods. "I got cauliflower ear from being on the phone," one activist explained. "Morning, noon and night we talked, talked, talked."[55]

A few opponents of sprawl even engaged in the sort of deliberate vandalism that novelist Edward Abbey eventually termed "monkey wrenching." In 1959, a small band of Arizonans began to attack development along one of the roads from Flagstaff to the Grand Canyon. (The youngest member of the group was a 12-year-old boy who later became a well-known Earth First! monkey wrencher.) In the next five years, the group destroyed more than 500 billboards. Their favorite targets were advertisements for a subdivision – Fort Valley – built in a floodplain: The tract of ranchettes epitomized everything the group abhorred.[56]

Well before 1970, therefore, the destruction of open space had led many middle-class Americans to reassess the costs and benefits of economic growth. The millions of new homes in the suburbs were signs of progress, the most striking evidence of the blessings brought by the postwar boom, and yet, as William Whyte warned in 1957, "much more of this kind of progress and we shall have the paradox of prosperity lowering our real standard of living." By the early 1960s, advocates of open-space preservation often set the word

55. Bagdikian, "The Rape of the Land," 26–29, 86.
56. Susan Zakin, *Coyotes and Town Dogs: Earth First! and the Environmental Movement* (1993; reprint, New York: Penguin, 1995), 41–45. In 1971, the Tucson Eco-Raiders continued the tradition of antisprawl monkey wrenching. "We bear a grudge against developers who go in and flatten out everything," one explained. "In general, if we see a nice area of the desert being destroyed, we'll do something about it." Like the Grand Canyon defenders a decade earlier, the Eco-Raiders cut down billboards. But the group of college-age boys went much farther. As Zakin explains, they "pulled up survey stakes from housing sites, poured lead in the locks of developer's offices, ripped out electrical and plumbing fixtures in unsold houses, broke windows, sabotaged bulldozers," and trashed everything that symbolized urban sprawl. See 59. Edward Abbey's *The Monkey Wrench Gang* (Philadelphia: Lippincott, 1975) was the first popular celebration of eco-sabotage.

"progress" in quotation marks to express their intensifying doubts. For many activists, the doubts about the postwar pattern of development eventually led to anger, often expressed in a recognizably environmentalist rhetoric of destruction, murder, and despoliation. "If this 'progress' were true progress," one wrote in 1964, "no one would have cause for complaint. But, in fact, 'progress' has come to stand for stupidity, greed, graft, malice, and moral debasement. We have imperiled the charms of our cities; now the countryside is being laid waste."[57]

Occasionally, the rhetoric of open-space advocacy was even more intimate. In the Senate hearing on the open-space provision of the Housing Act of 1961, the executive director of the American Society of Landscape Architects tentatively spoke of the destruction of the countryside as a "rape." By the mid-1960s, the word had become common in public debate about the fate of open space, as articles and book chapters decried "the rape of the land" and "the rape of the countryside."[58]

The new emotional tone is especially evident in a passage from Margo Tupper's *No Place to Play*. Like millions of Americans, Tupper moved with her family to the suburbs after World War II:

> At that time our house was second from the last on a dead-end street. Beyond were acres of untouched woodlands which were a refuge for children – a place to play in natural surroundings. Youngsters in the neighborhood would go there, build dams or catch minnows in a little creek, gather wildflowers and pick blossoms from the white dogwoods. They built tree houses, picnicked under the tall tulip trees, and dug jack-in-the-pulpits, wild fern and violets to transplant to their gardens. . . .
>
> Then one day my little girl, Jan, ran into the house shouting, "Mother, there's a bulldozer up the street. The men say they're going to cut down the trees. They can't do that. They're my trees! Where will we play? Please, mother, please stop them." Jan ran frantically out the door, shouting, "I'll

57. The quotations are from Whyte, *The Exploding Metropolis*, 133; Boyle, "America Down the Drain," 80. In addition, see Gulick, "The City's Challenge in Resource Use," 127; Grady Clay, "'Fighting the Rise': Consider the Hillsides and their Needs," *Landscape Architecture* 50 (Winter 1959–1960): 75; Shomon, *Open Land for Urban America*, ix; Udall, *The Quiet Crisis*, 160.

58. U.S. Senate, *Housing Legislation of 1961*, 606; Bagdikian, "The Rape of the Land," 25–29, 86–94; Tupper, *No Place to Play*, 17–37; Whyte, "A Plan to Save Vanishing U.S. Countryside," 90; Jesse J. Dukeminier, Jr., "Legal Control of Landscape: The Bluegrass," *Landscape Architecture* 50 (1959): 13.

get Susan, Georgie, Sissy and all the other children. If they're going to take our woods away we'll have to save all we can." The children returned several hours later pulling wagons loaded with flowers and plants. Jan brought home a small dogwood tree and planted it among the wildflowers in the south garden. . . .

Indeed the bulldozers did come! These huge earth-eating machines raped the woods, filled up the creek, buried the wildflowers and frightened away the rabbits and the birds. The power saws came too and took part in the murder of the woodlands near our home. Dynamite blasted out the huge tree roots; trucks roared past our house carrying the remains, sections of murdered trees and tons of earth in which were buried vines, shrubs, and flowers. Then the dozers came to level the earth and power shovels to dig great holes. In less than a month the first of two hundred look-alike, closely-set small houses rose to take the place of our beautiful forest.

The outraged language of Tupper owed much to the rhetoric of earlier preservation campaigns – for John Muir, to cite a famous example, the proponents of the Hetch Hetchy dam were "temple destroyers" – but the charge of rape also pointed in a new direction. The ravagers were not far away, building a massive structure in a valley of sacred beauty – they were next door, doing everyday work, and they threatened the well-being of families at home.[59]

As Tupper's account suggests, the destruction of open space also provided a powerful new symbol of technology run amuck. "To the right-thinking suburbanite," the landscape critic J. B. Jackson wrote in 1966, "the bulldozer is the very embodiment of ruthless destruction." Jackson did not share that view, but he clearly was in the minority among commentators on the new metropolitan landscape. By the mid-1960s, the literature on suburbia was full of attacks on "the age of the bulldozer," "the bulldozer blitz," and "the bulldozer mentality." To a number of observers, the bulldozed landscape brought to mind the desolation of a battlefield. Again and again, the critics tallied the losses. "The bulldozerite . . . tears down in one swoop what nature has caused to grow over the ages," a dismayed architect wrote in 1964. "Trees and bushes, meadows and

---

59. Tupper, *No Place to Play*, 18–19; the chapter in which the story appears is entitled "The Rape of the Land." In her introduction, Tupper cites Muir's attack on the "temple destroyers." See 12.

flowers, brooks and rivers are torn out or leveled, and the operation is admired as a triumph of technology."[60]

Often, the attacks on the bulldozer were supported by stark aerial photographs of the construction of subdivisions. In one famous
series of photographs, reproduced in Peter Blake's 1964 polemic
God's Own Junkyard, the first image was simply a vast expanse
of dirt crisscrossed by bulldozer tracks, with no topographical features, no vegetation – indeed, no visible life of any kind. The image of bulldozers tearing down hills appeared repeatedly in the work
of open-space activists. The moral was clear: The bulldozer was a
tool of arrogance, a symbol of the nation's devastating disregard
for nature.[61]

By the late 1960s, therefore, the effort to preserve open space and
the environmental movement had become intertwined in complex
ways. The emergence of a popular ecological consciousness strengthened the conservation argument for open space. At the same time,
the campaign for open space increased the range of support for the
environmentalist cause. Indeed, the image of the bulldozer in the
countryside became a shorthand for one of the basic dichotomies
in environmentalist argument, a dichotomy now almost a cliché –
the opposition of prodevelopment and proenvironment.

At first, few people defined the open-space issue in such oppo-
sitional terms. In the late 1950s, the can-do optimism of William

60. For the long quotations, see J. B. Jackson, "The New American Countryside: An Engi-
neered Environment," in Ervin H. Zube and Margaret J. Zube, editors, *Changing Rural
Landscapes* (Amherst: University of Massachusetts Press, 1977), 33; Victor Gruen, *The
Heart of Our Cities: The Urban Crisis: Diagnosis and Cure* (New York: Simon and
Schuster, 1964), 102–103. The quoted phrases come from Russell Lord, *The Care of the
Earth: A History of Husbandry* (New York: Thomas Nelson & Sons, 1962), 343, 347;
Degnan, "Santa Clara," 242, 245; F. Fraser Darling and John P. Milton, editors, *Future
Environments of North America: Transformation of a Continent* (Garden City, NY:
Natural History Press, 1966), 318, 329. For criticism of the bulldozer and the bulldozed
landscape, see also Gulick, "The City's Challenge to Resource Use," 127; John Keats,
The Crack in the Picture Window (Boston: Houghton Mifflin, 1956), xiv, 108; Owen,
Cities in the Motor Age, 5, 20; William O. Douglas, *A Wilderness Bill of Rights* (Boston:
Little, Brown and Company, 1965), 3, 10, 37; Rienow and Rienow, *Moment in the Sun,*
221; U.S. Department of Agriculture and U.S. Department of Housing and Urban Development, *Soil, Water, and Suburbia* (Washington: USGPO, 1968), 50.
61. For polemical photographs of bulldozers at work, see Peter Blake, *God's Own Junkyard:
The Planned Deterioration of America's Landscape* (New York: Holt, Rinehart and
Winston, 1964), 76–77, 106–107; Whyte, "A Plan to Save Vanishing U.S. Countryside,"
88; Gruen, *The Heart of Our Cities,* 102–103; Tucker, *The Crisis in Open Land,* front
cover.

Whyte was still common. Though Whyte often argued that the time for action was short, he never suggested that the issue called into question any fundamental aspect of American society. Instead, he argued that the nation could save enough open space if good people would just get to it. But the problem proved to be more intractable than Whyte expected. When the campaigns for open-space acquisition and cluster development did not work, many open-space advocates began to think more broadly and deeply about the roots of the problem. For some, the rethinking led to a call for a redefinition of the rights and responsibilities of property ownership. For others, the result was a new sense of the environmental irresponsibility of American culture.

Figures 1–4. In 1950, William Garnett took a series of aerial photographs of the construction of Lakewood, a California suburb, and four of Garnett's images soon became iconic. At first, the photographs were symbols of the skill of American business in meeting the demand for affordable housing. By the mid-1960s, however, the four images instead symbolized the environmental devastation wrought by suburban development. Credit: William Garnett. Reprinted by permission.

TIME

THE WEEKLY NEWSMAGAZINE

HOUSE BUILDER LEVITT
For sale: a new way of life.

Figure 5. On July 3, 1950, *Time* celebrated a postwar hero, homebuilder William Levitt. *Time* was not alone. For decades, business leaders and public officials had worried about the inability of the building industry to meet the demand for low-cost shelter, and the use of new mass-production techniques in Levittown won acclaim throughout the nation. Because tract housing satisfied so many economic, social, and political needs, the environmental critics of the new way of building always faced formidable obstacles. Credit: Copyright 1950 Time Inc. Reprinted by permission.

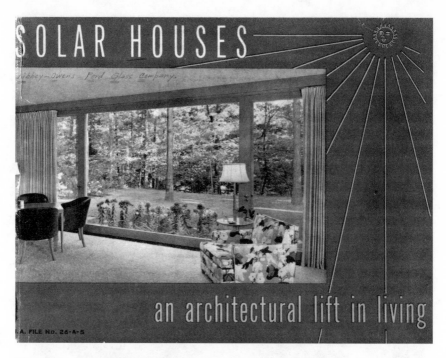

Figure 6. During World War II, a number of architects, architectural critics, and journalists began to promote solar homes. The need to conserve fuel in wartime prompted much of the interest in energy-saving design. But the advocates of solar architecture also promised homeowners a new closeness to nature, as the cover of this 1945 pamphlet suggests. Credit: Used by permission of Libbey-Owens-Ford Company, copyright 1945.

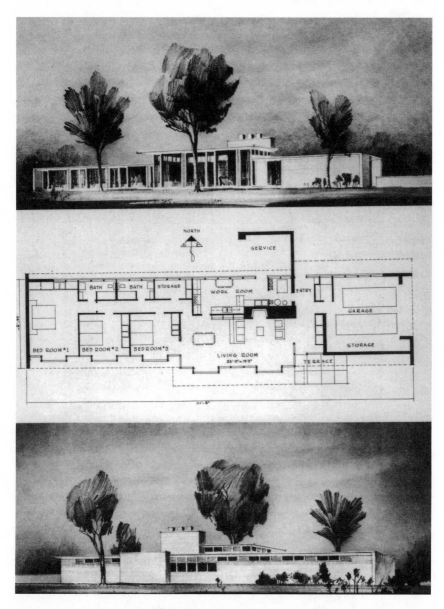

Figure 7. In the 1940s, George Fred Keck was a leading proponent of solar architecture. This plan is his contribution to *Your Solar House* (New York: Simon and Schuster, 1947). The book was sponsored by the Libbey-Owens-Ford Glass Company and featured a solar house for every state in the union. Credit: Used by permission of Libbey-Owens-Ford Company, copyright 1947.

Figure 8. In the late 1950s, the residents of many septic-tank subdivisions were shocked to find foam coming out of their kitchen faucets. The foam came from laundry detergents, which had leached from septic tanks into drinking wells. The concern about the health effects of "white beer" and "detergent cocktails" helped to make the problem of water pollution a national issue. This photograph of a glass of water in suburban Suffolk County, New York, was used as an illustration in one of the first popular books about the threat of water pollution: Donald E. Carr's *Death of the Sweet Waters* (New York: W. W. Norton, 1966). Credit: Wide World Photos.

Figure 9. To many critics of tract-house construction, the bulldozing of trees was especially appalling. Even homebuilders sometimes viewed the treeless tracts with dismay. The contrast in this photograph between the old and the new landscape led a homebuilder outside Washington, D.C., to urge members of the industry to reconsider "the economics of trees," and the trade publication *House and Home* used the photograph in April 1953 to illustrate the builder's argument. But the wholesale destruction of trees continued. Credit: *House and Home.*

Figure 10. The loss of "open space" to suburban development led to both grassroots protest and official action. In 1962, seven-year-old Scott Turner sent a plea for help to President John Kennedy, and the boy's handwritten letter soon became a symbol of the growing concern that fewer and fewer Americans would grow up with any appreciation for nature. The letter was reproduced in several books about the threat to open space. This illustration appeared in a booklet published by the U.S. Department of the Interior: *The Race for Inner Space* (Washington: U.S. Government Printing Office, 1964). Credit: U.S. Department of Interior.

Figure 11. In California, especially, the growth of suburbia often came at the expense of farms and orchards, and the bulldozing of prime agricultural lands became a subject of public concern. In addition to the loss of a vital productive resource, the critics argued, the nation also risked the loss of a deep-rooted source of cultural values. This drawing illustrated a story in the March 8, 1965, issue of *The Nation* about "the bulldozer crop." Credit: *The Nation*.

SECOND IN A SERIES ON THE AMERICAN ENVIRONMENT

THE RAPE OF THE LAND

As our cities spread out cancerously in all directions, we are destroying—for profit—too many of the green and open places we need to make life livable.

Figure 12. In the 1960s, open-space activists began to use a recognizably environmentalist rhetoric. The image of the bulldozer in the countryside became a powerful symbol of the environmental irresponsibility of American culture. The idea that development was a form of rape also became common in the 1960s. This photograph strikingly illustrated a featured story in the June 18, 1966, issue of the *Saturday Evening Post*. Credit: I. C. Rapoport. Reprinted by permission.

Figure 13. By 1960, a variety of Americans had begun to argue that homebuilders should not build on wetlands, steep hillsides, and flood-plains. The critics of hillside development often illustrated their arguments with aerial photographs of "mountain cropping" – the use of earthmoving equipment to create flat building sites on steep slopes. This photograph of the construction of Trousdale Estates in Beverly Hills, California, appeared in an *Architectural Forum* essay on "Bulldozer Architecture" in August 1960 and in Peter Blake's *God's Own Junk-yard: The Planned Deterioration of America's Landscape* (New York: Holt, Rinehart and Winston, 1964). Credit: Spence Air Photos, UCLA Department of Geography Air Photo Archives.

SEPTEMBER 1968
Vol. 33, No. 2

soil
conservation
DEVOTED TO THE WISE USE OF LAND AND WATER RESOURCES

Soil
water
and
suburbia

SOIL CONSERVATION SERVICE   U. S. DEPARTMENT OF AGRICULTURE

Figure 14. The Soil Conservation Service was one of three federal natural-resource agencies to take a keen interest in the environmental problems of suburban development in the 1950s and 1960s. In 1967, the agency played a leading role in a conference on "Soil, Water, and Suburbia" co-sponsored by the Department of Agriculture and the Department of Housing and Urban Development. The agency's journal devoted a special issue to the subject of the conference in 1968. Credit: Soil Conservation Service.

Figure 15. This photograph of soil erosion at a subdivision site in suburban Maryland illustrates the urbanization of the conservation movement – the recognition in the 1950s and 1960s that a range of problems once identified only with forests and farms also plagued the nation's metropolitan areas. The photograph was reproduced in Spenser W. Havlick, *The Urban Organism: The City's Natural Resources from an Environmental Perspective* (New York: Macmillan, 1974). Credit: U.S. Department of Housing and Urban Development.

"I'll tell you what else in there deserves to be protected: $744,000 of mine!"

Figure 16. In the early 1970s, a variety of reformers sought to expand the scope of government regulation of land use, and their efforts to institutionalize an "urban land ethic" led to heated debate about the rights of private property owners. This cartoon by William Hamilton appeared in a landmark report sponsored by the Rockefeller Brothers Fund: *The Use of Land: A Citizens' Policy Guide to Urban Growth* (New York: Thomas Y. Crowell, 1973). Though the cartoon gave voice to the sentiments of aggrieved landowners, *The Use of Land* offered a forceful argument in favor of land-use regulation. Credit: Reprinted by permission of the Rockefeller Brothers Fund.

Figures 17 and 18. To reduce the environmental costs of metropolitan growth, the federal Council on Environmental Quality in the early 1970s became a forceful advocate for national land-use legislation. These photographs of the outskirts of Philadelphia were published in the Council's fifth annual report in 1974. Together, the two photographs made vivid the explosive growth of suburbia after World War II. Both were taken in the 1950s. Credit: Aero Service, Philadelphia, Pennsylvania.

Figure 19. The questions first raised by critics of tract-house development in the 1950s and 1960s continue to be issues of public debate. For cartoonist Tom Toles, the environmental costs of suburban sprawl are a pressing concern. In this 1993 cartoon, Toles drew on the powerful image of the bulldozer in the countryside. Credit: Toles Copyright 1993 The Buffalo News. Reprinted with permission of universal press syndicate. All rights reserved.

5

Where Not to Build:
The Campaigns to Protect Wetlands,
Hillsides, and Floodplains

"The great issue in planning is not where to build," planner S. B. Zisman wrote in 1965, "but where not to build."[1]

With that dictum, Zisman summarized a dramatic change in the planning profession. For decades, the principal task of urban planners was to decide where to allow residential, commercial, and industrial development. What areas should be restricted in use, and what areas should be open to all forms of building? On planning and zoning maps, a different color represented each type of land use, while open space – as yet unzoned and undeveloped – was typically white. But the explosive growth of suburbia after World War II changed the way planners thought about the white spaces on city maps. Year after year, as cities consumed more land, people began to appreciate the value of open space. "The chief lesson to be learned," Zisman argued, "is that open space is a functional land use – open space is not the left-over land, or the vacant land, the unused land or the waste land. It is of an equal order of consideration with any kind of development." That meant that planners now needed to ask a new question. What sites were more valuable as open space than as subdivisions, shopping centers, or factories?[2]

1. S. B. Zisman, "Open Spaces in Urban Growth," in Southwestern Legal Foundation, *Proceedings of the 1964 Institute on Planning and Zoning* (New York: Matthew Bender and Company, 1965), 115.
2. For the quotation, see S. B. Zisman, "Urban Open Space," in James B. Trefethen, editor, *Transactions of the Thirty-First North American Wildlife and Natural Resources Conference* (Washington: Wildlife Management Institute, 1966), 430. In addition, see Zisman, "Open Spaces in Urban Growth," 115–128; S. B. Zisman, Delbert B. Ward, and Catherine H. Powell, *Where Not To Build: A Guide for Open Space Planning* [Technical Bulletin 1] (Washington: U.S. Bureau of Land Management, 1968). Zisman's "Open Spaces in Urban Growth" also appeared in the *AIA Journal* 44 (December 1965): 49–54.

The answers were not obvious. The more people thought about the where-not-to-build question, the longer the list of valuable open spaces became. Yet three kinds of places stood out. In the decades after World War II, developers built to an unprecedented extent on wetlands, steep slopes, and floodplains, and in time the construction of tract housing on all three kinds of land became controversial.[3]

The arguments against wetland, hillside, and floodplain development came from people in a variety of fields, including geography, ecology, civil engineering, geology, hydrology, and landscape architecture. Their critiques had much in common. In each case, the argument against development depended on a new understanding of the costs of disregarding natural processes. If we continued to build insensitively, the critics argued, we would lose a number of gifts of nature, from clear streams to valuable wildlife habitat; we also would increase the likelihood of losses from "natural" disasters, especially floods and landslides. We needed instead to "design with nature."[4]

The Value of Wetlands

"Many good building sites are going unnoticed because developers and builders see them only as swamps, tidal marshes or low land along lakes or rivers," *House and Home* wrote in 1958. "Some of these are in areas close to town that have been passed over while higher land all around has skyrocketed in price. Yet the marshy land can sometimes be bought and filled in for much less than the cost of the surrounding land." In the next six pages, the magazine illustrated the opportunities open to smart builders. In Florida, a new Venice was under construction in a mangrove swamp; on Long Island, 106 fine houses were rising on 44 newly filled acres; in

3. For a sense of the variety of places considered worthy of protection, see Charles Thurow, William Toner, and Duncan Erley, *Performance Controls for Sensitive Lands: A Practical Guide for Local Administrators* [American Society of Planning Officials Planning Advisory Service Reports 307 and 308] (Chicago: American Society of Planning Officials, 1975); Jon A. Kusler, *Regulating Sensitive Lands: A Guidebook* (Cambridge: Ballinger Publishing Company, 1980).
4. The injunction to "design with nature" comes from Ian L. McHarg, *Design with Nature* (1969; reprint, Garden City, NY: Doubleday, 1971).

Connecticut, a builder had shown how to transform a small tract of water into profitable building lots; in Ohio, a beautiful subdivision was replacing marshland along Lake Erie; and in New Jersey, a marsh was becoming a summer home resort. As the editors argued in a second article, "millions of premium homesites can be reclaimed from under water with today's new and more durable dredges – more land than even the Dutch have empoldered with all their dikes."[5]

Even as the trade press pointed out the opportunities, however, a diverse effort to preserve wetlands was beginning to take form. The popularity of hunting, the recognition of the role of wetlands in controlling floods, the desire to enjoy wild places, and the scientific study of wetland productivity – all led to a new appreciation of marshes, swamps, and bogs. The preservation effort never focused solely on urban and suburban development. Indeed, the greatest threat to wetlands throughout the postwar period was drainage for agricultural purposes. But the new appreciation of wetlands contributed to the evolving environmental critique of the building industry.[6]

The first groups of people to express concern about the destruction of wetlands were sport hunters, birders, and fish-and-game officials. "If we permit too much habitat to be destroyed," the president of the Wildlife Management Institute told members of the National Audubon Society in 1959, "waterfowl are doomed to become curiosities that may be seen by occasional enthusiastic or very fortunate bird watchers." The concern was not new. The first alarms about the destruction of waterfowl habitat had sounded around the turn of the century, and both federal and state officials had already

5. The first quotation is the opening to "Need Land? Then Take a Look at Marshland," *House and Home* 13 (April 1958): 146–152. For the second quotation, see "Most of the Land Shortage Talk You Hear Is Nonsense: Here Are Seven Big Reasons Why," *House and Home* 18 (August 1960): 106. In addition, see "With Today's Machines, You Can Reclaim Marshland and Even Create Land Where There Was None Before," *House and Home* 18 (August 1960): 164b–164c.
6. Throughout this section, I draw on Joseph V. Siry, *Marshes of the Ocean Shore: Development of an Environmental Ethic* (College Station: Texas A & M University Press, 1984); Ann Vileisis, *Discovering the Unknown Landscape: A History of America's Wetlands* (Washington: Island Press, 1997). Samuel P. Hays has a short but insightful analysis of the changing view of wetlands. See *Beauty, Health, and Permanence: Environmental Politics in the United States, 1955–1985* (New York: Cambridge University Press, 1987), 148–151.

created numerous wildlife refuges around the country. But the threat seemed more pressing in the years after World War II. On the one hand, the number of sport hunters was increasing rapidly – doubling, by some counts, just since the 1930s. On the other hand, the loss of habitat was accelerating. Together, the two trends portended a crisis.[7]

The U.S. Fish and Wildlife Service was especially vigorous in drawing attention to the problem. In 1954, the agency conducted a nationwide survey of wetlands, and the study identified a handful of new threats to waterfowl habitat. In addition to agricultural drainage and flood-control projects, the expansion of cities had also destroyed great numbers of marshes, swamps, and bogs. The use of wetlands for housing developments, airports, and industrial waste dumps all had increased tremendously. In publications and speeches, the Fish and Wildlife staff urged a redoubled effort to limit the losses. The agency's summary of the wetlands inventory put the point plainly: "Never before in the Nation's history has it been so necessary to plan for the setting aside of land and water areas to serve the future needs of fish and wildlife, as well as to provide for the recreational needs of people who depend on these resources."[8]

In the late 1950s, a number of open-space planners, scientists, and public officials began to argue that wetlands played a vital role in the metropolitan hydrological system. Wetlands often recharged underground aquifers. Perhaps more important, wetlands helped to limit the destructiveness of floods. In a 1960 study of the value of open space, for example, botanist William Niering defended

7. The quotation is from Ira N. Gabrielson, "The Future of North American Waterfowl," *Audubon* 62 (1960): 15. For the increasing loss of waterfowl habitat and the growing number of sport hunters, see also J. Clark Salyer II, "Gains and Losses in the Waterfowl Game," in James B. Trefethen, editor, *Transactions of the Twenty-First North American Wildlife Conference* (Washington: Wildlife Management Institute, 1956), 100, 111. In addition, see Ludlow Griscom, "The Future of Our Waterfowl," *Audubon* 56 (1954): 64–65, 82–83; Harold Titus, "Conservation: Wetlands Campaign," *Field and Stream* 60 (December 1955): 112. For the history of concern about game birds, see Phillip O. Foss, *Recreation* (New York: Chelsea House, 1971), 16–91.

8. For the quotation, see Samuel P. Shaw and C. Gordon Fredine, *Wetlands of the United States: Their Extent and Their Value to Waterfowl and Other Wildlife* [Circular 39] (Washington: U.S. Fish and Wildlife Service, 1956), 9. A year later, two New York conservation officials paraphrased the passage in a plea for wetlands preservation. See Dirck Benson and Don Foley, "Wetlands, Water and Wildlife," *The New York State Conservationist* 12 (August-September 1957): 17. For the threat to wetlands from housing construction, see also Salyer, "Gains and Losses in the Waterfowl Game," 101.

wetlands as "the basic component in a natural system of flood control." With just a 6-inch rise in level, a 10-acre marsh could store 1,500,000 gallons of water. In a heavy rainstorm, therefore, a wetland acted as a reservoir protecting cities and suburbs downstream. Yet a wetland required no money to construct and very little to maintain. To demonstrate the practical benefits of wetland preservation, Niering told a story about the devastating floods of 1955: In eastern Pennsylvania, the torrents washed out hundreds of bridges, but two bridges survived, and both were just downstream of the Cranberry Bog preserve. By 1960, a number of communities had used the flood-control argument to justify acquisition of marshes.[9]

At first, the argument about the hydrological value of wetlands was rudimentary, relying on a kind of common sense. But a number of scientific studies in the 1960s and 1970s corroborated the insight, at least in part, and eventually the nation's flood-control experts acknowledged the functional value of wetlands preservation. In the early 1970s, the Army Corps of Engineers decided to buy 8,500 acres of wetlands instead of building a reservoir or a system of dikes to control flooding outside of Boston. "Nature has already provided the least cost solution to future flooding in the form of

9. The first quotation comes from William A. Niering, *Nature in the Metropolis: Conservation in the Tri-State New York Metropolitan Area* (New York: Regional Plan Association, 1960), 7. In addition, see 40, 57. For the story about the 1955 flood, see *The Life of the Marsh: The North American Wetlands* (New York: McGraw-Hill, 1966), 190. In addition, see Paul B. Sears, "Natural and Cultural Aspects of Floods," *Science* 125 (1957): 807; Peter Farb, "Let's Plan the Damage," *National Municipal Review* 49 (1960): 240; Barbara B. Paine, "Challenge to Suburbia," *Nature Magazine* 51 (1958): 430. Fish-and-game officials sometimes mentioned the functional value of wetlands. See Shaw and Fredine, *Wetlands of the United States,* 1; Benson and Foley, "Wetlands, Water and Wildlife," 16. By the mid-1960s, the hydrological role of wetlands was also a basic tenet of open-space planning. See Lawrence Levine, "Land Conservation in Metropolitan Areas," *Journal of the American Institute of Planners* 30 (1964): 204–216; Christopher Tunnard and Boris Pushkarev, *Man-Made America: Chaos or Control?* (New Haven: Yale University Press, 1963), 370. For the flood-control argument as a justification for wetlands acquisition by local governments, see Shirley Adelson Siegel, *The Law of Open Space: Legal Aspects of Acquiring or Otherwise Preserving Open Space in the Tri-State New York Metropolitan Region* (New York: Regional Plan Association, 1960), 26. The hydrological role of wetlands also justified the first state preservation law. See Office of Technology Assessment, *Wetlands: Their Use and Regulation* (Washington: Office of Technology Assessment, 1984), 39, note 2. The authors of two works on wetlands note that the flood-control argument became common in the late 1950s and early 1960s. See Phillip E. Greeson, John R. Clark, and Judith E. Clark, editors, *Wetland Functions and Values: The State of Our Understanding* (Minneapolis: American Water Resources Association, 1979), v; Ralph W. Tiner, Jr., *Wetlands of the United States: Current Status and Recent Trends* (Washington: USGPO, 1984), 1.

extensive wetlands which moderate extreme highs and lows in stream flow," the Corps explained. "Rather than attempt to improve on this natural protection mechanism, it is both prudent and economical to leave the hydrologic regime established over the millennia undisturbed."[10]

The new appreciation of wetlands in the 1950s was also tied to the rise of a new aesthetic. For decades, outdoor enthusiasts had prized the sublime, but few people thought that marshes, swamps, and bogs possessed breathtaking grandeur. Even in 1932, for example, a prominent conservationist dismissed the Florida Everglades as a place with "mighty little that was of special interest, and absolutely nothing that was picturesque or beautiful." The Everglades "were not as ugly or repulsive as some other swamps I have seen," he acknowledged, but "a swamp is a swamp." As roads crisscrossed more and more of the country, however, wetlands became more attractive: Because they were hard to develop, they often offered the increasingly valuable satisfactions of wilderness.[11]

The first prominent sign of a new way of seeing marshes came in a celebrated essay by Aldo Leopold – "Marshland Elegy" – first published in 1937 in *American Forests* and then reprinted in 1949 in the conservation classic *A Sand County Almanac*. "A dawn wind stirs on the great marsh," Leopold began. "With almost imperceptible slowness it rolls a bank of fog across the wide morass. Like the white ghost of a glacier the mists advance, riding over phalanxes of tamarack, sliding across bogmeadows heavy with dew. A single silence hangs from horizon to horizon." Describing the first stirrings of the marsh, Leopold focused on the approach of a great for-

10. For the quotation, see Anne Whiston Spirn, *The Granite Garden: Urban Nature and Human Design* (New York: Basic Books, 1984), 154–155. The Corps purchase is also described in detail by Frank Notardonato and Arthur F. Doyle, "Corps Takes New Approach to Flood Control," *Civil Engineering* 49 (June 1979): 65–68. For a similar discussion of "natural storage" of floodwaters, see Richard L. Phillips, "Solving Flooding and Drainage Problems," *Agricultural Engineering* 51 (December 1970): 701. For scientific studies of the role of wetlands in reducing the severity of floods, see Virginia Carter, M. S. Bedinger, Richard P. Novitzki, and W. O. Wilen, "Water Resources and Wetlands," in Greeson, Clark, and Clark, *Wetland Functions and Values*, 348–349; Office of Technology Assessment, *Wetlands*, 43–46; Tiner, *Wetlands of the United States*, 21–23.

11. The quotation comes from Alfred Runte, *National Parks: The American Experience* [2d edition] (Lincoln: University of Nebraska Press, 1987), 131. The movement to create a federal system of wilderness areas became formidable in the 1950s and early 1960s. See Roderick Nash, *Wilderness and the American Mind* [3d edition] (New Haven: Yale University Press, 1982), 200–237.

mation of cranes, first flying "on motionless wings," then settling "in clangorous descending spirals to their feeding grounds." For Leopold, the quality of the scene went beyond mere beauty to "values as yet uncaptured by language." The cranes in the marsh were symbols "of our untameable past, of that incredible sweep of millennia which underlies and conditions the affairs of birds and men." Thus, the marsh offered a rare encounter with a humbling form of natural history. In the wildness of the marsh, Leopold suggested, we can feel a fundamental truth: We are as much a part of the evolutionary world of nature as the cranes.[12]

In 1957, a former colleague of Leopold's, Paul Errington, sounded similar themes in a book titled *Of Men and Marshes*. Like Leopold, Errington deplored the drainage of marshes to create cropland. He also argued that the conservation efforts of hunters and fur traders were too limited: Marshes were not valuable only as habitat for duck and muskrat. Instead, Americans needed to appreciate "how interesting and beautiful marshes are as marshes." To suggest the possibilities, Errington described in loving detail the seasons of the prairie marshes he knew best. But the soul of the book was a meditation on the value of marshes as forms of wilderness. "They have their own life-rich genuineness," Errington wrote, "and reflect forces that are much older, much more permanent, and much mightier than man." Indeed, like more celebrated forms of wilderness, marshes offered a kind of peace of mind, a chance to escape for a time from the futilities and conceits of human civilization. "The lessons as well as the beauties of marshes await the perceptive," Errington concluded, "as do the lessons and beauties of the skies, of the seas, of the mountains, and of the other places remaining where man can still reflect upon lessons and beauties that are not of human making."[13]

12. Aldo Leopold, *A Sand County Almanac, and Sketches Here and There* (New York: Oxford University Press, 1949), 95–101. For the publication history of the essay, see Curt Meine, *Aldo Leopold: His Life and Work* (Madison: University of Wisconsin Press, 1988), 330, 377, 459.
13. Paul L. Errington, *Of Men and Marshes* (New York: Macmillan, 1957), viii, 116, 150. Errington mentions on 113 that he was a friend of Leopold's. According to Leopold's biographer, Leopold was also a mentor and collaborator. See Meine, *Aldo Leopold*, 274–275. For another example of writing about marshes in the late 1950s, see Dudley Cammett Lunt, *Thousand Acre Marsh: A Span of Remembrance* (New York: Macmillan, 1959).

Though both Leopold and Errington were scientists, they wrote as defenders of wildness, and their words spoke for a growing number of people around the country. In 1965, for example, conservationist William O. Douglas devoted a section of *A Wilderness Bill of Rights* to wetlands. From Massachusetts to California, people fought to save bogs, marshes, and swamps as small remnants of a wilder world.[14]

The science of ecology also changed popular perceptions of wetlands. In the late 1950s, a pioneer in the field, Eugene Odum, began to study the flow of energy in the tidal marshes off the Georgia coast. Like a number of earlier studies of smaller natural systems, the Odum project on Sapelo Island gave special attention to the efficiency of microorganisms, plants, and animals in turning the sun's energy into living matter. The results suggested, in Odum's words, that the tidal marsh ecosystem was one of "the most naturally fertile areas of the world." The estuary was a hundred times more productive than the deep ocean, and ten times more productive than a typical grassland, forest, or wheat field. How was that possible? First, the mixing of waters in the estuary created a "nutrient trap." Second, the estuary produced a variety of basic sources of food for organisms – marsh grasses, mud algae, and phytoplankton. Third, the production was year-round, not just the harvest of a season or two. Thus, the estuary could support a vast array of life. Like a complex civilization, the estuary benefited from a kind of trade, with nutrients and organisms going back and forth across a wide area. In the transport process, the marshes were key. "By analogy," Odum wrote in 1961, "we could think of the marshes, and probably also the mud and sand flats, as the great 'wheat fields' which feed the teeming 'cities' of fish and other organisms living in the creeks and sounds."[15]

The research received considerable publicity in both scientific and

14. William O. Douglas, *A Wilderness Bill of Rights* (Boston: Little, Brown and Company, 1965), 144–146; Office of Technology Assessment, *Wetlands*, 39.
15. The most succinct summary of the Georgia studies is Eugene P. Odum, "The Role of Tidal Marshes in Estuarine Production," *The Conservationist* 15 (June-July 1961): 12–15, 35. For the quotations, see 12 and 14. For the development of the science of ecology, see Donald Worster, *Nature's Economy: A History of Ecological Ideas* [2d edition] (New York: Cambridge University Press, 1994), 291–315; Joel B. Hagen, *An Entangled Bank: The Origins of Ecosystem Ecology* (New Brunswick, NJ: Rutgers University Press, 1992).

nonscientific circles. Already renowned as the author of the leading textbook on ecology, Odum used the Sapelo Island study as a heuristic device. He was a great advocate of the ecosystem as a conceptual and managerial tool, and he often described the workings of estuaries to illustrate the importance of understanding complex systems as functional wholes. "Because of the importance of tidal action in nutrient cycling and production," he argued, "the entire estuarine system, including marshes, flats, creeks, and bays, must be considered as *one* ecosystem or productive unit." That last phrase was important. Odum believed that the science of ecology should guide human efforts to exploit natural resources, including estuaries. The agricultural model was no guide to the best use of a complex ecosystem. If people used farming methods to increase the harvest of a few estuarine crops, Odum predicted, the result would be a destructive cycle of boom and bust. But if people took the insights of ecosystem ecology into account, the estuary could provide a rich and enduring variety of products.[16]

To many people, however, the productivity of the coastal marsh was most important as a kind of metaphor. The new ecological understanding directly countered the oldest image of wetlands – the swamp as wasteland. In a time when Americans were obsessed with the growth of gross national product, the very word "productivity" also conveyed a powerful message. The marsh was efficient, amazingly productive, abundant – in other words, the marsh was a miniature of the United States. It already was a highly evolved community, and so it did not need to be "developed." Instead, the marsh should be admired and applauded.

The defenders of marshes again and again described the ecosystem's extraordinary abundance. "One reason for protecting our wetlands lies in their biological *productivity*," William Niering wrote in a 1966 work in the World Book series "Our Living World of Nature." Three years later, John and Mildred Teal devoted a chapter to "Marsh Production" in *Life and Death of the Salt Marsh,* a classic joining of natural history and ecological science. The productivity of marshes also figured in almost every magazine article

16. "The Role of Tidal Marshes in Estuarine Production," 12, 15, 35. For the role of Odum in the development of the field, see Worster, *Nature's Economy,* 362–371; Hagen, *An Entangled Bank,* 122–145.

on wetlands in the late 1960s and early 1970s. "The shallow edge of the sea where salt water mingles with fresh, commonly called the estuarine zone, is the most productive acreage known to man," a 1968 *Life* editorial proclaimed. In *Atlantic Monthly, Reader's Digest,* and *National Geographic,* the findings of marine ecologists and biologists were discussed at length. For a number of marsh advocates, indeed, the authority of science provided a key rhetorical support. "Technology has taught us to conquer," one told the *National Geographic,* "and many marshes have lain undisturbed only because man at first couldn't modify them. Now wetlands are prime areas of development – for housing, recreation, industry. Scientists say, for nature's sake – and for man's sake – don't blacktop it all. The scales must tip in favor of conservation and restoration."[17]

Though the new ways of thinking about wetlands were evident across the country, the effort to preserve marshes, swamps, and bogs was strongest in a handful of places. The coastal wetlands attracted far more attention than the inland prairie potholes. Because estuaries provided most of the nation's fish and shellfish harvests, the coastal wetlands had obvious economic value. The complexity of estuarine systems attracted ecological researchers. The coastal wetlands also were closest to the great centers of population, where the demands for outdoor recreation were most intense. The first state to pass a wetlands-preservation law was Massachusetts. In California, the filling-in of San Francisco Bay provoked protests. But the connection between local and national activism was strongest in New York.[18]

The 1954 Fish and Wildlife Service survey of wetland losses sug-

17. For the quotations, see Niering, *The Life of the Marsh,* 165; "Editorial: Endangered Edge of the Sea," *Life* 65 (July 19, 1968): 4; Stephen W. Hitchcock, "Can We Save Our Salt Marshes," *National Geographic* 141 (1972): 762. In addition, see Alfred Perlmutter, "Our Changing Shoreline," *The New York State Conservationist* 14 (October–November 1959): 12–15; Polly Redford, "Vanishing Tidelands," *Atlantic Monthly* 219 (June 1967): 76–77; John and Mildred Teal, *Life and Death of the Salt Marsh* (1969; reprint, New York: Ballantine Books, 1971), 179–196; Adrian Hope, "Cradle of Life," *Life* 72 (March 17, 1972): 67. The Redford article was reprinted in *Reader's Digest* 91 (September 1967): 134–137.

18. For brief descriptions of the wetlands preservation campaigns in California and Massachusetts, see Siry, *Marshes of the Ocean Shore,* 164–167, 171–172. In addition, see Harold Gilliam, *Between the Devil and the Deep Blue Bay: The Struggle to Save San Francisco Bay* (San Francisco: Chronicle Books, 1969); League of Women Voters Education Fund, *The Big Water Fight: Trials and Triumphs in Citizen Action on Problems of Supply, Pollution, Flooding, and Planning across the U.S.A.* (Brattleboro, VT: Stephen Greene Press, 1966), 174–177.

gested that the urban northeast might soon have almost no habitat for waterfowl. The danger seemed particularly acute in Long Island, where residential and commercial development were proceeding at a rapid pace. Because the Long Island wetlands were the heart of one of the principal migratory pathways for duck and geese, the federal government had a stake in the region: The United States was bound by two international treaties to protect the Atlantic flyway. In 1957, therefore, the Fish and Wildlife Service joined with the New York State Conservation Department to campaign for preservation of the Long Island wetlands. The campaign soon won the support of conservation groups and hunting and fishing clubs. In 1959, the legislature passed a law to enable the state to help towns and counties preserve wetlands.[19]

But the destruction continued at a relentless pace. In 1959, a resurvey of the island showed the loss of one-eighth of the wetlands of highest value to waterfowl. The construction of houses accounted for the largest share of the loss – 35 percent. Five years later, a third survey offered even more shocking evidence of the vulnerability of the region's marshes. In just 10 years, almost one-third of Long Island's wetlands had been drained or filled to provide land for houses, recreational facilities, marinas, airports, industrial plants, roads, parking lots, and dumps.[20]

The 1964 survey stunned legislators into action. The most valuable wetlands in Long Island were owned by a few towns, and a number of New York representatives decided that the town governments could not be trusted to protect what remained. Accordingly, the representatives introduced legislation in Congress to enable the federal government to create a 16,000-acre wetlands reserve in Long Island. Not long afterward, Representative John Dingell of Michigan introduced a bill to allow the Department of the Interior to acquire a nationwide system of wetlands refuges. In 1966, the House subcommittee on fisheries and wildlife conservation held hearings on the bills, and the hearings became a national forum on the value of wetlands.[21]

19. John E. Harney, "Wetlands Preservation on Long Island," *The Conservationist* 15 (February–March 1961): 13–14.
20. For the 1959 survey, see Harney, "Wetlands Preservation on Long Island," 13. The 1964 survey is summarized in Teal and Teal, *Life and Death of the Salt Marsh*, 242.
21. The Long Island bill was introduced separately by nine representatives. For the provisions of the legislation, see U.S. House of Representatives, *Estuarine and Wetlands Legislation:*

The testimony brought together all the major arguments for preservation. Though only two speakers noted the value of wetlands as protection against the fury of storms, the witnesses spoke again and again about the harvest of the coastal fisheries, the growing popularity of hunting, the role of Long Island in the Atlantic flyway, the importance of saving a few "unspoiled" places of natural beauty, and the lessons of ecology. Some offered statistics about the fish and shellfish catch, and others cited the number of hunting licenses issued in Long Island every year. A few people described the splendor of the marshes at dawn. In a variety of ways, the testimony also introduced the work of the ecosystem ecologists. One speaker quoted Eugene Odum's textbook, while another summarized the results of the Sapelo Island study. A New York representative introduced a booklet prepared by the Nassau County Museum of Natural History entitled "The Super Farm – The Wetlands." A few witnesses even described in detail the mechanisms of marsh productivity. "Nature's incredible efficiency and ingenuity in maintaining the maximum possible 'bio-mass' on each unit of the earth's surface reaches its ultimate heights in the estuarine ecosystem," one concluded. "Of course she had some two or three billion years to perfect the 'factory' and fashion each of its living cogs so they mesh perfectly. However, it is still an awesome achievement."[22]

The ecological argument had broad appeal. Indeed, a number of Long Island residents and public officials cited the salt marshes as examples of "the lesson of ecology." Everything was connected: "Once we disturb one link in the chain of life," the chairman of the Nassau County Planning Commission testified, "we endanger it all." The hearings also made clear that scientific evidence could be used to support appreciation of the wilderness qualities of salt marshes. In one passage from the Museum of Natural History booklet, the ecology of Odum joined the philosophy of Leopold and Errington:

Hearings on H. R. 11236, H. R. 11245, H. R. 11305, H. R. 11307, H. R. 11309, H. R. 11417, H. R. 13296, H. R. 15676, H. R. 15770, and H. R. 13447 before the Subcommittee on Fisheries and Wildlife Conservation of the Committee on Merchant Marine and Fisheries, 89th Congress, 2nd session, 1966, 1–3, 11–12.

22. For a sampling of the arguments, see U.S. House of Representatives, *Estuarine and Wetlands Legislation,* 21, 65, 90, 124–125, 127, 174, 176, 233, 243–244, 247–248, 268, 274–276, 296–297. The Dingell bill singled out for protection areas "relatively unspoiled or undisturbed by the technological advance of man." See 11. The quotation about the productivity of estuaries is on 276.

"Perhaps one reason man often sees the salt marsh as useless land is that he sees no human activity in the marsh – no houses, no parks, no roads – only the occasional hunter. The marsh needs no human help. It plants, harvests, and fertilizes itself. Man is an extra and so far he has been able to do little but destroy. It is hard for man to realize he is unnecessary and unwanted. Perhaps the psychological message of the salt marsh is as important as the biological. It says man is not the center of nature."[23]

Though Congress did not pass a wetlands-preservation law until 1968, the hearings drew national attention to the issue. The testimony also dramatized the role of homebuilders in the loss of tidal marshes. On Long Island, as witness after witness pointed out, the principal threat to wetlands was residential development. Throughout the 1950s, one conservationist testified, builders "seeking new lands to develop looked on the salt marshes on the upland side of Long Island as a cheap supply of marginal land – with a convenient and very low cost source of fill right next door by simply dredging up the bay bottom and pumping this material onto the marshes." The Long Island suburbs were not unique. From New Jersey to California, wetlands were fast falling victim to urban sprawl.[24]

The hearings did not consider long-term solutions to the problem of wetlands loss, but a New York representative voiced the conclusion of a growing number of people across the country. "No reasonable man would argue that we do not need new homes, new industry to accommodate our population," he said, "but neither would he deny that we must plan the growth and plan it wisely to protect the natural resources of the Nation as we grow. We must plan so that the communities we build may be livable, that we will be left with water to drink, air to breathe, fish and fowl to eat." Ten years later, at least 15 states and 1,000 local governments had passed regulations to protect wetlands.[25]

23. For the first quotation, see U.S. House of Representatives, *Estuarine and Wetlands Legislation*, 127. In addition, see 73, 268, 296. The second quotation is on 125.
24. The hearings figured prominently in the first major piece about wetlands in a national publication. See Redford, "Vanishing Tidelands," 76–77. For the quotation, see U.S. House of Representatives, *Estuarine and Wetlands Legislation*, 233–234. In addition, see 16, 21, 73, 78, 127, 162, 176, 243–246, 274, 296.
25. For the quotation, see U.S. House of Representatives, *Estuarine and Wetlands Legislation*, 76. The statistics about wetlands regulation are from Kusler, *Regulating Sensitive Lands*, 32.

The Hazards of Hillside Development

"With level land near cities getting scarce and costly," *House and Home* reported in 1953, "many builders are taking to the hills. Big islands of rolling land left high and dry in the first waves of expansion are getting a second look for development. New earth-moving equipment and techniques are making hill building possible as never before."[26]

To hit pay dirt on steep slopes, the magazine suggested, builders could borrow a host of proven ideas from architect-designed homes. The split-level offered countless possibilities. But builders could also adapt the traditional two-story house for hillside projects. The basement could be built into the slope to create a nice playroom. The lower floor could have a carport with a deck or enclosed porch on top. Thus, the hillside house could provide more space at little extra cost.[27]

The bulldozer also allowed ranch-house builders to exploit hilly ground. In 1951, the Kenbo Corporation bought 182 acres of the Coyote Hills in Monterey Park, California, for a 625-house project. The tract cost $2,000 less per acre than flat land, so the builder could still make a fine profit despite extra costs for site preparation. With a fleet of 26 earth-moving machines, Kenbo completely reshaped the rolling contours to create wide terraces. In all, the company moved more than a million cubic yards of dirt. Since the new lots were flat, Kenbo could use standard "flatland" designs for the houses, which sold for $13,500 to $17,500. The steplike terraces of the development still allowed homebuyers to enjoy "the view, breeze, and added privacy of hillside lots."[28]

To a number of observers, however, the bulldozing of hillsides was abominable. "Mountain cropping," the critics called the practice. Indeed, the critics vied to come up with memorable phrases to decry the "bulldozer blight." In a book on "man's prodigal meddling

---

26. "How to Hit Pay Dirt on a Hillside," *House and Home* 4 (December 1953): 91. In addition, see "Most of the Land Shortage Talk You Hear Is Nonsense," 106.
27. "How to Hit Pay Dirt on a Hillside," 92–97, 110–115. In addition, see "Nine Hillside Houses," *House and Home* 1 (April 1952): 82–107; "What's Happening in Split Levels," *House and Home* 5 (April 1954): 124; "20 Ways to Find Land," *House and Home* 8 (August 1955): 116.
28. "How to Hit Pay Dirt on a Hillside," 106–109.

with his environment," the California nature writer Richard Lillard ridiculed builders who bragged about the gargantuan task of turning "goatland" into "Mt. Olympus." "The lords of subdivision, replanners of the earth's surface, rationalize their doings as 'improvements of appearance,'" Lillard wrote. But the result was a desecration, "part of a tasteless trend that violates inherent charm and natural beauty and makes much of the 'Southland' not worth living in."[29]

The associate editor of *Landscape Architecture*, Grady Clay, agreed. The machine-made plateaus were ugly, and the ugliness was especially appalling because the hills surrounding a city established "the visual character" of the community. "You slice the hills open," Clay argued in 1959, "and the scars show for miles and miles. You turn them into dumps, and the visual stench reaches into the next county. Let them erode, and silt and mud pollute the waters of towns in the next state downstream. Hillside damage is community damage; a slipping slope may undermine a whole neighborhood. And visual pollution encourages everyone within sight – which might include a million or so people – to go and do likewise."[30]

As the mention of silt and mud in the *Landscape Architecture* editorial suggested, the critics of hillside development also pointed to environmental costs. The bulldozed slope was highly vulnerable to erosion – the steep grade and the lack of natural vegetation increased the destructive force of water – and erosion caused a

29. For a relatively temperate discussion of "mountain cropping," see Reyner Banham, *Los Angeles: The Architecture of Four Ecologies* (1971; reprint, London: Penguin, 1973), 106–109. Banham borrowed the phrase from William Bronson, *How to Kill a Golden State* (Garden City, NY: Doubleday & Company, 1968), 135–137. The "battle over steep landscapes" was the theme of a special issue of *Landscape Architecture* – volume 50 (Winter 1959–1960) – which included seven stories on the subject. For the critique of "bulldozer blight," see especially Tracy H. Abell, "'View Lots' Replace Natural Mountain Landscapes," 94; Ruth Jaffe, "Following the Trail of the 'Cat,'" 90. Though a number of architects wrote about the potential artfulness of "landshaping," the commentary in the architectural journals also warned about the devastation that the new machines often produced. See, for example, "A New Approach to Landshaping," *Architectural Forum* 106 (January 1957): 96–103; Richard A. Miller, "Bulldozer Architecture," *Architectural Forum* 113 (August 1960): 90. The Lillard quotations come from Richard G. Lillard, *Eden in Jeopardy: Man's Prodigal Meddling with His Environment: The Southern California Experience* (New York: Alfred A. Knopf, 1966), 17, 115, 271. As I noted in chapter four, the image of a bulldozed slope was the most common illustration in magazine articles about the destruction of open space.
30. Grady Clay, "'Fighting the Rise': Consider the Hillsides and their Needs," *Landscape Architecture* 50 (Winter 1959–1960): 75.

number of problems below. The downhill flow of soil might silt up reservoirs, drainage channels, and harbors. Thus, the development of hillsides could threaten the quality of drinking water, increase the likelihood of flood damages, and impair commercial navigation. The erosion of steep slopes could also upset the ecology of streams and lakes, and so diminish habitat for a host of creatures.[31]

Though a few of the costs of hillside erosion were easy to miss, the risk of landslides soon became front-page news in dozens of communities. The disasters took a variety of forms, but all could be deadly. In some cases, houses literally slid down slopes. In other cases, they were battered and even buried by tidal waves of sediment. Houses also collapsed when structural supports slipped. The property damage often totaled hundreds of thousands of dollars. In the worst cases, the losses ran into the millions.[32]

For homeowners, the loss could be a burden for years, because few home insurance policies covered landslides. The story of Mr. and Mrs. Robert Scott was typical. The couple bought a $30,000 home in Alexandria, Virginia, in 1957, but the hillside above the house began to slip three years later after a heavy rain. The next winter, the hill slipped further, and – as one chronicler of the disaster wrote – it did not stop slipping until the Scotts' house was leveled. The homes of nine neighbors were damaged seriously. Despite the disaster, however, the Scotts still had to pay the mortgage: "A pile of rubble at 419 Bluebill Lane mocks the Scotts' monthly payments."[33]

The suburbs of Washington, Cincinnati, and Pittsburgh all had serious landslides in the 1950s and 1960s, but the problem was most pressing in California, where homebuilders were especially quick to

31. Ann Louise Strong, "Incentives and Controls for Open Space," in David A. Wallace, editor, *Metropolitan Open Space and Natural Process* (Philadelphia: University of Pennsylvania Press, 1970), 101–103. For testimony about stream damage, see U.S. House of Representatives, *The Land Use Planning Act of 1973: Hearings on H.R. 4862 and Related Bills Before the Subcommittee on Environment of the Committee on Interior and Insular Affairs,* 93rd Congress, 1st session, 1973, 372.

32. For a short description of the damages from a relatively small landslide, see A. A. Klingebiel, "Bases for Urban Development: Soil," *Planning 1963* (Chicago: American Society of Planning Officials, 1963), 44. I describe the worst disasters below.

33. For the quotation, see Selden Lee Tinsley, "Planning for Conservation in the Suburbs," in U.S. Department of Agriculture, *A Place to Live: The Yearbook of Agriculture 1963* (Washington: USGPO, 1963), 391. The story of the Scotts was also recounted in U.S. Department of Agriculture and U.S. Department of Housing and Urban Development, *Soil, Water, and Suburbia* (Washington: USGPO, 1968), 13.

bulldoze the high ground. In Los Angeles, a few pioneers had begun to build hillside homes in the 1920s, and the hills became the site of mass building after World War II: In the 1950s, two-thirds of the city's new homes were on hillside lots. The uplands of San Francisco were also transformed in the 1950s, as subdivisions replaced forests, orchards, and pastures.[34]

In Los Angeles, the bulldozed slopes did not remain stable for long. In the winter of 1951–52, the city received 26 inches of rain – the average winter brought just 10 – and the rush of water caused $7.5 million in damage from erosion and landsliding. The city then passed a hillside grading ordinance, but the regulations turned out to be too lax. In 1956, the city again suffered tremendous damage after a heavy rain. In Los Angeles County, the 1956 rains also reactivated an old landslide in Portuguese Bend, and the slipping slopes eventually damaged or destroyed nearly 150 homes. The destruction of utilities and roads brought the total cost of the disaster to $10 million. The city of Los Angeles passed a more stringent hillside development ordinance in 1963, a year after a rush of landslides killed two people, threatened a hundred houses, and caused millions of dollars of damage. By the early 1960s, indeed, the "residential ills in the heartbreak hills of southern California" had received considerable publicity in both professional and popular forums.[35]

34. The Los Angeles statistic is from "Landslides Wreck Another Two Los Angeles Homes," *House and Home* 16 (October 1959): 55. In addition, see Ben H. Bagdikian, "The Rape of the Land," *Saturday Evening Post* 239 (June 18, 1966): 27. The history of hillside housing in southern California is sketched in Dominique Rouillard, *Building the Slope: Hillside Houses, 1920–1960* (Santa Monica, CA: Arts and Architecture Press, 1987). For the postwar transformation of the San Francisco uplands, see Robert D. Brown, Jr. and William J. Kockelman, *Geological Principles for Prudent Land Use: A Decisionmaker's Guide for the San Francisco Region* [Geological Survey Professional Paper 946] (Washington: USGPO, 1983), 31. The Earth Satellite Corporation also made a case study of hillside development in California: See *Land Use Change and Environmental Quality in Urban Areas* (Washington: Council on Environmental Quality, 1973), 180–184. For the problem in Cincinnati, see Rex L. Baum and Arvid M. Johnson, *Overview of Landslide Problems, Research, and Mitigation, Cincinnati, Ohio, Area* [U.S. Geological Survey Bulletin 2059–A] (Washington: USGPO, 1996), A1, A10. The major landslide areas are described in Duncan Erley and William J. Kockelman, *Reducing Landslide Hazards: A Guide for Planners* [Planning Advisory Service Report Number 359] (Chicago: American Planning Association, 1981), 1.

35. For the history of landslides in Los Angeles, see Robert W. Fleming, David J. Varnes, and Robert L. Schuster, "Landslide Hazards and Their Reduction," *Journal of the American Planning Association* 45 (1979): 434–435. The estimate of the Portuguese Bend damages comes from Richard Merriam, "Portuguese Bend Landslide, Palos Verdes Hills, California," *Journal of Geology* 68 (1960): 140. For the devastation of the 1962 Los

What were the lessons of the California landslides? The bull-dozed slope surely was a challenge to gravity. As two Los Angeles engineers wrote, the development of hillsides brought people "into direct collision with nature." But the implications of that insight were not obvious. Was the construction of housing on steep slopes a form of hubris? Were hillside developments simply gambles? Or could homebuilders and homebuyers win the battle against nature with proper preparation?[36]

The aesthetic critics of hillside development often treated the landslides as morality plays. Lillard's biting description of the 1952 disaster was typical:

Rivers of rain on denuded hillsides picked up rocks and soil and roared down. Sometimes as the mud flows gave way they pulled the foundations out of houses just above them. More often they piled up around the houses below them, new spick-and-span all-glass contemporary homes, and then when the mudslides slopped up deep and heavy enough, they went on through the houses, pushing in walls and windows, filling swimming pools, carrying away terraces and plants and trees and all the accumulated objects of Home, Sweet Home, and Garden Beautiful. Hundreds of cars were washed into storm channels or covered to their windows with mud, sticks, and slime. Throughout the newly built sections of the Hollywood Hills and the Santa Monica Mountains, streets were blocked for days, and the equipment that had excavated and shoved on the hilltops, now worked below cleaning up the belly-deep messes on the boulevards and private drives and lawns.

Angeles storm, see F. Beach Leighton, "Landslides and Hillside Development," in Richard Lung and Richard Proctor, editors, *Engineering Geology in Southern California* (Glendale, CA: Association of Engineering Geologists, 1966), 149–151. The Portuguese Bend disaster was described in "Landslides Wreck Another Two Los Angeles Homes," 55. The article was reprinted several times: See Robert A. Clark, *Hillside Development* [Planning Advisory Service Information Report 126] (Chicago: American Society of Planning Officials, 1959), 3; Jaffe, "Following the Trail of the 'Cat,'" 93. In addition, see Edward Higbee, *The Squeeze: Cities Without Space* (New York: William Morrow and Company, 1960), 122; John T. McGill, *Growing Importance of Urban Geology* [Geological Survey Circular 487] (Washington: USGPO, 1964), 2. For descriptions of less destructive California landslides, see "Mudslides," *Newsweek* 61 (January 14, 1963): 26; "Don't Water the Daisies!," *Time* 85 (June 18, 1965): 43. The quotation is the title of a piece by Richard H. Jahns in the Caltech Alumni Magazine: See *Engineering and Science* 22 (December 1958): 13–20.

36. For the quotation, see G. Austin Schroter and Ray O. Maurseth, "Hillside Stability – The Modern Approach," *Civil Engineering* 30 (June 1960): 67.

The lesson seemed clear: The disaster was a kind of judgment on the desecrators of the hills.[37]

To most engineers and geologists, however, the landslide losses argued for a more rigorous application of scientific knowledge in the planning of subdivisions. The courts supported the argument. In a series of decisions in cases prompted by the Portuguese Bend disaster, for example, the courts ultimately held that the landslide was not an act of God: Instead, it was the result of human negligence. The judicial decisions encouraged builders, engineers, geologists, and public officials to think hard about the soundness of hillside developments. "Millions of dollars of litigation grimly testify to the seriousness of the problems of landsliding and slope stability," a 1960 article in *Civil Engineering* began. Accordingly, the profession needed to give more thought to the causes of landslides. What could be done to prevent costly and deadly disasters?[38]

The list of potential problems was quite long. Some soils and geologic formations were naturally unstable. Builders could destabilize a hillside by steepening the slope, by increasing the height, by adding too much weight at the top, by undercutting the base, or by removing natural supports from the bedding planes. Blasting might set material moving. When builders created terraces by cutting and filling, the fill had to be sufficiently compact to bear the load: If the fill included too much vegetation or trash, if the fill was not layered properly, or if the fill retained water because the subdrainage system was inadequate, then the terrace might collapse. Water was a grave threat. When wet, clay soils could turn into slippery gels. The sheer weight and pressure of a saturated slope could cause the ground to move. Below the surface, water even could act as a lubricant, allowing bedrock to slip and slide.[39]

37. Lillard, *Eden in Jeopardy,* 112.
38. The quotation comes from Schroter and Maurseth, "Hillside Stability," 66. In addition, see John A. Lambie, "Hillside Subdivisions," *American City* 74 (May 1959): 157–158; David D. Bohannon, "Hillside Development," *Urban Land* 18 (January 1959): 3–5; Leighton, "Landslides and Hillside Development," 178; Clark, *Hillside Development*, 3.
39. Leighton, "Landslides and Hillside Development," 157–169; Jahns, "Residential Ills in the Heartbreak Hills of Southern California," 15–20; Donald H. Gray, "Soil and the City," in Thomas R. Detwyler and Melvin G. Marcus, editors, *Urbanization and the Environment: The Physical Geography of the City* (Belmont, CA: Duxbury Press, 1972), 158. In addition, see Erley and Kockelman, *Reducing Landslide Hazards*, 5–8.

To protect against disaster, therefore, a builder needed to think carefully about every phase of the construction process. The land needed to be inspected by professionals before the start of the project. To avoid excessive weight on the slope, the density of the development needed to be appropriate for the topography and geology of the site. Of course, the work of site preparation required special attention. The siting of the roads, the layout of the subdivision, and even the landscaping of the lots needed to be planned to ensure that storm runoff did not cause potentially disruptive drainage problems. Because leaching fields kept the ground saturated, the use of septic tanks might be problematic.[40]

Throughout the 1960s, engineers and geologists urged local governments to require sound construction practices. At the least, a community with steep hills should pass a grading ordinance to regulate cuts and fills. Subdivision regulations might include special hillside provisions for street and lot layout, drainage, and waste disposal. Officials also could require engineering and geological surveys before construction and professional supervision on site. With proper planning and oversight, the risks of disaster could be dramatically reduced or eliminated.[41]

Yet the promise of better engineering did not satisfy everyone. By 1970, a variety of experts were expressing doubts about the unprecedented transformation of the landscape. Like gods, we had exalted valleys and made rough places plain, but at what cost? Did we need to push the envelope, to strive unceasingly to overcome natural limits? "It could be argued," a professor of civil engineering wrote, "that the real need [is] simply to prohibit intensive develop-

40. Leighton, "Landslides and Hillside Development," 178–191; Schroter and Maurseth, "Hillside Stability," 66–69; Clark, *Hillside Development,* 2–30; Jahns, "Residential Ills in the Heartbreak Hills of Southern California," 15–20; Lambie, "Hillside Subdivisions," 157–158; Robert Stone, "Geology and Hillside Appraisal," *Residential Appraiser* 29 (1961): 9–11.

41. Leighton, "Landslides and Hillside Development," 190; Clark, *Hillside Development,* 2–30; Jahns, "Residential Ills in the Heartbreak Hills of Southern California," 20; Lambie, "Hillside Subdivisions," 158; C. Michael Scullin, "History, Development, and Administration of Excavation and Grading Codes," in Lung and Proctor, *Engineering Geology in Southern California,* 227–236; Charles A. Yelverton, "The Role of Local Governments in Urban Geology," in Donald R. Nichols and Catherine C. Campbell, editors, *Environmental Planning and Geology: Proceedings of the Symposium on Engineering Geology in the Urban Environment* (Washington: USGPO, 1971), 76–81; "Mounting Danger to Homes: Floods, Quakes and Slides," *U.S. News and World Report* 67 (December 15, 1969): 78–79.

ment on steep, slide-susceptible slopes." In a 1970 conference on environmental planning and geology, several participants offered similar comments. One urged cities and counties to outlaw "the old-fashioned form of pad cut into a steep hillside for a conventional ranch house – which is, in my judgment, a crime against nature." A planner and a geologist argued that potentially unstable land should often be left undeveloped, to serve as open space. A University of California geographer even chastised engineering geologists for helping developers to do what should not be done. "You are not solving problems," he argued; "you are part of the disaster."[42]

Adjusting to Nature in Floodplains

Though the trade press of the homebuilding industry never touted the promise of floodplains as subdivision sites, the construction of homes in flood-prone areas became much more common after World War II. In some fast-growing regions, the increase was phenomenal. In Denver, the residential acreage in floodplains jumped by 250 percent in the 1960s. In Dallas, the number of single-family homes in the floodplains of the Trinity River rose by 641 percent from 1936 to 1957; in the Pico-Rivera section of Los Angeles, the increase was 867 percent. Though compilers of floodplain statistics focused on construction along major rivers, a few analysts also noted a tremendous increase in building along creeks and streams.[43]

42. The first question paraphrases a passage in Banham, *Los Angeles*, 107. The quotations come from Gray, "Soil and the City," 155; Nichols and Campbell, *Environmental Planning and Geology*, 49, 97–98, 188–189. In addition, see Nathaniel T. Kenney, "Southern California's Trial by Mud and Water," *National Geographic* 136 (October 1969): 555–557.

43. The Denver statistic is from Earth Satellite Corporation, *Land Use Change and Environmental Quality in Urban Areas*, 198. For Dallas and Los Angeles, see Gilbert F. White, Wesley C. Calef, James W. Hudson, Harold M. Mayer, John R. Sheaffer, and Donald J. Volk, *Changes in Urban Occupance of Flood Plains in the United States* [Department of Geography Research Paper 57] (Chicago: University of Chicago Department of Geography, 1958), 205–206. For the problem in smaller drainages, see 231–232. In addition, see Aelred J. Gray, "Communities and Floods," *National Civic Review* 50 (1961): 134; Lee Wright, "Put Flood-Plain Management First to Avoid the Disaster of a River on the Rampage," *American City* 82 (November 1967): 98; Glenn B. Anderson, "Soil Erosion – A Major Menace to Urban-Fringe Conservation," *Journal of Soil and Water Conservation* 20 (1965): 184; Tom Dale, "Under All Is The Land," *Soil Conservation* 23 (October 1957): 53; Andrew M. Spieker, *Water in Urban Planning, Salt Creek Basin, Illinois: Water Management as Related to Alternative Land-Use Practice* [Geological

For the construction of subdivisions, floodplains offered substantial advantages. The land was usually cheap. Without a lot of effort, developers could piece together substantial tracts. Because the land was flat, the costs of site preparation were also minimal.

If people had refused to buy homes in floodplains, the opportunities for profitable development would have come to nothing, but builders found a ready market. Many homebuyers did not know about the hazard. Floodplain maps were not yet available, and real estate agents were not required to disclose the risk. In a number of cases, boosters suppressed evidence of past flooding by covering or removing high-water marks on buildings. Even when the flood potential was obvious, however, people often discounted the danger.[44]

Until the late 1950s, the issue seldom concerned local officials. In 1955, only a handful of cities and counties had strong laws to control floodplain building. But the climate of opinion had already begun to change.[45]

In the early 1950s, the devastation from flooding reached all-time highs. In 1951, a series of floods in the midwest forced almost 90,000 people to evacuate their homes and caused $870 million in damages. In 1955, nearly 200 people died when floods struck the northeast, and damage to property totaled $750 million. For the five-year period from 1950 to 1955, the annual losses averaged $500 million.[46]

The damage was particularly galling because the federal govern-

Survey Water Supply Paper 2002] (Washington: USGPO, 1970), 72; S. E. Rantz, *Urban Sprawl and Flooding in Southern California* [Geological Survey Circular 601–B] (Washington: USGPO, 1970), B3; John Savini and J. C. Kammerer, *Urban Growth and the Water Regimen* [Geological Survey Water Supply Paper 1591–A] (Washington: USGPO, 1961), A-35.

44. Francis C. Murphy, *Regulating Flood-Plain Development* [Department of Geography Research Paper 56] (Chicago: University of Chicago Department of Geography, 1958), 136–137; S. Kenneth Love, "Bases for Urban Development: Water," *Planning 1963* (Chicago: American Society of Planning Officials, 1963), 53; White et al., *Changes in Urban Occupance of Flood Plains*, 219.

45. Murphy, *Regulating Flood-Plain Development*, 44.

46. The statistics come from Samuel Davis Sturgis, Jr., "Floods," *Annals of the American Academy of Political and Social Science* 309 (January 1957): 18; Hoyt Lemons, "Physical Characteristics of Disasters: Historical and Statistical Review," *Annals of the American Academy of Political and Social Science* 309 (January 1957): 7. The property loss figures for the early 1950s exceeded earlier losses even when corrected for inflation and population growth. See Natural Hazards Research and Applications Information Center, *Floodplain Management in the United States: An Assessment Report* [Volume 1] (Boulder, CO: Federal Emergency Management Agency, 1992), 17.

ment had made a commitment in the 1930s to prevent flooding on the nation's rivers. The Flood Control Acts of 1936 and 1938 authorized a decades-long, multibillion-dollar public-works program later likened to the construction of the Great Wall of China. Eventually, the nation would spend over $14 billion to construct 260 reservoirs, 6,000 miles of levees and floodwalls, and 8,000 miles of stream channel improvements. By the late 1950s, the expenditures had reached nearly $4 billion. Yet flood losses continued to mount. What had gone wrong?[47]

To a considerable extent, the expert answers to that question built on work done before the war by a young geographer, Gilbert White. In 1934, while still a graduate student at the University of Chicago, White moved to Washington, D.C., to work for a new water resources planning agency, and he soon became interested in the issue of flood control. Colorado, Texas, Nebraska, and New York all suffered terrible floods in 1935. The next year, record floods hit New England and Appalachia. White doubted that the new policy of dam and levee building would end flood losses. In a short piece published in 1937, he argued for a more comprehensive approach to the flood problem, with land-use planning as a fundamental element. By 1942, he had developed the argument in detail in his dissertation, "Human Adjustment to Floods."[48]

"It has become common in scientific as well as popular literature to consider floods as great natural adversaries which man seeks persistently to over-power," White wrote in the introduction to his dissertation. "According to this view, floods always are watery marauders which do no good, and against which society wages a bitter battle. The price of victory is the cost of engineering works necessary to confine the flood crest; the price of defeat is a continuing chain of flood disasters." The truth was more complex. To reduce flood damages, the nation did not need to have impregnable lines of defense. The stereotype of rampaging rivers obscured the crucial

47. For a succinct summary of the federal flood-control program, see Rutherford H. Platt, "Floods and Man: A Geographer's Agenda," in Robert W. Kates and Ian Burton, editors, *Geography, Resources, and Environment: Themes from the Work of Gilbert F. White* [Volume Two] (Chicago: University of Chicago Press, 1986), 29–31, 35, 37–48.
48. For White's early career, see Platt, "Floods and Man," 32–35. The short piece is Gilbert F. White, "Notes on Flood Protection and Land-Use Planning," *Planner's Journal* 3 (1937): 57–61.

role of human decision making. Though rivers could be capricious and violent, the victims of flooding were rarely innocent. "Floods are 'acts of God,'" White explained, "but flood losses are largely acts of man. Human encroachment upon the flood plains of rivers accounts for the high annual toll of flood losses."[49]

In White's view, therefore, the nation's policy-makers needed to think more deeply about the ways people used floodplains. What types of occupancy would yield maximum returns to society with minimum social costs? Some uses simply were unsound: The benefits of locating in the floodplain did not outweigh the costs of providing flood protection or relief. Other uses made sense only if officials took steps to reduce the public liability for flood damages – requiring property owners to buy insurance, for example, or to design structures to withstand high water. If the government made no effort to oversee floodplain development, however, the policy of building protective works and providing disaster relief would inevitably promote misuse of flood-prone lands.[50]

White's work had extraordinary influence. The University of Chicago published the dissertation in a limited edition in 1945, then reissued the work in 1953. Again and again, people writing about the flood problem in the 1950s paraphrased White's comments about floodplains. "Nature makes floods," ecologist Paul Sears began a 1957 article in the journal *Science,* "but man makes flood hazards." "The flood plain is the place where nearly all flood damage occurs," hydrologists Luna Leopold and Thomas Maddock wrote in a 1954 analysis of the flood-control issue, "because man grows crops or has built buildings on an area which the river must at times cover with water. Man has encroached on a part of the river, and when he gets flooded out he berates the river for the destruction brought." In a 1960 work on urban planning, geographer Edward Higbee made the argument more pointedly: "The plaintive theme song is that floods are calamities of Nature," he wrote, but

49. Gilbert Fowler White, *Human Adjustment to Floods: A Geographical Approach to the Flood Problem in the United States* [Department of Geography Research Paper 29] (1945; reprint, Chicago: University of Chicago Department of Geography, 1953), 1–2. The original publication date appears on the title page of the 1953 edition, but the publication dates of earlier and later volumes in the series make clear that the volume was actually published in 1953.
50. Ibid., 34–35, 191–195, 205–212.

in fact flood damage occurs "because Man trespasses where Nature has clearly warned him to stay away." "The greater number of floods that have destroyed residential and industrial properties in recent years are not due to increased sunspots, nuclear explosions, or a switch in ancient storm tracks," Higbee added, "but only to the simple fact that more foolish people have built in places where Nature intended that high water run occasionally."[51]

White's dissertation also inspired a chapter on "Man's Adaptation to Floods" in the preeminent work on flooding written in the 1950s: William Hoyt and Walter Langbein's *Floods*, published in 1955. "Our present practice," the two hydrologists wrote, "is to adjust rivers to man's convenience, without stopping to think whether there is merit to the opposite idea embodied in the title of a too-little-known book by Gilbert White." Yet the nation's flood-control engineers ignored a fundamental truth. "Floods are as much a part of the phenomena of the landscape as are hills and valleys; they are natural features to be lived with, features which require certain adjustments on our part." Accordingly, the federal government needed to encourage cities and counties to adopt floodplain zoning – a policy which "could be more accurately termed sensible adjustment of land use to the flood peril." Though Hoyt and Langbein did not spell out the details of a good zoning ordinance, the two listed several appropriate uses of floodplains, including pastures and parks. "Home-building, on the other hand, is an example of the most unwise use of flood land."[52]

By 1955, floodplain zoning had the support of a handful of important institutions. The Tennessee Valley Authority began to provide flood-hazard information to state authorities in the early 1950s, and the American Society of Planning Officials published a guide to floodplain regulation in 1953. Both organizations offered a pragmatic rather than a philosophical argument for zoning. Though the

51. For the quotations, see Paul B. Sears, "Natural and Cultural Aspects of Floods," *Science* 125 (1957): 806; Luna B. Leopold and Thomas Maddock, Jr., *The Flood Control Controversy: Big Dams, Little Dams, and Land Management* (New York: Ronald Press Company, 1954), 9; Higbee, *The Squeeze*, 123. In addition, see Walter M. Kollmorgen, "Settlement Control Beats Flood Control," *Economic Geography* 29 (July 1953): 208–215.

52. William G. Hoyt and Walter B. Langbein, *Floods* (Princeton: Princeton University Press, 1955), 9, 91, 94, 100.

federal government had built a massive system of protective works in the Tennessee River basin, a TVA community planner explained, the region still had thousands of acres vulnerable to flooding: If local officials permitted residential or commercial developments in the unprotected areas, "the flood damage potential in the valley would be increased in spite of the river control system." The American Society of Planning Officials guide argued that floodplain regulations would save taxpayers money. When people built in floodplains, "the local community and the nation may be asked to pay for damage that should not have been *allowed* to occur."[53]

White was not content to leave a largely academic legacy. In 1955, after a ten-year stint as president of Haverford College, he returned to the University of Chicago with a keen desire to influence the nation's flood-control policy. He quickly made the geography department a leading center for research in the field. He directed a six-person study of changes in urban occupancy of floodplains, and he arranged for a member of the Army Corps of Engineers to spend a year at the university doing a pioneering analysis of floodplain regulation. In 1958, he organized a national conference on floodplain management in conjunction with the Council of State Governments, the American Society of Planning Officials, the American Institute of Planners, and the American Society of Civil Engineers. He published articles in the late 1950s and early 1960s in a variety of professional journals. He also served as a consultant for a congressional water-resources committee.[54]

53. The first quotation is from Gray, "Communities and Floods," 135. In addition, see Aelred J. Gray, "Planning for Local Flood Damage Prevention," *Journal of the American Institute of Planners* 22 (1956): 11–16. For the second quotation, see American Society of Planning Officials, *Flood Plain Regulation* [Planning Advisory Service Information Report 53] (Chicago: American Society of Planning Officials, 1953), 1.
54. The studies were White et al., *Changes in Urban Occupance of Flood Plains;* Murphy, *Regulating Flood-Plain Development.* White's publications included "Strategic Aspects of Urban Flood Plain Occupance," *Journal of the Hydraulics Division, Proceedings of the American Society of Civil Engineers* 86 (HY2, 1960): 89–102; "The Control and Development of Flood Plain Areas," in Southwestern Legal Foundation, *Proceedings of the 1960 Institute on Planning and Zoning* (New York: Matthew Bender and Company, 1961), 93–107; "A New Attack on Flood Losses," *State Government* 32 (Spring 1959): 121–127. He also contributed to report 29 of the Senate Select Committee on National Water Resources, 87th Congress, 1st session, 1961. For a summary of flood-control research at the University of Chicago in the late 1950s and early 1960s, see Platt, "Floods and Man," 50–51. In addition, see Martin Reuss, *Water Resources People and Issues: Interview with Gilbert F. White* (Fort Belvoir, VA: U.S. Army Corps of Engineers, 1993), 35–42.

Eventually White reached a mass audience. In 1961, *Reader's Digest* reprinted an article from the *National Civic Review* which drew heavily on his work. "Let's *Plan* the Damage Out of Floods," the headline urged. Like a host of pieces on the flood problem, the article began by comparing flood losses before and after the federal commitment to control flooding. Despite the expenditure of more than $4 billion on dams and levees, the problem had become worse, not better. Why? The gains from flood-control works were offset by a great increase in floodplain development. But the cure was elementary. "*Instead of trying to keep the rivers away from man, keep man away from the rivers.*" To support the point, the article quoted White in condensed form: "Floods are acts of God – but flood *losses* are acts of man, a payment which nature exacts in return for his occupation of her flood plain."[55]

The *Reader's Digest* piece also described the benefits of preserving floodplains in a relatively undeveloped state. For a fraction of the cost of protective works, a community could turn potential disaster areas into points of pride. In Milwaukee, for example, the county was buying 5,000 acres along rivers and streams to create a system of nature trails, wildlife refuges, and recreation areas. If a flood someday submerged the land, the damage would be slight – a small price to pay for the everyday pleasures of living with water.[56]

Though not new, the argument became more common in the early 1960s, when Americans rediscovered the aesthetic possibilities of waterways. Landscape architects and urban planners promoted the idea of creating greenbelts along metropolitan streams. Outdoor-recreation activists and conservationists sought legislation to protect "wild and scenic" rivers. In 1965, the White House Conference on Natural Beauty included a session on water and waterfronts: With imaginative planning, a number of participants argued, the

55. Peter Farb, "Let's *Plan* the Damage Out of Floods," *Reader's Digest* 78 (May 1961): 224–227. The original version of the article is "Let's Plan the Damage," *National Municipal Review* 49 (1960): 238–241. For a sample of articles which begin similarly, see Harriet Holt Cooter, "To Stay Out of Floods," *National Civic Review* 50 (1961): 534–539; Wright, "Put Flood-Plain Management First to Avoid the Disaster of a River on the Rampage," 98–99; James E. Goddard, "Flood-Plain Management Must Be Ecologically and Economically Sound," *Civil Engineering* 41 (September 1971): 81–85.
56. Farb, "Let's *Plan* the Damage Out of Floods," 225–226. In addition, see Wright, "Put Flood-Plain Management First to Avoid the Disaster of a River on the Rampage," 99; Gray, "Communities and Floods," 138.

land along the nation's streams and rivers could give millions of Americans rich opportunities to play, to exercise, and to enjoy the wonders of nature.[57]

The policy of floodplain management thus gained important new constituencies. In 1962, the Outdoor Recreation Resources Review Commission recommended floodplain zoning as a way "to preserve attractive reaches of rivers and streams for public recreation." The commission also pointed out that sound regulations would help control the problem of flooding. The rapid growth of cities and suburbs was "creating new pressures to utilize inviting but hazardous flood plains for subdivisions, shopping centers, commercial establishments, and other improvements," the commission argued. "This mushrooming trend is creating new flood-damage potential faster than construction works can add to existing protection."[58]

Conservationists made similar arguments. "Wherever you have a flood plain that is undeveloped, *do everything possible to keep it undeveloped,*" the authors of one piece on river conservation argued. "This is the cheapest and by far the most beneficial means of flood control. It's not simply that building on the flood plain is almost literally the same as building on the river, an open invitation to disaster; or that it destroys some of the finest land we have left for wildlife, recreation, and agriculture. It's also that when we crowd houses and factories onto the plain we're making inevitable the building of costly dams, thus forcing the general taxpayer to subsidize the developers."[59]

By the mid-1960s, then, a significant group of scholars, scientists, planners, civil engineers, outdoor-recreation enthusiasts, and environmentalists had criticized the tacit federal support of floodplain development. The nation's leaders acknowledged the criticism in 1966, when a presidential task force headed by Gilbert White rec-

---

57. For the renewed appreciation of waterways, see White House Conference on Natural Beauty, *Beauty for America* (Washington: USGPO, 1965), 7, 113, 143, 144, 149, 156, 167, 642. The growing interest of cities and counties in floodplain parks is discussed in Earth Satellite Corporation, *Land Use Change and Environmental Quality in Urban Areas,* 137.

58. Outdoor Recreation Resources Review Commission, *Outdoor Recreation for America* (Washington: USGPO, 1962), 8, 177.

59. James Nathan Miller and Robert Simmons, "Crisis on Our Rivers," *Reader's Digest* 97 (December 1970): 81. In addition, see Bagdikian, "The Rape of the Land," 88–89; William H. Whyte, *The Last Landscape* (Garden City, NY: Doubleday, 1968), 40–41.

ommended a more comprehensive program to control flood losses, with land-use regulation as a vital tool. In the next decade, a series of executive orders and legislative acts turned the task-force recommendations into national policy. Hundreds of local governments also moved to regulate floodplain development. By 1970, almost a sixth of the nation's cities and suburbs had taken action. After the federal government made floodplain zoning a requirement for participation in the subsidized flood-insurance program, the number of communities with floodplain regulations increased dramatically. Though analysts disagreed about the effectiveness of the local floodplain-management effort, the basic principle was widely accepted: Builders should avoid floodplains.[60]

Ian McHarg's Call to "Design with Nature"

For the landscape architect and regional planner Ian McHarg, the arguments against building on wetlands, steep hillsides, and floodplains all exemplified a single great insight, the need to respect "natural processes." Indeed, McHarg almost singlehandedly made that phrase part of the lexicon of planning. In his classes at the University of Pennsylvania, in his speeches and writings, in his work as a partner in a landscape architecture and planning firm, he argued that development should be restricted to "areas that were intrinsically suitable, where dangers were absent and natural processes unharmed." But McHarg did not simply call for public officials to set where-not-to-build standards. He argued for a new way of building.[61]

McHarg began to think about the problem of urban growth in the mid-1950s. After finishing his master's degree at Harvard, he worked for four years as a city planner in his native Scotland, then returned to the United States in 1954 to teach in Philadelphia. He

---

60. For the number of communities with floodplain ordinances in 1970, see Goddard, "Flood-Plain Management Must Be Ecologically and Economically Sound," 84. The shifts in federal policy are summarized in Natural Hazards Research and Applications Information Center, *Floodplain Management in the United States,* 24–26. On the effectiveness of local regulations, see Raymond J. Burby and Steven P. French, *Flood Plain Land Use Management: A National Assessment* (Boulder, CO: Westview Press, 1985).
61. McHarg, *Design with Nature,* 55–56.

was shocked by the sprawl of tract housing and strip development. In the four years he was away, thousands of acres had become ranch houses, split-levels, diners, and billboards. As he looked at the new landscape in dismay, he found his life mission. What could be done to stop the remorseless transformation of the countryside? By the end of the decade, McHarg was convinced that the answer lay in a combination of philosophical inquiry and hands-on planning.[62]

"Clearly," McHarg explained, "if there was to be a remedy there must be a profound change in social values, notably, attitudes toward nature and conceptions of what constitutes a humane environment." Accordingly, McHarg decided in 1959 to offer a new course on "Man and Environment." The heart of the course was a study in values. Why did people exploit the land? What did religion, philosophy, science, history, and art teach about the human relationship with nature? Because the Harvard program in landscape architecture did not address those questions, McHarg saw the "Man and Environment" course as a form of continuing education. He would learn – as his students learned – from a host of guest lecturers. He focused especially on the lessons of ecology.[63]

In 1959, McHarg also began to prepare a plan for open-space preservation in metropolitan Philadelphia. He saw the project as a chance to consider "the place of nature in the metropolis." On the one hand, nature did important work – providing water, air, wildlife habitat, and agricultural produce. On the other hand, nature threatened human health and well-being – creating floods, forest fires, landslides, and hurricanes. McHarg concluded that a sound open-space plan would ensure the continued operation of beneficial "natural processes" while protecting people from natural hazards. Relying on both common sense and ecological science, McHarg then identified seven types of land especially worthy of preservation. Rivers and streams were sources of drinking water, beauty, and recreation. Wetlands nourished wildlife and stored water during storms. Because rivers and streams periodically overflowed their banks, floodplains were too hazardous for intense development. Aquifers provided pure water: To protect aquifers from pollution,

---

62. Ian L. McHarg, *A Quest for Life: An Autobiography* (New York: John Wiley & Sons, 1996), 155–156.
63. Ibid., 156–157.

the points of interchange between surface and underground water also required protection. If developed improperly, steep slopes could become landslide hazards; a denuded slope also might increase the severity of floods and pollute surface waters with eroded soil. The richest agricultural soils offered a great bounty. Forests shaped the microclimate, played a key role in the hydrological cycle, and sheltered wildlife.[64]

For McHarg, however, the principles of open-space planning had a broader significance. The "values and prohibitions" created by natural processes should guide "the positive pattern of development." McHarg first had a chance to illustrate the point in 1963 when he joined with partner David Wallace to prepare a development plan for two rural valleys northwest of Baltimore. The clients – a group of valley landowners concerned about the approach of septic-tank subdivisions – wanted to find a way to accommodate development without destroying the character of the place. What could be done?[65]

The McHarg-Wallace plan began with a vision of the unplanned future. "Uncontrolled growth, occurring sporadically, spreading without discrimination, will surely obliterate the valleys, inexorably cover the landscape with its smear, irrevocably destroy all that is beautiful or memorable," the two wrote. "No matter how well designed each individual subdivision may be, no matter if small parks are interfused with housing, the great landscape will be expunged and remain only as a receding memory."[66]

To counter "the spectre," McHarg and Wallace proposed a plan inspired by "the genius of the site." No development would be allowed in the valleys: The valleys were too beautiful, and the aquifer under the valleys was likely to be polluted by septic tanks. No construction would be permitted on the banks of the streams, in the floodplains, or on slopes steeper than 25 percent. Where the valley

---

64. The study was eventually the basis for Wallace, *Metropolitan Open Space and Natural Process*. McHarg also describes the project in *Design With Nature*, 55–65. For the origins of the study, see McHarg, *A Quest for Life*, 141.
65. The quotation is from McHarg, *Design with Nature*, 57. For a succinct description of the project, see Ian L. McHarg and David A. Wallace, "Plan for the Valleys vs. Spectre of Uncontrolled Growth," *Landscape Architecture 55* (1964): 179–181. McHarg also describes the plan in *Design with Nature*, 79–93.
66. McHarg and Wallace, "Plan for the Valleys vs. Spectre of Uncontrolled Growth," 179.

walls were forested, only houses on three-acre lots would be allowed; the bare slopes would be left undeveloped. On the wooded plateau, McHarg and Wallace would permit one house per acre. In a few promontory locations, however, tower apartments would be appropriate. The open plateau would have no restrictions. With proper planning, McHarg and Wallace concluded, a handful of large communities, a country town, and several villages and hamlets could meet the needs of the expected influx of population.[67]

To stand a chance of succeeding, McHarg and Wallace knew, their plan had to provide incentives to all the landowners in the valleys. Ordinarily, only the owners of developable acreage would profit, but the two planners proposed a radical alternative to business as usual: The valley landowners should form a real estate syndicate. In return for stock, the landowners would cede to the syndicate the development rights for their land. The syndicate would retain the rights to the parcels McHarg and Wallace proposed to leave undeveloped. In accordance with the McHarg-Wallace plan, the syndicate would then oversee the development of the rest of the land, and the stockholders would share the proceeds. Everyone would gain financially, McHarg and Wallace argued, and everyone would have the satisfaction of living harmoniously with the land.[68]

"The Plan for the Valleys" won considerable acclaim. Though the valley landowners ultimately chose not to follow the McHarg-Wallace recommendations, McHarg soon had a national reputation as a leading proponent of a new way of planning. In the mid-1960s, he made the case for "ecological determinism" in a variety of forums, from *Audubon Magazine* to the *Annals of the American Academy of Political and Social Science*. He relentlessly attacked the ideology of development – "the concept of conquest and exploitation." The prevailing way of thinking, he wrote, "would seem to suggest that water is made to be befouled, air to be polluted, marshes to be filled, streams to be culverted, rivers to be dammed, farms subdivided, forests felled, flood plains occupied and wildlife eradicated."[69]

67. Ibid., 179–180.
68. Ibid., 180–181. For the response of the landowners, see McHarg, *A Quest for Life*, 179–180.
69. McHarg's publications include "The Place of Nature in the City of Man," *Annals of the American Academy of Political and Social Science* 352 (March 1964): 1–12; "Blight or a Noble City?," *Audubon Magazine* 68 (1966): 47–52; "Ecological Determinism," in

But McHarg's target was not simply the developers – "the despoilers." He criticized planners and conservationists, too. In different ways, he argued, each group had failed to respond to the environmental challenge posed by urban growth. Planners typically knew nothing about environmental science, nothing about the value of natural processes. But conservationists also were to blame. "The proponents of nature emphasize preservation," he wrote, "a negative position, one of defense, which excludes positive participation in the real and difficult tasks of creating noble and ennobling cities in fair landscapes." To stop the despoliation of the countryside, he concluded, conservationists needed to widen their field of concern "to include, not only wild environments, but those dominated by man."[70]

At least a few conservationists agreed. In 1966, the president of the Conservation Foundation invited McHarg to write a book about ecology and planning. The result was a classic. Published in 1969, *Design with Nature* joined philosophy and hands-on planning, the two key elements of McHarg's response to the problem of urban growth. In the philosophical chapters, McHarg criticized the commodity view of land, assailed the hubris of western attitudes toward nature, considered the significance of human dependence on natural processes, pondered the true meaning of creativity, explored the forms of life, and argued for a more ecological understanding of "health." The hands-on chapters showed how McHarg had applied the principles of ecological planning to projects of different scales, from the routing of a highway to the development of a metropolitan region. He described in detail the Philadelphia open-space study and the Plan for the Valleys.[71]

The book brought McHarg new renown. Though not the only landscape architect to argue in the 1960s for a new kind of planning, McHarg became the preeminent figure in the field after the publication of *Design with Nature*. The book was reprinted several

F. Fraser Darling and John P. Milton, editors, *Future Environments of North America* (Garden City, NY: Natural History Press, 1966), 526–538; "Values, Process, and Form," in Smithsonian Institution, editor, *The Fitness of Man's Environment* (1968; reprint, New York: Harper & Row, 1970), 207–227. For the quotations, see "Values, Process, and Form," 214; "Blight or the Noble City," 49.
70. McHarg, "Blight or the Noble City," 49; McHarg, "Ecological Determinism," 537.
71. For the origins of *Design with Nature*, see McHarg, *A Quest for Life*, 199–200.

times before the end of 1969, and eventually sold over 350,000 copies. McHarg also made the book into a documentary for the Public Broadcasting Service. *Time* and *Life* did short features on McHarg's work; *Smithsonian* and *The Nation* published longer profiles. McHarg was even invited to talk about designing with nature on the "Tonight" and "Today" shows.[72]

The articles and interviews often highlighted McHarg's most provocative or outrageous comments. But most of the pieces about McHarg struck a hopeful chord. At a time of deepening anxiety about the fate of the planet – *Design with Nature* appeared less than a year before the first Earth Day – his work suggested that we might solve our environmental problems without wrenching social dislocations. Though he could sound like Jeremiah when blasting "anthropocentric clods" for a multitude of environmental sins, he was no mere chastiser: He was also a skilled problem solver.[73]

As one article proclaimed, McHarg had "a sensible plan," a thoughtful approach to a pressing dilemma. "There is a fundamental, still unanswered question that hangs over almost every conservation battle now being fought in this country," the article began. "Whether it's a local group trying to keep an oil refinery out of an

72. For a sense of McHarg's reputation in the late 1960s and early 1970s, see "Ian McHarg vs. Us Anthropocentric Clods," *Life* 67 (August 15, 1969): 48B–48D; "How to Design with Nature," *Time* 94 (October 10, 1969): 70–71; Irene Kiefer, "An Angry Advocate for Nature's Plans," *Smithsonian* 2 (January 1972): 54–57; Dennis Farley, "Land Politics: Ian McHarg," *Atlantic Monthly* 233 (January 1974): 10–17; Anthony Bailey, *Through the Great City: Impressions of Megalopolis* (New York: Macmillan, 1967), 212–216. McHarg discusses the response to *Design with Nature* in *A Quest for Life*, 203–208. In the 1960s, landscape architect Philip Lewis, Jr., was a respected advocate of a kind of ecological planning, and commentators often considered Lewis and McHarg together. The two also spoke together at conferences. See Whyte, *The Last Landscape*, 182–195; Harvard University Landscape Architecture Research Office, *Three Approaches to Environmental Resource Analysis* (Washington: Conservation Foundation, 1967); White House Conference on Natural Beauty, *Beauty for America*, 481–487. Like McHarg, Lewis began by thinking about open-space preservation. He described his method in two important essays: "Quality Corridors for Wisconsin," *Landscape Architecture* 54 (1964): 100–107; "Nature in Our Cities," in Bureau of Sport Fisheries and Wildlife, *Man and Nature in the City* (Washington: USGPO, 1968), 22–27. In addition, see Philip H. Lewis, Jr., *Tomorrow by Design: A Regional Design Process for Sustainability* (New York: John Wiley and Sons, 1996).
73. McHarg continues to inspire people. Recently, for example, a philosopher proposed McHarg as a "patron saint" of the environmental movement. See Alastair S. Gunn, "Rethinking Communities: Environmental Ethics in an Urbanized World," *Environmental Ethics* 20 (1998): 341–360.

estuary, or a state legislature debating . . . the location of a jetport, the questions are the same: Will we be forced to slow or stop our economic growth in order to preserve our environment? Where can we put the damn things?" McHarg was one of the few people who had done more than theorize about the problem. "For the past dozen years," the article continued, "while he has been warning of approaching environmental disaster, McHarg has also been at work developing a fundamentally new approach to environmental problems: an ingenious set of analytical techniques, mapping procedures and computer programs whose aim is to take all of the paraphernalia of a growing economy – from highways and sewage plants to houses and country clubs – and fit them decently into the environment."[74]

From hard experience, McHarg knew that many of the boosters of *Design with Nature* underestimated the difficulty of changing the postwar pattern of suburban growth. The key to "sensible" building was not simply new analytical techniques. To use the new tools wisely, McHarg believed, developers, planners, and citizens needed a new set of values. They needed to reconsider the relationship between human communities and the nonhuman world. They also needed to confront what McHarg called "economic determinism" – the idea that the only function of land was to provide profits. Those kinds of intellectual shifts would not come easily.

By the time McHarg's book appeared in 1969, however, many Americans had already begun to think differently about urban and suburban land. They had concluded that the value of wetlands, steep hillsides, and floodplains should not be assessed solely in economic terms. In several ways, indeed, the where-not-to-build debate of the 1950s and 1960s broke new ground.

Before World War II, preservationists and conservationists mainly sought to preserve places of extraordinary natural beauty and conserve important natural resources. The where-not-to-build activists of the 1950s and 1960s similarly used aesthetic and economic arguments to justify restrictions on private development of "sensitive lands." But the where-not-to-build campaigns also depended to an unprecedented extent on ecological arguments. For the critics of

74. James Nathan Miller, "A Sensible Plan," *National Civic Review* 59 (1970): 371. The Miller piece also appeared in *Reader's Digest* 97 (August 1970): 77–81.

suburban development, the importance of wetlands, hillsides, and floodplains did not lie primarily in their beauty or resources – all three kinds of land were most important as parts of natural processes.

The growing regard for natural processes in the 1950s and 1960s also led to new thinking about the balance between public and private interests. In the late 19th and early 20th centuries, the preservation and conservation movements focused on acquiring and managing public land – national parks, forests, and wildlife refuges. In the postwar decades, in contrast, the where-not-to-build debate went beyond the issue of public ownership. Though a number of cities and states acquired wetlands, steep hillsides, and floodplains as open space, the critics of building on sensitive lands ultimately sought to restrict the use of private property. The where-not-to-build campaigns of the 1950s and 1960s thus planted the seeds of future controversies over property rights.

6

Water, Soil, and Wildlife: The Federal Critiques of Tract-House Development

In 1967, the U.S. Department of Agriculture and the U.S. Department of Housing and Urban Development cosponsored a conference on "Soil, Water, and Suburbia." To some observers, no doubt, the partnership of the two agencies seemed odd. The agricultural bureaucracy was one of the oldest in the capital, but the creation of HUD had come only two years before. What had brought the departments together?[1]

The conference was a sign of a new "urban consciousness" in Washington. In the postwar decades, almost all the nation's population growth had come in cities and suburbs, and intellectuals and policymakers slowly began to come to terms with the growing power of metropolitan America. Historian George Mowry summed up the momentous transformation in the title of a survey of the United States from 1920 to 1960: *The Urban Nation*. To meet the needs of the metropolitan majority, legislators and administrators around the country struggled to rethink the responsibilities of government, and the reconceptualization affected everything from the apportionment of legislative seats to the structure of government departments. To remain relevant, the old bureaucracies with rural roots started to pay more attention to the urban environment. The joint conference in 1967 thus was important as a bridge between the past and the future.[2]

1. U.S. Department of Agriculture and U.S. Department of Housing and Urban Development, *Soil, Water, and Suburbia* (Washington: USGPO, 1968), 16.
2. In *A Nation of Cities: The Federal Government and Urban America, 1933–1965* (New York: Oxford University Press, 1975), Mark I. Gelfand first described the new urban consciousness of postwar policymakers. See 276–307. Though Gelfand does not discuss the three natural resource agencies that are the focus of this chapter, all three well illustrate

The gathering also had a more specific purpose. Secretary of Agriculture Orville Freeman succinctly explained the mission in the opening session. In the 1930s, after generations of reckless pillaging of the land, the nation's farmers faced disastrous dust storms and floods, and the federal government responded by establishing the Soil Conservation Service. "The urban and suburban exploitation of land in the past two decades has been equally devastating," the secretary argued. "Damage is occurring at blinding speed." Accordingly, the two departments had to act with "crusading spirit and drive" to encourage conservation in metropolitan areas. "The new conservation must have a town-and-country look."[3]

In truth, the nation's leaders were not prepared to crusade against the destructiveness of suburban sprawl. The federal government had contributed to the problem in several ways, from encouraging the purchase of single-family homes to building the interstate highway system, and a number of government programs still stood in the way of reform. But the call to action at the Soil, Water, and Suburbia conference was not simply rhetoric. By 1967, a handful of federal natural resource agencies already were leaders in the effort to reduce the environmental cost of tract-house development.

The Geological Survey, the Soil Conservation Service, and the Fish and Wildlife Service made the greatest contributions. For all three agencies, the conservation effort in fast-growing metropolitan areas required a break with tradition. The Geological Survey was established after the Civil War to inventory the land and water resources of the sparsely settled regions of the West. The first mission of SCS was the protection of agricultural productivity. The Fish and Wildlife Service was the result of a merger between a Department of Commerce office organized to promote the fishing industry and a Department of Agriculture bureau responsible for enforcing game-protection laws and controlling agricultural predators and pests. To

his argument. In addition, see George E. Mowry, *The Urban Nation: 1920–1960* (New York: Hill and Wang, 1965).

3. Freeman's remarks are in U.S. Department of Agriculture and U.S. Department of Housing and Urban Development, *Soil, Water, and Suburbia,* 16. Part of this passage paraphrases Selden Lee Tinsley, "Planning for Conservation in the Suburbs," in U.S. Department of Agriculture, *A Place to Live: The Yearbook of Agriculture 1963* (Washington: USGPO, 1963), 393. In 1968, a presidential task force also called for a new urban conservation. See Charles M. Haar, editor, *The President's Task Force on Suburban Problems: Final Report* (Cambridge: Ballinger, 1974), xxix, 13, 33, 66–67, 175–180.

varying degrees, however, all three organizations saw the postwar growth of cities and suburbs as a challenge. Though none had the power to regulate homebuilding, all sought to improve the process by providing important information to citizens, builders, and local officials.[4]

Hydrology and Urban Growth

In 1956, the editor of the Soil Conservation Service magazine told the story of Max Bader, a resident of a fast-growing suburb of Washington:

He bought a home in a new development on the flood plain of a small creek. The realtor who sold him the home assured him, truthfully, that the area hadn't flooded in 20 years. But Bader's basement was filled with muddy floodwater the first spring after he moved into the house. He was angry, and the realtor was perplexed. They hadn't taken into consideration the fact that hundreds of new homes had been built in the creek watershed, during the past year. All of the shingled roofs, the bare yards with their heavy clay soils, and the paved streets shed runoff water into the creek as rapidly as the rain fell. So the creek flooded the area for the first time in more than 20 years; and it continues to do so with each heavy rain.

The editor's lesson was straightforward: People should be more careful about building in floodplains. But the story also suggested a more complicated point. Apparently, urban growth made floods more frequent.[5]

Was that really true? In the 1950s, a number of people began to argue that urbanization increased the volume of storm water in a watershed. The argument was logical. In a field or a forest, the ground absorbed rain and slowed runoff; once builders replaced the natural cover with smooth impervious surfaces, however, a hard rain could quickly become a torrent. The evidence seemed to support the argument. In a number of watersheds transformed by development, residents and officials reported that streams, creeks,

---

4. For the early history of the three agencies, see A. Hunter Dupree, *Science in the Federal Government: A History of Policies and Activities to 1940* (Cambridge: Belknap Press, 1957).

5. Tom Dale, "Under All Is The Land," *Soil Conservation* 23 (October 1957): 51.

and runs were flooding more often. But the evidence was both scanty and unscientific. No one had studied the issue. Though the reports of increased flooding were plausible, a team of Geological Survey researchers concluded in 1958, the observations might be misleading. Since the use of floodplains was increasing, "floods may appear larger and more frequent because the damage possibilities have been increased and damage occurs more frequently. This may happen even though the actual flood magnitudes have not increased." Accordingly, the relationship between urbanization and flooding required systematic study.[6]

The Geological Survey was prepared to investigate the issue. For decades, the agency's water-resources division had collected data about stream flows in hundreds of parts of the country. Though the field of hydrology had rural roots, the agency's hydrologists now recognized the need to consider the role of water in the nation's rapidly growing metropolitan areas. In 1961, the agency began publishing a pioneering series of studies of "the hydrological effects of urban growth." To provide information to planners, the agency also established an urban water program and issued a series of reports on "water in the urban environment."[7]

The first publication in the series on hydrology – "Urban Growth and the Water Regimen" – succinctly explained the survey's new focus. "The growth of population in city and suburb during the past half century has been tremendous and the trend is continuing," the

---

6. The quotation comes from Sulo W. Wiitala, Karl R. Jetter, and Alan J. Somerville, *Hydraulic and Hydrologic Aspects of Flood-Plain Planning* [Open-File Report] (Harrisburg, PA: U.S. Geological Survey, 1958), 87–88. For examples of the argument about urbanization and runoff, see Bernard Frank and Anthony Netboy, *Water, Land, and People* (New York: Alfred A. Knopf, 1950), 42–43; D. A. Williams, "Urbanization of Productive Farmland," *Soil Conservation* 22 (October 1956): 60, 63–64; Marion Clawson, R. Burnell Held, and Charles H. Stoddard, *Land for the Future* (Baltimore: Johns Hopkins University Press, 1960), 121; Jean Gottmann, *Megalopolis: The Urbanized Northeastern Seaboard of the United States* (New York: Twentieth Century Fund, 1961), 338.

7. For a description of the survey's urban water program, see William J. Schneider, "The U.S. Geological Survey Urban Water Program," in Walter L. Moore and Carl W. Morgan, editors, *Effects of Watershed Changes on Streamflow* (Austin: University of Texas Press, 1969): 165–168. The studies of the "hydrological effects of urban growth" were published periodically as parts of Geological Survey Water-Supply Paper 1591 (Washington: USGPO, 1961–1968). For the reports on "Water in the Urban Environment," see Geological Survey Circular 601 (Washington: USGPO, 1970–1973) and the third and fourth parts of Geological Survey Water-Supply Paper 2001 (Washington: USGPO, 1970–1974).

study began. "At the same time, the social, political, and economic problems resulting from this growth have become increasingly complex. Basic to many of these problems is man's need for land and water, and his effect upon these resources as he occupies and builds, with ever-increasing density, upon land once occupied only by field or forest. This report is a preliminary appraisal of some of the effects of urban man's activities upon his water resources as they occur both on and beneath the surface of the ground."[8]

The list of topics was long. How much water did cities and suburbs consume, and where did the water come from? Were the sources likely to prove sufficient to meet the growing needs of the urban and suburban population? What was the impact of urbanization on aquifers? Did the use of septic tanks and the irrigation of lawns significantly change surface and underground flows of water? What were the principal threats to water quality in metropolitan watersheds? What percent of the nation's developed land lay in floodplains? Were the risks of damage from flooding greater in cities and suburbs?

For a number of reasons, the survey's hydrologists gave special attention to the issue of storm drainage. The subject had great economic importance. If the peak flow of streams increased as a result of development, then the historic flood record had little value for designers of drainage systems. To reduce flood losses, engineers and planners needed to know more about the likely effects of urbanization on the volume and speed of storm runoff. The subject was also fundamental to a thorough understanding of urban hydrology, since runoff affected the supply of groundwater and the character

---

8. John Savini and J. C. Kammerer, *Urban Growth and the Water Regimen* [Geological Survey Water Supply Paper 1591–A] (Washington: USGPO, 1961), A-1. The survey's chief hydrologist offered a similar explanation in the foreword to the reports collected in Geological Survey Circular 601:

Urbanization – the concentration of people in urban areas and the consequent expansion of these areas – is a characteristic of our time. It has brought with it a host of new or aggravated problems that often make new demands on our natural resources and our physical environment. Problems involving water as a vital resource and a powerful environmental agent are among the most critical. These problems include the maintenance of both the quantity and quality of our water supply for consumption, for recreation, and general welfare and the alleviation of hazards caused by floods, drainage, erosion, and sedimentation.

of streams. Runoff also affected water quality both above and below the surface.[9]

The survey began to explore the runoff issue in a handful of places in the mid-1950s, and the research effort soon expanded. By 1970, the agency's staff had completed more than a dozen studies of watersheds in fast-growing areas in California, New York, Virginia, Maryland, Michigan, Illinois, North Carolina, and Mississippi. The runoff investigations took two forms. In some studies, researchers compared the flow of streams in rural and urban regions within a watershed. In other studies, investigators were able to analyze the water regimen before and after development. Either way, the studies showed a dramatic increase in flood potential in the wake of suburban growth. The change in land use doubled, tripled, or quadrupled the volume of runoff. The speed of the storm flow also increased sharply. Because a much greater amount of water ran off the land in less time, the result was likely to be more frequent and more damaging floods.[10]

9. In *Urban Growth and the Water Regimen,* for example, Savini and Kammerer concluded that runoff was the most important issue in urban hydrology. See A-38.
10. For a sampling of the survey's work on runoff in the 1950s and 1960s, see S. W. Wiitala, *Some Aspects of the Effect of Urban and Suburban Development upon Runoff* [Open-File Report] (Lansing, MI: U.S. Geological Survey, 1961); R. W. Carter, "Magnitude and Frequency of Floods in Suburban Areas," in *Short Papers in the Geologic and Hydrologic Sciences* [Geological Survey Professional Paper 424-B] (Washington: USGPO, 1961): B9–11; Arvi O. Waananen, "Hydrologic Effects of Urban Growth – Some Characteristics of Urban Runoff," in *Short Papers in the Geologic and Hydrologic Sciences* [Geological Survey Professional Paper 424–C] (Washington: USGPO, 1961): C353–356; R. M. Sawyer, "Effect of Urbanization on Storm Drainage and Groundwater Discharge in Nassau County, New York," in *Short Papers in Geology and Hydrology* [Geological Survey Professional Paper 475–C] (Washington: USGPO, 1963): C185–187; E. E. Harris and S. E. Rantz, *Effect of Urban Growth on Streamflow Regimen of Permanente Creek, Santa Clara County, California* [Geological Survey Water-Supply Paper 1591–B] (Washington: USGPO, 1964); John R. Crippen, "Changes in Character of Unit Hydrographs, Sharon Creek, California, after Suburban Development," in *Geological Survey Research 1965* [Geological Survey Professional Paper 525–D] (Washington: USGPO, 1965): D196–198; K. V. Wilson, "A Preliminary Study of the Effect of Urbanization on Floods in Jackson, Mississippi," in *Geological Survey Research 1967* [Geological Survey Professional Paper 575–D] (Washington: USGPO, 1967): D259–261; Luna B. Leopold, *Hydrology for Urban Land Planning – A Guidebook on the Hydrologic Effects of Urban Land Use* [Geological Survey Circular 554] (Washington: USGPO, 1968), 1–11; Lawrence A. Martens, *Flood Inundation and Effects of Urbanization in Metropolitan Charlotte, North Carolina* [Geological Survey Water-Supply Paper 1591–C] (Washington: USGPO, 1968); G. E. Seaburn, *Effects of Urban Development on Direct Runoff to East Meadow Brook, Nassau County, Long Island, New York* [Geological Survey Professional Paper 627–B] (Washington: USGPO, 1969); Daniel G. Anderson, *Effects of Urban Development on Floods in Northern Virginia* [Geological Survey Water-

In part, the increase in flood potential was due simply to the increase in impervious area. By analyzing aerial photographs of suburbanizing areas, a number of survey researchers were able to give fairly precise estimates of the change in area covered by structures and pavement. The increase usually was both substantial and rapid. In one California watershed, the impervious surface jumped from about 4 percent in 1945 to 19 percent in 1958. In some suburban areas, the degree of imperviousness even reached 30 percent.[11]

But the change in impervious surface was not the only important variable. Though the survey hydrologists hoped to provide a universal method of calculating the effect of urbanization on runoff, the task proved impossible: The increase in flood peaks was never a simple function of the increase in road, sidewalk, and roof area. Instead, the runoff in newly suburbanized watersheds depended on a variety of factors, including the design decisions of developers. Indeed, although the survey's researchers rarely highlighted the role of builders, the evidence in the runoff reports added up to a serious challenge to the postwar pattern of development.

With the help of bulldozers, builders eliminated the natural drainage channels in subdivision tracts. They filled in creeks, brooks, and runs to create flat construction sites. In a watershed in a rapidly growing county outside of Washington, builders had destroyed

Supply Paper 2001–C] (Washington: USGPO, 1970); Andrew M. Spieker, *Water in Urban Planning, Salt Creek Basin, Illinois: Water Management as Related to Alternative Land-Use Practices* [Geological Survey Water-Supply Paper 2002] (Washington: USGPO, 1970), 37–38.

11. The California statistics come from Harris and Rantz, *Effect of Urban Growth on Streamflow Regimen of Permanente Creek*, B9–13. For examples of areas with higher figures, see Anderson, *Effects of Urban Development on Floods in Northern Virginia*, C9–10. Though the survey reports did not contrast the imperviousness of suburbs built before and after World War II, the postwar communities had more pavement. In most prewar suburbs, the streets were gravel, with side swales or ditches – as a result, a fair amount of rain could soak into the ground. See D. Earl Jones, Jr., "Where Is Urban Hydrology Practice Today?," *Journal of the Hydraulics Division, Proceedings of the American Society of Civil Engineers* 97 (HY2, February 1971): 258. Between 1950 and 1965, local governments built 290,000 miles of roads – more than twice the total for the period from 1921 to 1940. See U.S. Bureau of the Census, *Historical Statistics of the United States, Colonial Times to 1970* (Washington: USGPO, 1975), 710. In postwar subdivisions, the streets also tended to be wider than in prewar neighborhoods. In San Francisco, for example, the streets in postwar suburbs were typically 40 to 50 feet wide, compared to 32 to 36 feet in prewar communities. See Michael Southworth and Peter M. Owens, "The Evolving Metropolis: Studies of Community, Neighborhood, and Street Form at the Urban Edge," *Journal of the American Planning Association* 59 (1993): 281.

60 percent of the streams by the late 1960s. But the elimination of streams was problematic. "In most conventional urban developments," a Geological Survey circular explained in 1971, "the land is stripped of much of its vegetation and divided into rectangular lots in a regular grid pattern. This method of development obliterates many of the smaller drainage channels, and they must be replaced by enclosed storm sewers. While the storm sewers are generally adequate to handle the runoff from minor and moderate storms, the sewers overflow during the occasional severe storm and flood streets and basements."[12]

Even when the storm sewers in a subdivision worked properly, the survey investigations demonstrated, the artificial drainage system could cause problems downstream. The outlet for storm drains was generally the nearest large stream, so the sewer system forced the stream to carry a tremendous burden after a hard rain. Instead of soaking into the ground or evaporating or flowing into a network of drainage channels, the storm water in the sewered area rushed to the stream in a few minutes or hours. Thus, the sewer system solved a problem in one area by creating a problem in another place: The increased stream flow made houses in downstream communities more vulnerable to flooding.[13]

Though the survey was most interested in the issue of flooding, the runoff investigations suggested that the use of streams as storm sewer outlets might have a variety of environmental impacts. The temperature of storm water in suburban areas sometimes exceeded the temperature of outlet streams by 10 degrees – a difference great enough to endanger certain types of fish. The increased speed and volume of flow might also transform the character of the stream. As a survey guide to urban hydrology noted, a stream "which is

---

12. For the quotation, see David A. Rickert and Andrew M. Spieker, *Real-Estate Lakes* [Geological Survey Circular 601–G] (Washington: USGPO, 1971), G3. Savini and Kammerer also argued that the elimination of streams contributed to flooding problems in urbanized watersheds. See *Urban Growth and the Water Regimen*, A8. The statistic about stream loss is cited by Harold E. Thomas and William J. Schneider, *Water as an Urban Resource and Nuisance* [Geological Survey Circular 601–D] (Washington: USGPO, 1970), D3.

13. For the effect of sewer systems on the peak flows in nearby streams, see Seaburn, *Effects of Urban Development on Direct Runoff to East Meadow Brook, Nassau County, Long Island, New York*. In addition, see Arvi O. Waananen, "Urban Effects on Water Yield," in Moore and Morgan, *Effects of Watershed Changes on Streamflow*, 181.

gradually enlarged owing to the increased floods caused by urbanization, tends to have unstable and unvegetated banks, scoured or muddy channel beds, and unusual debris accumulations. These all tend to decrease the amenity value of the stream."[14]

Inevitably, the survey studies neglected a number of important issues. The research lacked a rigorous historical component. Though a careful reading of the results suggested that the tract-house form of development sharply increased the peak flow of streams, the survey investigators never compared the hydrology of prewar and postwar suburbs.

The runoff studies also did not consider in sufficient detail the issue of imperviousness. Were all structures and paved surfaces equally impervious? If not, why not? Similarly, the survey's researchers seldom distinguished between types of vegetative groundcover. What allowed the greatest absorption of storm water? In a 1963 study published in *Public Works,* a county conservation official and a U.S. Forest Service scientist demonstrated that water ran off grass lawns quite quickly. Indeed, lawns behaved more like slabs of concrete than sponges. Why? Unlike the ground in a forest or a field, the soil in a suburban yard was usually quite compact, with little ability to absorb rain, because it was made by bulldozers, not by natural processes. In other words, the way the typical tract-house builder prepared a site for construction exacerbated the drainage problem. If a house had a septic tank, the ability of the lawn to slow runoff could be reduced further: The ground was often saturated with waste water from toilets, showers, laundries, and sinks. But the Geological Survey did not follow up these insights.[15]

14. The quotation comes from Leopold, *Hydrology for Urban Land Planning,* 2. For the impact of artificial drainage systems on stream temperatures, see also 17. In addition, see E. J. Pluhowski, *Urbanization and Its Effect on the Temperature of the Streams on Long Island, N. Y.* [Geological Survey Professional Paper 627–D] (Washington: USGPO, 1970).

15. In a 1975 review of research in the field, a task force of the American Society of Civil Engineers pointed out the lack of detailed work on imperviousness. See Task Committee on the Effects of Urbanization on Low Flow, Total Runoff, Infiltration, and Ground-Water Recharge of the Committee on Surface-Water Hydrology, "Aspects of Hydrological Effects of Urbanization," *Journal of the Hydraulics Division, Proceedings of the American Society of Civil Engineers* 101 (HY5, May 1975): 458. The head of the task force was a Geological Survey hydrologist. For the study of lawn drainage, see Paul M. Felton and Howard W. Lull, "Suburban Hydrology Can Improve Watershed Conditions," *Public Works* 94 (1963): 94. The first survey report on urban hydrology noted the effect of septic tanks on drainage, but the runoff researchers did not pursue the subject.

Despite the oversights, however, the survey's research had considerable influence. To a great extent, the agency helped to establish urban hydrology as a distinct area of inquiry. The research on the flood characteristics of fast-growing areas was especially important. In a 1969 review of the field conducted by a task force of the American Society of Civil Engineers, a fifth of the works cited in the annotated bibliography were survey publications. In a chronological guide to major studies of storm runoff in urbanizing watersheds, 10 of the first 15 were conducted by survey hydrologists. By the late 1960s, the general conclusion of the survey investigations was widely accepted in professional circles: The process of urbanization increased the volume and speed of runoff. Thus, the agency's work encouraged engineers and urban planners to consider "the possibility of deliberate modification of land-development and drainage practices to reduce the peak rates of storm runoff from urbanizing areas."[16]

What could be done to reduce the flood potential created by suburban construction? With a few exceptions, the Geological Survey did not address that question directly. Though the runoff studies were often intended to provide city, county, and state officials with decision-making information – many were conducted with the cooperation of local agencies – the survey investigators rarely contemplated alternatives: They simply described and analyzed the hydrological changes in urbanizing watersheds. In the late 1960s, however, the agency began to publish guides for urban planners and

See Savini and Kammerer, *Urban Growth and the Water Regimen,* A20–21. As Savini and Kammerer observed, the heavy watering of lawns also added to suburban drainage problems. The problem was not limited to residential areas; the irrigation of golf courses increased runoff in some areas. See Crippen, "Changes in Character of Unit Hydrographs, Sharon Creek, California, after Suburban Development," D198; Waananen, "Urban Effects on Water Yield," 179.

16. For the annotated bibliography, see Task Force on Effect of Urban Development on Flood Discharges, "Effect of Urban Development on Flood Discharges – Current Knowledge and Future Needs," *Journal of the Hydraulics Division, Proceedings of the American Society of Civil Engineers* 95 (HY1, January 1969): 293–308. For the chronological list of runoff studies, see Eugene J. Riordan, Neil S. Grigg, and Robert L. Hiller, *Development of a Drainage and Flood Control Management Program for Urbanizing Communities – Part II* (Fort Collins: Colorado State University Environmental Resources Center, 1978), 178–179. The survey was responsible for the first, second, third, fourth, sixth, seventh, tenth, eleventh, thirteenth, and fourteenth studies. For the quotation, see William H. Espey, Jr., David E. Winslow, and Carl W. Morgan, "Urban Effects on the Unit Hydrograph," in Moore and Morgan, *Effects of Watershed Changes on Streamflow,* 215.

developers, and the publications often included suggestions about ways to improve drainage conditions.[17]

In a 1968 guide to "hydrology for urban land planning," for example, survey hydrologist Luna Leopold suggested a half-dozen methods for slowing and storing storm water in new developments. Instead of installing paved gutters and curbs, builders could use street-side swales to trap water temporarily. Builders could create small reservoirs in subdivisions by partially damming streams – the farm pond offered a model. Alternatively, builders could construct ponds, fountains, or drainage basins to serve as storage areas outside of the stream channel. Of course, builders could also preserve natural systems of drainage.[18]

A handful of Leopold's suggestions became a new ideal – "blue-green development." The phrase was coined in the mid-1960s by a Federal Housing Administration official, and the concept soon had the support of civil engineers and landscape architects. The basic idea was to combine storm water storage and open space. "Rather than constructing large artificial drainage channels in urbanizing areas," explained the authors of one of the Geological Survey reports on water in the urban environment, "the developer preserves the natural drainage channels and flood plains and creates artificial lakes by impoundment or by a combination of impoundment and excavation. These lakes serve the purposes of providing recreation, an esthetically pleasing environment, and space for the temporary storage of storm runoff." By the early 1970s, the idea had shaped the development of a number of projects, from a low-cost subdivision in El Paso to the celebrated "new town" of Woodlands, Texas.[19]

---

17. In addition to the works cited in the next two notes, the guides include William J. Schneider, David A. Rickert, and Andrew M. Spieker, *Role of Water in Urban Planning and Management* [Geological Survey Circular 601-H] (Washington: USGPO, 1973). For the studies done with the cooperation of local agencies, see the works by Harris and Rantz, Martens, Seaburn, Anderson, and Spieker cited earlier.
18. Leopold, *Hydrology for Urban Land Planning*, 11.
19. The quotation is from Rickert and Spieker, *Real-Estate Lakes*, G3. In addition, see D. Earl Jones, Jr., "Urban Hydrology – A Redirection," *Civil Engineering* 37 (August 1967): 59–61; U.S. Department of Agriculture and U.S. Department of Housing and Urban Development, *Soil, Water, and Suburbia*, 63; Richard H. McCuen and Harry W. Piper, "Hydrologic Impact of Planned Unit Developments," *Journal of the Urban Planning and Development Division, Proceedings of the American Society of Civil Engineers* 101 (UP1, May 1975): 93–102. Jones describes the El Paso development. For the blue-green concept in Woodlands, see Anne Whiston Spirn, *The Granite Garden: Urban Nature and Human Design* (New York: Basic Books, 1984), 163–166.

Soil Erosion in Suburbia

In the late 1950s, a group of homeowners around Lake Barcroft in Fairfax County, Virginia, began to worry about silt. The lakeshore was often muddy, and the lake seemed to be filling up with sediment. What was causing the problem? The age-old response was to blame poor farming practices, but the region had few farms – the county was developing rapidly into a major suburb of Washington. The perplexed homeowners asked the Soil Conservation Service to investigate.

At the time, no city or state sought to control soil erosion in metropolitan areas. If erosion from a construction site caused damage to a nearby property, the property owner could sue the developer. Because the plaintiffs in erosion cases sometimes won, a handful of construction engineers had begun to recommend erosion-control measures for large projects. But the overwhelming majority of builders were not worried about the problem. There was also little public interest in the issue.[20]

The Soil Conservation Service report on Lake Barcroft turned out to be a catalyst for change. Because the lake was built in 1915 as a water-supply reservoir, the study could compare the rate of sedimentation over a span of more than 40 years, and the results showed a dramatic intensification of the problem in the 1940s and 1950s. From 1915 to 1938, when the surrounding area was mostly farmland, the deposition of silt from erosion caused the lake to shrink by just four-tenths of an acre. But in the period after 1938, when nearly 70 percent of the lake's watershed was transformed into suburban neighborhoods, the lake shrank by six acres.[21]

The study strongly suggested that erosion during the construction of houses, streets, and shopping centers could be a significant

20. In the early 1960s, a survey of builders in Maryland found little concern about soil erosion during the construction of subdivisions, although a few consulting engineers acknowledged the problem. See M. Gordon Wolman, *Problems Posed by Sediment Derived from Construction Activities in Maryland* (Annapolis: Maryland Water Pollution Control Commission, 1964), 60. Wolman also discusses the law of sediment. See 82–84.
21. J. N. Holeman and A. F. Geiger, *Sedimentation of Lake Barcroft, Fairfax County, Virginia* (Washington: Soil Conservation Service, 1959). The study is summarized by Harold P. Guy and George E. Ferguson, "Sediment in Small Reservoirs Due to Urbanization," *Journal of the Hydraulics Division, Proceedings of the American Society of Civil Engineers* 88 (HY2, March 1962): 29–30.

problem. Yet the SCS investigators did not address a number of broader questions raised by the study. Did some ways of building cause more soil erosion than others? What sort of standard should be used to gauge the severity of erosion from suburban construction sites? Besides the filling-in of lakes and reservoirs, what were the costs of erosion from development?

For a number of reasons, the Soil Conservation Service was slow to follow up the Lake Barcroft study. The principal mission of the agency was outreach – the provision of technical advice – more than research. Perhaps more important, the agency's traditional way of explaining the need for erosion control did not apply to erosion from urban and suburban construction. With erosion from farmland, the cost was easy to define, since the eroding soil was a scarce productive resource. But the soil lost from construction sites was not productive, and the loss was not borne by the owner of the land – instead, the burden fell off-site.

In contrast to the Soil Conservation Service, the Geological Survey was well equipped to consider the problem of erosion in rapidly urbanizing areas. Because the principal repositories for sediment were rivers, lakes, and estuaries, the problem was partly a matter of hydrology, and the survey's hydrologists were trained to assess changes in the character of the nation's water. Early in 1959, survey hydrologist Harold Guy began the first of a series of studies of erosion in fast-growing areas outside of Washington. The results were striking. In rural regions of Pennsylvania and Virginia, the rate of erosion was generally about 200 tons per square mile, Guy soon reported, but the figures for a housing construction site in Maryland went as high as 50,000 tons per square mile. Though he did not make a detailed comparison of erosion rates from different types of construction, Guy also argued that the problem was less severe in developments with "custom-built" houses than in tract-house subdivisions. The methods used to build "mass housing" exposed more land for a longer time, while the longer drainage channels in the typical subdivision increased the amount of sediment carried away by storm runoff.[22]

Throughout the early 1960s, survey researchers found similar

22. Guy and Ferguson, "Sediment in Small Reservoirs Due to Urbanization," 32–35.

evidence at a number of sites around the region. Again and again, the construction of subdivisions led to erosion five or ten times higher than that in nearby fields and forests. In a few cases, the sediment losses were hundreds of times as severe. The variation in the results from study to study was apparently caused by a variety of factors – the type of soil, the slope of the land, and the extent of precipitation, especially. But the similarities were more important than the differences, because the worst erosion figures came from sites where builders had bulldozed away all vegetation at the start of construction. The exposed soil was generally subsoil, lacking the roots and organic material which helped to protect topsoil against rain, so the ground was especially vulnerable to erosion. Often, builders made the problem even more severe by leaving the land bare for more than a year.[23]

Because the survey had a strong interest in water quality, the hydrologists studying urban erosion often defined sediment as a form of water pollution. The point was not entirely new. In the 1940s, a number of people interested in the fate of the nation's waters began to write about sediment pollution. But the earlier studies of the problem focused on erosion from farming, ranching, logging, and mining – the survey scientists were the first people to point to urbanization as a major cause of sediment pollution. In a 1962 report to the federal outdoor recreation commission, for example, the survey devoted a small section to urban erosion. Thousands of acres of woodlands and grasslands had been "scraped to the bare ground" by mass builders, the report argued, and the exposed soils then ran off during storms to the nearest streams. The result was

23. Frank J. Keller, "Effect of Urban Growth on Sediment Discharge, Northwest Branch Anacostia River Basin, Maryland," *Geological Survey Professional Paper 450–C* (Washington: USGPO, 1962), 129–131; Harold P. Guy, "Residential Construction and Sedimentation at Kensington, MD," in Agricultural Research Service, *Proceedings of the Federal Inter-Agency Sedimentation Conference 1963* [Miscellaneous Publication 970] (Washington: U.S. Department of Agriculture, 1965), 30–37; J. W. Wark and F. J. Keller, *Preliminary Study of Sediment Sources and Transport in the Potomac River Basin* [Technical Bulletin 1963–11] (Washington: Interstate Commission on the Potomac River Basin, 1963); Harold P. Guy, Norman E. Jackson, Kenneth Jarvis, Carl J. Johnson, Carl R. Miller, and Wilber W. Steiner, *A Program for Sediment Control in the Washington Metropolitan Region* [Technical Bulletin 1963–1] (Washington: Interstate Commission on the Potomac River Basin, 1963). In addition, see M. Gordon Wolman and Asher P. Schick, "Effects of Construction on Fluvial Sediment, Urban and Suburban Areas of Maryland," *Water Resources Research* 3 (1967): 451–464, which reports earlier studies of the relationship of erosion to the length of time the ground lay exposed during construction.

serious damage to water quality. By reducing the amount of sunlight able to penetrate the water, sediment decreased the growth of a number of forms of aquatic plant life and lowered the oxygen content of the water. When the oxygen level changed, the balance of fish species might change as well, with game fish giving way to "coarse fish." Sediment could also reduce both fish and shellfish populations by burying nests, spawn, and food supplies. Eventually populations of game fowl might fall as well.[24]

The research done by the survey immediately attracted the attention of officials responsible for controlling water pollution in the Washington area. The Interstate Commission on the Potomac River Basin asked the survey to suggest ways to deal with the sediment problem, and the agency responded in 1963 with two major reports. Both pointed to suburbanization as a major source of sediment pollution. The Maryland Water Pollution Control Commission also hired a former survey scientist to report on the problem of soil erosion in fast-growing suburbs. The report concluded that "the tonnage of sediment derived from an acre of ground under construction in developments and highways may exceed 20,000 to 40,000 times the amount eroded from farms and woodlands in an equivalent period of time." Accordingly, the report recommended a vigorous state effort to encourage builders to use erosion-control measures. Because the three studies were soon cited in a variety of professional publications, they had impact well beyond the region.[25]

24. For a good example of early writing on sediment pollution, see Harold A. Kemp, "Soil Pollution in the Potomac River Basin," *Journal of the American Water Works Association* 41 (1949): 792–796. In addition, see Interstate Commission on the Potomac River Basin, *Teamwork on the Potomac: The Story of Water Pollution Control* (Washington: Interstate Commission on the Potomac River Basin, 1958), 53. For the discussion of urban erosion, see U.S. Geological Survey, *Water for Recreation – Values and Opportunities: Report to the Outdoor Recreation Resources Review Commission* [ORRRC Study Report 10] (Washington: USGPO, 1962), 15. In addition, see H. A. Swenson, "Sediment in Streams," *Journal of Soil and Water Conservation* 19 (1964): 223–226.
25. The three reports are Wark and Keller, *Preliminary Study of Sediment Sources and Transport in the Potomac River Basin;* Guy, Jackson, Jarvis, Johnson, Miller, and Steiner, *A Program for Sediment Control in the Washington Metropolitan Region;* Wolman, *Problems Posed by Sediment Derived from Construction Activities in Maryland.* The quotation from the third report is on iii. For citations of these studies, see David R. Dawdy, "Knowledge of Sedimentation in Urban Environments," *Journal of the Hydraulics Division, Proceedings of the American Society of Civil Engineers* 93 (HY6, November 1967): 235–245; Wolman and Schick, "Effects of Construction on Fluvial Sediment, Urban and Suburban Areas of Maryland," 313, 323; Robert K. Davis and David B. Brooks, "Some Economic Aspects of Urban Sedimentation," *Land Economics* 43 (1967): 312; Harold

By the mid-1960s, indeed, the problem of sediment pollution was beginning to receive publicity in nonprofessional forums. In 1966, one of the first popular books on water pollution included a strongly worded indictment of the building industry. "Silting is usually blamed on the farmer and the logger," the author argued, "but the most recent villain is the real estate developer. In the clearing of vast acreages for urban housing projects the bulldozer is allowed to tear the soil to pieces. Trees are seldom preserved. A whole area is leveled and replanted later. This leaves large sections of raw ground open to heavy erosion for a critical year or two." The consequences could be severe: "The sudden silting of rivers and reservoirs that results from an ambitious real estate project can assassinate a river. Aside from the fact that the river becomes a sort of brown molasses 'too thick to navigate and too thin to cultivate,' the silting has a murderous effect on water life and the ability of the river to assimilate organic waste."[26]

Belatedly, the Soil Conservation Service also began to sound alarms. "The erosion crisis, which in the 1930s spurred a vigorous soil conservation effort, today is moving from the Nation's farmlands to its rapidly growing urban and suburban areas," an SCS official warned in 1965. "The builder's bulldozer bids fair to become the modern successor to the farmer's plow as the instrument of soil destruction." But the devastation could be stopped. If citizens

P. Guy, *Sediment Problems in Urban Areas* [Geological Survey Circular 601–E] (Washington: USGPO, 1970), E7–8; Harold P. Guy and George E. Ferguson, "Stream Sediment: An Environmental Problem," *Journal of Soil and Water Conservation* 25 (1970): 219–221; Glenn B. Anderson, "Soil Erosion – A Major Menace to Urban-Fringe Conservation," *Journal of Soil and Water Conservation* 20 (1965): 184–185; Leopold, *Hydrology for Urban Land Planning*, 11–14; U.S. Department of Agriculture and U.S. Department of Housing and Urban Development, *Soil, Water, and Suburbia*, 48.

26. The quotation comes from Donald E. Carr, *Death of the Sweet Waters* (New York: W. W. Norton, 1966), 128–129. In addition, see Lawrence S. Hamilton, "An Ecological Perspective on Urban Sprawl," *American Forests* 69 (June 1963): 40; William O. Douglas, *A Wilderness Bill of Rights* (Boston: Little, Brown and Company, 1965), 11; President's Council on Recreation and Natural Beauty, *From Sea to Shining Sea* (Washington: USGPO, 1968), in Phillip O. Foss, *Recreation* (New York: Chelsea House, 1971), 463; Dwight F. Rettie, "Let's Urbanize Conservation Education," in James B. Trefethen, editor, *Transactions of the Thirty-Third North American Wildlife and Natural Resources Conference* (Washington: Wildlife Management Institute, 1968), 467–468; David Zwick and Marcy Benstock, *Water Wasteland: Ralph Nader's Study Group Report on Water Pollution* (1971; reprint, New York: Bantam Books, 1972), 106; Don Gill and Penelope Bonnett, *Nature in the Urban Landscape: A Study of City Ecosystems* (Baltimore: York Press, 1973), 31.

made erosion a public issue, the official argued, builders would adopt erosion-control measures.[27]

The agency's renewed interest in suburban erosion was tied to a decade-long redefinition of mission. Throughout the 1950s, as millions of acres of farmland were transformed into suburbs, the soil-conservation clientele had shrunk. At first, SCS employees responded by calling for a more cautious, land-conserving approach to development. But the spread of the nation's metropolitan areas continued unabated. Slowly, the agency's leaders began to see professional opportunities in the transformation of the countryside, not simply threats. One of the first signs of the new thinking came in the 1963 *Yearbook of Agriculture,* which included several essays on land use at the rural-urban border. In a piece entitled "Planning for Conservation in the Suburbs," an SCS official argued that a variety of environmental problems in fast-growing areas – septic-tank failures, flooding, landslides, and erosion – all stemmed from inadequate attention to soil science. As a result, the nation's soil conservationists had a chance to improve the quality of the suburban environment by showing developers and planning officials how to work more successfully with nature. The agency responded to the challenge. By the mid-1960s, hundreds of SCS county agents no longer offered technical advice solely to farmers. Instead, as the SCS administrator explained in 1968, the agency sought to help both rural and urban landowners "make the right land-use decisions."[28]

Unlike the Geological Survey hydrologists, the employees of the Soil Conservation Service were expected to be adept at public

---

27. Verne M. Bathurst, "Soil Erosion in Urban Areas," *Soil Conservation* 30 (July 1965): 274–275.
28. The SCS magazine *Soil Conservation* published a number of pieces about the loss of farmland in the 1950s. See Henry C. Lint, "Buildings or Farms?," 16 (September 1950): 42–43; D. A. Williams, "Urbanization of Productive Farmland," 22 (October 1956): 60–65; A. B. Beaumont, "A Look at Urbanization," 24 (August 1958): 3–7. The yearbook article is Tinsley, "Planning for Conservation in the Suburbs," 391–398. For the expanding mission of SCS, see U.S. Department of Agriculture and U.S. Department of Housing and Urban Development, *Soil, Water, and Suburbia,* 102. In addition, see D. A. Williams, "Conservation Challenges in New Urban Areas," *Soil Conservation* 32 (1966): 95; Charles E. Kellogg and H. C. Enderlin, "What Urban Building Does to Soil and Water," *Soil Conservation* 35 (November 1969): 86; Norman A. Berg, "What's New with Conservation Districts," *Soil Conservation* 35 (February 1970): 147–149. Though not an SCS employee, Joseph L. Fisher also argued that soil conservationists had opportunities to serve a new clientele in fast-growing suburbs. See "An Expanding Future for Soil Conservation," *Journal of Soil and Water Conservation* 25 (1970): 212–216.

relations, and SCS officials preached the new gospel with passion. In 1966 and again in 1968, the SCS magazine *Soil Conservation* published special issues on the conservation problems of fast-growing urban areas. In 1967, the agency also had a prominent role in the national conference on "Soil, Water, and Suburbia." In several counties, SCS agents led publicity campaigns to dramatize the consequences of erosion in urbanizing areas. They wrote articles for newspapers, appeared on local television programs, and gave talks to builders, civic groups, and municipal officials. Occasionally, SCS officials addressed national audiences of professionals in urban planning. Because the agency had a staff of photographers, SCS employees routinely illustrated talks and articles with dramatic photographs of gullied subdivisions, sediment-choked storm drains, and muddy lakes. The agency even provided funding for a film documentary about urban and suburban erosion: "Mud."[29]

The SCS materials often tallied the direct economic costs of erosion from construction sites. When sediment clogged storm drains or filled lakes, rivers, and harbors, the result might be increased flooding, reduced navigability, or destruction of recreational areas. To avoid those problems, property owners or public agencies had to remove the sediment at a cost of thousands or millions of dollars. Thus, while acknowledging the effects of sediment on water quality, SCS officials emphasized engineering issues.[30]

29. For the issues of *Soil Conservation* devoted to urbanization, see 32 (November 1966); 34 (September 1968). The second issue was tied to the "Soil, Water, and Suburbia" conference. For descriptions of SCS publicity efforts, see John W. Neuberger, "Conservation Programs in the Urban Fringe," *Journal of Soil and Water Conservation* 24 (1969): 216–218; Glenn B. Anderson and Carolyn Johnston, "Conservation in New Urban Areas," *Soil Conservation* 32 (November 1966): 75–77, 90–91; Glenn B. Anderson, "How to Stop Suburban Soil Erosion," *American City* 82 (December 1967): 102–105; "New Motion Picture on Suburban Problems," *Soil Conservation* 34 (September 1968): 29. In 1963, officials from both the Soil Conservation Service and the Geological Survey spoke about erosion at the national conference of the American Society of Planning Officials. See "Bases for Urban Development: Air, Soil, Water," *Planning 1963* (Chicago: American Society of Planning Officials, 1963), 45, 54. For striking examples of SCS photographs of suburban erosion, see Spenser W. Havlick, *The Urban Organism: The City's Natural Resources from an Environmental Perspective* (New York: Macmillan, 1974), 14, 158; Donald H. Gray, "Soil and the City," in Thomas R. Detwyler and Melvin G. Marcus, editors, *Urbanization and the Environment: The Physical Geography of the City* (Belmont, CA: Duxbury Press, 1972), 141–142.

30. For discussion of the costs of dredging sediment, see Anderson, "Soil Erosion," 185; Anderson, "How to Stop Suburban Soil Erosion," 104; U.S. Department of Agriculture and U.S. Department of Housing and Urban Development, *Soil, Water, and Suburbia,* 14. Neuberger, "Conservation Programs in the Urban Fringe," also discusses "property damage problems" caused by eroding soil from construction sites. See 216–217.

SCS employees also highlighted the nuisance of sediment. They told the story of a church graveyard buried under silt after builders denuded a nearby tract. They described the transformation of recreational lakes into mud flats. They recalled the complaints of outraged citizens. "You've seen it happen," an SCS agent wrote in the journal *American City.* "A developer moves in, bulldozing away all the trees and natural ground cover in order to make the land fit his plans. Then it rains. Soil from the tract he denuded flows over paved roads, neighboring lawns and parks. It converts once clear streams into muddy, flooding torrents. Disrupted drainage patterns ruin recreation and even pollute water supplies. The telephone rings. Angry voices insist on quick action. What do *you* do? What *can* you do?"[31]

The Soil Conservation Service also publicized ways to prevent erosion during construction. Developments could be designed to suit the topography, and site preparation could be planned to leave the ground bare for the shortest possible time. To protect the soil after bulldozing, subdivision developers could plant temporary vegetation and cover the ground with mulch. Trees could be preserved – or planted after construction. To trap eroding soil at the site, builders also could dig small debris basins, install terraces, or plant grass in drainage channels. The total cost would often be $150 per acre or less.[32]

The publicity made a difference. In Fairfax County, SCS agent Glenn Anderson was instrumental in effecting the passage of a pioneering erosion-control ordinance in 1966. He demonstrated the practicality of a variety of measures to hold soils in place. He also worked closely with civic groups to marshal popular support. Because sediment from construction sites had reduced the recreational value of two county lakes, the Soil Conservation Service approach

31. For the quotation, see Anderson, "How to Stop Suburban Soil Erosion," 102. On 104, Anderson also describes a 130–acre lake turned into a 90–acre mud flat. The story about the graveyard is in Tinsley, "Planning for Conservation in the Suburbs," 391; U.S. Department of Agriculture and U.S. Department of Housing and Urban Development, *Soil, Water, and Suburbia,* 13–14.
32. See, for example, Tinsley, "Planning for Conservation in the Suburbs," 395; Anderson, "How to Stop Suburban Soil Erosion," 103; Anderson, "Soil Erosion," 185; Anderson and Johnston, "Conservation in New Urban Areas," 90; Theodore H. Ifft, "Solving Erosion and Sedimentation Problems," *Agricultural Engineering* 51 (December 1970): 701–702. The Geological Survey reports on erosion made similar recommendations. See Guy, Jackson, Jarvis, Johnson, Miller, and Steiner, *A Program for Sediment Control in the Washington Metropolitan Region,* 31–37; Guy, *Sediment Problems in Urban Areas,* E6.

to the erosion problem struck a chord with residents. The Northern Virginia Conservation Council – a grassroots group devoted to the preservation of open space – lobbied for the ordinance. The local League of Women Voters was especially active, preparing a slide show and providing speakers for public meetings.[33]

The Fairfax County ordinance soon became a model. It was easy to copy, since it simply required builders to secure county approval of erosion-control plans and to put money in escrow as a guarantee that the plans would be followed. But the origins of the ordinance were atypical. Across the country, the public relations work of the SCS was less important in the passage of erosion-control legislation than the hydrological research of the Geological Survey.

The influence of the Geological Survey was especially evident in Maryland, the first state to put the erosion issue on the policy agenda. In the early 1960s, the state's policymakers defined sediment as a water pollutant. In 1965, Montgomery County established the nation's first suburban erosion-control program as part of a campaign to clean up Rock Creek. The first state law dealing with sediment in urban areas – which applied to only one watershed – was an addition to Maryland's water-quality act. In 1970, when the Maryland legislature passed the nation's first statewide sediment-control bill, the Department of Water Resources was chosen to administer the legislation. Because of sediment deposition, the preamble to the 1970 act explained, the state's watersheds "are being polluted and despoiled to such a degree that fish, marine life, and recreational uses of the waters are being adversely affected."[34]

---

33. Stuart Finley, "Soil Conservation Goes to Town," *Soil Conservation* 34 (September 1968), 38; Anderson and Johnston, "Conservation in New Urban Areas," 76; Anderson, "How to Stop Suburban Soil Erosion," 104.

34. Arnold C. Hawkins, "Maryland's Sediment Control Law," *Journal of Soil and Water Conservation* 26 (1971): 28–29. Hawkins reprints the text of the 1970 law. In addition, see Edward R. Keil, "Urban Sediment-Control Program Adopted by Maryland County," *Soil Conservation* 32 (November 1966): 81–83; William J. Davis, "Watershed Management and Sediment Control in Montgomery County," in David T. Y. Kao, editor, *Proceedings of the National Symposium on Urban Rainfall and Runoff and Sediment Control* (Lexington: University of Kentucky Office of Research and Engineering Services, 1974), 211–217. Like the erosion-control campaign in Fairfax County, the campaign to save Rock Creek had the support of conservationists and citizens' groups, including the League of Women Voters; the Soil Conservation Service was also involved. See League of Women Voters Education Fund, *The Big Water Fight: Trials and Triumphs in Citizen Action on Problems of Supply, Pollution, Flooding, and Planning across the U.S.A.* (Brattleboro, VT: Stephen Greene Press, 1966), 81–90.

The statewide legislation in Maryland was a sign of things to come. By 1970, a significant number of scientists and public officials had begun to think of sediment pollution as "an environmental problem." The Federal Water Quality Administration issued a guide for builders and planners entitled *Urban Soil Erosion and Sediment Control*. The newly established Environmental Protection Agency investigated the issue. In 1972, the Federal Water Pollution Control Act required states to develop plans for controlling erosion. Eventually, every state passed some sort of legislation intended to address the problem.[35]

The harm done by urban and suburban erosion would not have become a public issue if a variety of factors had not come together in the 1960s. The growing concern about water pollution was a prerequisite for action. The desire to protect recreational open space also increased interest in the erosion problem. To some extent, the issue even had resonance for people dismayed at the spread of the treeless subdivision, since trees helped to hold soil in place. But the role of the federal government was critical. The nation's first erosion-control laws were enacted in two fast-growing counties outside of Washington, and the work of federal employees played a key role in both cases.[36]

35. The quotation comes from the subtitle of Guy and Ferguson, "Stream Sediment." The federal publications include National Association of Counties Research Foundation, *Urban Soil Erosion and Sediment Control* (Washington: Federal Water Quality Administration, 1970); Robert E. Thronson, *Control of Erosion and Sediment Deposition from Construction of Highways and Land Development* (Washington: Environmental Protection Agency, 1971). For the importance of the 1972 water pollution act, see James D. Mertes, "Trends in Government Control of Erosion and Sedimentation in Urban Development," *Journal of Soil and Water Conservation* 44 (1989): 550–551.

36. The best example of the tie between the erosion issue and the tree-saving campaign is Charlton Ogburn, Jr., "The Battle to Save the Trees," *Saturday Evening Post* 234 (January 28, 1961): 29, 68.

In our country, with its history of rampaging rivers and gullied hillsides, no one should have to be reminded of the function of natural plant cover in holding soil and water. The story of erosion and of the siltation of streams and rivers, which destroys aquatic life, clogs channels, and causes floods, has been told frequently and well, but generally in terms of bad farming practices. Less well understood is the extent to which the damage is compounded by bulldozing off the vegetation and topsoil, during the development of subdivisions. The District of Columbia's famous Rock Creek, which winds through its chief park after draining an adjacent part of Maryland, tends to flood twice as badly as it did twenty years ago. You know why when you read a statement by Harold P. Guy of the United States Geological Survey pointing out how the water-holding capacity of the watershed has been reduced, as for example in a subdivision in Kensington, Maryland, from which "nearly all of the trees were removed and the natural waterways were

The Fate of Wildlife in the Exploding Metropolis

The construction of tract housing worked havoc on wildlife communities. The bulldozed landscape offered little nourishment or shelter to birds. Though a residential subdivision eventually would support a new population of birds adapted to human settlement, the overall diversity of species often declined. By clearing away vegetation and by filling or channeling streams, builders also eliminated habitat for turtles, snakes, salamanders, frogs, and fish. When construction sediments and septic-tank effluents polluted nearby streams, the threat to wildlife populations increased. Occasionally, the spread of new developments destroyed habitat for larger animals: In Florida, for example, the postwar building boom endangered the panther.[37]

In the first two decades after World War II, however, Americans made very little effort to protect wildlife in rapidly suburbanizing areas of the country. The very word "wildlife" seemed to place the subject outside the ken of urban planners and developers – the metropolis was the home of civilization, not wildness. The nation's wildlife managers and researchers similarly neglected the cities and suburbs. The first session devoted to urban problems at the annual conference of the Wildlife Management Institute was not held until 1967; the first study of the impact of suburbanization on amphibians and reptiles did not appear until 1968. The journal *Urban Ecology* only began publication in 1975.[38]

altered." After this scalping, each inch of runoff from rain falling on the area carried about 250 tons of sediment into Rock Creek, or about fifty times as much as from an equivalent undeveloped watershed. Further reading tells you that in the Washington area as a whole streams now move about 1,000,000 tons of sediment a year, helping to explain why game fishing has suffered so severely in the lower Potomac and why experts debated the ways and means of keeping the Washington harbor open in the future.

37. James B. Trefethen, *An American Crusade for Wildlife* (New York: Winchester Press, 1975), 270; Dale L. Keyes, *Land Development and the Natural Environment: Estimating Impacts* (Washington: Urban Land Institute, 1976), 99–100; Daniel L. Leedy, Robert M. Maestro, and Thomas M. Franklin, *Planning for Wildlife in Cities and Suburbs* [Planning Advisory Service Report 331] (Chicago: American Society of Planning Officials, 1978), 7–9; Richard D. Taber, Richard H. Cooley, and William F. Royce, "The Conservation of Fish and Wildlife," in James A. Bailey, William Elder, and Ted D. McKinney, editors, *Readings in Wildlife Conservation* (Washington: The Wildlife Society, 1974), 479; Ian Douglas, *The Urban Environment* (London: Edward Arnold, 1983), 136.
38. For the pathbreaking nature of the 1967 wildlife conference, see A. J. W. Scheffey, "Farm and Urban Resources: Remarks of the Chairman," in James B. Trefethen, editor, *Trans-*

The U.S. Fish and Wildlife Service was no exception to the rule. In the 1950s, the agency's responsibility for protecting the international flyways forced a limited reckoning with the destructiveness of suburbanization. The rapid development of Long Island came at the expense of thousands of acres of waterfowl habitat, and the agency joined with local conservationists and state officials to try to save the region's surviving wetlands. But the Fish and Wildlife effort in New York did not lead to a more encompassing program to preserve wildlife habitat in cities and suburbs.[39]

The administrative obstacles were formidable. The principal concern of the federal fish and wildlife bureaucracy was the management of public refuges, not the use of private property. The agency's mandate also neglected the vast majority of the nation's wild species. From 1957 to 1974, the Fish and Wildlife Service was called the Bureau of Sport Fisheries and Wildlife, and the name made clear the limits of the agency's responsibilities: The bureau had to be far more concerned about trout and quail than opossums, bluebirds, or salamanders. Throughout the 1950s, indeed, the agency's director of research could not secure funding for work on urban wildlife.[40]

In the mid-1960s, the Fish and Wildlife Service began to feel pressure to assume new responsibilities. The pressure came from two directions. First, a growing number of Americans wanted the chance simply to enjoy wildlife – to watch wild creatures in the outdoors. The demand was especially great in metropolitan areas. Second, a growing number of scientists and conservationists wanted the government to act to protect endangered species. The need was urgent,

actions of the Thirty-Second North American Wildlife and Natural Resources Conference (Washington: Wildlife Management Institute, 1967), 49–50. Sherman A. Minton, Jr., "The Fate of Amphibians and Reptiles in a Suburban Area," *Journal of Herpetology* 2 (December 1968): 113–116, was the first article on the subject. In addition, see Paul N. Orser and Donald J. Shure, "Effects of Urbanization on the Salamander Desmognathus Fuscus Fuscus," *Ecology* 53 (1972): 1148–1154, which was the first work of its kind to appear in a leading scientific journal.

39. I describe the Long Island campaign in chapter five.
40. For the difficulty of securing funding for research on urban wildlife, see Lowell W. Adams and Daniel L. Leedy, editors, *Wildlife Conservation in Metropolitan Environments* (Columbia, MD: National Institute for Urban Wildlife, 1991), 5. The Fish and Wildlife Service publications about the value of wetlands sometimes listed nongame birds and animals which relied on marshes or swamps, but the lists were secondary. See, for example, Samuel P. Shaw and C. Gordon Fredine, *Wetlands of the United States: Their Extent and Their Value to Waterfowl and Other Wildlife* [Circular 39] (Washington: U.S. Fish and Wildlife Service, 1956), 40–42.

the supporters of new legislation argued, because the destruction of wildlife habitat was accelerating rapidly. Again, the problem focused professional attention on the attitudes of urban and suburban residents. "If we want room for wild animals in the wild places of our country," ecologist Raymond Dasmann argued at a 1966 meeting of the American Association for the Advancement of Science, "we will need an interest in wild animals among our city voters."[41]

The new thinking dominated the inaugural session on urban resources at the 1967 wildlife conference. In the first paper, Stuart Davey, a federal Bureau of Outdoor Recreation official, spoke forcefully about the narrowness of the fish and game model of wildlife management. Millions of people had begun to appreciate wildlife "as a recreational and esthetic resource and as an integral element of man's total environment," he argued. "More people are interested in just observing, preserving, and protecting wildlife." The evidence was considerable. The membership of the National Wildlife Federation quadrupled in the mid-1960s. Sales of bird feed to homeowners were up. A 1965 survey conducted by the Bureau of Outdoor Recreation found over eight million bird watchers and three million wildlife photographers. The survey also found a 19-percent increase in nature walking since 1960. In 1966, Congress passed the first Endangered Species Act.[42]

To Davey, the moral was clear. "[W]ildlife managers should broaden their approach to wildlife management," he said. "Wildlife managers should think more about people – urban people and their great interest in birds and mammals. Wildlife managers should work with other professions – urban planners, architects, landscape architects, city administrators, housing developers, and economists. Wildlife managers should give *further* attention to preserving and providing for all wildlife, and not just game species."[43]

In Davey's long list of "should"s, the reference to housing developers might have slipped by unnoticed. But Davey returned to

41. For the change in both popular and professional attitudes toward wildlife in the 1950s and 1960s, see Thomas R. Dunlap, *Saving America's Wildlife: Ecology and the American Mind, 1850–1990* (Princeton: Princeton University Press, 1988), 98–110 and 142–155. The quotation comes from Stuart P. Davey, "Role of Wildlife in an Urban Environment," in Trefethen, *Transactions of the Thirty-Second North American Wildlife and Natural Resources Conference*, 59.
42. Davey, "Role of Wildlife in an Urban Environment," 52–53.
43. Ibid., 50–51.

the point in a discussion of the opportunities awaiting wildlife professionals. "Housing developers in general aren't noted for their enhancement of wildlife in the countryside," he argued, "but have wildlife managers tried to point out the ways to retain some natural amenities in suburbia?" Unfortunately not. Indeed, the professional challenge was scientific as well as administrative. To help people build wildlife into cities and suburbs, Davey concluded, wildlife managers needed to give more thought to the habitat requirements of hundreds of nongame species.[44]

The Fish and Wildlife Service responded to the challenge in several ways. The agency hired a specialist in urban bird habitat. In 1966, the agency also published a 550-page collection of essays titled *Birds in Our Life*. Though a sequel to a work on the future of waterfowl, the 1966 collection offered scientific, literary, and philosophical reflections on birds of all kinds, not simply game species, and the volume included a celebrated essay on the importance of birds in the metropolis: "Amid Brick and Asphalt."[45]

Perhaps most significantly, the bureau organized a pioneering conference in 1968 to consider the relationship of "Man and Nature in the City." As director John Gottschalk explained, the subject was "complex, dynamic, and poorly understood. Yet we know . . . that many major problems of conservation and environmental management today stem from urban areas and their inhabitants. We also know that conservation decisions will soon be made by people who know only the environment of the city." Accordingly, the agency had to do more to meet the needs of the ever-increasing metropolitan population. If the bureau continued to work only in the nation's wide open spaces, Gottschalk told the conference participants, "I believe it would soon find itself in a very questionable orientation to society."[46]

The conference focused on ways to encourage nature appreciation

44. Ibid., 54, 56–57. In addition, see Forest W. Stearns, "Wildlife Habitat in Urban and Suburban Environments," in Trefethen, *Transactions of the Thirty-Second North American Wildlife and Natural Resources Conference*, 61–69; Robert H. Twiss, "Wildlife in the Metropolitan Landscape," in Trefethen, *Transactions of the Thirty-Second North American Wildlife and Natural Resources Conference*, 69–74.

45. Irston R. Barnes, "Amid Brick and Asphalt," in Alfred Stefferud, editor, *Birds in Our Lives* (Washington: USGPO, 1966), 414–424. The essay was reprinted in Bailey, Elder, and McKinney, *Readings in Wildlife Conservation*, 631–635.

46. Bureau of Sport Fisheries and Wildlife, *Man and Nature in the City* (Washington: USGPO, 1968), iii, viii.

in cities and suburbs. One session considered "Nature and the Ghetto Dweller," while another focused on "Urban Youth and Natural Environments." The conference also included a long discussion of the psychology of human–nature relations. The organizers thus responded to the growing concern among scientists that the fate of wildlife conservation depended on the nation's metropolitan majority.[47]

In one session, however, the conference addressed the role of wildlife in urban planning. For a number of years, a few open-space advocates had argued that the preservation of wetlands, steep hillsides, and floodplains would protect valuable habitat for wildlife, and the session built on that foundation. The principal speaker, landscape architect Philip Lewis, focused on regional open-space planning. He began with a call to action: "The monumental task of assuring nature in the new urban fabric now sprawling into the lovely countryside is not as well understood nor supported as it must be if we are to prevent duplication of the environmental mistakes now prevalent in our core cities." But Lewis did not consider the possibility of incorporating wildlife habitat into subdivisions. Instead, he argued that the key to successful planning lay in the use of "open-space corridors" to shape the geography of growth.[48]

The list of speakers included only one developer – Morton Hoppenfeld of the Rouse Company, which was building the new town of Columbia, Maryland – but Hoppenfeld's participation led to the most original discussion of the conference. During a question-and-answer session, someone asked how the Bureau of Sport Fisheries and Wildlife could "participate more effectively in urban planning," and the moderator directed the question to Hoppenfeld. "[B]y doing it," he answered. Indeed, Hoppenfeld had already made the point at lunch, when a bureau official asked him pointedly why the Rouse Company was not doing more to provide wildlife habitat in Columbia. "I allowed that we have perhaps made mistakes by not doing things, or perhaps we did them poorly, out of ignorance, but that he knew better how to do it and he shouldn't just sit around

47. Ibid., 1–21, 43–51, 63–74.
48. Philip H. Lewis, Jr., "Nature in Our Cities," in Bureau of Sport Fisheries and Wildlife, *Man and Nature in the City,* 22–27. The quotation is on 23. In addition, see White House Conference on Natural Beauty, *Beauty for America* (Washington: USGPO, 1965), 115, 483.

and wait for us." Instead, the official should offer his help. The point held for the wildlife profession generally, not just the staff of the Bureau of Sport Fisheries and Wildlife. "Come to people in the development process," Hoppenfeld said. "Some will turn you away for any number of reasons, but others, and I would include our company among them, would welcome you with open arms. . . . Leave the ivy halls and come out and join the fight for the things you value because that is really what happens. It is a battle of values."[49]

The discussion bore fruit. In 1969, the Rouse Company asked the Fish and Wildlife Service to help improve the design of Columbia. The development plan already called for 3,200 acres of open space – 20 percent of the project – but the company's executives now understood that the provision of open space did not necessarily ensure a large and diverse wildlife population. The bureau responded with a variety of suggestions. The company should preserve streams and streamside vegetation. To maintain the natural richness of bird life, the company should retain a portion of the mature forests, fallow fields, croplands, grassy patches, and hedgerows in the tract. The development should include a new lake, and perhaps even a man-made marsh. To increase ecological diversity, the company also should create a number of small clearings in the woods and at the edges of the fields. The recreational facilities of the community – the golf course, for example, and the playing fields – should be adjacent to the natural areas to provide protection from the heavy traffic of the residential and commercial zones.[50]

The plan for Columbia had the potential to be a breakthrough. Slowly, the Fish and Wildlife Service developed some expertise in urban wildlife management. The agency continued to work with the Rouse Company to study the ecology of the new town. Soon, the bureau's urban birdlife specialist began to publish studies of habitat patterns in suburban neighborhoods. In 1978, the agency joined

---

49. Bureau of Sport Fisheries and Wildlife, *Man and Nature in the City*, 76. Hoppenfeld returned to the point later in the discussion. What kind of information would he need from wildlife professionals in order to plan and develop better cities? "[Y]ou know what," he answered, "I don't know. I am so ignorant on the subject of wildlife that I really can't answer your question. But I would be grateful to anyone who would be sufficiently motivated to get in touch with us and help us in the future to ask those questions and seek the answers." See 81–82.
50. For a description of the Columbia plan, see Gill and Bonnett, *Nature in the Urban Landscape*, 129–131.

with the American Society of Planning Officials to publish the first guide to "planning for wildlife in cities and suburbs."[51]

Despite the signs of a new commitment to urban wildlife, however, the Fish and Wildlife Service never made a sustained effort to provide advice to developers and urban planners. Indeed, the 1978 guide perfectly illustrated the strengths and weaknesses of the agency's response to the challenge of suburban growth. It was thoughtful and thorough, with chapters on subdivision design, regional planning, and landscaping in older communities. Yet the Fish and Wildlife Service had little to do with the guide's content. Though the agency provided a large share of the funding for the project, the authors were all affiliated with the Urban Wildlife Research Center, a nonprofit organization formed in 1973 to encourage the preservation of wildlife habitat in fast-growing cities and suburbs. The center's staff included several former employees of the Fish and Wildlife Service who had concluded that the government agency never would make a major commitment to urban issues.

With a relatively small staff and a budget tied to revenues from hunters, the Fish and Wildlife Service needed a new legislative mandate in order to take on a significant new mission. Still, the bureau managed to make something out of almost nothing in the late 1960s and early 1970s. Years later, the organizers of urban wildlife meetings often looked back at the 1968 "Man and Nature in the City" conference as a pathbreaking event. The plan for Columbia also became a model. By encouraging debate about the ecological impacts of urbanization, the agency helped to redefine the agenda for wildlife managers and researchers.[52]

51. For a pioneering example of a habitat study by a Fish and Wildlife specialist, see Aelred D. Geis, "Effects of Urbanization and Type of Urban Development on Bird Populations," in John H. Noyes and Donald R. Progulske, editors, *A Symposium on Wildlife in an Urbanizing Environment* (Amherst: Massachusetts Cooperative Extension Service, 1974), 97–105. The study was based on work in Columbia from 1966 to 1971. The guide is Daniel L. Leedy, Robert M. Maestro, and Thomas M. Franklin, *Planning for Wildlife in Cities and Suburbs* (Washington: U.S. Fish and Wildlife Service, 1978). The guide was also published by the American Society of Planning Officials.
52. For the budget constraints faced by the Fish and Wildlife Service, see Trefethen, *American Crusade for Wildlife,* 352, 358, 363. For the importance of the 1968 conference, see Lowell W. Adams and Daniel L. Leedy, editors, *Integrating Man and Nature in the Metropolitan Environment: Proceedings of a National Symposium on Urban Wildlife* (Columbia, MD: National Institute for Urban Wildlife, 1987), 3, 245. The Columbia plan is offered as a model by Gill and Bonnett, *Nature in the Urban Landscape,* 129–131; Spirn, *The Granite Garden,* 224.

The Federal Contribution

In *The American Conservation Movement,* Stephen Fox dismisses the work of government conservationists in a few perfunctory sentences. Though he acknowledges that conservation agencies gave the environmental movement expertise and organizational staying power, he concludes that "the driving force" of environmental activism almost always came from outside the government: The outsiders provided "high standards, independence, integrity." In contrast, the conservation bureaucracies were hampered by inertia, political compromise, and self-justifying commitments to outworn ideas.[53]

Historians of the environmental movement have generally accepted the basics of Fox's argument. At best, the government followed belatedly and perhaps reluctantly along paths blazed by engaged citizens. At worst, as the postwar records of the Bureau of Reclamation and the Forest Service make clear, the government actively opposed the goals of environmentalists. Yet the story of the federal conservation effort in the suburbs demonstrates that the truth is more complex.[54]

The Geological Survey, the Soil Conservation Service, and the Fish and Wildlife Service were not stuck in the rut of old ideas. Though traditionally concerned only with rural regions, all three agencies recognized that the rapid suburbanization of the countryside had far-reaching environmental consequences. All three agencies drew

53. Stephen Fox, *The American Conservation Movement: John Muir and His Legacy* (1981; reprint, Madison: University of Wisconsin Press, 1985), 333–334.
54. As I noted in the introduction, both Samuel P. Hays, *Beauty, Health, and Permanence: Environmental Politics in the United States, 1955–1985* (New York: Cambridge University Press, 1987) and Hal K. Rothman, *The Greening of a Nation?: Environmentalism in the United States Since 1945* (Fort Worth: Harcourt Brace College Publishers, 1998) discuss the opposition of federal resource management agencies to environmentalism. For the Forest Service, see also Paul W. Hirt, *A Conspiracy of Optimism: Management of the National Forests since World War Two* (Lincoln: University of Nebraska Press, 1994). Like Fox, Hays also argues that environmental concerns arose from a broad base "and worked their way from the middle levels of society outward, constantly to press on a reluctant leadership." See 13. But Thomas Dunlap neatly challenges Fox's argument in *Saving America's Wildlife*, xiii: "We have too often characterized 'government' as an inert lump that must be moved by (usually high-minded and pure-souled) conservation organizations, and we neglect the complex interplay of people within and without the government and the ways in which agencies have roused public support – which then 'forced' them to take action. There is an anti-institutional bias in much historical work."

attention to new environmental problems. At a time when the United States had few institutional sources of environmental research, the Geological Survey took the leading role in investigating the hydrological effects of urban growth. The Soil Conservation Service mobilized a nationwide network of agents to encourage homebuilders to adopt conservation measures. The Fish and Wildlife Service used the prestige of the federal government to give more weight to important questions about wildlife habitat in fast-growing regions.

The three agencies were not equally able to meet new demands. The Geological Survey had the easiest task. To begin a new line of research, the agency did not need a new mandate, only a new set of priorities. The Soil Conservation Service had to develop new ways to explain the value of erosion-control measures, yet the agency could address the problems caused by urban and suburban development without a fundamental redefinition of purpose: SCS officials simply needed to decide to reach out to a new clientele. In contrast, the principal responsibilities of the Fish and Wildlife Service were to manage wildlife refuges and enforce fish and game laws, and the bureau's research and outreach efforts largely supported the management and enforcement missions. The FWS staff thus had little opportunity to work with developers and urban planners.

Yet the three agencies shared a few key traits. All focused on a specific resource, and all compiled information from across the country. Though none had the kind of holistic vision prized by environmentalists, all encouraged a kind of integrative thinking. What determined the fate of water, soil, or wildlife in fast-growing regions? In each case, the answer was many-faceted, so officials in the three agencies took a much broader view of homebuilding than most open-space planners. They focused on how builders worked, not simply where. They considered a range of issues, from site preparation to storm-water management. As a result, each agency made a distinctive contribution to the critique of suburban sprawl.

Because the Geological Survey, the Soil Conservation Service, and the Fish and Wildlife Service were part of the federal government, all three agencies also had ready access to the network of national policy-making. The water, soil, and wildlife experts provided information to presidential commissions and congressional committees. Beginning in 1970, the three agencies often advised the Council on Environmental Quality and the Environmental Protection Agency, both of which sought to integrate the expertise of a multiplicity of disciplines. As the Soil, Water, and Suburbia conference demonstrated, the agencies could bring a variety of officials together to make a more powerful case for action.

The work of the three agencies soon emboldened activists and policy-makers. Because the nation seemed to be developing a sophisticated and comprehensive understanding of the environmental costs of suburban development, people could imagine ambitious new efforts to address the issue. In the early 1970s, the expertise of the water, soil, and wildlife agencies helped to make possible a new kind of town building, with interdisciplinary teams of environmental specialists contributing to the design of entire communities. The new critiques also helped to inspire a five-year campaign to enact a national land-use bill. For the first time, the environmental impact of metropolitan growth became a prominent subject of debate in Washington's great corridors of power.

7

Toward a Land Ethic: The Quiet Revolution in Land-Use Regulation

On January 1, 1970, President Richard Nixon inaugurated a new decade and a new era by signing the National Environmental Policy Act. The act declared a national interest in protecting and restoring environmental quality, required officials to prepare environmental-impact assessments for federal projects, and established a Council on Environmental Quality to advise the president. Seven months later, President Nixon sent the CEQ's first annual report to Congress. The report was "a historic milestone." For the first time, the president explained, Americans had paused to consider carefully "the state of the Nation's environment."[1]

The CEQ marveled at the moment. "Historians may one day call 1970 the year of the environment," the report began. "They may not be able to say that 1970 actually marked a significant change for the better in the quality of life; in the polluting and the fouling of the land, the water, and the air; or in health, working conditions, and recreational opportunity. Indeed, they are almost certain to see evidence of worsening environmental conditions in many parts of the country." Yet 1970 surely was "a turning point, a year when the quality of life has become more than a phrase; environment and pollution have become everyday words; and ecology has become almost a religion to some of the young. Environmental problems, standing for many years on the threshold of national prominence, are now at the center of nationwide concern. Action to improve the

---

1. Council on Environmental Quality, *Environmental Quality: The First Annual Report of the Council on Environmental Quality* (Washington: USGPO, 1970), v.

environment has been launched by government at all levels. And private groups, industry, and individuals have joined the attack."[2]

The CEQ also saw signs that Americans were taking a more sophisticated approach to environmental issues. In the past, each issue "was treated in an ad hoc fashion, while the strong, lasting interactions between various parts of the problem were neglected. Even today most environmental problems are dealt with temporarily, incompletely, and only after they have become critical." Yet activists and policymakers were beginning to appreciate the complex relationships between issues.[3]

The critics of tract-house development fit the pattern. For two decades, officials had tried to solve one problem at a time. To preserve open space, the federal government provided funds for open-space acquisition. To restrict development on steep hillsides, cities and counties enacted hillside-development ordinances. To control soil erosion from suburban construction, states passed sediment-control laws. By 1970, however, a number of people had begun to see the environmental costs of homebuilding as disparate elements of a mega problem: land use. To deal with so vast a problem, the critics concluded, the nation needed to develop a new land ethic.

The CEQ's first annual report provided a particularly good example of the new way of thinking. The report included a section on land use, and the section began with a brief description of the environmental costs of suburban development:

Although the impact of the rural-to-suburban shift of land use varies greatly throughout the country, certain effects tend to be common to this change. Open space is continuously eaten up by housing, which, with most present subdivision practices, provides few parks but instead only offers each family its individual front and back yard. Space is likewise diminished by other facilities required by suburban development. Shopping centers and highway interchanges, made necessary by dependence on the automobile and truck, consume large portions of land. Airports, commonly constructed in suburban or exurban areas and constantly growing in size and number, pose similar problems on an even larger scale, attracting a vast conglomeration of light industry and housing. Consequently, the growing suburban population finds less and less public open space.

Building and construction practices, together with the quickened pace

2. Ibid., 5.   3. Ibid., 18.

of development and complementary zoning, often end in severe abuse of the land and are ultimately costly to the public. The popular practice of stripping subdivisions of all cover before commencing construction destroys tree and plant cover and can trigger heavy soil runoff. Sedimentation from this runoff in urbanizing areas loads nearby streambeds and ultimately river channels. This can cause costly downstream dredging, upstream flood control and destruction of the esthetic quality of lakes and rivers.

Public pressure for flood control projects is often spurred by suburban development along flood plains, which usually contain fertile soil supporting an abundant variety of native plant and animal life. Construction over aquifer recharge areas, where the groundwater is normally replenished, accelerates rapid runoff, increases flooding, and contributes to water shortages.

Suburban development often spreads across ridges and slopes which should be left alone because of their beauty and because their trees and plant cover absorb rain and inhibit flooding. Trees are not only important for their esthetic qualities and as habitat for birds and wildlife, but they affect temperature and air pollution as well. Building on steep slopes can affect soil stability, causing severe erosion which then undermines foundations. Nevertheless, few cities or counties adequately control development of flood plains, steep slopes, or land above aquifer recharge areas. Important data concerning aquifers, subsoil composition, cover, wetlands, and wildlife are not considered by many planning and zoning boards.

Esthetically, this current pattern of growth triggers at least three adverse consequences. First, much commercial development along roads and highways through suburbs is of cheap and unimaginative construction. Gaudy neon signs, billboards, powerlines, and clutter characterize this development. Second, many residential subdivisions are visually boring – block after block of treeless lawns, uniform setbacks, and repetitious housing designs and street layouts. Finally, wooded streambeds, slopes, and ridges, which could help break the monotony of uniform housing developments, are often destroyed.

The CEQ's accounting was incomplete. The report did not mention the pollution caused by septic tanks, for example, or the energy inefficiency of tract-house design. Yet the CEQ analysis clearly suggested that the problem of land use demanded attention.[4]

4. Ibid., 171–172. In addition, see Elizabeth H. Haskell, "Land Use and the Environment: Public Policy Issues," in U.S. Senate, *Readings on Land Use Policy: A Selection of Recent Articles and Studies on Land Use Policy Issues and Activities in the United States*, 94th

In a message accompanying the CEQ report, President Nixon seconded the CEQ's argument about the importance of the land-use issue. "We have treated our land as if it were a limitless resource," the president wrote. "Traditionally, Americans have felt that what they do with their own land is their own business. This attitude has been a natural outgrowth of the pioneer spirit. Today, we are coming to realize that our land is finite, while our population is growing. The uses to which our generation puts the land can either expand or severely limit the choices our children will have. The time has come when we must accept the idea that none of us has a right to abuse the land, and that on the contrary society as a whole has a legitimate interest in proper land use."[5]

The president returned to the subject in a February 1972 message on the environment. In the interim, he had endorsed a national land-use bill, and he pressed Congress to approve the legislation. "In recent years," he wrote, "we have come to view our land as a limited and irreplaceable resource. No longer do we imagine that there will always be more of it over the horizon – more woodlands and shorelands and wetlands – if we neglect or overdevelop the land in view. A new maturity is giving rise to a land ethic which recognizes that improper land use affects the public interest and limits the choices that we and our decedents [sic] will have. Now we must equip our institutions to carry out the responsibility implicit in this new outlook. We must create the administrative and regulatory mechanism necessary to assure wise land use and to stop haphazard, wasteful, and environmentally damaging development."[6]

The emphatic call to action was a sign of the times. Though Nixon's commitment to environmentalism was open to question, the most knowledgeable commentators on environmental issues shared the president's sense that a new attitude toward land was taking hold across the nation. The evidence was considerable. To reduce the environmental costs of residential, commercial, and in-

Congress, 1st session, 1975, 8–12; Walter A. Rosenbaum, *The Politics of Environmental Concern* (New York: Praeger, 1973), 281; Soil Conservation Society of America, *National Land Use Policy: Objectives, Components, Implementation* (Ankeny, IA: Soil Conservation Society of America, 1973), 21.

5. Ibid., xii–xiiii.
6. Council on Environmental Quality, *Environmental Quality: The Third Annual Report of the Council on Environmental Quality* (Washington: USGPO, 1972), 373.

dustrial development, a handful of states had established ambitious programs to regulate land use. The result was – in the words of a widely cited study commissioned by the CEQ – a "quiet revolution." The revolution in the legislatures was accompanied by a noticeable change in legal thinking about property rights. In Congress, members of both parties supported national land-use legislation. The reform effort also had the support of important foundations, professional organizations, and editorial boards. As the *Washington Post* argued in 1970, land use was "the key to all the rest of our environmental problems."[7]

The Rise of State Land-use Regulation

The state land-use programs were responses to a variety of concerns. In the late 1960s and early 1970s, the far-reaching environmental effects of power plants, airports, strip mines, and oil refineries began to trouble both citizens and policymakers. But the most common concern was urban sprawl – the "haphazard, wasteful, and

7. For a critical assessment of Nixon's commitment to environmentalism, see John Brooks Flippen, "Containing the Urban Sprawl: The Nixon Administration's Land Use Policy," *Presidential Studies Quarterly* 26 (Winter 1996): 197–207. The CEQ study of the state land-use laws is Fred Bosselman and David Callies, *The Quiet Revolution in Land Use Control* (Washington: USGPO, 1971). The literature on the state programs quickly became extensive. For good overviews, see Robert G. Healy, *Land Use and the States* (Baltimore: Johns Hopkins University Press, 1976); Nelson Rosenbaum, *Land Use and the Legislatures: The Politics of State Innovation* (Washington: Urban Institute, 1976); Frank J. Popper, *The Politics of Land-Use Reform* (Madison: University of Wisconsin Press, 1981); and John M. DeGrove, *Land, Growth, and Politics* (Chicago: American Planning Association, 1984). The literature on the national debate is also extensive. For a sense of the variety of the work on the subject, see Noreen Lyday, *The Law of the Land: Debating National Land Use Legislation, 1970–75* (Washington: Urban Institute, 1976); James C. Hite, *Room and Situation: The Political Economy of Land-Use Policy* (Chicago: Nelson-Hall, 1979); Gordon C. Bjork, *Life, Liberty, and Property: The Economics and Politics of Land-Use Planning and Environmental Controls* (Lexington, MA: Lexington Books, 1980); Judith I. de Neufville, editor, *The Land Use Policy Debate in the United States* (New York: Plenum Press, 1981); Richard A. Walker and Michael K. Heiman, "Quiet Revolution for Whom?," *Annals of the Association of American Geographers* 71 (1981): 67–83; Sidney Plotkin, *Keep Out: The Struggle for Land Use Control* (Berkeley: University of California Press, 1987). Perhaps because the campaign for national legislation ultimately failed, environmental historians have neglected the land-use debates of the late 1960s and early 1970s. But Samuel P. Hays discusses the issue in *Beauty, Health, and Permanence: Environmental Politics in the United States, 1955–1985* (New York: Cambridge University Press, 1987), 164–170, 450–453. The *Washington Post* editorial is quoted in Haskell, "Land Use and the Environment," 5.

environmentally damaging" construction of subdivisions and shop-ping centers. "In the city fringe areas," the president of the Council of State Planning Agencies wrote in a 1971 essay on land-use regulation, "vegetation is stripped, topsoil is buried, streams are channeled into culverts, hills are leveled, valleys and marshes are filled and whole new communities occupy areas which were formerly forested or farmed. The adverse impact of these phenomena on human and natural life and resources is what we call the environmental crisis."[8]

Hawaii was the first state to act. With the rise of jet travel in the 1950s, the state's economy boomed, and the city of Honolulu soon seemed a sprawling threat to the beauty and productivity of the countryside. To protect the state's pineapple and sugarcane plantations, the legislature passed a land-use law in 1961. The act created a land-use commission to divide the entire state into urban, rural, agricultural, and conservation districts. Once the commission defined each zone, the territorial expansion of the state's cities would be limited to the urban district. The act also gave the land-use commission the power to regulate development in the rural and agricultural districts, while the Department of Land and Natural Resources controlled the use of the state's conservation lands.[9]

The political economy of Hawaii was unique, and the Hawaiian system of statewide zoning never became a national model. In the mid-1960s, however, a number of states imposed limited restrictions on development. The restrictions took several forms, yet all evidenced a new concern about the environmental consequences of growth. Often the state initiatives sought to protect a type of land of critical importance. Between 1963 and 1968, for example, Mass-

8. The Storm King generating plant and the Everglades jetport were among the most controversial projects during the late 1960s and early 1970s. For accounts of those two controversies, see Allan R. Talbot, *Power Along the Hudson: The Storm King Case and the Birth of Environmentalism* (New York: E. P. Dutton & Company, 1972); Luther J. Carter, *The Florida Experience: Land and Water Policy in a Growth State* (Baltimore: Johns Hopkins University Press, 1974), 187–227. The long quotation is from Richard H. Slavin, "Toward a State Land-Use Policy: Harmonizing Development and Conservation," *State Government* 44 (1971): 4.
9. Bosselman and Callies, *The Quiet Revolution*, 5–53; DeGrove, *Land, Growth, and Politics*, 9–63; Daniel R. Mandelker, *Environmental and Land Use Controls Legislation* (Indianapolis: Bobbs-Merrill, 1976), 269–322. The rural district actually was established by a separate vote shortly after the land-use act passed, but I have followed the majority of commentators in treating the two measures together.

achusetts approved a series of acts to provide public oversight of development in wetlands. Wisconsin passed a law in 1966 to counter the ill effects of second-home construction along the state's lakeshores. States also acted to control development in fast-growing regions. In 1965, California created a commission to regulate all filling and construction projects in San Francisco Bay. Because of intense development, legislators feared, the Bay might soon become a mere river, surrounded by "tract housing, supermarkets, filling stations, hamburger stands, and factories." Two years later, Minnesota established a Twin Cities metropolitan council with the power to address several of the worst problems caused by urban sprawl, including the loss of open space and the contamination of drinking water by septic tanks.[10]

Vermont and Maine took the next steps in 1970 by approving statewide land-use regulations. In Vermont, the principal concern was the environmental impact of building recreational subdivisions in timber country, whereas the Maine law largely was a response to a spate of proposals for offshore energy facilities. But the two initiatives were quite alike. In both cases, the state required a permit for residential, commercial, and industrial projects of significant size. (To protect the aesthetic and ecological qualities of the Green Mountains, Vermont also required a permit for all development above 2,500 feet.) In both states, the criteria for granting or rejecting permits included a variety of environmental factors, from the suitability of the soil to the likely effect on nearby streams.[11]

The Vermont and Maine laws received considerable publicity. In July 1971, the journal of the American Institute of Planners cited both as exemplars of a significant new trend in state policy. A few months later, Fred Bosselman and David Callies gave the trend a name in their influential study, *The Quiet Revolution in Land Use Control*. "This country is in the midst of a revolution in the way

10. Bosselman and Callies use these examples in *The Quiet Revolution*. See 108–163, 205–261. The quotation comes from Wesley Marx, *The Frail Ocean* (1967; reprint, New York: Ballantine, 1969), 162.
11. Bosselman and Callies discuss Vermont and Maine in *The Quiet Revolution*, 54–107, 187–204. For the Vermont act, see in addition Healy, *Land Use and the States*, 35–63; DeGrove, *Land, Growth, and Politics*, 65–98; Mandelker, *Environmental and Land Use Controls Legislation*, 323–391; Phyllis Myers, *So Goes Vermont: An Account of the Development, Passage, and Implementation of State Land-Use Legislation in Vermont* (Washington: Conservation Foundation, 1974).

we regulate the use of land," the two attorneys wrote. "It is a peaceful revolution, conducted entirely within the law. It is a quiet revolution, and its supporters include both conservatives and liberals. It is a disorganized revolution, with no central cadre of leaders, but it is a revolution nonetheless."[12]

The trend soon became even more distinct. In 1972, Florida passed a new kind of statewide land-use act, and several states then followed Florida's lead: In different ways, the laws all gave state agencies the power to regulate land use in "areas of critical state concern" and to review proposals for "developments of regional impact." The land-use acts of the mid-1960s also served as models for legislation in the early 1970s. New York established a regional agency to regulate the use of privately owned lands in the vast Adirondack State Park. By 1975, the number of states with acts to protect wetlands or shorelands had risen to 23. Though a number of legislatures turned down land-use measures, the cause often had powerful support.[13]

In Oregon, for example, the land-use issue was the most important item on Governor Tom McCall's legislative agenda in 1973. "There is a shameless threat to our environment and to the whole quality of life – the unfettered despoiling of the land," McCall told the legislature. "Sagebrush subdivisions, coastal 'condomania,' and the ravenous rampage of suburbia in the Willamette Valley all threaten to mock Oregon's status as the environmental model for the nation. We are in dire need of a state land use policy, new subdivision laws, and new standards for planning and zoning by cities and counties. The interests of Oregon for today and in the future must be protected from the grasping wastrels of the land." The legislature agreed.[14]

12. The piece on the new trend in state policy is Elizabeth Haskell, "New Directions in State Environmental Planning," *Journal of the American Institute of Planners* 37 (July 1971): 253–258. In addition, see Elizabeth H. Haskell and Victoria S. Price, *State Environmental Management: Case Studies of Nine States* (New York: Praeger, 1973), 169–209. For the Bosselman and Callies quotation, see *The Quiet Revolution,* 1.
13. Rosenbaum analyzes the adoption of land-use legislation in *Land Use and the Legislatures:* The states with wetlands and shorelands legislation are listed on 69 and 72. For the history of the Florida law, see DeGrove, *Land, Growth, and Politics,* 99–176; Healy, *Land Use and the States,* 103–138; Carter, *The Florida Experience.* The New York act is one of the measures Popper considers in *The Politics of Land-Use Reform:* For a summary of the act's provisions, see 81–83.
14. Popper quotes McCall in *The Politics of Land-Use Reform,* 59. In addition, see DeGrove,

In California, in contrast, the legislature three times rejected bills to protect the state's 1,100-mile coastline. Yet a Coastal Zone Conservation Act passed anyway as a result of a ballot initiative. The Santa Barbara oil spill, the construction of second-home subdivisions and high-rise apartments on bluffs overlooking the water, the increasing number of proposals for power plants, the destruction of estuaries and the decline of fisheries, the aesthetic blighting of public beaches – all contributed to popular support for state action. The 1972 initiative established regional and state commissions with extraordinary power to oversee development along the coast. Though a coalition of developers, electric utilities, and oil companies spent lavishly to defeat the measure, it was approved by 55 percent of the voters.[15]

Everywhere, the state acts were rebellions against a decades-old tradition of local control of development. Though the states held the ultimate authority to regulate land use, all had given cities and counties the power to enact zoning and subdivision regulations. The supporters of state land-use legislation argued that local regulation had proven "woefully inadequate" to the task of environmental protection. Cities typically used zoning to uphold property values and promote economic development, not to prevent environmental degradation. Worse yet, many counties did not use their regulatory powers at all. Even when local officials tried to adapt zoning and subdivision regulations to serve environmental goals, their efforts were often insufficient. The boundaries of cities and counties seldom followed the patterns of nature, so local governments usually lacked the jurisdiction to control the fate of mountain ranges, valleys, lakes, floodplains, or estuaries: Only regional or state authorities could protect many ecologically important areas.[16]

Land, Growth, and Politics, 235–290; Charles E. Little, *The New Oregon Trail: An Account of the Development and Passage of State Land-Use Legislation in Oregon* (Washington: Conservation Foundation, 1974); Brent Walth, *Fire at Eden's Gate: Tom McCall & the Oregon Story* (Portland: Oregon Historical Society Press, 1994), 242–249, 351–361.

15. DeGrove, *Land, Growth, and Politics*, 177–234; Healy, *Land Use and the States*, 64–102; Melvin B. Mogulof, *Saving the Coast: California's Experiment in Intergovernmental Land Use Control* (Lexington, MA: Lexington Books, 1975).

16. The quoted phrase comes from Bosselman and Callies, *The Quiet Revolution*, 3. But the critique of local regulation was common. See, for example, Slavin, "Toward a State Land-Use Policy," 2–11; Council on Environmental Quality, *First Annual Report*, 184–188; Haskell, "New Directions in State Environmental Planning," 255; Robert Cahn

Yet the quiet revolution was not just about shifting power from one level of government to another. The state laws gave public agencies a much greater say in decisions about the use of privately owned lands. In effect, the states had concluded that the question of land use was not truly "private," since a landowner's decision to develop a piece of property might threaten the public good. The quiet revolution thus challenged the traditional understanding of the rights of property ownership.[17]

Property Rights and the Public Good

"So great . . . is the regard of the law for private property," the English legal scholar William Blackstone wrote in the 18th century, "that it will not authorize the least violation of it; no, not even for the general good of the whole community." In fact, the common law never was so one-sided. Yet Blackstone memorably expressed a view that shaped the American legal system from the start. To the founders of the nation, the ability to own land was a safeguard against oppression, a source of social order, and a stimulus to enterprise. Accordingly, the Constitution sought in many ways to protect the freedom of property owners.[18]

and William K. Reilly, "Fighting to Save the Land," *National Wildlife* 12 (August–September 1974): 14.

17. The preambles to the state laws often stated forthrightly that the use of land was no longer a private decision. The best example comes from the Maine law: "The Legislature finds that the economic and social wellbeing of the citizens of the State of Maine depend upon the location of commercial and industrial developments with respect to the natural environment of the State; that many developments because of their size and nature are capable of causing irreparable damage to the people and the environment in their surroundings; that the location of such developments is too important to be left only to the determination of the owners of such developments; and that discretion must be vested in state authority to regulate the location of developments which may substantially affect environment." The text of the law is reproduced as an appendix in Bosselman and Callies, *The Quiet Revolution*.

18. Fred Bosselman, David Callies, and John Banta cite Blackstone in *The Taking Issue: A Study of the Constitutional Limits of Governmental Authority to Regulate the Use of Privately-Owned Land Without Compensation* (Washington: USGPO, 1973), 90. I am summarizing here an interpretation of the American legal tradition that was common in the late 1960s and early 1970s. See, for example, John E. Cribbet, "Changing Concepts in the Law of Land Use," *Iowa Law Review* 50 (1965): 247–253; Lynton K. Caldwell, "Rights of Ownership or Rights of Use? – The Need for a New Conceptual Basis

The state land-use laws restricted that freedom, and aggrieved landowners soon asked the courts to rule the laws unconstitutional. The plaintiffs often focused on the meaning of a clause in the Fifth Amendment to the Constitution which prohibited the government from taking private property for public use without paying just compensation. In the landmark case of Pennsylvania Coal Company v. Mahon, decided in 1922, the Supreme Court interpreted the takings clause in a way that called into question the government's power to regulate land use. If a regulation severely decreased the value of a piece of property, the court held, then the regulation amounted to a taking. But the land-use cases never were simply disputes about property values. As a Wisconsin court explained, the suits compelled judges to weigh "the public interest in stopping the despoliation of natural resources" against "an owner's asserted right to use his property as he wishes." In a number of important decisions in the early 1970s, courts accepted the arguments for state land-use regulation. Together, the decisions constituted "a quiet judicial revolution."[19]

Well before the courts took up the land-use cases, however, a movement had begun in legal circles to redefine the rights of property. The impetus again was anxiety about the transformation of the metropolitan landscape. What could be done to stop the blight of the slums? What could be done to control the explosion of the suburbs? In the late 1950s and early 1960s, those questions led many legal scholars to ponder "the public interest" in private decisions about the use of land. In 1965, for example, the *Iowa Law Review* and the *UCLA Law Review* both published a special issue on land use, urban planning, and the law, and the two publications

for Land Use Policy," *William and Mary Law Review* 15 (1974): 761–762; John W. Ragsdale, Jr. and Richard P. Sher, "The Court's Role in the Evolution of Power over Land," *Urban Lawyer* 7 (1975): 63–64. For a subtle, up-to-date analysis of the subject, see Gregory S. Alexander, *Commodity or Propriety: Competing Visions of Property in American Legal Thought, 1776–1970* (Chicago: University of Chicago Press, 1997).

19. For the quotation from the Wisconsin court, see Virginia Curtis, editor, *Land Use and the Environment: An Anthology of Readings* (Washington: Environmental Protection Agency, 1973), 191. Bosselman, Callies, and Banta discuss "the quiet judicial revolution" in *The Taking Issue*, 212–229. In addition, see David E. Hess, "Institutionalizing the Revolution: Judicial Reaction to State Land Use Laws," in James H. Carr and Edward E. Duensing, *Land Use Issues of the 1980s* (New Brunswick, NJ: Center for Urban Policy Research, 1983), 99–112.

demonstrated the deepening scholarly discontent with the Black-stonian conception of property.[20]

In the lead article of the Iowa symposium, John Cribbet force-fully attacked the idea of "laissez-faire." The laissez-faire philosophy had left landowners free to degrade the environment: "Minerals could be exploited, forests could be destroyed, streams could be polluted, water could be wasted, air could be contaminated, and buildings could be constructed in growing cities without regard to elementary principles of health (to say nothing of aesthetics), all in the sacred name of private property." Though the laissez-faire tradition had begun to give way in the early 1900s to "a modernized philosophy of property," the growth of suburbia had made all the more obvious the need for "regulation of land as a social asset." The law needed especially to define the duties of ownership. "We are not abandoning our historical emphasis on individual rights in property," Cribbet argued, "but we are expanding our emphasis on public rights."[21]

Jesse Dukeminier's introductory essay in the UCLA review similarly called for "the development of new concepts of urban land ownership." The traditional approach to property rights allowed the market to determine the shape of the metropolis, Dukeminier wrote, yet the market failed to account for the "social costs" of development. The result was a pattern of land use without beauty or permanence. But the future need not be like the recent past. "Although land is still mainly thought of as a commodity in the free market," Dukeminier concluded, "the public is beginning to think of land as a *basic community resource.* As land use comes to be

20. The editors of both issues explicitly tied the renewed interest in property law to the post-war transformation of the nation's cities and suburbs. See Charles M. Haar, "Foreword," *Iowa Law Review* 50 (1965): 243–244; The Editors, "For the Record," *UCLA Law Review* 12 (March 1965): vii–viii. For a sampling of earlier reflections on the legal challenge of the metropolis, see Allison Dunham, "A Legal and Economic Basis for City Planning," *Columbia Law Review* 58 (1958): 650–671; Allison Dunham, "Flood Control Via the Police Power," *University of Pennsylvania Law Review* 107 (1959): 1098–1132; Jan Z. Krasnowiecki and James C. N. Paul, "The Preservation of Open Space in Metropolitan Areas," *University of Pennsylvania Law Review* 110 (1961): 179–239; Burton Danziger, "Control of Urban Sprawl or Securing Open Space: Regulation by Condemnation or by Ordinance?," *California Law Review* 50 (1962): 483–497.
21. Cribbet, "Changing Concepts in the Law of Land Use," 245–278. For the quotations, see 246, 253, 268, 275.

viewed as a matter of the most serious community concern, and vital to the maximization of all community values, legal institutions must accommodate this change."[22]

Neither Cribbet nor Dukeminier offered a truly ecological view of property, and neither followed ecologist Aldo Leopold in arguing for "a land ethic." Yet both helped to push the law closer to a Leopoldian understanding of the rights and responsibilities of ownership. The next big push came in the early 1970s, when a handful of legal scholars began to ponder the implications of a fundamental "law" of ecology: Everything is connected.[23]

"Property does not exist in isolation," Joseph Sax argued in the *Yale Law Journal* in 1971. "Particular parcels are tied to one another in complex ways, and property is more accurately described as being inextricably part of a network of relationships that is neither limited to, nor usefully defined by, the property boundaries with which the legal system is accustomed to dealing." Two years later, Donald Large made a similar argument in the *Wisconsin Law Review.* "We now realize," he wrote, "that whatever the state of its title, one parcel of land is inextricably intertwined with other parcels, and that causes and effects flow across artificially imposed divisions in the land without regard for legal boundaries. The land simply cannot be neatly divided into mine and yours."[24]

To give weight to such abstractions, Sax and Large cited a number of examples of land uses with effects outside the bounds of ownership. When a coal company strip-mined a steep hillside, a piece of land downslope might begin to erode or a nearby stream might begin to silt up. When a developer filled a wetland to build housing, fisheries might suffer, floods might do greater damage, and waterways might become more polluted. When a farmer used powerful

22. Jesse Dukeminier, Jr., "The Coming Search for Quality," *UCLA Law Review* 12 (1965): 707–718. For the quotations, see 710, 714, 716.
23. Barry Commoner offered a famous statement of the laws of ecology in *The Closing Circle: Nature, Man, and Technology* (1971; reprint, New York: Bantam Books, 1972), 29–44. For Aldo Leopold's argument about the need for a land ethic, see *A Sand County Almanac, and Sketches Here and There* (New York: Oxford University Press, 1949), 201–226.
24. Joseph L. Sax, "Takings, Private Property and Public Rights," *Yale Law Journal* 81 (December 1971): 152; Donald W. Large, "This Land Is Whose Land? Changing Concepts of Land as Property," *Wisconsin Law Review* (1973): 1045.

pesticides, birds might fail to reproduce hundreds of miles away. No piece of property was an island.[25]

What followed from that insight? Though Sax and Large drew different conclusions, both argued that "the ecological facts of life" rendered traditional conceptions of property untenable. Both also argued that the interconnectedness of seemingly discrete tracts of land strengthened the claim of "public rights" in private property. As Large concluded, the law needed to reflect "a more communal view of land." Otherwise, "the preservation of ecologically vital yet economically valueless systems" would be impossible, since the idea of land as a commodity failed to recognize the importance of land as a source of life.[26]

The ecological view of property played a key role in the revolutionary court decisions of the early 1970s. In a 1970 decision affirming the power of the San Francisco Bay commission, the California Court of Appeals accepted the state's argument about the complex unity of the bay. In the words of the court, "the legislature has determined that the bay is the most valuable single natural resource of the entire region and changes in one part of the bay may affect all other parts; that the present uncoordinated, haphazard way in which the bay is being filled threatens the bay itself and is therefore inimical to the welfare of both present and future residents of the bay area; and that a regional approach is necessary to protect the public interest in the bay." The Wisconsin Supreme Court offered a similar argument in Just v. Marinette County, a 1972 decision upholding the state's Shoreland Protection Act. For the court, a controlling factor in the case was "the interrelationship of the wetlands, the swamps and the natural environment of the shorelands to the purity of the water and to such natural resources as navigation, fishing, and scenic beauty." The court also pointed to the growing recognition of the importance of swamps and wetlands in "the balance of nature."[27]

The Just v. Marinette County decision was especially important because the court directly challenged the idea "that an owner has

25. Sax, "Takings, Private Property and Public Rights," 154; Large, "This Land Is Whose Land?," 1047.
26. Sax, "Takings, Private Property and Public Rights," 155; Large, "This Land Is Whose Land?," 1081.
27. Bosselman, Callies, and Banta, *The Taking Issue*, 216, 219.

a right to use his property in any way and for any purpose he sees fit." To comply with the Shoreland Protection Act, the county had prohibited the filling of wetlands near lakes and streams without a permit, and the plaintiffs claimed that the permit requirement unconstitutionally reduced the value of their lakefront land. The court readily acknowledged that wetlands were worth more when filled to make building sites. Yet the court rejected the claim that the plaintiffs were entitled to the profits of development. "An owner of land," the court held, "has no absolute and unlimited right to change the essential natural character of his land so as to use it for a purpose for which it was unsuited in its natural state and which injures the rights of others." To protect the health and welfare of the public, the government had the right to limit "the use of private property to its natural uses."[28]

The court's respect for the "natural character," "natural state," and "natural uses" of land was a startling break with traditional thinking. In a well-known 1963 decision, for example, the New Jersey Supreme Court struck down a local zoning ordinance that limited the use of swampland in a Meadows Development Zone. As the court explained, the ordinance allowed only "passive" activities: "All in all, about the only practical use which can be made of property in the zone is a hunting or fishing preserve or a wildlife sanctuary, none of which can be considered productive." Since a regulation that prohibited all "worthwhile" uses of a piece of property was a taking, the court concluded, the ordinance was unconstitutional. In Just v. Marinette County, however, the Wisconsin Supreme Court rejected the assumption that only profitable uses of the land deserved judicial consideration. The court noted that the Marinette County ordinance did not render shorelands valueless: The plaintiffs could still use their land to collect plants, fish, hunt, hike, or ride on horseback. Beyond that, the plaintiffs had no claim. "Too much stress is laid on the right of an owner to change commercially valueless land," the court argued, "when that change does damage to the rights of the public." That was a radical idea.[29]

---

28. The court's decision is reprinted in Curtis, *Land Use and the Environment,* 189–194. For the quotations, see 192 and 193.
29. In my discussion of the New Jersey case, I have followed David B. Hunter, "An Ecological Perspective on Property: A Call for Judicial Protection of the Public's Interest in

Though the court's ruling was binding only in Wisconsin, Just v. Marinette County soon became well known throughout the country. The case was analyzed in dozens of law review articles about property rights. In several states, judges used the arguments of the Wisconsin court to support their own decisions upholding land-use regulations. The Environmental Protection Agency reprinted the Just v. Marinette County decision in a collection of readings about land use and the environment, and local officials quoted passages in planning documents. The case was also discussed in the committee rooms of Congress, since the issue of property rights became a key point of contention in the debate about national land-use legislation.[30]

A National Debate about Land-use Regulation

Senator Henry Jackson of Washington opened the debate in January 1970 by proposing a National Land Use Policy Act. As chairman

Environmentally Critical Resources," *Harvard Environmental Law Review* 12 (1988): 344–345. In addition, see Bosselman, Callies, and Banta, *The Taking Issue,* 155–159; Jon A. Kusler, "Open Space Zoning: Valid Regulation or Invalid Taking," *Minnesota Law Review* 57 (November 1972): 39–43. I also have drawn on the discussion of the Just v. Marinette County decision in Eric T. Freyfogle, *Bounded People, Boundless Lands: Envisioning a New Land Ethic* (Washington: Island Press, 1998), 107–108. For the quotation, see Curtis, *Land Use and the Environment,* 192.

30. For a sampling of commentary on the decision, see Bosselman, Callies, and Banta, *The Taking Issue,* 217–221; Large, "This Land Is Whose Land?," 1074–1081; Jon A. Kusler, "Land Use: Persuasion or Regulation? – Regulation," in Soil Conservation Society of America, *Land Use: Persuasion or Regulation?* (Ankeny, IA: Soil Conservation Society of America, 1974), 148–149; Sondra E. Berchin, "Regulation of Land Use: From Magna Carta to a *Just* Formulation," *UCLA Law Review* 23 (1976): 928–935; Natural Resources Defense Council, *Land Use Controls in the United States: A Handbook on the Legal Rights of Citizens* (New York: The Dial Press, 1977), 257–258. One commentator even suggested that the decision could provide the text for a constitutional amendment protecting the environment. See Daniel R. Fusfeld, "Next Steps in Land Policy," in Richard N. L. Andrews, *Land in America: Commodity or Natural Resource?* (Lexington, MA: Lexington Books, 1979), 58. The Just v. Marinette decision did not win universal acclaim. For a sympathetic discussion of the argument for the plaintiffs, see Bernard H. Siegan, *Other People's Property* (Lexington, MA: Lexington Books, 1976), 101–104. The influence of the case on judges in other states is discussed by Hunter, "An Ecological Perspective on Property," 353–357. According to one commentator, however, the decision did not have much influence on local officials even in Wisconsin. See David P. Bryden, "A Phantom Doctrine: The Origins and Effects of Just v. Marinette County," *American Bar Foundation Research Journal* 1978 (1978): 397–513. For an example of the quotation of the decision in a local planning document, see Stephen Sussna, "Developing Land in the Midst of the Environmental, Energy, Exclusionary, and Bureaucratic Maze," in Southwestern Legal Foundation, *Proceedings of the Institute on Planning, Zoning, and Eminent Domain: 1974* (New York: Matthew Bender, 1975), 1.

of the Senate Interior Committee, the Democratic senator had struggled to resolve bitter disputes between developers and environmentalists, and he hoped his bill would provide a way to harmonize the two interests. Jackson also had a more ambitious goal. Only a few weeks before, President Nixon had signed the National Environmental Policy Act, and Jackson saw land-use legislation as "the next logical step in our national effort to promote a quality life in a quality environment for present and future generations." Though NEPA required officials to prepare environmental-impact assessments for federal projects, the act did not directly affect the actions of individuals, corporations, or state and local governments. Jackson therefore sought to ensure that "*all* future development" would be "in harmony with sound ecological principles." Because he believed that the key to good development was adequate information, his bill provided federal aid to states for comprehensive land-use planning: The states would gather data about the ecological characteristics of their land and then suggest where different kinds of development should go.[31]

Jackson held hearings on the land-use issue in the spring and summer of 1970, but the policy debate did not begin in earnest until the winter of 1971, when the Nixon administration offered an alternative to Jackson's bill. The administration had little faith in planning. The heart of the land-use problem was not a lack of information, the administration argued, but a lack of effective public oversight of private enterprise. Local governments were not doing the job. Accordingly, the administration bill – drafted by the Council on Environmental Quality – sought to improve land-use regulation: The federal government would encourage the states to control "development of more than local significance" and regulate land use in "areas of critical environmental concern."[32]

Despite the obvious differences in approach, the two proposals

31. For Jackson's comments, see U.S. Congress, *Congressional Record* 116, part 2 (January 29, 1970): 1757; U.S. Senate, *National Land Use Policy: Hearings on S. 3354 Before the Subcommittee on Environment and Land Resources of the Committee on Interior and Insular Affairs,* 91st Congress, 2nd session, 1970, part 1, 393. Lyday offers a fine summary of Jackson's thinking in *The Law of the Land,* 1–15.

32. The administration bill is reprinted as the first appendix in Bosselman and Callies, *The Quiet Revolution.* For a good summary of the administration's thinking about the issue, see Lyday, *The Law of the Land,* 17–26.

had much in common. Unlike the landmark antipollution acts of the early 1970s, neither the Jackson bill nor the CEQ bill required action. Instead, both bills offered the carrot of federal aid to encourage state officials to address the land-use issue. The similarities allowed compromise, and the Democratic senator and the Republican administration soon agreed to support a new measure that combined the principal provisions of the original proposals: The federal government would provide funds to any state willing to inventory its land and then establish a system of land-use regulation. The compromise bill – introduced with bipartisan support in 1972 – was the subject of debate for the next three years.[33]

For most of the supporters of land-use legislation, the impact of urban growth was a major concern. The first witnesses to testify in the 1970 Senate hearings made that clear. Governor Francis Sargent of Massachusetts began by calling for a new kind of conservation effort in the nation's cities and suburbs. Though the conservation movement had always concentrated on mountains, forests, and seashores, Sargent explained, the need had changed: "We must take the tools of the conservationists and apply them to the problems of urban areas." The presidents of the American Institute of Architects, the American Society for Landscape Architects, and the American Institute of Planners also testified about the need to improve land-use planning in metropolitan regions. To illustrate the need, a representative of the AIA's committee on urban growth policy made a slide presentation, and almost all the slides depicted environmental impacts of homebuilding. One made vivid the erosion caused by development on steep hillsides in San Francisco. Several slides showed a bulldozer preparing the land for a subdivision in the desert outside Tucson, while others showed the filling of wetlands in Florida to build homes and factories.[34]

Like the first witnesses to testify before Jackson's committee, the Council on Environmental Quality was especially concerned about the impact of uncontrolled suburban development. The agency repeatedly discussed the subject in its annual reports. To buttress the

33. The best short account of the debate is Lyday, *The Law of the Land*, 27–53. Though the last congressional vote on a land-use bill came in 1975, the subject inspired speeches, articles, and books for the rest of the decade.
34. U.S. Senate, *Hearings on S. 3354,* 30, 44–46, 61–62.

argument for land-use legislation, the CEQ also commissioned two important reports. The first – *The Costs of Sprawl* – was a theoretical assessment of the economic and environmental impacts of different patterns of urban development. The second study used data from the 1960s to analyze the relationship between land-use change and environmental quality in fast-growing metropolitan areas.[35]

The costs of urban growth were also the focus of one of the most influential reform documents of the early 1970s – *The Use of Land,* published in 1973. The document was the work of a task force supported by the Rockefeller Brothers Fund and directed by a former CEQ staff member, William Reilly. As Reilly explained, the reform effort was motivated by a deep disappointment with the postwar pattern of development. Accordingly, the task force argued for legislation to ensure that the next wave of development would be better than the sprawl that followed World War II: "The massive urban growth foreseeable by the end of the century must be managed without destroying what we most value in the distinctiveness of our neighborhoods and communities; the beauty of our countryside, coastal lands, and mountains; and the delicate rhythms of nature."[36]

Because the proposed bill would not force the states to act, a number of environmentalists doubted that the legislation would solve the worst land-use problems. The critics wanted a bill with sticks as well as carrots. Like the antipollution bills, the land-use bill needed to set national standards: The federal government should require the states to preserve open space, to protect prime farmland, and to prevent development of floodplains, wetlands, and steep hillsides. But the bill's sponsors believed that a tougher measure would fail. The key task was to put the land-use issue on

35. In addition to the analysis of suburban development in the first CEQ report, which I quoted earlier, see *Environmental Quality: The Fourth Annual Report of the Council on Environmental Quality* (Washington: USGPO, 1973), 295–325; *Environmental Quality: The Fifth Annual Report of the Council on Environmental Quality* (Washington: USGPO, 1974), 1–92. The commissioned studies are Real Estate Research Corporation, *The Costs of Sprawl: Environmental and Economic Costs of Alternative Residential Development Patterns at the Urban Fringe* [Two volumes] (Washington: USGPO, 1974); Earth Satellite Corporation, *Land Use Change and Environmental Quality in Urban Areas* (Washington: Council on Environmental Quality, 1973).
36. For the quotation, see William K. Reilly, editor, *The Use of Land: A Citizens' Policy Guide to Urban Growth* (New York: Thomas Y. Crowell, 1973), 9–10. In addition, see Reilly's comments in Soil Conservation Society of America, *Land Use: Tough Choices in Today's World* (Ankeny, IA: Soil Conservation Society of America, 1977), 20–21.

the national agenda. Even without federal standards, the proposed bill was strong enough to make a difference.[37]

The bill's supporters hoped especially that federal action would change the way Americans thought about land use. One of Jackson's advisers, political scientist Lynton Caldwell, expressed that hope in the first Senate hearing on the land-use issue. "No man made the land," Caldwell testified, "and none will possess it beyond a lifetime." Yet Americans frequently had used land carelessly. Now, "in their own ultimate interest," the nation's citizens needed to "develop a land ethic that is consistent with our best knowledge of the natural world, including the full range of human needs in land and environment. The National Land Use Policy Act, as law, would be a major step toward the development of a popular land ethic."[38]

Throughout the five-year debate over the legislation, indeed, much of the discussion focused on the pressing need to stimulate new thinking about the land. The congressional testimony of CEQ chairman Russell Train was typical. "The country needs this legislation now," Train told a Senate subcommittee in February 1973. "While there are honest differences of opinion over certain provisions, we cannot afford delay. What we need most is a new perception about the land. We have tended to take the land for granted, perhaps because of our frontier tradition. We need now to develop a sense of stewardship for the land."[39]

37. For the testimony of the bill's environmentalist critics, see U.S. House of Representatives, *The Land Use Planning Act of 1973: Hearings on H.R. 4862 and Related Bills Before the Subcommittee on Environment of the Committee on Interior and Insular Affairs*, 93rd Congress, 1st session, 1973, 366–368, 373–375, 385–386, 391–392. In addition, see Roger P. Hansen, "A National Land Use Policy: Toward a New Land Ethic," in Curtis, *Land Use and the Environment*, 121–122. Lyday also discusses the debate over national standards in *The Law of the Land*. See especially 25–26, 31, 35–36, 41.

38. U.S. Senate, *Hearings on S. 3354*, part 1, 37. The reports of the Senate and House committees with jurisdiction over land use also suggested that the legislation should stimulate new thinking about the importance of land. See, for example, U.S. Senate, *Land Use Policy and Planning Assistance Act of 1972: Report of the Committee on Interior and Insular Affairs, Together with Minority and Additional Views, to Accompany S. 632*, 92nd Congress, 2nd session, 1972, 32–33; U.S. House of Representatives, *National Land Policy, Planning, and Management Act of 1972: Report of the Committee on Interior and Insular Affairs to Accompany H. R. 7211*, 92nd Congress, 2nd session, 1972, 22; U.S. Senate, *Land Use Policy and Planning Assistance Act: Report of the Committee on Interior and Insular Affairs, Together with Minority and Additional Views, to Accompany S. 268*, 93rd Congress, 1st session, 1973, 72–73.

39. Train's testimony was reprinted in a summary of Congressional debate on the issue. See "Pro and Con: Should the Senate-Passed Land Use Policy and Planning Act Be Enacted

As Train's testimony suggested, the bill's supporters often argued that the development of a stewardship ethic required a reckoning with the nation's frontier heritage. For much of American history, the overwhelming abundance of land had encouraged wasteful and destructive attitudes. We felt free to exploit the earth – to do whatever we pleased with our property – because we were blessed with so much. When we used up the resources of a place, we could always move on, to the West, to start anew on fresh land. But the population explosion and the sprawl of suburbia made "the pioneer ethic" a dangerous anachronism.[40]

The recognition that Americans no longer could treat land as a limitless bounty led to a more radical rejection of tradition. "Basically," Bosselman and Callies explained in *The Quiet Revolution,* "we are drawing away from the 19th century idea that land's only function is to enable its owner to make money." In the debate about land-use legislation, the advocates of regulation argued repeatedly that land was not merely a commodity. Land – even privately owned land – was also a public resource. *The Use of Land* made that argument succinctly. "It is time to change the view that land is little more than a commodity to be exploited and traded," the report argued. "We need a land ethic that regards land as a resource which, improperly used, can have the same ill effects as the pollution of air and water, and which therefore warrants similar protection." In a variation on the theme, the supporters of land-use legislation occasionally quoted a now-famous passage from Aldo Leopold's *A Sand County Almanac:* "We abuse land because we regard it as a commodity belonging to us. When we see land as a community to which we belong, we may begin to use it with love and respect."[41]

Into Law?," *Congressional Digest* 52 (December 1973): 310. Train offered similar testimony in the 1974 hearings in the House. See U.S. House of Representatives, *Land Use Planning Act of 1974: Report of the Committee on Interior and Insular Affairs, Together with Additional, Dissenting, and Minority Views, to Accompany H. R. 10294,* 93rd Congress, 2nd session, 1974, 26.

40. For examples of the critique of the frontier ethic, see "Pro and Con," *Congressional Digest,* 306; U.S. Senate, *National Land Use Policy: Background Papers on Past and Pending Legislation and the Roles of the Executive Branch, Congress, and the States in Land Use Planning,* 92nd Congress, 2nd session, 1972, 3, 21; Denis Binder, "Taking Versus Reasonable Regulation: A Reappraisal in Light of Regional Planning and Wetlands," *University of Florida Law Review* 25 (Fall 1972): 13, note 96.

41. For the first quotation, see Bosselman and Callies, *The Quiet Revolution,* 314. The second quotation is from Reilly, *The Use of Land,* 7. For quotations from *A Sand County*

The popular reporting on the land-use debate highlighted the challenge to long-held ideas. In a 1972 special report on "The Land Use Battle that Business Faces," for example, *Business Week* argued that business leaders needed to respond skillfully to changing national values. "More than a century ago," the report began, "Alexis de Tocqueville wrote that the fledgling American republic's basic source of strength was its 'boundless continent.' Americans have since treated their land as though it were indeed boundless, a commodity for unrestrained private exploitation. Today, however, this deep-rooted tradition is being challenged by a new idea: Land is a depletable resource, not a renewable commodity."[42]

The press also highlighted the issue of property rights. In a 1973 report illustrated with photographs of new housing developments, *Time* quoted two members of *The Use of Land* task force to suggest the force of the challenge. Conservationist Laurance Rockefeller told the magazine that land-use planning was essential to environmental quality and good urban growth, "and to this end, the public good must transcend individual property rights." Developer James Rouse agreed: "We are in the midst of the most rapid, radical change in the concept of property rights in our history. It's good. There may

Almanac, see U.S. House of Representatives, *Report to Accompany H. R. 7211,* 22; U.S. House of Representatives, *Report to Accompany H. R. 10294,* 25; U.S. Senate, *Report to Accompany S. 632,* 72; Hansen, "A National Land Use Policy," 119; Morris K. Udall, "Land Use: Why We Need Federal Legislation," in Institute for Contemporary Studies, *No Land Is an Island: Individual Rights and Government Control of Land Use* (San Francisco: Institute for Contemporary Studies, 1975), 74. Though not directly a contribution to the national debate about land-use legislation, Carter also cites Leopold in *The Florida Experience,* vi, 337. For examples of the commodity versus resource argument, see also Bosselman and Callies, 315–319; Council on Environmental Quality, *First Annual Report,* 166; Albert Mayer, "It's Not Just the Cities: Land as a Public Resource vs. Speculative Commodity," *Architectural Record* 147 (June 1970): 137–142; U.S. Senate, *Report to Accompany S. 632,* 32–33; U.S. Senate, *National Land Use Policy: Hearings on S. 632 and S. 992 Before the Subcommittee on Environment and Land Resources of the Committee on Interior and Insular Affairs,* 92nd Congress, 1st session, 1971, 395; Soil Conservation Society of America, *Land Use: Tough Choices in Today's World,* 170, 307; James Nathan Miller, "Hawaii's 'Quiet Revolution' Hits the Mainland," *National Civic Review* 62 (1973): 412. The subtitle of Andrews, *Land in America: Commodity or Natural Resource?,* suggests just how common the dichotomy became.
42. "The Land Use Battle that Business Faces," *Business Week* (August 26, 1972): 40. In addition, see Gladwin Hill, "New Land Ethic: Its Spread Raises Political and Legal Issues to Be Resolved by Public," *New York Times* (September 4, 1973): 23; "The New American Land Rush," *Time* 102 (October 1, 1973): 80–99; "'Stop' Signs for Developers Going Up All Over U.S.," *U.S. News and World Report* 76 (January 21, 1974): 40–42; John H. Douglas, "How Shall We Use the Land?," *Science News* 104 (October 27, 1973): 268; James Nathan Miller, "Hawaii's 'Quiet Revolution' Hits the Mainland," *Reader's Digest* 103 (October 1973): 128.

be excesses, but in a great rush our society is saying that we won't squander the land any more."[43]

By 1973, then, the land-use bill had become the symbol of a revolution in progress. A vote for the bill, the press suggested, was a vote for sweeping changes in the way Americans regarded the nature of property ownership. Several of the principal supporters of the land-use bill encouraged that view by urging judges and lawyers to reconsider the meaning of the takings clause. *The Use of Land* included a chapter on adapting the old law of property to new ideals, and the CEQ published a 300-page report on the takings issue. To protect critical environmental values, *The Use of Land* explained, "tough new restrictions will have to be placed on the use of privately owned land. These restrictions will be little more than delaying actions if the courts do not uphold them as reasonable measures to protect the public interest, in short, as restrictions which landowners may fairly be required to bear without payment by the government."[44]

To many opponents of land-use legislation, the talk about the need for a new ethic sounded alarms. Representative Steve Symms warned the House of Representatives in 1974 that passage of the land-use bill would begin a slow but sure erosion of the rights of property ownership. "For this bill will lay the groundwork for a New Feudalism," Symms argued. "The duke and baron of old will be replaced by the State, supposedly acting in the name of 'the people.' Today's independent landowner will become the serf of tomorrow's New Feudalism. Under the New Feudalism all real property will be not owned, but merely 'held,' at the sufferance of the State. Whatever the State thinks the landholder must do in the people's interest, he will be forced to do. The New Feudalism will recreate the misery and bondage of an age long since mercifully forgotten."[45]

In a 1975 essay on "The New Feudalism," the president of the

43. "The New American Land Rush," 97, 98. In addition, see "'Stop' Signs for Developers Going Up All Over U.S.," 40.
44. Reilly, *The Use of Land,* 145–175; Bosselman, Callies, and Banta, *The Taking Issue.* For the quotation from *The Use of Land,* see 23. *The Use of Land* analysis went well beyond the commentary on the takings issue in the law reviews: The often-cited report called for the courts to overturn "outmoded" precedents, to expand the definition of the public purposes justifying regulation, and to shift the burden of proof in land-use cases so that property owners would have to demonstrate that development would not degrade the environment.
45. U.S. House of Representatives, *Report to Accompany H. R. 10294,* 104.

Institute for Liberty and Community, John McClaughry, elaborated Symms's argument. McClaughry began by reciting the "catechism of slogans" used to justify land-use regulation. "Land is a resource, not a commodity." "The public has rights as well as property owners." For McClaughry, the real meaning of those slogans was clear: The reformers sought "the centralization of all power over land in state – and ultimately federal – regulatory agencies." The reformers also intended to institutionalize "the idea of social property." That theory held that land belonged to society, McClaughry explained, and individuals could use land only at the sufferance of the government. To demonstrate the danger, McClaughry again cited a number of comments by supporters of land-use regulation. "We will have to stop thinking in terms of land ownership and start thinking of land holdership." "When it comes to ownership of land, we are nothing more, and never should be anything more, than very temporary trustees with a direct responsibility for its protection and use." In McClaughry's judgment, the words needed almost no interpretation: "These public statements illustrate the basic social property approach of the New Feudalism."[46]

The issue of property rights also sparked grassroots activism. In New York and Vermont, thousands of landowners joined organizations to oppose state land-use regulation, and the Vermont activists soon mobilized against the national legislation. The editors of the *Vermont Watchman* – the journal of the state's most influential property-rights organization – warned that the bill would "turn loose upon the hapless citizens of the various states a horde of planners and lawyers, paid by the taxpayers, whose advancement requires success in preventing those citizens from making normal use of their own property." If the bill passed, the editors concluded,

46. John McClaughry, "The New Feudalism: State Land Use Controls," in Institute for Contemporary Studies, *No Land Is an Island*, 38, 50. In addition, see John McClaughry, "Farmers, Freedom, and Feudalism: How to Avoid the Coming Serfdom," *South Dakota Law Review* 21 (1976): 486–541. Robert H. Nelson also criticizes the new feudalism of land-use regulation in *Zoning and Property Rights: An Analysis of the American System of Land-Use Regulation* (Cambridge: MIT Press, 1977), 124–125, 152–153. In McClaughry's home state of Vermont, a grassroots organization used a similar argument to oppose the state land-use law. "If the environmentalists win," the group warned, "private property will be replaced by 'social property' and all landowners will be allowed to act only as the state permits. If they are defeated, the ideas on which Vermont was founded – private property, individual liberty, and a republican form of government – will prevail." See Myers, *So Goes Vermont*, 27.

"it may well be seen years from now as perhaps the most significant action of the century in destroying the institution of private property."[47]

Of course, much of the concern about the land-use bill had little to do with property rights. The legislation directly affected a number of industries, and representatives of dozens of trade organizations testified about the cost of land-use regulation in jobs, profits, and community well-being. The Chamber of Commerce lobbyist repeatedly called for Congress to balance economic and environmental considerations. An executive of the National Association of Realtors spoke about the likely effect of regulation on housing costs, and a spokesperson for the National Association of Home Builders voiced the fear that the bill would become "a Federal 'seal of approval' on the no-growth movement."[48]

To defeat the bill, the Chamber of Commerce organized a lobbying coalition, the Coordinating Committee on Land Use Control. The committee membership was dominated by organizations representing landowners and business interests that profited from homebuilding and development, including the American Land Development Association, the National Crushed Stone Association, the National Sand and Gravel Association, the Associated General Contractors of America, the National Association of Home Builders, the National Forest Products Association, the National Association of Electric Companies, the National Cattlemen's Association, and the American Farm Bureau Federation. In regular meetings, the chamber lobbyist argued repeatedly that the land-use bill would affect the economic interests of the member organizations in unexpected

47. The *Vermont Watchman* is quoted in Plotkin, *Keep Out*, 196, 306, note 72. The opposition in New York organized the League for Adirondack Citizen Rights. See David Helvarg, *The War Against the Greens: The 'Wise-Use' Movement, the New Right, and Anti-Environmental Violence* (San Francisco: Sierra Club Books, 1994), 207. In Vermont, the best known opponents of land-use regulation were the Landowners Steering Committee and the Green Mountain Boys. See McClaughry, "The New Feudalism," 39–49; Meyers, *So Goes Vermont*, 91; Calvin Trillin, "U.S. Journal: Vermont," *New Yorker* 50 (November 4, 1974): 128–135.
48. U.S. House of Representatives, *Hearings on H.R. 4862*, 543–544, 557–558; U.S. Senate, *The Land Use Policy and Planning Assistance Act: Hearings on S. 268 Before the Subcommittee on Environment and Land Resources of the Committee on Interior and Insular Affairs*, 93rd Congress, 1st session, 1973, Part 3, 266–271; U.S. House of Representatives, *The Land Use Planning Act of 1974: Hearings on H.R. 10294 Before the Subcommittee on Environment of the Committee on Interior and Insular Affairs*, 93rd Congress, 2nd session, 1974, 135.

and damaging ways, since the legislation had strong antigrowth implications.[49]

The Chamber of Commerce also worked to stir up opposition at the grassroots. In a 1974 "action" letter sent to roughly 2,500 local and state affiliates, for example, the national organization stressed the economic threat to small property owners. "Suppose you own land in the country, near a major metropolitan area," the mailing began. "You bought this land with your savings, many years ago, as an investment . . . maybe to put the kids through college, when the time comes. . . . Up to now, if the government wanted this land of yours for public purposes . . . it had to pay a fair price for it." Then came the kicker: "What if the government declares it in the public interest to 'preserve open space' and says you may continue to own your land, but you may not build anything on it?" "Believe it or not," the mailing concluded, "there are 'experts' in Washington advocating such policies." The appeal succeeded. By all accounts, the offices of senators and representatives were soon flooded with letters and phone calls opposing the land-use bill.[50]

Yet the most intense attacks on the proposed legislation were ideological. In the 1974 House committee report on the bill, the dissenters argued that the trend toward public control over the use of private property threatened the American system of free enterprise and individual liberty. The minority statement in the 1973 Senate committee report also defined the issue as a defense of the American way. The bill would "jeopardize the one single characteristic of American life, the right of private ownership of property, that so distinguishes our lives from those of people in other countries." By stifling private ownership, the bill would stifle the great "stimulus to man's initiative" that had made "the standard of living of America the envy of all the world."[51]

The intensity of the opposition was not apparent at first. Even many of the business lobbyists initially assumed that passage of some

---

49. "Land Use Legislation: A Precarious Future," *Congressional Quarterly Weekly Report* 33 (March 1, 1975): 430. In addition, see Lyday, *The Law of the Land*, 47.

50. Lyday quotes the Chamber of Commerce alert in *The Law of the Land*, 47. For the letters and phone calls, see also "Land Use Legislation," 431.

51. U.S. House of Representatives, *Report to Accompany H. R. 10294*, 155, 156; U.S. Senate, *Report to Accompany S. 268*, 74–75. In addition, see U.S. House of Representatives, *Hearings on H.R. 10294*, 67.

sort of land-use bill was inevitable. The only question was what the legislation would require. In September 1972, the Senate approved the Land Use Policy and Planning Assistance Act by a vote of 60–18. When the House did not take up the measure, the Senate passed the bill again, 64–21, in June 1973. The House Interior Committee overwhelmingly endorsed the legislation in January 1974. But a few months later, President Nixon abruptly withdrew the administration's support. In June, the House voted 211–204 not to allow debate on the bill. Representative Morris Udall attempted to revive the legislation in 1975, without success.[52]

The defeat shocked the bill's supporters. Yet the legislative effort was not futile. In the early 1970s, the Clean Air Act, the Clean Water Act, and the Endangered Species Act all gave federal agencies new power to regulate land use. Though lawmakers rejected the all-encompassing National Land Use Policy Act, the Coastal Zone Management Act of 1972 provided federal assistance to states willing to control land use on the nation's coasts. The strong support for national action also encouraged the trend toward state regulation of land use. While Congress was debating the issue, the number of legislatures considering land-use bills increased dramatically, and several states passed sweeping reform measures. The debate in Washington likewise drew attention to the effort in legal circles to redefine the rights and responsibilities of property ownership. The CEQ report on the takings issue quickly became a classic. The likelihood that Congress would pass a major land-use bill even inspired the National Science Foundation to sponsor a research initiative on "environment" as a guide to land-use planning. In many ways, therefore, the five-year debate had a lasting impact on the landscape.[53]

52. For the votes, see Lyday, *The Law of the Land*, 30, 36, 38–39.
53. For the land-use provisions in the legislation of the early 1970s, see Harvey M. Jacobs, editor, *Who Owns America?: Social Conflict Over Property Rights* (Madison: University of Wisconsin Press, 1998), 148; Bruce Yandle, editor, *Land Rights: The 1990s Property Rights Rebellion* (Lanham, MD: Rowman & Littlefield, 1995), 296; Carr and Duensing, *Land Use Issues of the 1980s*, 120–122. The federal research initiative is the subject of Donald M. McAllister, editor, *Environment: A New Focus for Land-Use Planning* (Washington: National Science Foundation, 1973). In addition, see Edward J. Kaiser, Karl Elfers, Sidney Cohn, Peggy A. Reichert, Maynard M. Hufschmidt, and Raymond E. Stanland, Jr., *Promoting Environmental Quality Through Urban Planning and Controls* (Washington: Environmental Protection Agency, 1973).

The Lessons of Defeat

With the defeat in Washington, the movement to institutionalize a land ethic lost momentum. Though the quiet revolution went forward in the courts, the reform effort in the states slowed considerably. The number of state land-use regulations continued to increase, partly in response to the federal pollution and coastal-zone initiatives – but the push for comprehensive state land-use programs hit a wall. What had happened?[54]

In 1973, the economy began to slump, and then the oil embargo led to a dramatic increase in energy prices. The economic crisis quickly changed the political situation. For the first time, the nation began to suffer both serious inflation and rising unemployment. The housing market was hit especially hard. Housing starts dropped from nearly 2.4 million in 1972 to barely 1 million in 1974. As a result, the idea of regulating development became much harder to sell. "Land use may be a kind of luxury in a depression year," one supporter of federal legislation noted in 1975. "If you've got lots of people in the construction trades out of work, they're not going to be very fastidious about where and how growth takes place."[55]

The campaign for land-use legislation was also hurt by a backlash against the environmental movement's early triumphs. For a few years, protecting the environment was supporting "apple pie and motherhood": Though environmentalists often said and wrote things in 1970 that pointed toward radical change, the radicalism of the movement was lost in the widespread and seemingly incontrovertible conviction that we needed to take better care of the earth. By 1974, however, a significant number of business and political leaders believed that the first round of environmental laws had had more far-reaching and disruptive consequences than anyone anticipated. When a federal court ruled, for example, that the Clean Air Act required the Environmental Protection Agency to draw up regulations limiting development in heavily polluted areas, the rul-

54. For a superb analysis of the course of regulation, see Frank J. Popper, "Understanding American Land Use Regulation Since 1970: A Revisionist Interpretation," *Journal of the American Planning Association* 54 (1998): 291–301.
55. For the quotation, see "Land Use Legislation," 428. A number of commentators have pointed to the economic downturn in explaining the defeat of land-use legislation. For a good example of the argument, see Plotkin, *Keep Out*, 194–197.

ing sent shivers down a lot of spines. In the debate about land-use legislation, the opposition argued repeatedly that the economic and social costs of reform would be much higher than the bill's proponents allowed. "Lest we be accused of needlessly crying 'Wolf,'" the dissenters wrote in the 1973 Senate report on the bill, "consider the surprising consequences, unimagined and unintended by the Congress which passed it, of the court interpretation and bureaucratic administration of the National Environmental Policy Act." Eight members of the House offered a similar warning in 1974: "The dangers arise, because, as we are beginning to realize in the case of air and water pollution laws, the effects of such laws go far beyond cleaning the air and water."[56]

Though the antienvironmental backlash was important, the reform effort of the early 1970s also suffered from a kind of immaturity. The supporters of land-use legislation underestimated the complexity of the task. To many environmentalists, the misuse of land was "just another form of pollution," and a federal land-use bill seemed the obvious next step after the passage of the two great antipollution acts. But that assumption was flawed: The problem of land use was quite different from the problem of pollution.[57]

Because both the Clean Air Act and the Clean Water Act required industry to produce less pollution, the most difficult battles in the antipollution campaign involved the prerogatives of corporate management. Yet the rights of management were not nearly so sacred as the rights of property. Indeed, the threat to property rights became a powerful rallying cry for opponents of environmentalism in the decades to come, and the property rights activists of the 1980s and 1990s often drew on arguments first used against the

---

56. U.S. Senate, *Report to Accompany S. 268,* 156; U.S. House of Representatives, *Report to Accompany H. R. 10294,* 73. For similar comments, see the testimony of Senator Carl Curtis in "Pro and Con," *Congressional Digest,* 303. The Chamber of Commerce lobbyist was especially vigorous in arguing that the land-use bill was not "apple pie and motherhood." See "Land Use Legislation," 430; Lyday, *The Law of the Land,* 45–46. In *Other People's Property,* Siegan also argues that the backlash against the effects of earlier environmental acts helped to defeat the bill. See 70.

57. For the quotation, see Luther J. Carter, "Land Use Law: Congress on the Verge of a Modest Beginning," *Science* 182 (November 16, 1973): 692. CEQ chairman Russell Train again and again defined land-use legislation as the top priority for environmentalists after the creation of a regulatory structure to deal with pollution. In the introduction to *The Use of Land,* William Reilly made a similar argument.

National Land Use Policy Act in the early 1970s, especially the attack on the "new feudalism."[58]

The antipollution campaign could also target a distant, impersonal elite – "corporate polluters." But the nation had far more landowners than industrial corporations. Though advocates of land-use regulation might attack "the grasping wastrels of the land," the land-use issue did not fit neatly into the classic populist mold of Us versus Them, the suffering many against the greedy few. As one supporter of the national land-use bill acknowledged, "the dream of selling one's land for a big capital gain is, in a modest way, the dream of many Americans." That dream allowed the Chamber of Commerce to win the support of a host of ordinary folks, from farmers to retirees.[59]

Despite the enormity of the pollution problem, the solution seemed to many policymakers largely a matter of technology. With smokestack scrubbers, catalytic converters, and waste-treatment plants, industry could make the air and the water cleaner. But the land-use problem could not be solved simply by mandating the adoption of new production techniques. Unlike the goods produced in pollution generating factories, the urban landscape was not manu-

58. By the early 1990s, hundreds of property rights groups were active across the nation, and journalists were writing about "the property-rights movement." In 1991, Steve Symms – then a U.S. senator – introduced a Private Property Rights Act to require the federal government to weigh the impact of all federal actions on the value of privately owned land: Though never enacted, the act twice passed the Senate. The issue of property rights was also debated in dozens of state legislatures: Another veteran of the land-use battles of the early 1970s, John McClaughry, was the first legislator to propose a state property rights bill, in Vermont. The property rights campaign also included legal challenges to state land-use laws. For the enduring appeal of the "new feudalism" argument, see Bruce Yandle, "Escaping Environmental Feudalism," *Harvard Journal of Law and Public Policy* 15 (1992): 517–539; Richard J. Lazarus, "Debunking Environmental Feudalism: Promoting the Individual Through the Collective Pursuit of Environmental Quality," *Iowa Law Review* 77 (1992): 1739–1774; Dennis J. Coyle, *Property Rights and the Constitution: Shaping Society Through Land Use Regulation* (Albany: State University of New York Press, 1993): 213–237; Yandle, *Land Rights*, 109; Jacobs, *Who Owns America?*, 31. The Symms bill is discussed briefly in John Echeverria and Raymond Booth Eby, editors, *Let the People Judge: Wise Use and the Private Property Rights Movement* (Washington: Island Press, 1995), 159–160; Philip D. Brick and R. McGreggor Cawley, editors, *A Wolf in the Garden: The Land Rights Movement and the New Environmental Debate* (Lanham, MD: Rowman & Littlefield, 1996), 67. For McClaughry's career, see Helvarg, *The War Against the Greens*, 66, 202–204, 320.

59. The quotation comes from Soil Conservation Society of America, *National Land Use Policy*, 129. On the difficulty of making urban sprawl a populist issue, see also Paul Ylvisaker, "The Villains Are Greed, Indifference – and You," *Life* 59 (December 24, 1965): 96.

factured in a controlled environment designed by engineers. Instead, the pattern of urban growth was the result of countless decisions made by a variety of people, and builders were only one part of the equation. The environmental impact of urban growth depended on where people built, not just how.

The cost of solving the two problems was also different. The improvement in the quality of life from antipollution legislation came at a price that most Americans clearly were willing to pay. Though consumers ultimately paid more for utilities and for countless products, the increases seldom were overwhelming. Even the price of new cars did not rise that much, despite the dire predictions of the automakers. But if land-use regulation increased the cost of developing subdivisions, the effects might be more onerous. The purchase of a house was often a once-in-a-lifetime decision, and the added cost might change the lives of a significant number of people. To many business and political leaders, the issue raised a troubling question: Would land-use regulation reverse the postwar trend toward rising rates of homeownership?[60]

To overcome so many obstacles, the supporters of land-use legislation surely needed to provide unforgettable examples of the hazards of unregulated development. The costs of inaction had to become at least as clear as the dangers of living with polluted air and water. Yet the witnesses in the congressional hearings on land use rarely provided detailed evidence of the environmental impact of sprawl. The evidence was there, but the advocates of regulation too readily assumed that the problem was obvious, and only the solution needed to be debated. In the words of the official report on the 1973 Senate hearings, "little discussion was directed to the question of whether or not a national land-use policy was desirable."[61]

The reformers also stumbled in defining the goal of land-use

60. Though published a few years after the defeat of the national land-use bill, Bernard J. Frieden's *The Environmental Protection Hustle* (Cambridge: MIT Press, 1979) is the best example of the argument that land-use regulation threatened "the American dream" of homeownership. See especially 1–15. For a summary of the early literature on the impact of regulation on the housing market, see Arthur P. Solomon, *The Effect of Land Use and Environmental Controls on Housing: A Review* (Cambridge: Joint Center for Urban Studies of the Massachusetts Institute of Technology and Harvard University, 1976).

61. U.S. Senate, *National Land Use Policy Legislation: An Analysis of Legislative Proposals and State Laws*, 93rd Congress, 1st session, 1973, 79.

legislation. In part, the difficulty was unavoidable. The land-use ideal was much harder to define than "clean air" or "clean water." Scientists could measure pollution with some precision. Even where the air or the water was polluted, people sometimes could remember a time when the skies were blue or the streams were clear. But what was good land use? "There is no physical ideal of 'pure land' to guide us or even to indicate when we are making progress," the authors of *The Use of Land* acknowledged. Though environmentalists readily listed a few basic principles of good land use – don't build on steep hillsides, preserve open space, minimize water pollution, control erosion – the lists did not provide a compelling vision of sound development.[62]

The task of envisioning good land use was made more difficult by the long-standing environmentalist habit of setting nature apart from the city. When environmentalists described landscapes where people lived in harmony with the nonhuman world, the scenes were almost always rural: The English countryside, the hillside villages of the Mediterranean, the Pennsylvania Dutch country. But the problem of land use was predominately urban. What would environmentally sound development look like? Though Ian McHarg made a start toward answering that question in *Design with Nature,* few environmentalists followed McHarg's lead until the 1980s.[63]

No doubt, the advocates of land-use regulation thought the idea of "a land ethic" offered a defining vision for the future, but the phrase meant different things to different people. Aldo Leopold

---

62. The quotation is from Reilly, *The Use of Land,* 1. For a good illustration of the inadequacy of lists of land-use principles, see Haskell, "Land Use and the Environment." After offering a thoughtful sketch of basic "do"s and "don't"s, Haskell concluded with a vague summary of the goals of regulation: "Land use management is a positive force for creating the type of development we want, not just stopping that we don't want. It must be more than mere conservation of existing resources; it must create physical and social environments that will be satisfying in the future." See 7. At least one environmentalist criticized the land-use reformers for failing to address the issue of acceptable development. See Robert L. Sansom, *The New American Dream Machine: Toward a Simpler Lifestyle in an Environmental Age* (Garden City, NY: Anchor Books, 1976), 186–187.
63. I drew my examples of idyllic landscapes from the work of Rene Dubos. See *So Human an Animal* (New York: Charles Scribner's Sons, 1968), 201–208; *The Wooing of Earth* (New York: Charles Scribner's Sons, 1980), 113. For the urban land-use visions of the next generation of environmentalists, see Anne Whiston Spirn, *The Granite Garden: Urban Nature and Human Design* (New York: Basic Books, 1984); Michael Hough, *City Form and Natural Process: Towards a New Urban Vernacular* (1984; reprint, London: Routledge, 1989).

argued that a land ethic required a deeply felt obligation to something larger than society: We needed to see the land as a community where humans were plain members and citizens, not conquerors. To some supporters, however, a land ethic simply meant acknowledging that the public had a vital interest in private decisions about land use. For most reformers, the idea of a land ethic also involved a Pinchotian sense that land was a scarce and valuable resource that ought to be conserved. But the resource argument did not go deep enough. Though a real advance over the idea that land was a limitless bounty for individuals to exploit, the call to acknowledge the ecological value of land ultimately played on fear. Yet, as Leopold understood, a lasting ethic could only come from a hard-won change in popular "loyalties, affections, and convictions."[64]

64. For Leopold's views, see *A Sand County Almanac,* viii, 204, 209–210.

Conclusion

In 1950, economist K. William Kapp published a pioneering book entitled *The Social Costs of Private Enterprise*. He did not mention homebuilding at all, and he devoted only a page to urban land use, yet his work offered a powerful analysis of the environmental problems caused by the postwar pattern of development.[1]

The capitalist system contained a fundamental flaw, Kapp argued, since businesses routinely forced members of society to pay a significant part of the costs of production. To illustrate the point, Kapp considered a handful of environmental issues, including air and water pollution, soil erosion, destruction of wildlife, and waste of energy. Because no one charged for the use of air as a waste depository, manufacturers sent dirty, destructive, and deadly pollutants into the skies. Manufacturers also destroyed aquatic life, contaminated drinking supplies, and marred the aesthetic qualities of water by pouring wastes into rivers, lakes, and oceans. To reduce the costs of logging, timber companies often left steep slopes to erode, and so increased the siltation of streams and the severity of floods. In the race to exploit limited oil, gas, and coal resources, extractive firms used inefficient means of production and abandoned wells and mines prematurely. Market hunters also took for today without thought of tomorrow. For a number of species, from the passenger pigeon to the whale, the result of competitive exploitation was extinction or near-extinction.[2]

Though some entrepreneurs were more public-minded than

1. K. William Kapp, *The Social Costs of Private Enterprise* (1950; reprint, New York: Schocken Books, 1971).
2. Ibid., 67–145.

others, Kapp wrote, the disregard of social costs was not a matter of individual character. The problem inhered in capitalist economies. To make more money, entrepreneurs habitually sought to maximize the difference between revenues and outlays for labor, materials, and borrowed capital. Unless restrained by legal action, by organized opposition, or by government regulation, profit-driven enterprises had a clear financial incentive to reduce the costs of production no matter what the social burden in diminished health, damage to property, depletion of natural resources, or despoliation of places of beauty and tranquillity. Indeed, Kapp concluded, "capitalism must be regarded as an economy of unpaid costs, 'unpaid' in so far as a substantial portion of the actual costs of production remain unaccounted for in entrepreneurial outlays; instead, they are shifted to, and ultimately borne by, third persons or by the community as a whole."[3]

The building industry was no exception to Kapp's rule. In 1950, homebuilders rarely had to take environmental costs into account. Though many cities and counties had subdivision codes and zoning ordinances, the two forms of regulation dealt mainly with economic and social issues – the technical standards for streets and utilities, the shape of lots, or the location of residential, commercial, and industrial land. To cut costs, therefore, homebuilders were free to cause a variety of environmental problems. To take advantage of the cheap, unsewered land at the fringes of cities, they could install septic tanks on tiny lots, in unsuitable soils, or near streams or wells. To reduce land acquisition costs, builders could level hills, fill wetlands, and build in floodplains. To maximize the number of lots in a tract, they could design subdivisions with no open space. To speed the work of site preparation, builders could clear the ground of vegetation. To save on material and labor, they could design and build houses without much protection against heat and cold.

The social circumstances of the postwar period greatly intensified the competitive pressure to reduce production costs by ignoring environmental burdens. The nation was desperately short of housing. The homebuilding industry had all but shut down during the Depression and the war, so almost a generation had passed with little

3. Ibid., 231.

construction, yet millions of newly married and recently reunited couples keenly desired the space to start families. Newspapers, magazines, radio shows, and movie newsreels all told horror stories about couples forced to double up with relatives in tiny apartments or temporary shelters. According to a congressional investigation, the housing shortage forced hundreds of thousands of veterans to find shelter in garages, trailers, barns, and – shockingly – chicken coops.

For many business and government leaders, the housing issue was also tied to powerful concerns about the strength of the nation's economic and political structure. In the 1920s, Secretary of Commerce Herbert Hoover had launched a campaign to promote homeownership as a bulwark of individual freedom and national prosperity. "Maintaining a high percentage of individual homeowners is one of the searching tests that now challenge the people of the United States," Hoover wrote in 1923, and the argument only became more resonant in the late 1940s. The lingering memories of the bitter class conflict during the Depression and the onset of the Cold War encouraged a desire to increase the rate of homeownership, which had remained at roughly 40 percent since the turn of the century. As one commentator noted later, the nation's postwar leadership saw widespread homeownership as a major way to overcome "the unmistakable contradiction between actual social inequalities and an egalitarian ideology."[4]

To respond to the social, economic, and political demands of the late 1940s and early 1950s, the building industry sought to produce houses quickly and cheaply. Though a few highbrow critics lambasted the monotonous rows of little boxes in the new subdivisions and suburbs, the initial response of most commentators was to acclaim the Model T method of building. In 1947, *Fortune* touted Levittown as a sign that "the industrial revolution" had finally come to the world of homebuilding. *Reader's Digest* reprinted the *Fortune* story with the exuberant headline, "The Way to More – and Cheaper – Houses." *Life* published huge spreads of Levittown

---

4. For the Hoover quotation, see Gwendolyn Wright, *Building the Dream: A Social History of Housing in America* (Cambridge: MIT Press, 1981), 193. The second quotation is from Constance Perin, *Everything in Its Place: Social Order and Land Use in America* (Princeton: Princeton University Press, 1977), 79.

photographs, and *Time* put Levittown on the cover. As *Time* acknowledged in 1950, the new suburb had problems, especially the lack of a few essential public facilities. "But most Levittowners think the disadvantages are far outweighed by the advantages," the magazine reported. "Said ex-G.I. Wilbur Schaetzl, who lived with his wife and a relative in a one-room apartment before he moved to Levittown: 'That was so awful I'd rather not talk about it. Getting into this house was like being emancipated.' Bill Levitt puts it in his own brash way: 'In Levittown 99% of the people pray for us.'"[5]

In the 1950s and 1960s, however, a variety of people began to tally the environmental costs of mass-produced housing. The accounting was not systematic or concerted. Indeed, the course of criticism had many twists and turns. Architects were more interested in energy-conserving design in 1950 than in 1965. The way the critics defined the issues often changed over time. The open-space movement was especially protean. In the late 1950s, the grassroots protests against suburban sprawl were rooted in aesthetic and social concerns, yet the open-space issue soon helped to inspire the first efforts at environmental planning. Though a few people took a panoramic look at the new suburban landscape, the environmental critique of tract housing ultimately brought together the ideas of a diverse group of specialists. Some of the critics of tract housing were mainly concerned about public health, while others worried only about soil erosion or species preservation.

In every case, though, the critics of homebuilding had to grapple with a basic question: What could be done to remedy the problems they saw? Occasionally, the critics concluded that they needed to educate homebuyers, to convince the public to demand a different kind of construction. To preserve open space, for example, William Whyte made a pitch to homebuyers about the advantages of cluster subdivisions. But both activists and policymakers generally thought that the heart of the problem – the key to reform – was the building

5. For the quotation, see "Up from the Potato Fields," *Time* 56 (July 3, 1950): 69–70. The story was also published in *Reader's Digest* 57 (October 1950): 105–108. In addition, see "The Industry Capitalism Forgot," *Fortune* 36 (August 1947): 61–67, 167–170; "The Way to More – and Cheaper – Houses," *Reader's Digest* 51 (October 1947): 45–50; "Nation's Biggest Housebuilder," *Life* 25 (August 8, 1948): 75–78. For a more critical view, see Eric Larrabee, "The Six Thousand Houses That Levitt Built," *Harper's* 197 (September 1948): 79–88.

industry. Builders made the most important decisions about how and where to build. How could they be persuaded or compelled to reduce the environmental costs of development?

From the first, a variety of experts hoped that tract-house development could be improved without recourse to government regulation, and their hopes were expressed most ambitiously in the 1960s in a campaign to encourage a new kind of community building. The typical land-use regulation was a prohibition, the proponents of the "new communities" ideal argued, yet a list of "don't"s tended to stifle imaginative thought about ways to improve the overall pattern of development. Perhaps the answer lay instead in planning on a large scale – the construction of new suburbs designed by interdisciplinary teams of professionals to meet environmental goals?

The new community ideal had historic roots. In turn-of-the-century England, Ebenezer Howard advocated the construction of "garden" communities as a solution to the problems of dirty, congested cities, and the English planning ideal soon crossed the Atlantic. In the 1920s, a New York philanthropic corporation sponsored the building of Radburn, New Jersey, to suggest the possibilities of community design. A New Deal agency built three "greenbelt" towns in the 1930s. By the late 1950s and early 1960s, a handful of large-scale developers saw a potential market for new open-space communities with thousands of acres of nature trails, water, and recreational facilities, and the innovative "new towns" of Reston, Virginia, and Columbia, Maryland, received considerable publicity. Though the American new towns used only a few principles of environmental design, the experiments encouraged the hope that a national program of planned community building would counter the destructive effects of sprawl.[6]

The Housing and Home Finance Agency sought legislation in 1964 to provide federal loan guarantees to developers of new communities. If government assistance could reduce the burden of meeting start-up costs, the agency argued, then the construction of new communities might become common. The measure failed, yet the idea rapidly gained support. In 1968, the American Institute of

6. The literature on the new town idea is extensive. For a succinct history of the idea, see Raymond J. Burby, III and Shirley F. Weiss, *New Communities U.S.A.* (Lexington, MA: Lexington Books, 1976), 37–38, 47–53.

Architects called for a major federal commitment to encourage the construction of planned cities. In addition to serving a number of social goals, the organization argued, a new communities program would help meet the need for developments that "are less hostile to man and nature, that continuously reduce the pollution of land, air, and water, and that maintain open spaces and greenbelts for recreation and tranquillity." In 1968 and 1969, three national commissions also endorsed the proposal as a critical way to deal with the problems of uncontrolled urban growth. Despite some doubts, Congress agreed. The Urban Growth and New Community Development Act of 1970 provided a variety of forms of financial assistance to developers willing to build socially integrated, environmentally sensitive cities.[7]

The federal program helped to make possible one outstanding example of environmental planning – a new community thirty miles north of Houston developed by a subsidiary of entrepreneur George Mitchell's oil-and-gas company. In the late 1960s, Mitchell began to envision a new community of 180,000 people on a well-wooded 20,000-acre tract, but the financing proved difficult to arrange. With the prospect of government loan guarantees, however, Mitchell decided to go ahead with the project in 1970. After reading *Design with Nature,* he hired Ian McHarg's firm to do the environmental design for the new suburb: Woodlands, Texas.[8]

After investigating the site, McHarg proposed to build around a few key natural elements. The tract included two creeks lined with a magnificent collection of trees – evergreen magnolias, water and willow oaks, towering pines. Though most of the land had poorly drained soil, the soil in a few wooded locations allowed water to seep below and replenish two important aquifers. The creek banks, the floodplains, and the well-drained land therefore would provide recreational open space for the community. Because the open space formed a rich wildlife corridor, the development could continue to support white-tailed deer, opossum, armadillos, and even bobcats.

7. For the quotation, see James Bailey, editor, *New Towns in America: The Design and Development Process* (New York: John Wiley & Sons, 1973), 150. Burby and Weiss provide a succinct history of the effort to pass a federal new communities act. See *New Communities U.S.A.,* 57–62.
8. George T. Morgan, Jr., and John O. King, *The Woodlands: New Community Development, 1964–1983* (College Station: Texas A & M University Press, 1987), 6–9, 22–29.

McHarg placed the major roads and the most intense development along the ridges of the tract. The land between the floodplain and the ridges would provide sites for low-density housing. To avoid the expense and ecological disruption of storm-sewer construction, McHarg also designed an innovative drainage and flood-control system. In addition to the creeks and floodplains, the system included a large reservoir and a series of small ponds and swales.[9]

The Woodlands soon became a model of environmental planning. Yet the hopes of the new community proponents never were fulfilled. The government ultimately provided loan guarantees, to just 13 developers for projects with a total of 250,000 housing units: The developments would have housed only 785,000 people. By 1973, the Nixon administration had become concerned about the financial viability of the thirteen communities, and two years later federal housing officials decided not to make further loan commitments. Eventually all but one of the communities – the Woodlands was the exception – defaulted. In 1981, the Reagan administration decided to eliminate the program and it was killed in 1984.[10]

The developers of new communities faced formidable financial obstacles. The initial investment for land, planning, site improvements, and infrastructure could total tens of millions of dollars, yet the first profits might not come for ten or fifteen years. Even with federal aid, few companies were willing to invest so much in projects with such long-delayed payoffs. To put together a large tract at a low price, the developer usually had to locate a new town at a considerable distance from existing centers of population, and the long commute frequently made for slow sales at the start. Often, the developer had to pay for facilities ordinarily provided by local governments. Because the project might take more than a decade to complete, the developer also faced the prospect of changing economic and political conditions. In the early 1970s, especially, a

9. Anne Whiston Spirn, *The Granite Garden: Urban Nature and Human Design* (New York: Basic Books, 1984), 163–166.
10. For a succinct history of the program, see Evan McKenzie, *Privatopia: Homeowner Associations and the Rise of Residential Private Government* (New Haven: Yale University Press, 1994), 102–103. In addition to loan guarantees to make land acquisition easier and cheaper, the government also provided $137 million in block grants to pay for infrastructure in the thirteen communities.

large number of new town developments failed because the oil crisis unexpectedly raised interest rates and gasoline prices.[11]

But the failures had deeper causes: The supporters of the new community program fundamentally misconceived the relationship between private interest and public good. Though intended to serve a public purpose, a new community was still a profit-making venture. Unless a developer chose willingly to accept a substandard rate of return, the cost of environmental planning and open-space preservation had to be included in the price of homes and development sites. Yet the benefits of environmental protection were not enjoyed solely by residents. Only a portion of the cost of undeveloped land went for recreational amenities, so only a portion of the cost of environmental design helped developers to market the community. Though a government loan guarantee might help to get the project off the drawing board, the federal aid program did not change the basic accounting equation. If the developer was not willing to treat the project as a philanthropic enterprise, then the homebuyers had to pay to provide a public good – environmental protection – out of the goodness of their hearts. That was asking a lot. As one housing expert concluded, the new communities required buyers to buy too much that they did not want.[12]

11. The Woodlands Development Corporation did not earn an operating profit until the seventh year of the project – even though the accounting of operating profits did not include interest, general and administrative expenses, and income taxes. See Morgan and King, *The Woodlands*, 148. For the obstacles to successful new town development, see Burby and Weiss, *New Communities U.S.A.*, 53–54; James A. Clapp, *New Towns and Urban Policy: Planning Metropolitan Growth* (New York: Dunellen Publishing Company, 1971), 132–139; Edward P. Eichler and Marshall Kaplan, *The Community Builders* (Berkeley: University of California Press, 1967), 140–159.
12. There is some debate among analysts about the reasons for the failure of the new community program. At least one defender of the idea blamed the Nixon administration for failing to support the program. See Helene V. Smookler, "Administration Hari-Kiri: Implementation of the Urban Growth and New Community Development Act," *Annals of the American Academy of Political and Social Sciences* 422 (November 1975): 129–140. But other commentators predicted in the 1960s that the planned city idea would fail, because homebuyers saw "planning" primarily as a way to protect their investment – not as a way to improve the environment. See Eichler and Kaplan, *The Community Builders*, 110–119. Eichler elaborated the argument in "Why New Communities?," in Bernard J. Frieden and William W. Nash, editors, *Shaping an Urban Future: Essays in Memory of Catherine Bauer Wurster* (Cambridge: MIT Press, 1969), 95–113. McKenzie seconded Eichler's argument in *Privatopia*. He cited the line from the housing expert that I paraphrase. See 98. McKenzie also argued that the new community program would not have fulfilled the hopes of proponents even if the developers had succeeded financially, because the government loan guarantees came without any oversight of design.

Long before the failure of the new community program, however, most critics of postwar homebuilding had concluded that carrots did not work as well as sticks. The first calls for regulation came in the 1950s, and the call became more common in the 1960s. Then the 1970s and 1980s saw an explosion of codes, regulations, and guidelines intended to limit the use of septic tanks; ensure the provision of open space; restrict the development of hillsides, wetlands, and floodplains; control erosion during construction; preserve trees in subdivisions; retain natural systems of drainage; protect wildlife; and encourage energy-efficient design of houses and neighborhoods.[13]

Indeed, the postwar sprawl of suburbia was a critical factor in a momentous shift in public policy – a shift analysts called "the quiet revolution in land use control." For generations, American landowners had enjoyed extraordinary freedom to decide how to use their property, but governments at every level began to restrict that freedom in the 1960s. Especially at the state and federal levels, the new land-use legislation affected countless industries, not just homebuilding. Some laws provided for public oversight of decisions by utilities about the location of power plants, for example, while others limited the ability of coal companies to strip-mine land. Yet the new laws all had a similar goal – to prevent private property owners from using land in ways contrary to the public good.

Did the revolution succeed? Despite the importance of the issue, few people have tried to measure the environmental impact of the land-use legislation enacted since the 1960s. Still, enough evidence

At best, the new communities offered more open space than the typical subdivision, since open space was marketable. Richard A. Walker and Michael K. Heiman came to a similar conclusion in "Quiet Revolution for Whom?," *Annals of the Association of American Geographers* 71 (1981): 79–81. In the 1960s, a few analysts also warned against expecting too much from "civic-minded" developers, since new communities would still have to compete in the marketplace against traditional developments. See Frederick Gutheim, "New Towns?," in Roger Revelle and Hans H. Landsberg, editors, *America's Changing Environment* (Boston: Houghton Mifflin, 1967), 199.

13. I describe most of the regulatory initiatives in chapters 3, 4, 5, 6, and 7. In addition, see Christopher J. Duerksen, *Tree Conservation Ordinances: Land-Use Regulations Go Green* [Planning Advisory Service Report Number 446] (Chicago: American Planning Association, 1993); Duncan Erley and David Mosena, "Energy-Conserving Development Regulations: Current Practice," in Robert W. Burchell and David Listokin, editors, *Energy and Land Use* (New Brunswick, NJ: Center for Urban Policy Research, 1982), 462–489.

exists to conclude that efforts to reduce the social costs of development have had only mixed success. "The programs have largely eliminated the worst, most flagrant, and most environmentally harmful development practices," one analyst concluded in 1981. "Yet more remains to be done." That assessment is still true today.[14]

In the case of homebuilding, the regulatory effort has had considerable effect. Developers no longer build 8,000-home subdivisions with septic tanks. The filling of wetlands in metropolitan areas has declined sharply. In a few states, indeed, the annual loss of coastal wetlands is now measured in tens of acres, not thousands. The massive stepping-stone form of hillside development is largely a thing of the past. In some communities, builders can no longer put houses on floodplains. Though no one has made a nationwide study of efforts to reduce soil erosion during building, a study of the first suburban county to require erosion-control measures found that sediment rates in county streams fell by more than a third. Officials in a few communities have required developers to set aside habitat for endangered species. In small ways, the design of the typical single-family house has also changed for the better: Builders use more insulation now, to cite just one example.[15]

But the failures are as significant as the successes. The sprawl of suburbia consumes more land now than ever before. According to the U.S. Department of Agriculture, the nation lost almost 1.4 million acres a year to development from 1982 to 1992. In the mid-1990s, the rate more than doubled, to nearly 3.2 million acres a year. The rush of development in the top five growth states alone accounted for the loss of more than 1 million acres a year. That is

14. Frank J. Popper, *The Politics of Land-Use Reform* (Madison: University of Wisconsin Press, 1981), 199. Popper also noted the paucity of evidence on the subject. See 193–194.
15. In addition to the evidence cited in earlier chapters, see David G. Burke, Erik J. Meyers, Ralph W. Tiner, Jr., and Hazel Groman, *Protecting Nontidal Wetlands* [Planning Advisory Service Report 412/413] (Chicago: American Planning Association, 1988), 14; Thomas H. Yorke, "Effects of Sediment Control on Sediment Transport in the Northwest Branch Anacostia River Basin, Montgomery County, Maryland," *Journal of Research of the U.S. Geological Survey* 3 (1975): 487–494; Timothy Beatley, "Reconciling Urban Growth and Endangered Species: The Coachella Valley Habitat Conservation Plan," in Rutherford H. Platt, Rowan A. Rowntree, and Pamela C. Muick, editors, *The Ecological City: Preserving and Restoring Urban Biodiversity* (Amherst: University of Massachusetts Press, 1994), 231–250; Eric Hirst, Jeanne Clinton, Howard Geller, and Walter Kroner, *Energy Efficiency in Buildings* (Washington: American Council for an Energy-Efficient Economy, 1986).

roughly the total for the entire nation in the 1950s, when the first critics of the bulldozed landscape began to call for land-saving methods of building.[16]

Because land-use regulation is still largely a local issue, the standards of environmental protection vary greatly from place to place. The number of septic tanks continues to rise nationwide, and septic tanks remain a major cause of groundwater contamination. Builders continue to build on sensitive lands. In many places, bare eroding earth still surrounds new subdivisions. Developers continue to replace streams with storm sewers. Though some developers now design open space for wildlife, most do not: Habitat loss is still the principal threat to endangered and threatened species in many parts of the country. Few builders follow the principles of energy-conserving design. Despite the rosy predictions of the early 1950s, less than 1 percent of the nation's homes rely on solar heating.[17]

The shortcomings have many causes. In part, the mixed record since 1970 testifies to changing economic and political circumstances. But the reform effort also ran into a phalanx of powerful interests and ideals.

In the early 1970s, the postwar economic boom ended, and a painful period of stagflation began. The rise in prices and interest rates had especially damaging consequences for the housing market. From 1974 to 1980, the average price of a new home jumped from $37,800 to over $70,000. Interest rates also doubled in the 1970s, so the average mortgage payment skyrocketed. For the first time in a generation, millions of young couples began to fear that they never would be able to buy a home. Builders worried about a

16. Weston Kosova, "The Race to Save Open Space," *Audubon* 102 (March–April 2000): 69.
17. David Listokin and Carole Walker offer a critical evaluation of the quality of subdivision design in *The Subdivision and Site Plan Handbook* (New Brunswick, NJ: Center for Urban Policy Research, 1989), 159. For the continued impact of septic tanks on groundwater, see Sierra Club Legal Defense Fund, *The Poisoned Well: New Strategies for Groundwater Protection* (Washington: Island Press, 1989), 42. For the problem of habitat loss, see "Cities and Suburbs: A Roundtable," *Harvard Magazine* 102 (January–February 2000): 110. The solar-heat statistic is from F. John Devaney, *Tracking the American Dream: 50 Years of Housing History from the Census Bureau* (Washington: U.S. Department of Commerce, 1994), 42. For the building industry's lack of interest in energy-conserving design, see Edward J. Kaiser, with Raymond J. Burby, "Energy Conservation Decisions for New Housing," in Raymond J. Burby and Mary Ellen Marsden, editors, *Energy and Housing: Consumer and Builder Perspectives* (Cambridge: Oelgeschlager, Gunn & Hain, 1980), 97.

catastrophic slowdown in the industry. The affordability of housing became a political issue, and public officials steadfastly reaffirmed the federal commitment to homeownership as a bulwark of freedom, prosperity, and national pride. "This is after all the land where more homes of better quality are owned by a higher percentage of people than anywhere else in the world," Secretary of Housing and Urban Development Carla Hills declared in 1975. "We intend to keep it that way." Accordingly, the building industry had less trouble persuading people that the costs of environmental protection were burdensome.[18]

The opponents of regulation also exploited a change in the debate about land-use regulations. In the early 1970s, a number of suburban communities began to use their regulatory powers to limit growth as well as to protect the environment. The shift was politically significant. Because the antigrowth initiatives often served the economic and social interests of the wealthy – keeping taxes down, increasing property values, shutting out unwanted classes of people – the regulations invited populist attacks on environmentalism. In a 1979 book entitled *The Environmental Protection Hustle,* for example, housing scholar Bernard Frieden offered a scathing critique of efforts to "regulate the American dream." Though the opponents of growth invariably spoke about the need to prevent pollution or harm to wildlife or destruction of natural resources, Frieden wrote, their arguments often masked other, less admirable motives: "In suburban America, preserving the environment usually means preserving the social status quo as well."[19]

From the start, the task of environmental reformers was made more difficult by the fragmented nature of political authority in the United States. Land-use regulation was a prerogative of local government, yet a large number of counties made no effort to control development. As a result, builders often took advantage of power vacuums. They built subdivisions and suburbs on unincorporated land, and the new communities did not become legal entities – with

---

18. For the statistics about housing costs and interest rates, see Wright, *Building the Dream,* 263. The quotation is from Perin, *Everything in Its Place,* 78.
19. Bernard J. Frieden, *The Environmental Protection Hustle* (Cambridge: MIT Press, 1979), 8, 129. Mike Davis makes a similar argument from the opposite end of the ideological spectrum in *City of Quartz: Excavating the Future in Los Angeles* (1990; reprint, New York: Vintage, 1992), 169–213.

regulatory powers – until the builders had completed the projects. Even in areas subject to city or county regulations, moreover, builders frequently operated with little public supervision. The great majority of local governments were small, with few resources for planning or regulating growth. The problem was already apparent in the early 1960s. As a group of analysts concluded in 1960, "the public agencies were not equipped or financed to keep abreast of private real estate development, much less to lead it."[20]

To overcome the obstacle of fragmented authority, a variety of activists and policy-makers attempted to centralize the power to regulate land use. Yet the effort was only partly successful. Several states passed important land-use acts in the 1960s and 1970s, but a five-year campaign to pass a federal land-use law came to nothing in 1975. The legislation lacked a wide and deep following. Though the nation's councils of government passed countless laws to reduce the environmental costs of development, environmentalists had not uprooted long-established ideas about the rights of property ownership. "Landowners expect to be able to develop their property as they choose," William Reilly argued in 1973, "even at the expense of scenic, ecological, and cultural assets treasured by the public." To a great extent, that remains true. Few property owners believe that a land-use ethic should be a publicly enforced responsibility rather than a matter of private choice. The legal and political battles over the "taking" of property, already years old when Reilly wrote, still rage. Even among those willing to accept regulation as a fact of life, few accept the argument that land is first and foremost a social resource.[21]

As K. William Kapp surely would have predicted, developers and builders have fought aggressively to maximize their freedom of action. They have opposed most land-use regulations, and they have worked hard to limit the effectiveness of laws passed despite

20. For the quotation, see Marion Clawson, R. Burnell Held, and Charles H. Stoddard, *Land for the Future* (Baltimore: Johns Hopkins University Press, 1960), 119.
21. The quotation comes from William K. Reilly, editor, *The Use of Land: A Citizens' Policy Guide to Urban Growth* (New York: Thomas Y. Crowell Company, 1973), 15. For a thoughtful analysis of the American commitment to property as an individual liberty rather than a social resource, see Sam Bass Warner, Jr., *The Urban Wilderness: A History of the American City* (1972; reprint, Berkeley: University of California Press, 1995), 15–52.

their objections. The building industry has also enjoyed the support of important allies. In contrast, the public pressure to force developers and builders to take account of environmental costs never has had a persistent and powerful source.[22]

Like developers and builders, rural landowners have proved staunch opponents of land-use regulation. To be sure, they have often favored subsidy programs and tax-law changes designed to reduce the financial burden of farming in rapidly urbanizing areas, but they have still insisted on the right to dispose of their lands as they see fit. The issue is largely economic. From the time of the first European settlements in North America, farmers have profited by speculating in land. For many farmers today, the option of selling out is a form of security for retirement. But the subject of land-use regulation also strikes emotional nerves. "If a man's home is his castle," a rural Pennsylvanian explained, "then his land is his fertility. To take away his rights in the land is nothing less than castration."[23]

The most consistent support for environmental regulation of homebuilding has come from professionals with expertise in related fields, yet scientists, planners, and architects inevitably play secondary parts in the decision-making process. To shape the landscape, the professionals have to win the support of the people with primary decision-making responsibility: builders, public officials, and homebuyers.

In the legislative and administrative debates over environmental regulation, public officials have always recognized the economic and political power of the construction industry. Developers and builders have well-established trade organizations with considerable resources. They are pillars of the economy. At the local level, developers and builders can play one community against another, since local officials often compete vigorously for new development: In the view of many scholars, city and county governments tend to be "growth machines."[24]

22. The opposition of builders to environmental regulation is summarized in a semiofficial history of the industry. See Joseph B. Mason, *History of Housing in the U.S., 1930–1980* (Houston: Gulf Publishing Company, 1982), 144–146.
23. For the quotation, see Popper, *The Politics of Land-Use Reform*, 211.
24. For a recent discussion of the politics of growth, see Kee Warner and Harvey Molotch, "Power to Build: How Development Persists Despite Local Controls," *Urban Affairs Review* 30 (1995): 378–406.

If homeowners or homebuyers had a compelling interest in reforming the homebuilding industry, then public officials might do more to compel developers and builders to take environmental costs into account. But neither homeowners nor homebuyers have acted consistently as a countervailing force. Indeed, both groups often weigh environmental issues in economic terms.

As Constance Perin argues in a classic study of the meaning of homeownership, homeowners are producers of used housing, so they have a financial interest in maintaining or increasing the resale value of their property. In some cases, that interest may lead homeowners to support stricter regulation of homebuilding. But in other cases, the desire to protect a substantial investment may work against innovation. Homeowners have given little support to campaigns to require construction of more energy-efficient housing, for example, and Perin's insight helps to explain their lack of enthusiasm: Because white elephants are difficult to sell at a profit, homeowners have a stake in ensuring that new homes are not radically superior to old homes, especially if the outmoded elements cannot be replaced at a reasonable cost.[25]

For homebuyers, the issue of environmental regulation is both more immediate and more complex. Though eager to be protected from potentially disastrous environmental hazards, homebuyers also want the greatest possible freedom of choice. Especially for the vast majority of buyers concerned about the cost of housing, however, regulation limits choice. Despite the risks, people continue to

25. Perin, *Everything in Its Place,* 129–162. Though Perin does not write about environmental issues, Ann Louise Strong once argued that the interest of homeowners in the "development value" of their property had important environmental consequences. See "Crisis Mentality and the Deteriorating Environment," in Roger Revelle and Hans H. Landsberg, editors, *America's Changing Environment* (Boston: Beacon Press, 1970), 86–87. The architectural critic Philip Langdon also cites the drive to resell at a profit as a principal cause of the design shortcomings of suburbia:

The builders and developers always fall back on the argument that if people didn't like what was produced, they wouldn't buy it. This is a vastly oversimplified version of what's really going on. Many homebuyers buy houses or communities that they know are flawed. They buy them because of the location, the quality of the local schools, or the price, even though they might prefer houses or communities very different from what the builders and developers are offering. People also buy into flawed houses or defective communities for another important reason: They expect to make money.

See *A Better Place to Live: Reshaping the American Suburb* (Amherst: University of Massachusetts Press, 1994), 78.

buy homes with septic tanks and homes in floodplains. In each case, the buyers are effectively choosing to discount the risks – and to ignore the environmental implications of their decisions – in order to get more house for the money.

Of course, the purchase of a house is never simply a matter of cost. What do Americans want in a house? The question points to a final reason for the limited success of efforts to reduce the environmental impact of homebuilding. For almost all Americans, the definition of a good house has not changed much since the rise of the environmental movement: A good house is a house with adequate and aesthetically satisfying space, in a pleasant neighborhood, in a good school district, with bearable taxes, and with a good chance of appreciating in value. That list of essential attributes still does not reflect a deep sense of our dependence on the larger living world of plants and animals and microbes, of soil and water and air.[26]

26. I was led to think about the definition of "a good house" by Richard Manning, *A Good House: Building a Life on the Land* (New York: Grove Press, 1993).

Selected Bibliography

The argument of this book rests on a vast body of evidence from trade publications, professional journals, general-interest magazines, and government documents. Because my notes are bibliographic, however, I chose to list here only a handful of the shorter sources I drew on in my research and I have selected the most important book-length primary and secondary sources. I also include a few works not cited in the notes that helped me think through the issues I address in the text.

Abrams, Charles. *The Future of Housing.* New York: Harper & Brothers, 1946.

Albrecht, Donald, editor. *World War II and the American Dream: How Wartime Building Changed a Nation.* Cambridge: MIT Press, 1995.

Andrews, Richard N. L., editor. *Land in America: Commodity or Natural Resource?* Lexington, MA: Lexington Books, 1979.

Aronin, Jeffrey Ellis. *Climate and Architecture.* New York: Reinhold, 1953.

Arsenault, Raymond. "The End of the Long Hot Summer: The Air Conditioner and Southern Culture." *Journal of Southern History* 50 (1984): 597–628.

Association for Applied Solar Energy. *Proceedings of the World Symposium on Applied Solar Energy.* Menlo Park: Stanford Research Institute, 1956.

Ayres, Eugene, and Scarlott, Charles A. *Energy Sources: The Wealth of the World.* New York: McGraw-Hill, 1952.

Bagdikian, Ben H. "The Rape of the Land." *Saturday Evening Post* 239 (June 18, 1966): 25–29, 86–94.

Bailey, Anthony. *Through the Great City: Impressions of Megalopolis.* New York: Macmillan, 1967.

Bailey, James, editor. *New Towns in America: The Design and Development Process.* New York: John Wiley & Sons, 1973.

Balogh, Brian. *Chain Reaction: Expert Debate and Public Participation in American Commercial Nuclear Power, 1945–1975.* New York: Cambridge University Press, 1991.

Banham, Reyner. *The Architecture of the Well-Tempered Environment.* Second edition. Chicago: University of Chicago Press, 1984.

Baxandall, Rosalyn, and Ewen, Elizabeth. *Picture Windows: How the Suburbs Happened.* New York: Basic Books, 2000.

Behrman, Daniel. *Solar Energy: The Awakening Science*. Boston: Little, Brown and Company, 1976.

Benfield, F. Kaid, Raimi, Matthew D., and Chen, Donald D. T. *Once There Were Greenfields: How Urban Sprawl Is Undermining America's Environment, Economy, and Social Fabric*. New York: Natural Resources Defense Council, 1999.

Blake, Peter. *God's Own Junkyard: The Planned Deterioration of America's Landscape*. New York: Holt, Rinehart, and Winston, 1964.

Blum, John Morton. *V Was For Victory: Politics and American Culture During World War II*. New York: Harcourt Brace Jovanovich, 1976.

Bosselman, Fred, and Callies, David. *The Quiet Revolution in Land Use Control*. Washington: USGPO, 1971.

Bosselman, Fred, Callies, David, and Banta, John. *The Taking Issue: A Study of the Constitutional Limits of Governmental Authority to Regulate the Use of Privately-Owned Land Without Compensation*. Washington: USGPO, 1973.

Bowles, Chester. *Tomorrow Without Fear*. New York: Simon and Schuster, 1946.

Bremner, Robert H., and Reichard, Gary W., editors. *Reshaping America: Society and Institutions, 1945–1960*. Columbus: Ohio State University Press, 1982.

Brinkley, Alan. *The End of Reform: New Deal Liberalism in Recession and War*. New York: Alfred A. Knopf, 1995.

Brown, Harrison. *The Challenge of Man's Future*. 1954. Reprint. New York: Viking Press, 1956.

Brown, Steven R., and Coke, James G. *Public Opinion on Land Use Regulation*. Columbus, OH: Academy for Contemporary Problems, 1977.

Building Research Advisory Board. *Weather and the Building Industry*. Washington: National Research Council, 1950.

Burby, Raymond J. [III], and French, Steven P. *Flood Plain Land Use Management: A National Assessment*. Boulder, CO: Westview Press, 1985.

Burby, Raymond J. [III], and Marsden, Mary Ellen. *Energy and Housing: Consumer and Builder Perspectives*. Cambridge: Oelgeschlager, Gunn & Hain, 1980.

Burby, Raymond J. III, and Weiss, Shirley F. *New Communities U.S.A.* Lexington, MA: Lexington Books, 1976.

Burchell, Robert W., and Listokin, David, editors. *Energy and Land Use*. New Brunswick, NJ: Center for Urban Policy Research, 1982.

Bureau of Sport Fisheries and Wildlife. *Man and Nature in the City*. Washington: USGPO, 1968.

Butti, Ken, and Perlin, John. *A Golden Thread: 2500 Years of Solar Architecture and Technology*. New York: Van Nostrand Reinhold, 1980.

Caldwell, Lynton Keith. *Environment: A Challenge to Modern Society*. 1970. Reprint. Garden City, NY: Anchor Books, 1971.

Caldwell, Lynton K., Hayes, Lynton R., and MacWhirter, Isabel M. *Citizens and the Environment: Case Studies in Popular Action*. Bloomington: Indiana University Press, 1976.

Carr, Donald E. *Death of the Sweet Waters*. New York: W. W. Norton, 1966.

Carr, James H., and Duensing, Edward E., editors. *Land Use Issues of the 1980s*. New Brunswick, NJ: Center for Urban Policy Research, 1983.

Carson, Rachel. *Silent Spring*. Boston: Houghton Mifflin, 1962.

Carter, Luther J. *The Florida Experience: Land and Water Policy in a Growth State*. Baltimore: Johns Hopkins University Press, 1974.

Chapin, F. Stuart Jr. *Urban Land Use Planning*. Second edition. Urbana: University of Illinois Press, 1965.

Checkoway, Barry. "Large Builders, Federal Housing Programmes, and Postwar Suburbanization." *International Journal of Urban and Regional Research* 4 (1980): 21–45.

Christian Science Monitor. *The Call of the Vanishing Wild*. Boston: Christian Science Publishing Society, 1967.

"The City's Threat to Open Land." *Architectural Forum* 108 (January 1958): 87–90, 164–166.

Clapp, James A. *New Towns and Urban Policy: Planning Metropolitan Growth*. New York: Dunellen Publishing Company, 1971.

Clark, Clifford Edward, Jr. *The American Family Home, 1800–1960*. Chapel Hill: University of North Carolina Press, 1986.

Clark, John G. *Energy and the Federal Government: Fossil Fuel Policies, 1900–1946*. Urbana: University of Illinois Press, 1987.

Clark, Robert A. *Hillside Development*. Planning Advisory Service Information Report 126. Chicago: American Society of Planning Officials, 1959.

Clark, Wilson. *Energy for Survival: The Alternative to Extinction*. Garden City, NY: Anchor Books, 1974.

Clawson, Marion. *Suburban Land Conversion in the United States: An Economic and Governmental Process*. Baltimore: Johns Hopkins University Press, 1971.

Clawson, Marion, and Hall, Peter. *Planning and Urban Growth: An Anglo-American Comparison*. Baltimore: Johns Hopkins University Press, 1973.

Coates, Donald R., editor. *Environmental Geomorphology and Landscape Conservation*. Volume II: Urban Areas. Stroudsburg, PA: Dowden, Hutchinson & Ross, 1974.

Colean, Miles L. *American Housing: Problems and Prospects*. New York: Twentieth Century Fund, 1944.

Can America Build Houses? New York: Public Affairs Committee, 1940.

Colten, Craig E., and Skinner, Peter N. *The Road to Love Canal: Managing Industrial Waste before EPA*. Austin: University of Texas Press, 1996.

Commission on Population Growth and the American Future. *Population and the American Future*. New York: Signet, 1972.

Commoner, Barry. *The Closing Circle: Nature, Man, and Technology*. 1971. Reprint. New York: Bantam Books, 1972.

Community Builders Council of the Urban Land Institute. *The Community Builders Handbook*. Washington: Urban Land Institute, 1956.

Conard, Rebecca. "Green Gold: 1950s Greenbelt Planning in Santa Clara County, California." *Environmental History Review* 9 (1985): 5–18.

274 *Selected Bibliography*

Conklin, Groff. *The Weather Conditioned House.* New York: Reinhold, 1958.
Cooper, Gail. *Air-conditioning America: Engineers and the Controlled Environment, 1900–1960.* Baltimore: Johns Hopkins University Press, 1998.
Cribbet, John E. "Changing Concepts in the Law of Land Use." *Iowa Law Review* 50 (1965): 245–278.
Cronon, William. *Nature's Metropolis: Chicago and the Great West.* New York: W. W. Norton, 1991.
    editor. *Uncommon Ground: Toward Reinventing Nature.* New York: W. W. Norton, 1995.
Curtis, Virginia, editor. *Land Use and the Environment: An Anthology of Readings.* Washington: Environmental Protection Agency, 1973.
Daniels, Farrington. *Direct Use of the Sun's Energy.* New Haven: Yale University Press, 1964.
Daniels, Farrington, and Duffie, John A., editors. *Solar Energy Research.* Madison: University of Wisconsin Press, 1955.
Darling, F. Fraser, and Milton, John P., editors. *Future Environments of North America.* Garden City, NY: Natural History Press, 1966.
Dasmann, Raymond F. *The Destruction of California.* New York: Macmillan, 1965.
Davies, Richard O. *Housing Reform During the Truman Administration.* Columbia: University of Missouri Press, 1966.
Davis, Mike. *City of Quartz: Excavating the Future in Los Angeles.* 1990. Reprint. New York: Vintage, 1992.
    Ecology of Fear: Los Angeles and the Imagination of Disaster. New York: Metropolitan Books, 1998.
DeGrove, John M. *Land, Growth, and Politics.* Chicago: American Planning Association, 1984.
deNeufville, Judith I., editor. *The Land Use Policy Debate in the United States.* New York: Plenum Press, 1981.
Detwyler, Thomas R., and Marcus, Melvin G., editors. *Urbanization and the Environment: The Physical Geography of the City.* Belmont, CA: Duxbury Press, 1972.
Devaney, F. John. *Tracking the American Dream: 50 Years of Housing History from the Census Bureau.* Washington: U.S. Department of Commerce, 1994.
Diggins, John Patrick. *The Proud Decades: America in War and Peace, 1941–1960.* New York: W. W. Norton and Company, 1988.
Donaldson, Scott. *The Suburban Myth.* New York: Columbia University Press, 1969.
Douglas, Ian. *The Urban Environment.* London: Edward Arnold, 1983.
Douglas, William O. *A Wilderness Bill of Rights.* Boston: Little, Brown and Company, 1965.
Downie, Leonard, Jr. *Mortgage on America.* New York: Praeger, 1974.
Duany, Andres, Plater-Zyberk, Elizabeth, and Speck, Jeff. *Suburban Nation: The Rise of Sprawl and the Decline of the American Dream.* New York: North Point Press, 2000.

Dukeminier, Jesse Jr. "The Coming Search for Quality." *UCLA Law Review* 12 (March 1965): 707–718.

Dunlap, Riley E., and Mertig, Angela G., editors. *American Environmentalism: The U.S. Environmental Movement, 1970–1990.* Washington: Taylor & Francis, 1992.

Dunlap, Thomas R. *DDT: Scientists, Citizens, and Public Policy.* Princeton: Princeton University Press, 1981.

    Saving America's Wildlife: Ecology and the American Mind, 1850–1990. Princeton: Princeton University Press, 1988.

Dupree, A. Hunter. *Science in the Federal Government: A History of Policies and Activities to 1940.* Cambridge: Belknap Press, 1957.

Dworsky, Leonard B., editor. *Pollution.* New York: Chelsea House, 1971.

Earth Satellite Corporation. *Land Use Change and Environmental Quality in Urban Areas.* Washington: Council on Environmental Quality, 1973.

Ehrlich, Paul R. *The Population Bomb.* New York: Ballantine Books, 1968.

Eichler, Edward P., and Kaplan, Marshall. *The Community Builders.* Berkeley: University of California Press, 1967.

Eichler, Ned. *The Merchant Builders.* Cambridge: MIT Press, 1982.

Erley, Duncan, and Kockelman, William J. *Reducing Landslide Hazards: A Guide for Planners.* Planning Advisory Service Report Number 359. Chicago: American Planning Association, 1981.

Faltermayer, Edmund K. *Redoing America: A Nationwide Report on How to Make Our Cities and Suburbs More Livable.* 1968. Reprint. New York: Collier, 1969.

Fellmeth, Robert C., editor. *Politics of Land: Ralph Nader's Study Group Report on Land Use in California.* New York: Grossman Publishers, 1973.

Findlay, John M. *Magic Lands: Western Cityscapes and American Culture After 1940.* Berkeley: University of California Press, 1992.

Fish, Gertrude Sipperly, editor. *The Story of Housing.* New York: Macmillan, 1979.

Fishman, Robert. *Bourgeois Utopias: The Rise and Fall of Suburbia.* New York: Basic Books, 1987.

Fitch, James Marston. *American Building: The Forces that Shape It.* Boston: Houghton Mifflin, 1948.

Fleming, Donald. "Roots of the New Conservation Movement." *Perspectives in American History* 6 (1972): 7–91.

Fleming, Robert W., Varnes, David J., and Schuster, Robert L. "Landslide Hazards and Their Reduction." *Journal of the American Planning Association* 45 (1979): 428–439.

Flippen, John Brooks. "Containing the Urban Sprawl: The Nixon Administration's Land Use Policy." *Presidential Studies Quarterly* 26 (Winter 1996): 197–207.

Foote, Nelson H., Abu-Lughod, Janet, Foley, Mary Mix, and Winnick, Louis. *Housing Choices and Housing Constraints.* New York: McGraw-Hill, 1960.

Ford, Katherine Morrow, and Creighton, Thomas H. *The American House Today.* New York: Reinhold, 1951.

Ford, Larry R. *Cities and Buildings: Skyscrapers, Skid Rows, and Suburbs.* Baltimore: Johns Hopkins University Press, 1994.

"Fortune," Editors of. *Housing America.* New York: Harcourt, Brace and Company, 1932.

Foss, Phillip O. *Recreation.* New York: Chelsea House, 1971.

Fox, Frank W. *Madison Avenue Goes to War: The Strange Career of American Advertising, 1941–1945.* Provo: Brigham Young University Press, 1975.

Fox, Kenneth. *Metropolitan America: Urban Life and Urban Policy in the United States, 1940–1980.* Jackson: University Press of Mississippi, 1986.

Fox, Stephen. *The American Conservation Movement: John Muir and His Legacy.* 1981. Reprint. Madison: University of Wisconsin Press, 1985.

Frank, Bernard, and Netboy, Anthony. *Water, Land, and People.* New York: Alfred A. Knopf, 1950.

Freyfogle, Eric T. *Bounded People, Boundless Lands: Envisioning a New Land Ethic.* Washington: Island Press, 1998.

Frieden, Bernard J. *The Environmental Protection Hustle.* Cambridge: MIT Press, 1979.

Friedman, Robert. "The Air-Conditioned Century." *American Heritage* 35 (August–September 1984): 20–33.

Garreau, Joel. *Edge City: Life on the New Frontier.* New York: Doubleday, 1991.

Gelfand, Mark I. *A Nation of Cities: The Federal Government and Urban America, 1933–1965.* New York: Oxford University Press, 1975.

Gill, Don, and Bonnett, Penelope. *Nature in the Urban Landscape: A Study of City Ecosystems.* Baltimore: York Press, 1973.

Gilliam, Harold. *Between the Devil and the Deep Blue Bay: The Struggle to Save San Francisco Bay.* San Francisco: Chronicle Books, 1969.

Girling, Cynthia L., and Helphand, Kenneth I. *Yard-Street-Park: The Design of Suburban Open Space.* New York: John Wiley & Sons, 1994.

Goldstein, S. N., Wenk, V. D., Fowler, M. C., and Poh, S. S. *A Study of Selected Economic and Environmental Aspects of Individual Home Wastewater Treatment Systems.* Washington: Mitre Corporation, 1972.

Goodwin, Craufurd D., editor. *Energy Policy in Perspective: Today's Problems, Yesterday's Solutions.* Washington: Brookings Institution, 1981.

Gordon, Mitchell. *Sick Cities.* New York: Macmillan, 1963.

Gottlieb, Robert. *Forcing the Spring: The Transformation of the American Environmental Movement.* Washington: Island Press, 1993.

Gottmann, Jean. *Megalopolis: The Urbanized Northeastern Seaboard of the United States.* New York: Twentieth Century Fund, 1961.

Gould, Lewis L. *Lady Bird Johnson and the Environment.* Lawrence: University Press of Kansas, 1988.

Goulden, Joseph C. *The Best Years: 1945–1950.* New York: Atheneum, 1976.

Graham, Frank, Jr. *Disaster by Default: Politics and Water Pollution.* New York: M. Evans and Company, 1966.

Graham, Otis L., Jr. *Toward a Planned Society: From Roosevelt to Nixon.* New York: Oxford University Press, 1976.

Grava, Sigurd. *Urban Planning Aspects of Water Pollution Control*. New York: Columbia University Press, 1969.

Gray, Aelred J. "Communities and Floods." *National Civic Review* 50 (1961): 134–138.

Greeson, Phillip E., Clark, John R., and Clark, Judith E., editors. *Wetland Functions and Values: The State of Our Understanding*. Minneapolis: American Water Resources Association, 1979.

Gries, John M., and Ford, James T., editors. *Housing Objectives and Programs*. Publications of the President's Conference on Home Building and Home Ownership, Volume XI. Washington: National Capital Press, 1932.

Slums, Large-Scale Housing and Decentralization. Publications of the President's Conference on Home Building and Home Ownership, Volume III. Washington: National Capital Press, 1932.

Gruen, Victor. *The Heart of Our Cities: The Urban Crisis: Diagnosis and Cure*. New York: Simon and Schuster, 1964.

Guy, Harold P. *Sediment Problems in Urban Areas*. Geological Survey Circular 601–E. Washington: USGPO, 1970.

Guy, Harold P., and Ferguson, George E. "Stream Sediment: An Environmental Problem." *Journal of Soil and Water Conservation* 25 (1970): 217–221.

Guy, Harold P., Jackson, Norman E., Jarvis, Kenneth, Johnson, Carl J., Miller, Carl R., and Steiner, Wilber W. *A Program for Sediment Control in the Washington Metropolitan Region*. Technical Bulletin 1963–1. Washington: Interstate Commission on the Potomac River Basin, 1963.

Haar, Charles M., editor. *The President's Task Force on Suburban Problems: Final Report*. Cambridge: Ballinger Publishing Company, 1974.

Hagen, Joel B. *An Entangled Bank: The Origins of Ecosystem Ecology*. New Brunswick, NJ: Rutgers University Press, 1992.

Halacy, D. S., Jr. *The Coming Age of Solar Energy*. Revised edition. New York: Harper and Row, 1973.

Hamilton, Richard W., editor. *Space Heating with Solar Energy*. Cambridge: Massachusetts Institute of Technology, 1954.

Harriss, C. Lowell, editor. *The Good Earth of America: Planning Our Land Use*. Englewood Cliffs, NJ: Prentice-Hall, 1974.

Haskell, Elizabeth H., and Price, Victoria S. *State Environmental Management: Case Studies of Nine States*. New York: Praeger, 1973.

Havlick, Spenser W. *The Urban Organism: The City's Natural Resources from an Environmental Perspective*. New York: Macmillan, 1974.

Hawley, Ellis W., editor. *Herbert Hoover as Secretary of Commerce: Studies in New Era Thought and Practice*. Iowa City: University of Iowa Press, 1981.

Hayden, Dolores. *Redesigning the American Dream: The Future of Housing, Work, and Family Life*. New York: W. W. Norton, 1984.

Hays, Samuel P. *Beauty, Health, and Permanence: Environmental Politics in the United States, 1955–1985*. New York: Cambridge University Press, 1987.

Healy, Robert G. *Environmentalists and Developers: Can They Agree on Anything?* Washington: Conservation Foundation, 1977.

    Land Use and the States. Baltimore: Johns Hopkins University Press, 1976.

Herber, Lewis. *Crisis in Our Cities.* Englewood Cliffs, NJ: Prentice-Hall, 1965.

Herbert, John H. *Clean Cheap Heat: The Development of Residential Markets for Natural Gas in the United States.* New York: Praeger, 1992.

Higbee, Edward. *The Squeeze: Cities Without Space.* New York: William Morrow and Company, 1960.

Hine, Thomas. *Populuxe.* New York: Alfred A. Knopf, 1986.

Hirsh, Richard F. *Technology and Transformation in the American Electric Utility Industry.* New York: Cambridge University Press, 1989.

Hirst, Eric, Clinton, Jeanne, Geller, Howard, and Kroner, Walter. *Energy Efficiency in Buildings: Progress and Promise.* Washington: American Council for an Energy-Efficient Economy, 1986.

Hise, Greg. *Magnetic Los Angeles: Planning the Twentieth-Century Metropolis.* Baltimore: Johns Hopkins University Press, 1997.

Hite, James C. *Room and Situation: The Political Economy of Land-Use Policy.* Chicago: Nelson-Hall, 1979.

Hodgins, Eric. *Mr. Blandings Builds His Dream House.* New York: Simon and Schuster, 1946.

Hodgson, Godfrey. *America in Our Time.* Garden City, NY: Doubleday and Company, 1976.

Horrigan, Brian. "The Home of Tomorrow, 1927–1945." In *Imagining Tomorrow,* edited by Joseph Corn, pp. 137–163. Cambridge: MIT Press, 1986.

Hough, Michael. *City Form and Natural Process: Towards a New Urban Vernacular.* 1984. Reprint. London: Routledge, 1989.

Housing and Home Finance Agency. *Climate and Architecture: Selected References.* Washington: Housing and Home Finance Agency, 1951.

    The Materials Use Survey. Washington: Housing and Home Finance Agency, 1953.

Hoyt, William G., and Langbein, Walter B. *Floods.* Princeton: Princeton University Press, 1955.

Hubbard, Alice Harvey. *This Land of Ours: Community and Conservation Projects for Citizens.* New York: Macmillan, 1960.

Huffman, Thomas R. *Protectors of Land and Water: Environmentalism in Wisconsin, 1961–1968.* Chapel Hill: University of North Carolina Press, 1994.

Hurley, Andrew. *Environmental Inequalities: Class, Race, and Industrial Pollution in Gary, Indiana, 1945–1980.* Chapel Hill: University of North Carolina Press, 1995.

"Individual Sewage Disposal Systems – Part I." In *HHFA Technical Bulletin Number 7,* pp. 21–41. Washington: Housing and Home Finance Agency, 1948.

"Individual Sewage Disposal Systems – Part II." In *HHFA Technical Bulletin Number 10,* pp. 17–32. Washington: Housing and Home Finance Agency, 1949.

"Individual Sewage Disposal Systems – Part III." In *HHFA Technical Bulletin Number 11,* pp. 19–37. Washington: Housing and Home Finance Agency, 1949.

Institute for Contemporary Studies. *No Land Is an Island: Individual Rights and Government Control of Land Use.* San Francisco: Institute for Contemporary Studies, 1975.

Jackson, Kenneth T. *Crabgrass Frontier: The Suburbanization of the United States.* New York: Oxford University Press, 1985.

Jarrett, Henry, editor. *Perspectives on Conservation: Essays on America's Natural Resources.* Baltimore: Johns Hopkins University Press, 1958.

Jewell, William J., and Swan, Rita, editors. *Water Pollution Control in Low Density Areas: Proceedings of a Rural Environmental Engineering Conference.* Hanover, NH: University Press of New England, 1975.

Jones, A. Quincy, and Emmons, Frederick E. *Builders' Homes for Better Living.* New York: Reinhold, 1957.

Jones, D. Earl, Jr. "Urban Hydrology – A Redirection." *Civil Engineering* 37 (August 1967): 58–62.

"Where Is Urban Hydrology Practice Today?" *Journal of the Hydraulics Division, Proceedings of the American Society of Civil Engineers* 97 (HY2, February 1971): 257–264.

Kaiser, Edward J., Elfers, Karl, Cohn, Sidney, Reichert, Peggy A., Hufschmidt, Maynard M., and Stanland, Raymond E., Jr. *Promoting Environmental Quality Through Urban Planning and Controls.* Washington: Environmental Protection Agency, 1973.

Kao, David T. Y., editor. *Proceedings of the National Symposium on Urban Rainfall and Runoff and Sediment Control.* Lexington: University of Kentucky Office of Research and Engineering Services, 1974.

Kaplan, Samuel. *The Dream Deferred: People, Politics, and Planning in Suburbia.* 1976. Reprint. New York: Vintage Books, 1977.

Kapp, K. William. *The Social Costs of Private Enterprise.* 1950. Reprint. New York: Schocken Books, 1971.

Keats, John. *The Crack in the Picture Window.* Boston: Houghton Mifflin, 1956.

Keith, Nathaniel S. *Politics and the Housing Crisis Since 1930.* New York: Universe Books, 1973.

Kelly, Barbara M. *Expanding the American Dream: Building and Rebuilding Levittown.* Albany: State University of New York Press, 1993.

editor. *Suburbia Re-examined.* Westport: Greenwood Press, 1989.

Kelly, Burnham, editor. *Design and Production of Houses.* New York: McGraw-Hill, 1959.

Kennedy, Robert Woods. *The House and the Art of Its Design.* New York: Reinhold, 1953.

Keyes, Dale L. *Land Development and the Natural Environment: Estimating Impacts.* Washington: Urban Land Institute, 1976.

Kunstler, James Howard. *The Geography of Nowhere: The Rise and Decline of America's Man-Made Landscape.* New York: Simon and Schuster, 1993.

Kusler, Jon A. *Regulating Sensitive Lands: A Guidebook.* Cambridge: Ballinger Publishing Company, 1980.

Lacey, Michael J., editor. *Government and Environmental Politics: Essays on*

Historical Developments Since World War Two. Washington: Woodrow Wilson Center Press, 1989.

Lader, Lawrence. "Chaos in the Suburbs." *Better Homes & Gardens* 36 (October 1958): 10–17, 121, 129, 166.

"Land Use Legislation: A Precarious Future." *Congressional Quarterly Weekly Report* 33 (March 1, 1975): 428–432.

Langdon, Philip. *A Better Place to Live: Reshaping the American Suburb*. Amherst: University of Massachusetts Press, 1994.

Langewiesche, Wolfgang. "So You Think You're Comfortable!" *House Beautiful* 91 (October 1949): 132–134, 230–240.

Large, Donald W. "This Land Is Whose Land? Changing Concepts of Land as Property." *Wisconsin Law Review* (1973): 1039–1083.

Lasch, Robert. *Breaking the Building Blockade*. Chicago: University of Chicago Press, 1946.

League of Women Voters Education Fund. *The Big Water Fight: Trials and Triumphs in Citizen Action on Problems of Supply, Pollution, Flooding, and Planning across the U.S.A.* Brattleboro, VT: Stephen Greene Press, 1966.

Leedy, Daniel L., Maestro, Robert M., and Franklin, Thomas M. *Planning for Wildlife in Cities and Suburbs*. Planning Advisory Service Report 331. Chicago: American Society of Planning Officials, 1978.

Lehman, Tim. *Public Values, Private Lands: Farmland Preservation Policy, 1933–1985*. Chapel Hill: University of North Carolina Press, 1995.

Leopold, Aldo. *A Sand County Almanac, and Sketches Here and There*. New York: Oxford University Press, 1949.

Leopold, Luna B. *Hydrology for Urban Land Planning – A Guidebook on the Hydrologic Effects of Urban Land Use*. Geological Survey Circular 554. Washington: USGPO, 1968.

Leopold, Luna B., and Maddock, Thomas, Jr. *The Flood Control Controversy: Big Dams, Little Dams, and Land Management*. New York: Ronald Press Company, 1954.

Leveson, David. *Geology and the Urban Environment*. New York: Oxford University Press, 1980.

Lewis, Philip H., Jr. *Tomorrow by Design: A Regional Design Process for Sustainability*. New York: John Wiley & Sons, 1996.

Libbey-Owens-Ford Glass Company. *Solar Heating for Post-War Dwellings*. Toledo: Libby-Owens-Ford Glass Company, 1943.

Solar Houses: An Architectural Lift in Living. Toledo: Libby-Owens-Ford Glass Company, 1945.

Lillard, Richard G. *Eden in Jeopardy: Man's Prodigal Meddling with His Environment: The Southern California Experience*. New York: Alfred A. Knopf, 1966.

Listokin, David, editor. *Land Use Controls: Present Problems and Future Reform*. New Brunswick, NJ: Center for Urban Policy Research, 1974.

Little, Charles E. *Challenge of the Land: Open Space Preservation at the Local Level*. 1968. Reprint. New York: Pergamon Press, 1969.

Little, Charles E., and Mitchell, John G., editors. *Space for Survival: Blocking the Bulldozer in Urban America.* New York: Pocket Books, 1971.

Little, Silas, and Noyes, John H., editors. *Trees and Forests in an Urbanizing Environment: A Symposium.* Amherst: University of Massachusetts Cooperative Extension Service, 1971.

Logan, Michael F. *Fighting Sprawl and City Hall: Resistance to Urban Growth in the Southwest.* Tucson: University of Arizona Press, 1995.

Lung, Richard, and Proctor, Richard, editors. *Engineering Geology in Southern California.* Glendale, CA: Association of Engineering Geologists, 1966.

Lyday, Noreen. *The Law of the Land: Debating National Land Use Legislation, 1970–75.* Washington: Urban Institute, 1976.

McAllister, Donald M., editor. *Environment: A New Focus for Land-Use Planning.* Washington: National Science Foundation, 1973.

McGauhey, P. H., and Winneberger, John H. *Causes and Prevention of Failure in Septic-Tank Percolation Systems.* Washington: Federal Housing Administration, 1964.

McGill, John T. *Growing Importance of Urban Geology.* Geological Survey Circular 487. Washington: USGPO, 1964.

McGucken, William. *Biodegradable: Detergents and the Environment.* College Station: Texas A & M University Press, 1991.

McHarg, Ian L. *Design With Nature.* 1969. Reprint. Garden City, NY: Doubleday, 1971.

A Quest for Life: An Autobiography. New York: John Wiley and Sons, 1996.

McKeever, J. Ross, editor. *The Community Builders Handbook: Anniversary Edition.* Washington: Urban Land Institute, 1968.

McKenzie, Evan. *Privatopia: Homeowner Associations and the Rise of Residential Private Government.* New Haven: Yale University Press, 1994.

McPhee, John. *The Control of Nature.* New York: Farrar, Straus and Giroux, 1989.

Encounters with the Archdruid. New York: Farrar, Straus and Giroux, 1971.

Maisel, Sherman J. *Housebuilding in Transition.* Berkeley: University of California Press, 1953.

Mandelker, Daniel R. *Environmental and Land Use Controls Legislation.* Indianapolis: Bobbs-Merrill, 1976.

Manning, Richard. *A Good House: Building a Life on the Land.* New York: Grove Press, 1993.

Marling, Karal Ann. *As Seen on TV: The Visual Culture of Everyday Life in the 1950s.* Cambridge: Harvard University Press, 1994.

Marx, Leo. *The Machine in the Garden: Technology and the Pastoral Ideal.* New York: Oxford University Press, 1964.

Marx, Wesley. *The Frail Ocean.* 1967. Reprint. New York: Ballantine Books, 1969.

Mason, Joseph B. *History of Housing in the U.S., 1930–1980.* Houston: Gulf Publishing Company, 1982.

Mason, Robert J. *Contested Lands: Conflict and Compromise in New Jersey's Pine Barrens.* Philadelphia: Temple University Press, 1992.

May, Elaine Tyler. *Homeward Bound: American Families in the Cold War Era*. New York: Basic Books, 1988.

Mayer, Martin. *The Builders: Houses, People, Neighborhoods, Governments, Money*. New York: W. W. Norton, 1978.

Meine, Curt. *Aldo Leopold: His Life and Work*. Madison: University of Wisconsin Press, 1988.

Melosi, Martin V. *Coping with Abundance: Energy and Environment in Industrial America*. Philadelphia: Temple University Press, 1985.

   "Lyndon Johnson and Environmental Policy." In *The Johnson Years: Vietnam, the Environment, and Science*, edited by Robert A. Divine, pp. 113–149. Lawrence: University Press of Kansas, 1987.

   "The Place of the City in Environmental History." *Environmental History Review* 17 (Spring 1993): 1–23.

   The Sanitary City: Urban Infrastructure in America from Colonial Times to the Present. Baltimore: Johns Hopkins University Press, 2000.

   editor. *Pollution and Reform in American Cities, 1870–1930*. Austin: University of Texas Press, 1980.

Mertes, James D. "Trends in Government Control of Erosion and Sedimentation in Urban Development." *Journal of Soil and Water Conservation* 44 (1989): 550–554.

Miller, Douglas T., and Nowak, Marion. *The Fifties: The Way We Really Were*. New York: Doubleday & Company, 1977.

Miller, James Nathan. "To Save the Landscape." *National Civic Review* 53 (1964): 354–359, 364.

Mitchell, J. Paul, editor. *Federal Housing Policy and Programs: Past and Present*. New Brunswick, NJ: Center for Urban Policy Research, 1985.

Moe, Richard, and Wilkie, Carter. *Changing Places: Rebuilding Community in the Age of Sprawl*. New York: Henry Holt & Company, 1997.

Montanari, John H., and Kusler, Jon A., editors. *Proceedings of the National Wetland Protection Symposium*. Washington: U.S. Fish and Wildlife Service, 1978.

Moore, Walter L., and Morgan, Carl W., editors. *Effects of Watershed Changes on Streamflow*. Austin: University of Texas Press, 1969.

Morgan, George T., Jr., and King, John O. *The Woodlands: New Community Development, 1964–1983*. College Station: Texas A & M University Press, 1987.

Morris, David. *Self-Reliant Cities: Energy and the Transformation of Urban America*. San Francisco: Sierra Club Books, 1982.

Morrison, Bonnie Maas. "Household Energy Consumption, 1900–1980: A Quantitative History." In *Energy and Transport: Historical Perspectives on Policy Issues*, edited by George H. Daniels and Mark H. Rose, pp. 201–233. Beverly Hills: Sage Publications, 1982.

Muller, Peter O. *Contemporary Suburban America*. Englewood Cliffs, NJ: Prentice-Hall, 1981.

Mumford, Lewis. *The Urban Prospect*. New York: Harcourt, Brace & World, 1968.

Murphy, Earl Finbar. *Governing Nature*. Chicago: Quadrangle Books, 1967.
   Water Purity: A Study in Legal Control of Natural Resources. Madison: University of Wisconsin Press, 1961.
Murphy, Francis C. *Regulating Flood-Plain Development*. Department of Geography Research Paper 56. Chicago: University of Chicago Department of Geography, 1958.
Nash, Roderick. *Wilderness and the American Mind*. Third edition. New Haven: Yale University Press, 1982.
Nathan, Robert R. *Mobilizing for Abundance*. New York: McGraw-Hill, 1944.
National Association of Counties Research Foundation. *Urban Soil Erosion and Sediment Control*. Washington: Federal Water Quality Administration, 1970.
National Commission on Urban Problems. *Building the American City*. Washington: USGPO, 1969.
National Committee on Housing. *Proceedings of the National Conference on Postwar Housing*. New York: National Committee on Housing, 1944.
National Resources Planning Board. *The Role of the Housebuilding Industry*. Washington: USGPO, 1942.
Natural Resources Defense Council. *Land Use Controls in the United States: A Handbook on the Legal Rights of Citizens*. New York: The Dial Press, 1977.
Nelson, Robert H. *Zoning and Property Rights: An Analysis of the American System of Land-Use Regulation*. Cambridge: MIT Press, 1977.
Newman, Dorothy K., and Day, Dawn. *The American Energy Consumer: A Report to the Energy Policy Project of the Ford Foundation*. Cambridge: Ballinger, 1975.
Nichols, Donald R., and Campbell, Catherine C., editors. *Environmental Planning and Geology: Proceedings of the Symposium on Engineering Geology in the Urban Environment*. Washington: USGPO, 1971.
Niering, William A. *The Life of the Marsh: The North American Wetlands*. New York: McGraw-Hill, 1966.
   Nature in the Metropolis: Conservation in the Tri-State New York Metropolitan Area. New York: Regional Plan Association, 1960.
Norcross, Carl. *Open Space Communities in the Marketplace*. Washington: Urban Land Institute, 1966.
Noyes, John H., and Progulske, Donald R., editors. *A Symposium on Wildlife in an Urbanizing Environment*. Amherst: Massachusetts Cooperative Extension Service, 1974.
Nye, David E. *Consuming Power: A Social History of American Energies*. Cambridge: MIT Press, 1998.
Odum, Eugene P. "The Role of Tidal Marshes in Estuarine Production." *The Conservationist* 15 (June–July 1961): 12–15, 35.
Office of Technology Assessment. *Wetlands: Their Use and Regulation*. Washington: Office of Technology Assessment, 1984.
Olgyay, Victor. *Design with Climate: Bioclimatic Approach to Architectural Regionalism*. Princeton: Princeton University Press, 1963.
   "The Temperate House." *Architectural Forum* 94 (March 1951): 179–194.

Olgyay, Victor, and Olgyay, Aladar. *Application of Climatic Data to House Design.* Housing Research. Washington: Housing and Home Finance Agency, 1954.

O'Neill, William L. *American High: The Years of Confidence, 1945–1960.* New York: Free Press, 1986.

Open Space Action Committee. *Stewardship: The Land, the Landowner, the Metropolis.* New York: Open Space Action Committee, 1965.

Osborn, Fairfield. *Our Plundered Planet.* Boston: Little, Brown and Company, 1948.

Outdoor Recreation Resources Review Commission. *Outdoor Recreation for America.* Washington: USGPO, 1962.

Owen, Wilfred. *Cities in the Motor Age.* New York: Viking, 1959.

Packard, Vance. *The Waste Makers.* New York: David McKay, 1960.

Paehlke, Robert C. *Environmentalism and the Future of Progressive Politics.* New Haven: Yale University Press, 1989.

Patterson, J. W., Minear, R. A., and Nedved, T. K. *Septic Tanks and the Environment.* Chicago: Illinois Institute of Technology, 1971.

Pells, Richard H. *The Liberal Mind in a Conservative Age: American Intellectuals in the 1940s and 1950s.* Second edition. Middletown, CT: Wesleyan University Press, 1989.

Perin, Constance. *Everything in its Place: Social Order and Land Use in America.* Princeton: Princeton University Press, 1977.

Petulla, Joseph M. *American Environmental History.* Second edition. Columbus, OH: Merrill Publishing Company, 1988.

Pincetl, Stephanie S. *Transforming California: A Political History of Land Use and Development.* Baltimore: Johns Hopkins University Press, 1999.

Platt, Harold L. *The Electric City: Energy and the Growth of the Chicago Area, 1880–1930.* Chicago: University of Chicago Press, 1991.

Platt, Rutherford H. "Floods and Man: A Geographer's Agenda." In *Geography, Resources, and Environment: Themes from the Work of Gilbert F. White,* volume two, edited by Robert W. Kates and Ian Burton, pp. 28–68. Chicago: University of Chicago Press, 1986.

  Open Land in Urban Illinois: Roles of the Citizen Advocate. DeKalb: Northern Illinois University Press, 1971.

Platt, Rutherford H., Rowntree, Rowan A., and Muick, Pamela C., editors. *The Ecological City: Preserving and Restoring Biological Diversity.* Amherst: University of Massachusetts Press, 1994.

Plotkin, Sidney. *Keep Out: The Struggle for Land Use Control.* Berkeley: University of California Press, 1987.

Popper, Frank J. *The Politics of Land-Use Reform.* Madison: University of Wisconsin Press, 1981.

  "Understanding American Land Use Regulation Since 1970: A Revisionist Interpretation." *Journal of the American Planning Association* 54 (1998): 291–301.

President's Materials Policy Commission. *Resources for Freedom.* Five volumes. Washington: USGPO, 1952.

Putnam, Palmer Cosslett. *Energy in the Future.* New York: Van Nostrand, 1953.

Pyle, Robert Michael. *The Thunder Tree: Lessons from an Urban Wildland.* Boston: Houghton Mifflin, 1993.

Radford, Gail. *Modern Housing for America: Policy Struggles in the New Deal Era.* Chicago: University of Chicago Press, 1996.

Real Estate Research Corporation. *The Costs of Sprawl: Environmental and Economic Costs of Alternative Residential Development Patterns at the Urban Fringe.* Two volumes. Washington: USGPO, 1974.

Regional Plan Association. *The Race for Open Space: Final Report of the Park, Recreation and Open Space Project.* New York: Regional Plan Association, 1960.

Reilly, William K., editor. *The Use of Land: A Citizens' Policy Guide to Urban Growth.* New York: Thomas Y. Crowell Company, 1973.

Resources for the Future. *The Nation Looks at Its Resources.* Washington: Resources for the Future, 1954.

Reuss, Martin. *Water Resources People and Issues: Interview with Gilbert F. White.* Fort Belvoir, VA: U.S. Army Corps of Engineers, 1993.

Rienow, Robert, and Rienow, Leona Train. *Moment in the Sun: A Report on the Deteriorating Quality of the American Environment.* New York: The Dial Press, 1967.

Rome, Adam W. "Building on the Land: Toward an Environmental History of Residential Development in American Cities and Suburbs, 1870–1990." *Journal of Urban History* 20 (1994): 407–434.

Rose, Mark H. *Cities of Light and Heat: Domesticating Gas and Electricity in Urban America.* University Park: Penn State Press, 1995.

Rosen, Christine Meisner, and Tarr, Joel Arthur. "The Importance of an Urban Perspective in Environmental History." *Journal of Urban History* 20 (1994): 299–310.

Rosenbaum, Nelson. *Land Use and the Legislatures: The Politics of State Innovation.* Washington: Urban Institute, 1976.

Rosenbaum, Walter A. *The Politics of Environmental Concern.* New York: Praeger, 1973.

Rosenman, Dorothy. *A Million Homes a Year.* New York: Harcourt, Brace and Company, 1945.

Rosenthal, Jon. *Cluster Subdivisions.* Planning Advisory Service Information Report Number 135. Chicago: American Society of Planning Officials, 1960.

Ross, Davis R. B. *Preparing for Ulysses: Politics and Veterans During World War II.* New York: Columbia University Press, 1969.

Rothman, Hal K. *The Greening of a Nation?: Environmentalism in the United States Since 1945.* Fort Worth: Harcourt Brace College Publishers, 1998.

Rowe, Peter G. *Making a Middle Landscape.* Cambridge: MIT Press, 1991.

Rydin, Yvonne. "Environmental Dimensions of Residential Development and the Implications for Local Planning Practice." *Journal of Environmental Planning and Management* 35 (1992): 43–61.

Sale, Kirkpatrick. *The Green Revolution: The American Environmental Movement, 1962–1992*. New York: Hill and Wang, 1993.

Sansom, Robert L. *The New American Dream Machine: Toward a Simpler Lifestyle in an Environmental Age*. Garden City, NY: Anchor Books, 1976.

Savini, John, and Kammerer, J. C. *Urban Growth and the Water Regimen*. Geological Survey Water Supply Paper 1591–A. Washington: USGPO, 1961.

Sax, Joseph L. "Takings, Private Property and Public Rights." *Yale Law Journal* 81 (December 1971): 149–186.

Scalf, Marion R., Dunlap, William J., and Kreissl, James F. *Environmental Effects of Septic Tank Systems*. Ada, OK: Environmental Protection Agency, 1977.

Scheffer, Victor B. *The Shaping of Environmentalism in America*. Seattle: University of Washington Press, 1991.

Schmitt, Peter J. *Back to Nature: The Arcadian Myth in Urban America*. New York: Oxford University Press, 1969.

Schrepfer, Susan R. *The Fight to Save the Redwoods: A History of Environmental Reform, 1917–1978*. Madison: University of Wisconsin Press, 1983.

Schuyler, David. *The New Urban Landscape: The Redefinition of City Form in Nineteenth-Century America*. Baltimore: Johns Hopkins University Press, 1986.

Scott, Mel. *American City Planning Since 1890*. Berkeley: University of California Press, 1969.

Scott, Randall W., editor. *Management and Control of Growth: Issues, Techniques, Problems, Trends*. Three volumes. Washington: Urban Land Institute, 1975.

Seeley, John R., Sim, R. Alexander, and Loosley, Elizabeth W. *Crestwood Heights: A Study of the Culture of Suburban Life*. New York: Basic Books, 1956.

Senn, Milton J. E., with Wylie, Evan McLeod. "We Must Stop Contaminating Our Water." *American Home* 66 (Winter 1963): 45–46, 72–74.

Shabecoff, Philip. *A Fierce Green Fire: The American Environmental Movement*. New York: Hill and Wang, 1993.

Shaw, Samuel P., and Fredine, C. Gordon. *Wetlands of the United States: Their Extent and Their Value to Waterfowl and Other Wildlife*. Circular 39. Washington: U.S. Fish and Wildlife Service, 1956.

Shomon, Joseph James. *Open Land for Urban America: Acquisition, Safekeeping, and Use*. Baltimore: Johns Hopkins University Press, 1971.

Siegan, Bernard H. *Other People's Property*. Lexington, MA: Lexington Books, 1976.

Siegel, Shirley Adelson. *The Law of Open Space: Legal Aspects of Acquiring or Otherwise Preserving Open Space in the Tri-State New York Metropolitan Region*. New York: Regional Plan Association, 1960.

Sierra Club Legal Defense Fund. *The Poisoned Well: New Strategies for Groundwater Protection*. Washington: Island Press, 1989.

Simon, Maron J., editor. *Your Solar House*. New York: Simon and Schuster, 1947.

Siry, Joseph V. *Marshes of the Ocean Shore: Development of an Environmental Ethic.* College Station: Texas A & M University Press, 1984.

Slavin, Richard H. "Toward a State Land-Use Policy: Harmonizing Development and Conservation." *State Government* 44 (1971): 2–11.

Smith, Edward Ellis, and Riggs, Durward S., editors. *Land Use, Open Space, and the Government Process: The San Francisco Bay Area Experience.* New York: Praeger, 1974.

Smith, Thomas G. "John Kennedy, Stewart Udall, and New Frontier Conservation." *Pacific Historical Review* LXIV (1995): 329–362.

Soil Conservation Society of America. *Land Use: Persuasion or Regulation?* Ankeny, IA: Soil Conservation Society of America, 1974.

Land Use: Tough Choices in Today's World. Ankeny, IA: Soil Conservation Society of America, 1977.

Solomon, Arthur P. *The Effect of Land Use and Environmental Controls on Housing: A Review.* Cambridge: Joint Center for Urban Studies of the Massachusetts Institute of Technology and Harvard University, 1976.

Spirn, Anne Whiston. *The Granite Garden: Urban Nature and Human Design.* New York: Basic Books, 1984.

Stanley, William E., and Eliassen, Rolf. *Status of Knowledge of Ground Water Contaminants.* Washington: Federal Housing Administration, 1960.

Stearns, Forest W. "Wildlife Habitat in Urban and Suburban Environments." In *Transactions of the Thirty-Second North American Wildlife and Natural Resources Conference,* edited by James B. Trefethen, pp. 61–69. Washington: Wildlife Management Institute, 1967.

Stein, Richard G. *Architecture and Energy.* Garden City, NY: Anchor Press, 1977.

Stephenson, R. Bruce. *Visions of Eden: Environmentalism, Urban Planning, and City Building in St. Petersburg, Florida, 1900–1995.* Columbus: Ohio State University Press, 1997.

Stilgoe, John. *Borderland: Origins of the American Suburb, 1820–1939.* New Haven: Yale University Press, 1988.

Straus, Nathan. *The Seven Myths of Housing.* New York: Alfred A. Knopf, 1945.

Strong, Ann Louise. *Open Space for Urban America.* Washington: U.S. Department of Housing and Urban Development, 1965.

Tansil, John, and Moyers, John C. "Residential Demand for Energy." In *Energy: Demand, Conservation, and Institutional Problems,* edited by Michael S. Macrakis, pp. 375–385. Cambridge: MIT Press, 1974.

Tarr, Joel A. "The Evolution of Urban Infrastructure in the Nineteenth and Twentieth Centuries." In *Perspectives on Urban Infrastructure,* edited by Royce Hanson, pp. 4–66. Washington: National Academy Press, 1984.

The Search for the Ultimate Sink: Urban Pollution in Historical Perspective. Akron: University of Akron Press, 1996.

Task Force on Effect of Urban Development on Flood Discharges. "Effect of Urban Development on Flood Discharges – Current Knowledge and Future

Needs." *Journal of the Hydraulics Division, Proceedings of the American Society of Civil Engineers* 95 (HY1, January 1969): 287–309.

Teaford, Jon C. *Post-Suburbia: Government and Politics in the Edge Cities.* Baltimore: Johns Hopkins University Press, 1997.

Teal, John and Mildred. *Life and Death of the Salt Marsh.* 1969. Reprint. New York: Ballantine Books, 1971.

Telkes, Maria. "Future Uses of Solar Energy." *Bulletin of the Atomic Scientists* 7 (1951): 217–219.

"A Review of Solar House Heating." *Heating and Ventilating* 46 (September 1949): 68–74.

Thomas, Harold E., and Schneider, William J. *Water as an Urban Resource and Nuisance.* Geological Survey Circular 601–D. Washington: USGPO, 1970.

Thomas, William L., Jr., editor. *Man's Role in Changing the Face of the Earth.* Chicago: University of Chicago Press, 1956.

Thronson, Robert E. *Control of Erosion and Sediment Deposition from Construction of Highways and Land Development.* Washington: Environmental Protection Agency, 1971.

Thurow, Charles, Toner, William, and Erley, Duncan. *Performance Controls for Sensitive Lands: A Practical Guide for Local Administrators.* American Society of Planning Officials Planning Advisory Service Reports 307 and 308. Chicago: American Society of Planning Officials, 1975.

Tiner, Ralph W., Jr. *Wetlands of the United States: Current Status and Recent Trends.* Washington: USGPO, 1984.

Tobey, Ronald C. *Technology as Freedom: The New Deal and the Electrical Modernization of the American Home.* Berkeley: University of California Press, 1996.

Trefethen, James B. *An American Crusade for Wildlife.* New York: Winchester Press, 1975.

Tucker, Walter A., editor. *The Crisis in Open Land.* Wheeling, WV: American Institute of Park Executives, 1959.

Tunnard, Christopher, and Pushkarev, Boris. *Man-Made America: Chaos or Control?* New Haven: Yale University Press, 1963.

Tupper, Margo. *No Place to Play.* Philadelphia: Chilton Books, 1966.

Twiss, Robert H. "Wildlife in the Metropolitan Landscape." In *Transactions of the Thirty-Second North American Wildlife and Natural Resources Conference,* edited by James B. Trefethen, pp. 69–74. Washington: Wildlife Management Institute, 1967.

Udall, Stewart L. *The Quiet Crisis.* New York: Holt, Rinehart and Winston, 1963.

Ullman, John E., editor. *The Suburban Economic Network: Economic Activity, Resource Use, and the Great Sprawl.* New York: Praeger, 1977.

Urban Land Institute and National Association of Home Builders. *Innovations vs. Traditions in Community Development: A Comparative Study in Residential Land Use.* Technical Bulletin 47. Washington: Urban Land Institute, 1963.

New Approaches to Residential Land Development: A Study of Concepts and Innovations. Technical Bulletin 40. Washington: Urban Land Institute, 1961.

U.S. Department of Agriculture. *A Place to Live: The Yearbook of Agriculture 1963.* Washington: USGPO, 1963.

U.S. Department of Agriculture and U.S. Department of Housing and Urban Development. *Soil, Water, and Suburbia.* Washington: USGPO, 1968.

U.S. Department of the Interior. *The Race for Inner Space.* Washington: USGPO, 1964.

U.S. Geological Survey. *A Study of Detergent Pollution in Ground Water.* Washington: Federal Housing Administration, 1959.

U.S. Public Health Service. *Ground Water Contamination: Proceedings of the 1961 Symposium.* Cincinnati: Robert A. Taft Sanitary Engineering Center, 1961.

Vennard, Edwin. *The Electric Power Business.* New York: McGraw-Hill, 1962.

Vietor, Richard H. K. *Energy Policy in America Since 1945: A Study of Business-Government Relations.* New York: Cambridge University Press, 1984.

Vileisis, Ann. *Discovering the Unknown Landscape: A History of America's Wetlands.* Washington: Island Press, 1997.

Vogt, William. *Road to Survival.* New York: William Sloane Associates, 1948.

Waldie, D. J. *Holy Land: A Suburban Memoir.* 1996. Reprint. New York: St. Martin's, 1997.

Walker, Richard A., and Heiman, Michael K. "Quiet Revolution for Whom?" *Annals of the Association of American Geographers* 71 (1981): 67–83.

Wallace, David A., editor. *Metropolitan Open Space and Natural Process.* Philadelphia: University of Pennsylvania Press, 1970.

Warner, Kee, and Molotch, Harvey. "Power to Build: How Development Persists Despite Local Controls." *Urban Affairs Review* 30 (1995): 378–406.

Warner, Sam Bass, Jr. *The Urban Wilderness: A History of the American City.* 1972. Reprint. Berkeley: University of California Press, 1995.

Weiss, Marc A. "Real Estate History: An Overview and Research Agenda." *Business History Review* 63 (1989): 241–282.

The Rise of the Community Builders: The American Real Estate Industry and Urban Land Planning. New York: Columbia University Press, 1987.

Welfeld, Irving. *Where We Live: A Social History of American Housing.* New York: Simon and Schuster, 1988.

Wellock, Thomas Raymond. *Critical Masses: Opposition to Nuclear Power in California, 1958–1978.* Madison: University of Wisconsin Press, 1998.

Wendt, Paul F. *Housing Policy – The Search for Solutions: A Comparison of the United Kingdom, Sweden, West Germany, and the United States since World War II.* Berkeley: University of California Press, 1963.

White, Gilbert Fowler. *Human Adjustment to Floods: A Geographical Approach to the Flood Problem in the United States.* 1945. Reprint. Department of Geography Research Paper 29. Chicago: University of Chicago Department of Geography, 1953.

White, Gilbert F., Calef, Wesley C., Hudson, James W., Mayer, Harold M., Sheaffer, John R., and Volk, Donald J. *Changes in Urban Occupance of Flood*

Plains in the United States. Department of Geography Research Paper 57. Chicago: University of Chicago Department of Geography, 1958.

White House Conference on Natural Beauty. *Beauty for America.* Washington: USGPO, 1965.

Whyte, William H., Jr. *The Last Landscape.* Garden City, NY: Doubleday, 1968.

"A Plan to Save Vanishing U.S. Countryside." *Life* 47 (August 17, 1959): 88–102.

editor. *The Exploding Metropolis.* 1958. Reprint. Berkeley: University of California Press, 1993.

Williams, Edward A. *Open Space: The Choices Before California.* The Urban-Metropolitan Open-Space Study, 1965. San Francisco: Diablo Press, 1969.

Williams, James C. *Energy and the Making of Modern California.* Akron: University of Akron Press, 1997.

Wingo, Lowdon, Jr., editor. *Cities and Space: The Future Use of Urban Land.* Baltimore: Johns Hopkins University Press, 1963.

Wolf, Peter. *Land in America: Its Value, Use, and Control.* New York: Pantheon, 1981.

Wolman, M. G[ordon]. "Erosion in the Urban Environment." *Hydrological Sciences Bulletin* 20 (1975): 117–125.

Problems Posed by Sediment Derived from Construction Activities in Maryland – Report to the Maryland Water Pollution Control Commission. Annapolis: Maryland Water Pollution Control Commission, 1964.

Wood, Robert C. *Suburbia: Its People and Their Politics.* Boston: Houghton Mifflin, 1958.

Wood, Samuel E., and Heller, Alfred E. *California Going, Going . . . : Our State's Struggle to Remain Beautiful and Productive.* Sacramento: California Tomorrow, 1962.

Worster, Donald. *Nature's Economy: A History of Ecological Ideas.* Second edition. New York: Cambridge University Press, 1994.

The Wealth of Nature: Environmental History and the Ecological Imagination. New York: Oxford University Press, 1993.

Wright, Gwendolyn. *Building the Dream: A Social History of Housing in America.* Cambridge: MIT Press, 1981.

Wurster, Catherine Bauer. "Framework for an Urban Society." In *Goals for Americans: Programs of Action in the Sixties,* pp. 225–247. President's Commission on National Goals. Englewood Cliffs, NJ: Prentice-Hall, 1960.

"The Urban Octopus." In *Wilderness: America's Living Heritage,* edited by David Brower, pp. 117–122. San Francisco: Sierra Club, 1961.

Yearwood, Richard M. *Land Subdivision Regulation: Policy and Legal Considerations for Urban Planning.* New York: Praeger, 1971.

Yellott, John I. "Solar Energy Today and Tomorrow." *Journal of the American Institute of Architects* 29 (April 1958): 198–206.

Zakin, Susan. *Coyotes and Town Dogs: Earth First! and the Environmental Movement.* 1993. Reprint. New York: Penguin, 1995.

Zisman, S. B. "Open Spaces in Urban Growth." *AIA Journal* 44 (December 1965): 49–54.

Zisman, S. B., Ward, Delbert B., and Powell, Catherine H. *Where Not To Build: A Guide for Open Space Planning.* Technical Bulletin 1. Washington: U.S. Bureau of Land Management, 1968.

Zwick, David, with Benstock, Marcy. *Water Wasteland: Ralph Nader's Study Group Report on Water Pollution.* 1971. Reprint. New York: Bantam, 1972.

Index

Abbey, Edward, 148
Abrams, Charles, 33–34
air conditioning, 64, 65–72, 85
air pollution, 47, 84, 137, 144, 146, 184, 223, 248–252, 255
American Academy of Arts and Sciences, 50
American Association for the Advancement of Science, 50, 212
American Institute of Architects, 60, 238, 259–260
American Institute of Planners, 178, 227, 238
American Society of Civil Engineers, 103, 178, 198
American Society of Landscape Architects, 129, 149, 238
American Society of Planning Officials, 129, 133, 177–178, 216
American Water Works Association, 103
Anderson, Glenn, 207
architecture, 9–10, 45–46, 54–55, 57–58, 60, 62, 63–64, 70, 122, 167n29, 238, 268
Arizona: desert development, 238; open-space preservation, 148; septic-tank use, 88; solar-energy conference, 50
Association for Applied Solar Energy, 50–52, 54n13
atomic energy, 5, 48, 53, 77
Atomic Energy Commission, 51, 53n13

Baker, John, 145
Banham, Reyner, 70
Better Homes for America, 23
Blake, Peter, 2, 151
Bombeck, Erma, 87
Bosselman, Fred, 227–228, 241
Bowles, Chester, 32–33
Buchheister, Carl, 145–156
Bureau of Outdoor Recreation, 212
Bureau of Reclamation, 217
Bureau of Sport Fisheries and Wildlife (U. S. Fish and Wildlife Service), 10, 156, 162–163, 190–191, 211, 213–219

Caldwell, Lynton, 240
California: farmland loss, 123; floodplain development, 173; hillside development, 97–99, 139, 166–167, 168–171, 238; land-use regulation, 227, 229, 234; open-space preservation, 128, 132, 134, 139, 146; solar technology, 49; tract-house builders, 1–2, 17n5; urban hydrology studies, 194, 195; wetlands preservation, 162, 227, 229, 234
Callies, David, 227–228, 241
Carrier Corporation, 65, 71
Carson, Rachel, 5, 9, 109
Clay, Grady, 167
Clean Air Act, 247–249
Clean Water Act (Federal Water Pollution Control Act), 110–112, 209, 247, 249

How do we measure economic growth?
— # of houses built is one way
  "housing starts"
why do we use these things to measure
economic growth
Living in places with inherent hazards